Intermediate GNVQ
Information and Communication
Technology Options

Intermediate GNVQ Information and Communication Technology Options

Peter Bradshaw, Alison Duff,
John Dunlop, Alan Jarvis,
Graham Redfern and Julia Wright

Series Editor: Jenny Lawson

An imprint of **Pearson Education**

Harlow, England · London · New York · Reading, Massachusetts · San Francisco
Toronto · Don Mills, Ontario · Sydney · Tokyo · Singapore · Hong Kong · Seoul
Taipei · Cape Town · Madrid · Mexico City · Amsterdam · Munich · Paris · Milan

In this book you will find helpful icons showing which Key Skills the Activities can be used for:

 Communication

 Application of number

 Working with others

 Problem solving

 Improving own learning and performance

Pearson Education Limited
Edinburgh Gate, Harlow
Essex CM20 2JE, England
and Associated Companies throughout the world

© Pearson Education Limited 2002

The right of Peter Bradshaw, Alison Duff, John Dunlop, Alan Jarvis, Graham Redfern and Julia Wright to be identified as authors of this work has been asserted by them in accordance with the Copyright, Designs and Patents Act 1988.

All rights reserved; no part of this publication may be reproduced, stored in any retrieval system, or transmitted in any form or by any means, electronic, mechanical, photocopying, recording, or otherwise without either the prior written permission of the Publishers or a licence permitting restricted copying in the United Kingdom issued by the Copyright Licensing Agency Ltd, 90 Tottenham Court Road, London W1P 0LP.

First published 2002

British Library Cataloguing in Publication Data
A catalogue entry for this title is available from the British Library

ISBN 0-582-36866-9

Set by 35 in Humanist, Rotis Sans and Caslon

Printed in Malaysia, CLP

Contents

		Page number
	About the authors	vii
	Introduction	xii
1	**Design project** Alan Jarvis	1
2	**Information resources** Alison Duff	21
3	**Communicating with multimedia** Alan Jarvis	57
4	**Graphics and desktop publishing** Julia Wright	97
5	**Computer-aided design** Alison Duff	123
6	**Numerical modelling using spreadsheets** Peter Bradshaw	153
7	**Databases** Peter Bradshaw	193
8	**Monitoring and control systems** John Dunlop	237
9	**Networks and communications** Graham Redfern	273

10	**Programming** *Alan Jarvis*	**307**
11	**Impact of ICT on society** *Alison Duff*	**353**
	Good Working Practice guide	**389**
	Portfolio guide	**393**
	Key Skills guide	**399**
	Examination guide	**401**
	Index	**411**

About the authors

The authors responsible for writing the eleven chapters of this book have, between them, more than 100 years of valuable experience of ICT:

- Within the computing industry
- As teachers delivering GNVQ and other vocational and academic courses
- As examiners, preparing course specifications, devising student assessment material, marking examinations and verifying students' portfolios
- As consultants on projects funded by government organisations such as QCA and FEDA

The authors have all worked for the GNVQ awarding bodies, many since the earliest days of GNVQ. Indeed, several are still very active in the preparation of examination materials. Between them, they therefore have in-depth knowledge of the specifications and assessment methods. They are all totally committed to the GNVQ qualification – only recently renamed as the Advanced Vocational Certificate of Education (AVCE) – and, as examiners, they know exactly what is expected of students on a Vocation A-level course.

Peter Bradshaw

BSc (Joint Hons) Mathematics and Physics with Computing and Education [1978]
PGCE Secondary [1979]

Peter has worked in IT education for 20 years. He has been a teacher, IT co-ordinator, advisory teacher, programme leader for BTEC National IT and GNVQ co-ordinator. Involved in GNVQ since the 1992 pilot, Peter has written and edited tests and unit specifications and is Chief Examiner for GNVQ IT Part One, at Foundation and Intermediate level.

Peter has also examined at GCSE and GCE A-level Computing and helped to write the new OCR ICT AS-level/A-level specifications. He currently works for ULTRALAB on learning, research and technology projects. A facilitator for the online NPQH, he has also worked on the Talking Heads project. Both of these are DfEE funded as part of the National College of School Leadership. This followed on from a secondment as a Tesco SchoolNet 2000 advisory teacher in which he worked with schools and on an Internet-based project for the Millennium Experience.

Peter has published material for Foundation GNVQ IT and has worked in all phases of education from first school to further education.

Outside of education, he co-ordinates a folk festival, is a Morris dancer and qualified signalman, croquet coach and coach driver!

Alison Duff

BEng Manufacturing Systems Engineering [1994]
PGCE Information Technology and Games [1995]

Alison Duff worked for Ford Motor Company during her degree course, studying design and engineering systems, and has worked in IT since completing her PGCE course. She teaches at the City Technology College, Kingshurst, co-ordinates the GNVQ ICT courses and internally verifies work across Levels 2 and 3; she also delivers Key Skills.

Alison was involved in the writing of the specifications for the RSA/C&G Optional Units, and also works for OCR writing full and Part One award GNVQ question papers.

She has more recently been involved with contributing to the TTA numerical question paper project. She works for SLDA as a consultant for Key Skills and has been involved with the writing of the new Key Skills IT Level 1 and 2 papers.

Outside of education, Alison is a keen scuba diver and skier and, whenever possible, follows these pursuits abroad.

John Dunlop

BEng (Hons) Electronics and Computer Control [1992]
PhD [1995]

John Dunlop has worked with IT-based control systems for 10 years and has been involved in many aspects of monitoring and control. He spent six years at Coventry University developing advanced control theory methods for engine testing. He now runs a company that designs and installs IT systems into large manufacturing companies around the world. He was involved in the writing of the unit specifications for OCR/AQA Optional Units for Intermediate and Advanced IT. When not working, John is a keen snowboarder and mountain cyclist.

Alan Jarvis

BSc [1979]
Cert.Ed. (FE) [1997]
MSc Business Information Technology [1999]

Alan spent 15 years in the commercial IT industry working in programming, user support and training. For the past five years, Alan has been working at Southgate College in North London as an IT lecturer and course manager on GNVQ and HNC courses.

Alan was involved in the writing of the unit specifications for OCR/AQA Optional Units for Intermediate and Advanced IT. Along with his partner, Neela Soomary, who also works at Southgate College, he has recently been involved in setting up the School of IT web site and ILT pilot project.

Graham Redfern

BSc Maths and Computing
PGCE [1977]

Initially, Graham taught Mathematics but, since 1979, he has been involved in the development and running of IT courses and cross-curricula IT.

Graham became involved in GNVQ IT from the very first syllabus development meeting in April 1993 and, as Principal Examiner for City and Guilds Advanced GNVQ IT, was involved in writing the unit specifications for the OCR/AQA Optional Units for Intermediate and Advanced IT.

Graham has extensive experience in writing and editing examination papers and, until January 2001, wrote the papers for Networks and Communications.

Julia Wright

BSc Management Sciences [1981]
PGCE Business Studies and Economics [1984]

Julia has taught Business and IT in Bradford Schools for 16 years and is currently Vocational Leader at Laisterdyke High School in Bradford.

She is a GNVQ External Verifier for OCR Examinations Board and a Key Skills Trainer for SLDA. She has also worked as an IT Scrutineer for QCA (1997) and as Lead Reviewer for the Part 1 GNVQ Controlled Assignment.

Julia has been involved in GNVQ delivery since 1994. She was involved in the writing of the unit specifications for OCR/AQA Optional Units, and test specifications for the new AVCE award. Julia has also been involved in unit test writing for both new and old GNVQ specifications.

Julia contributes to the Intermediate GNVQ ICT book and her next book, *The Key to IT Skills*, written with Jenny Lawson, is due to be published in September 2001.

Jenny Lawson (series editor)

BSc (Hons) Mathematics [1973]

Jenny has worked in a computing/IT environment for over 30 years, as a programmer, systems analyst, director of a software house, an IT trainer, a teacher and an examiner. She taught in schools and colleges for ten years, including five years as Head of Computing at Woking Sixth Form College.

As Chief Examiner and Vocational Advisor to the RSA, for many years Jenny worked on the IT GNVQ qualification – almost since its inception – being involved in all aspects of syllabus writing, test specification writing, examination paper production, marking and awarding, plus the training of other examiners.

For the last ten years, Jenny has been director of a publishing company, First Class Publishing Ltd, which provides editorial services to major publishers and organisations such as the ICAEW.

Her educational consultancy work continues and has included projects on AS-level/A-level ICT and Computing, and Key Skills. Currently Jenny is working as a consultant to the Skills and Learning Development Agency (SLDA), writing guidance materials for teachers of the IT Key Skill.

Jenny has already had published with Longman both *Foundation GNVQ ICT* and *Intermediate GNVQ ICT*, and as series editor has also overseen the preparation of books to support the optional units for Vocational A-level ICT. Her next publication, together with Julia Wright, is a text for IT Key Skills, *The Key to IT Key Skills*, due for publication in January 2002.

Introduction

As one of the Longman GNVQ series edited by Jenny Lawson, this book is written for students of the GNVQ qualification at Intermediate level, and supports the *GNVQ Intermediate Information and Communication Technology* book published in 2000.

The introduction to *GNVQ Intermediate Information and Communication Technology* gives full details of the GNVQ qualification and how to achieve Intermediate GNVQ in Information and Communication Technology.

GNVQ Intermediate Information and Communication Technology contains three chapters, each one covering a mandatory unit:

- Presenting Information
- Handling Information
- Hardware and Software

The Qualifications and Curriculum Authority developed these three mandatory units but the three awarding bodies – OCR, AQA and EdExcel – were allowed to develop their own suite of optional units. As a result, while each awarding body offers only six optional units, there are instead eleven chapters in this book, each one covering an optional unit from one or more of the three awarding bodies.

Details of which units relate to which awarding body, and how units are assessed, are given on page 259 of *GNVQ Intermediate Information and Communication Technology*.

The team of writers for this book were all involved in writing the specifications for the optional units for one or other of the awarding bodies, and have also been involved in writing examination papers and marking them, apart from their day-to-day teaching of this qualification.

The style of this book follows the style of the Longman GNVQ series:

- Each chapter presents information for one GNVQ unit, with notes on what you need to know and plenty of diagrams and examples, mostly based on case studies.
- Exercises provide stopping points for you to check you have understood what you have just been reading about.
- Activities test your understanding and help you to produce portfolio material.
- Revision questions offer a final check on a unit.

Towards the end of the book, as with the *GNVQ Intermediate Information and Communication Technology*, there are four guides:

- The Good Working Practice Guide
- The Portfolio Guide
- The Key Skills Guide
- The Examinations Guide

The first three provide basic details and refer you back to *GNVQ Intermediate Information and Communication Technology* and/or relevant websites for more information. The Examination Guide, though, includes material not published elsewhere in this series: valuable advice written by Jenny Lawson, who was until recently the Chief Examiner for GNVQ ICT, on how to prepare yourself for the external tests.

There is also a comprehensive index. The index lists all important words used in the book. Indexed words appear in bold within the text, or within headings. The index also includes cross references to help you find what you are looking for.

Acknowledgements

The authors would like to thank those who kindly contributed to the case studies. Thanks also to Alison Stanford at Pearson Education for seeing the book through its final stages and to Robert Chaundy of Bookstyle for such careful checking of the proofs.

Whilst every effort has been made to trace the owners of copyright material, we take this opportunity to apologise to any copyright holders whom we may not have been able to contact and whose rights we may have unwittingly infringed.

All trademarks used in this book are the property of their respective owners. The use of any trademark in this text does not vest in the author or publisher any trademark ownership rights in such trademarks, nor does the use of such trademarks imply any affiliation with or endorsement of this book by such owners.

Design project

1

- **Identifying an ICT project**
- **Defining the purpose of the project and planning how to undertake the work**
- **Using software to produce the required facilities**
- **Testing and evaluating your work**

You will need to create a computer application to carry out some useful task. To do this you will need to build on what you have learnt in other units.

You might decide to use what you have learnt about database systems to create an application to keep track of members of a sports club.

You could use the knowledge you gained about desktop publishing (DTP) to produce a template for a monthly newsletter.

You need to make sure you choose something which you can achieve with the resources and the time you have available. Your teacher will help you in this, but it will be to your benefit to choose something you are interested in. You will use software to design and create a product which meets a specified user need – so you will need to identify and define this need. The result may be a single product or a number of related products.

Identifying a suitable project

Although computers usually come with a range of general purpose application programs, such as word processing, spreadsheet and database programs, these usually need to be modified to meet the specific needs of particular users.

Microsoft Access provides powerful database facilities. If you gave a sports club secretary (who perhaps had only used a computer for typing letters and memos) a copy of the program and told them to use it to keep track of all the club's members, they would probably not be able to achieve very much on their own. However, if you were to set up the database for them, creating and linking the required tables, setting up all the screen forms, printed reports and queries they might need, then they would probably be able to make use of the database.

To complete this unit, you need to think of a suitable project that will help someone to make better use of the computer. Although you could use an imaginary person, it is probably better if you can find an actual person (a friend, member of your family or even yourself), because that way you will be able to get a clearer idea of what the person actually wants.

Exercise 1.1

Write a list of people that you know who have a computer. List some of the things that these people might like to be able to do with their computer. Ask yourself: could you produce something that would help them?

Whatever you decide to do, it is important to make sure that the project you choose is achievable.

- Is it within your own capabilities?

You might like to create your own full functional version of 'Tomb Raider' but you probably do not have the programming skills required (yet! – but in the future who knows . . . !)

- Is it possible within the resources you have available?

If your project will require special hardware or software, you need to check that this is available. Remember also that you only have a limited amount of time to complete this project.

- Is it interesting?

It makes sense to choose something that interests you. So, if you enjoy programming, and are hoping to follow a career in programming later on, then you may want to consider a project which includes some programming.

There are a number of ways your project can be structured:

- Several simple facilities
- A single product
- A large project

You could, for example, provide a range of facilities within a computer to make it easier for a novice to use. This would include several simple facilities. You may make a single larger product, by yourself.

Alternatively, you may choose to do something that would take too long to produce on your own. In this case, you may want to consider working in a group. This approach involves a number of additional complexities. You must choose a product that can be broken down into several smaller but more or less equal parts. This way, each member of the group can be allocated a separate part. Also, because you cannot guarantee that all members will complete their part, each part of the project must be sufficiently independent from the other parts for you to complete something worthwhile even if the other parts are not completed.

Activity 1.1

To help you to decide on a suitable project, ask yourself these questions.

★ What sort of projects do you think you could successfully tackle?

> Your teacher may be able to guide you here.

★ What types of problems do people have using computers, and could you produce something that would help them?

> You should try to speak to as many different computer users as you can to answer this question. Friends, family and students on other courses are just some of the people you could ask.

★ What sort of tasks have you completed so far on the course? Were there any that you would like to do some more of? Are there areas of ICT that you have not had time to explore that interest you?

Make notes on your answers and then discuss them with others in your group.

Jessica

Jessica's sister, Emma, has not long started school and she is learning to do addition and subtraction. Jessica decides to write a program using Visual Basic: an adding and subtracting game for her little sister to play.

Adam

Adam's uncle is a sculptor. He carves beautiful designs in wood and sometimes sells them to people. He knows nothing about computers but would like to have a web page created so his work can reach a wider audience.

If you are interested in web page design or programming, these types of projects may be the kind you should consider. On the other hand, if you enjoy using or creating databases then a project to provide a database for a friend or family member who has a specific requirement may be suitable. Creating spreadsheets, presentation materials or desktop published documents also provide possible areas for projects.

▼▼▼▼▼▼▼▼▼▼
Brainstorming is used when you have to create new ideas, and works best in groups.
▲▲▲▲▲▲▲▲▲▲

One technique that is very helpful in generating fresh ideas is called **brainstorming**.

Brainstorming is a method of free expression that can be great fun as well as very useful. One person's idea may not be brilliant, and it may not be the answer to the problem, but it can trigger a better idea from someone else in the group. In this way, brainstorming stimulates the production of ideas.

Did You Know?

The ideal group size should be somewhere between four and eight. Fewer people may not be able to generate enough ideas. With more than eight people it may become difficult for anyone to get a word in!

For any brainstorming session, you may be more successful if, before you start, you follow a few rules:

- **Have a clear idea of the problem** to be solved, before you start the brainstorming session

- **Agree who is in your group and appoint someone as 'leader'** – someone to make sure other rules are followed.

- **Appoint someone else as 'scribe'** – someone who will write down ideas as they are suggested.

When everyone is ready, remind yourself of the brainstorming 'goal posts':

- **Each member is asked for an idea in turn**. Sitting in a circle – or round a table – can be helpful in remembering whose turn it is next.

- **Each member can offer only one idea per turn** – if they have no idea to offer they say 'pass'.

- **All ideas are accepted** – even if at first they seem really silly – and written down. A flipchart is useful for this, because everyone can see it, and only one person has to take notes.

- **Questions are only asked if an idea is not clear**. It is best if only the person whose turn it is speaks, and everyone else just listens, until it is their turn.

- **No criticism, discussion, interruptions, comments or judgements are allowed** during this early stage. Interruptions can break the 'creative flow' and criticisms may inhibit some people to make their own suggestions known.

- **Ideas are not evaluated** during the brainstorming session at all – that is left until later. Later could even be another day, after everyone has time to think through all the ideas raised.

- **An informal atmosphere is best**. Even good-natured laughter helps to create the right environment for new ideas.

- **Exaggeration may be a useful tactic**. It adds humour and can also provoke new ideas.

When no more new ideas can be thought of or time runs out, it's time to evaluate the ideas and pick out the best ones.

Activity 1.2

Run a brainstorming session to generate ideas for projects you and the other students in your group could do.

Producing a project proposal

Once you have decided on the idea for your project, you will need to create a project proposal. This document will explain what you will do and what the result will be. You will need to present your proposal to your teacher to gain his/her approval before you can proceed with the project.

The project proposal needs to contain:

- A description of what the user needs
- An outline of how you intend to meet the user's needs
- A list of the resources you will need to complete the project

For the description of what the user needs, you need to explain what the requirements of the eventual user of your product are. You may need to spend some time with that user making sure you understand what problems they currently have.

For the outline of how you intend to meet the users needs, you need to explain how the product you are proposing to produce will meet the needs of the user and solve the problem you have outlined above.

Resources can include a variety of different things:

- Access to computer hardware, including special equipment like scanners, digital cameras, etc.
- Application and operating system software, including clip art files, CD-ROMS, etc.
- Text books and instruction manuals
- Consumables such as paper, disks, ink-jet cartridges, laser printer toner
- Access to the Internet, web page space and e-mail facilities
- People, and their time, to tell you what they require (users) or to give you assistance with problems
- Example of output from the product
- A time schedule showing how long each stage will take

The example output will only need to be in sketch form at this stage but you should be able to give some idea of how the resulting product will look and what it will produce.

You will need to break your project down into various stages and then estimate how long each stage will take. For this, you will have to use your own experience of how long similar task have taken you in the past. If you have never done anything similar, other people (your teacher would be a good place to start) may be able to help you. Remember the basic stages that any project will include:

- **Designing the product** – explained in the next section
- **Creating the product** – depending on what your product is this may involve writing programming code, creating documents, building databases, etc.
- **Testing the product** – making sure it works the way it should and does not give any unexpected results
- **Implementing the product** – giving it to the user, training him/her how to use it, sorting out any teething problems and evaluating it

Once your project proposal is complete, you need to present it to your teacher, and obtain their permission. You will need to convince your teacher that what you are proposing is worthwhile and achievable:

- **Worthwhile** – in that it meets some genuine user need
- **Achievable** – in that it is within your capabilities and can be completed with the time and resources available

Your teacher will ask you some searching questions about your project, so you must be clear in you own mind what you intend to do. You may have to argue your case, so make sure you have prepared well for the meeting. You may find it helpful to run through your proposal with a friend beforehand. Another person may see your product from a different point of view and identify problems that you have missed.

Activity 1.3

Create a project proposal for the project you are considering. Then, in groups of 3 or 4 present your proposals to each other and discuss the strengths and weaknesses of each proposal.

Jessica

Jessica arranges a meeting at Emma's primary school with her teacher. The teacher is very interested in the idea of a computer game to help the children practice their adding and subtracting. The teacher points out there is only one computer in the class room, so it would be helpful if the program recognised each child's name and remembered how well they had done last time they had used the program. It should also restrict the time each child spends on the program and prevent the same child using the game twice in a row. The program would only need to ask the children to do sums with whole numbers between 1 and 10. As the children receive 'smiley face' stickers for good work, it would be a good idea if the program also awarded smiley faces based on how well they did. At the end of each child's session, the program should print out a report showing the sums done and the smiley faces awarded.

Adam

Adam has a chat to his uncle about what kind of information he would like on his web site. Pictures of the sculptures he has previously done are obviously important. His uncle would also like some photos and information about himself. He would like a feedback form on the web site so people could comment on his work, make suggestions and perhaps even contact him to buy one of his sculptures or commission him to make one specially.

Planning the design

Once you have permission to proceed, the next stage is to design your project in more detail. Designing your project should take about a quarter of the time you spend on this unit. It is important that your design is good. Producing something from a poor design will never result in a successful project.

Your design needs to include, in the form of notes or drawings, all the details of the project. Use the following list as a guide, although you should bear in mind that not all of the items on the list may apply to your project:

- A list of all the information you will need and where you will get it from
- People who will help you planning the project, e.g. users, colleagues, teachers
- Sketches of screen layouts, reports, templates or documents
- Descriptions of programs or macros
- Design tools like storyboards, flowcharts, etc.
- Lists of graphics files to be used (and the source of graphics files)
- Sketches of graphic files you will produce.
- Examples of records, data types, calculations or formulae to be used
- Specifications for any search or sort requirements
- Layout of toolbars or menus to be created
- Ideas for testing each part of your work

Jessica

Because Jessica's project is based on programming, she needs to produce a program design for her product. She uses the techniques of flowcharting and sequence diagrams. She also produces a sketch of the screen design her program will use, and of the report it will print out. She remembers that she will need to find a clip art file of a smiley face. Jessica lists the resources she will need:

★ Regular access to a computer with Visual Basic installed

★ A book or manual on Visual Basic (her college library has several)

★ Some help and advice from her programming lecturer

★ Some time with Emma's teacher

Rebecca estimates that she needs about an hour with her teacher to demonstrate her prototype, and a couple of hours to show the finished product and help her to evaluate it.

Adam

Adam uses the storyboard technique he learnt in the multimedia unit to sketch out the design for the web pages he will create.

He also makes a list of the resources he will need:

★ Regular access to a computer with web page design software
★ Use of a digital camera (to take photographs of his uncle and his work)
★ A book or manual on using the web page design software
★ Some help and advice from his multimedia teacher
★ Time with his uncle to take the photographs and collect other information he wants on the web site
★ Internet access and web space to load the web site

Activity 1.4

Decide what details will you need to include in the design for your project. Make notes and discuss your ideas with others in your group.

You will also need to flesh out the time plan you produced in your project proposal. As you work on your design you should develop a better idea of all the tasks you need to complete. You need to develop your project plan showing when you will do each task (some tasks will have to be done in a certain order) and how long you estimate each task will take. One of the problems you may face during this project is completing everything on time. Your plan must show not only how long each task takes but also by which date each task will be completed. That way, once the project is underway, you can monitor your actual progress against your plan. Remember the project must be completed by a certain deadline date, so if some tasks take longer than expected you will have to try to make up time later on.

One useful project planning tool is the **Gantt chart** (Figure 1.1). This displays planned and actual progress against a horizontal time-scale. As well as showing when each task is due to begin and end, it shows the links between tasks, and from this a **'critical' path** of a project.

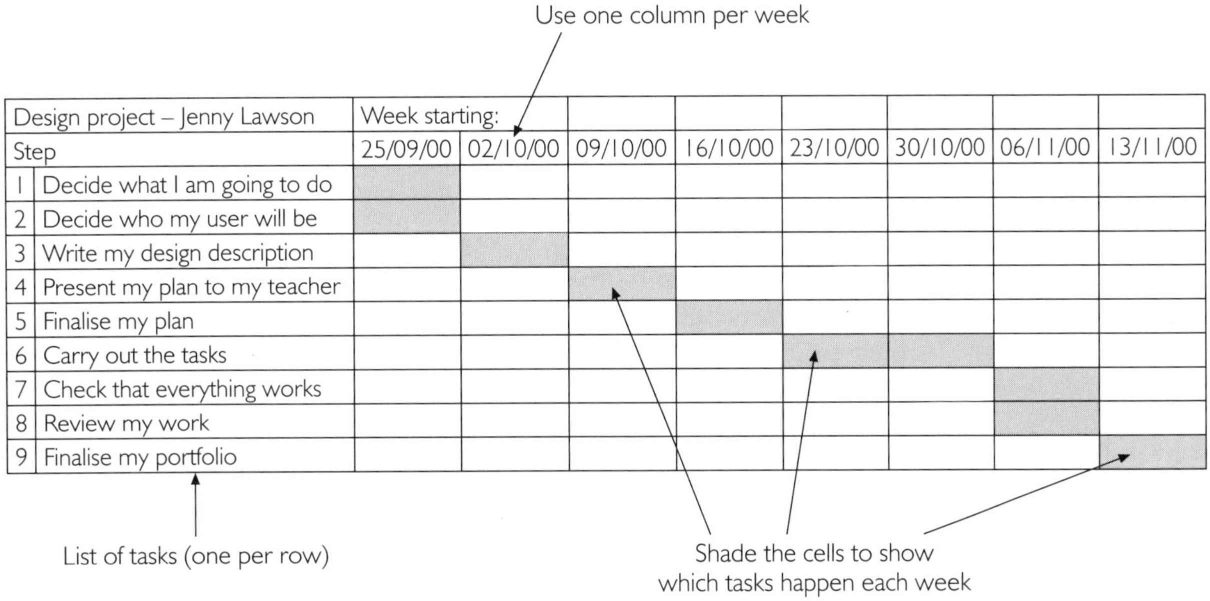

Use one column per week

Design project – Jenny Lawson	Week starting:							
Step	25/09/00	02/10/00	09/10/00	16/10/00	23/10/00	30/10/00	06/11/00	13/11/00
1 Decide what I am going to do	▓							
2 Decide who my user will be	▓							
3 Write my design description		▓						
4 Present my plan to my teacher			▓					
5 Finalise my plan				▓				
6 Carry out the tasks					▓	▓		
7 Check that everything works							▓	
8 Review my work								
9 Finalise my portfolio								▓

List of tasks (one per row)

Shade the cells to show which tasks happen each week

Figure 1.1 *Gantt chart*

When allocating a duration for each task, it is usually easier to work from the deadline backwards. If you then find you seem to have too much to do in the available time you may need to rethink your project. Are you taking on too much? Or do you need to allocate more time to the project?

The important thing is to be in control of the timing of the project. A last-minute rush may mean the quality of your product suffers. Leaving things to the last minute also means you may put yourself under stress.

Production and progress monitoring

Once the design is complete, you need to begin work on the product. The tasks you will have to complete will depend on the type of project you have chosen.

The design you have previously completed should guide your progress, but you will probably find there are problems or tasks that you did not anticipate at the design stage. You must go back to your time plan regularly, check your progress and amend your plan if things have not gone as you planned or you have needed to do some tasks you had not included in the original plan. Without this monitoring, you may find yourself bogged down in one small area of the project and when the deadline arrives, the rest of the project is incomplete.

Jessica

Jessica's project starts off well, and goes according to plan. However, four weeks into the project she has the flu and is off for a week, which puts her behind. She also underestimates how difficult the programming is and how many problems she will run into. This puts her another three weeks behind schedule. With the deadline approaching rapidly, she decides she will have to leave out the part of the program which prints a report on each child's progress. Unless she does this, her project will not be completed by the deadline.

Testing and documentation

As your product is nearing completion, you must begin to test that it works correctly and write both technical and user documentation for it.

Testing

When testing your product you need to be sure that it works both when it is being used correctly and when it is being used incorrectly. You should remember that the user of the product may not be an expert in using computers, so it needs to be easy to use and difficult to break, in other words, **robust** and **idiot proof**.

Your testing needs to be systematic and thorough. It can help to produce a **test plan**. The subject of testing and producing a test plan is covered on page 345 in Chapter 10: Programming.

Apart from testing the product yourself, it helps to have someone else test it as well. Because you have been working closely on the project, you may not notice if something is wrong. Someone who understands how the system works and yet is unfamiliar with it – someone with a fresh pair of eyes – may spot something you have missed.

Activity 1.5

Working with another student on your course, test each other's product.

★ While testing the product, write down anything which does not work the way you expect it to, or any improvements you think might be useful.

★ Once you have completed the testing, review your list of comments and write a summary of things that need attention.

★ Discuss each other's list and then make any amendments to your product that you feel are necessary.

Documentation

You need to produce two sets of documents:

- User documentation
- Technical documentation

User documentation explains to the user how the product is to be used. What you include will depend on the type of product you create:

- How to start and exit the product
- Examples of how the product can be used, including screen shots
- Explanations of the different types of input that can be made
- What various error messages mean
- The functions of menus, toolbars, buttons and icons
- How to produce different reports or documents

Remember to use language your users will be able to understand. Unless they are computer experts, technical jargon will only confuse them. Remember also that you may have to explain some things to novice users that would be obvious to computer experts.

Technical documentation explains how the product was created. Again, the content will depend on the type of product you have created:

- The document you created at the design stage
- Hardware and software requirements
- Listings of macros or programs
- Lists of names, locations and contents of files required
- Details of testing carried out – your test plan
- Designs of database tables
- Spreadsheet formulae

Activity 1.6

Prepare to write the user documentation for your project.

★ Start with a Contents page which lists everything that you need to include for the user.

★ Collect together all material that you have produced to date.

★ Check what extra information you might need to produce to complete this documentation.

Produce your user documentation using word-processing facilities. Then, swap documentation with a friend.

★ Read through each other's user documentation, while working with their product.

★ Make notes on how the documentation might be improved.

★ Then discuss any ways in which each other's documentation can be improved.

Make improvements to your own user documentation so that it is ready to present to your teacher.

Activity 1.7

Repeat Activity 1.6 for the technical documentation for your project.

TESTING AND DOCUMENTATION

Evaluation

When you present your project to your teacher, your work will be reviewed by your teacher and you will be given some feedback. However, it is important that you review your own work as well. Writing an evaluation helps you to understand what you have learned and what you might be able to do better next time. There are a number of areas you need to consider:

- How good was your design and planning?
- How well did you use time and resources?
- What did you learn?
- What does the user think of your product?

This last point is the real test of success. After all, your product should have been designed to meet the needs of a user. Before you present your product to your user, review what you have done to see if you can make any final improvements.

If you carry out an evaluation some time <u>before</u> you are scheduled to present your project to your teacher, you may have the opportunity to improve it some more, and to gain a higher grade.

Activity 1.8

Ask yourself these questions about your design and planning:

★ Was your project realistic? Did you run out of time? If so, why?

★ Did you follow your plan closely? Did you have to constantly modify your plan?

★ How closely does your finished product match your original design? If there are differences, why?

Make notes on your answers. In particular, prepare to answer these questions if your teacher asks them.

Activity 1.9

Ask yourself these questions about your use of time and resources:

★ How would you improve your product if you had more time?

★ Were you able to use the resources you needed, when you needed them?

★ How would you improve your product if you had more and better resources?

Make notes on your answers.

> If you still have some time before your deadline, you might decide to make some improvements.

Activity 1.10

Ask yourself these questions about what you learnt while doing the project:

★ What worked well and what worked not so well on your project, and why?

★ What techniques did you use which you might use again?

Make notes on your answers. You may soon be attempting another project, and you can benefit from this one, even if you felt it did not work as well as you had hoped.

EVALUATION

Activity 1.11

Present your product to your user and ask for feedback. Make notes on the response. After your presentation, ask yourself these questions:

★ How did the user react when they tried the product? Were they happy with it or not? If not, why not?

★ Did the user find the product easy to use? Was the user documentation suitable? If not, why not?

★ Did your product meet the needs of the user?

★ Were there any improvements the user could suggest to your product?

Write a report summarising your project performance and include it in your project documentation.

Information resources

2

- Use a wide range of resources to seek out information from articles and tables

- Draw together information from a variety of sources

- Investigate the types of information resources organisations use

- Draw conclusions about the importance and effectiveness of information resources to organisations today

- Consider the effects of information overload on individuals and organisations

The Internet is being used extensively as an information resource tool. Individuals and organisations alike can surf the Internet at a touch of a button. The Internet may seem to have replaced conventional methods of information resourcing, but is it a more effective research tool? This is the type of question this chapter will consider.

How and where to find information, and how to make use of it is the theme of this chapter. You will search for information on a topic of your choice, carrying out searches for the information using a variety of information sources, including paper-based and ICT-based sources. Whatever you find will be recorded and collected as an information pack, together with notes describing the content of the pack. You will distinguish between the information resources that organisations use to communicate internally and externally. You will use case studies to discuss the advantages and disadvantages of organisations' current information resources and suggest alternatives that these organisations may not have even thought of to date.

Up till now, the majority of information has been stored in printed form. This includes books, newspapers and other documents. Nowadays, much information is available electronically, especially on the Internet. While you may feel you will never need to refer to paper-based information, it will help you to make best use of electronic information if you first understand how to access and use paper-based information. Then you can compare this with electronic sources and see the good and bad points of both forms.

This chapter looks in detail at six topics.

- Paper-based sources of information
- ICT-based sources of information
- Finding information you need
- Methods of communicating information
- Information in organisations
- Information overload

This chapter complements the work in Intermediate Unit 1: *Presenting information* and builds on Unit 2, so information given in the Intermediate GNVQ ICT book will be useful to you, especially where it covers the detailed use of effective techniques for finding, analysing and using information.

Paper-based sources of information

Paper-based sources of information have been available for a long time. Do you know anything about the history of paper and printing?

Activity 2.1

Use the Internet to find the answers to these questions:

★ Before paper was invented how were facts recorded in writing?
★ What language was used for the earliest writings?
★ What material was paper first made from?
★ How did the knowledge of producing paper spread through the world?
★ When was the first paper mill established in England?
★ When was the printing press invented? Who invented it?

Keep a note of where you found the information, and details of any web sites that you might like to visit another time.

Did You Know?

Paper was first made in China, in AD105, by a eunuch called Ts'ai Lun, who was attached to the Eastern Han court of the Chinese emperor Ho Ti.

Activity 2.2

Working with others in a small group, imagine that you have been transported back in time to a period before the invention of paper.

★ Discuss what might happen during a typical school day. Brainstorm your ideas.
★ Then, individually, write a report on the differences that you imagine.

PAPER-BASED SOURCES OF INFORMATION

There are many different paper-based sources of information:

- Reference books
- Dictionaries
- Encyclopaedias
- Directories
- Card indexes
- Paper files

Exercise 2.1

What other types of paper-based sources of reference can you think of? Explain how each is used and where they are most commonly used.

Reference books

Reference books tend to be very large books that cannot be taken away from the library. These books are often very expensive, hence the library wanting to keep them in situ as opposed to lending them out.

Activity 2.3

With others in your group, visit your library.

★ Make a list of all the reference books that are relevant to your area of study. What reasons do you think that your library has for making those particular books reference only?

★ Find out what reference material can be found on-line. Make a list and compare it with what is available from the library.

★ Compare your findings with others in your group.

Dictionaries

> **Did You Know?**
>
> The British Computer Society (BCS) produces a *glossary* of computing terms.

Dictionaries list words in alphabetical order and, for each word, a definition of its meaning, and other forms of the word, including where it comes from. Dictionaries are available in lots of different languages: English, American English, French, German and so on. Dictionaries often have other useful information such as foreign phrases, abbreviations and symbols.

Dictionaries are also available for particular subject areas, although sometimes these are called **glossaries**.

Exercise 2.2

In The British Computer Society (BCS) *Glossary of Computing Terms*, look up the word 'Modem'. Copy its definition.

List five other types of glossaries, giving an example definition from each.

Check what dictionaries are available in your school and make a list. Which dictionaries do you think you would use the most and why?

Encyclopaedias

Encyclopaedias offer more than a dictionary. Instead of just defining words, encyclopaedias explain them.

For this reason, an encyclopaedia may be presented as lots of books in a series. It is also unusual for individuals to buy a complete set of encyclopaedias, because they cost such a lot and can soon become out of date. In libraries, encyclopaedias are kept in the reference section, so they can be looked at but not borrowed and taken away.

Exercise 2.3

Find information in an encyclopaedia about these topics: scanners, the silicon chip and the Internet.

How easy was the encyclopaedia to use?

PAPER-BASED SOURCES OF INFORMATION

Directories

▼▼▼▼▼▼▼▼▼

Telephone directory holds the name, address and telephone number of nearly everyone in a particular area.

▲▲▲▲▲▲▲▲▲

Did You Know?

Some people prefer <u>not</u> to have their telephone numbers included in a directory. Their numbers are called ex-directory.

Directories hold information to help you to contact people and organisations.

Entries in a directory are shown in alphabetical order of surname. Because people move house and change telephone numbers so frequently, **telephone directories** are published every year, but can still be out of date after a very short time.

It helps businesses if their contact details are presented under categories, so that someone wanting a particular kind of product or service can find them listed with other similar traders. For this reason, telephone directories sometimes have a business section. Special **trade directories** are also published, such as *Yellow Pages* and *Thomson Directory*. In these, businesses might also choose to pay for a larger entry including an advertisement. Then, when you turn to the category, their entries are noticed ahead of others.

Exercise 2.4

Use a telephone directory to find out the telephone numbers of five people in your class whose numbers you do not already know.

Use a business directory to find the contact details for: your local doctor, dentist, hospital, police station and veterinary surgery.

How easy were the directories to use?

Was the business directory easier to use than the telephone directory?

Explain your answer.

Card indexes

Card indexes are a useful way of keeping information. Each card relates to one thing: a person, a car, an event, or a topic that you have to revise for an examination. Depending on the situation, the cards may be arranged either alphabetically (e.g. by topic title), or numerically (e.g. in date order). Card indexes are often stored in a box, or in drawers. Sometimes they can be held on a circular stand, which allows you to see the contents of one card, for example while making a telephone call.

Card indexes are useful because you can hand write information as things change, and keep notes that are important to you. There is flexibility in how you present information on the card.

Many people use a card index for their address list. Adding an extra person's details is easy – you just add another card.

Sometimes libraries still use card indexes for their books. One card index is arranged in order of author – one card per book title. Another card index – with identical information – may be arranged in order of subject.

Having two card indexes allows you to look things up, according to how much you know. For the librarian, though, this means changes have to be recorded twice, once in each card index.

Activity 2.4

With others in your group, visit your local library to find out what indexing system is used.

★ If they still use card indexes, look up some details, e.g. books available for a GNVQ course. Make a note of what information is written on each card, and how these cards are arranged.

★ If the library now has a computerised system, ask the librarian how the card index system used to work, and how the new system improves on it.

★ Ask if he or she is completely happy with the computerised system. Is there anything that could be improved?

Libraries hold a lot of books and need to keep track of them. People who use libraries need to be able to locate books on a particular topic, so librarians catalogue the books. The main catalogue is based on the author of a book. So long as you know who wrote a book, you should be able to find out whether a library has a copy.

Often though, you are interested in finding books on a particular topic, and you don't know – and really don't mind – who wrote the books.

PAPER-BASED SOURCES OF INFORMATION

> **Did You Know?**
>
> In 1876, Melvil Dewey invented the **Dewey decimal system** of classifying books.

Under the Dewey decimal system, all knowledge is divided into ten main classes, and each is given a 100-number span. The first class is 000-099, and these numbers are used for encyclopaedias, newspapers and magazines. Each main class is then divided into 10 subclasses. So, the 800–899 class is for literature, but the 810s are for American literature, and 811 is for American poetry. More numbers then appear after a decimal point to give even more detail, e.g. a particular place, or period in history.

More recently, the **Library of Congress classification** has offered a system, which divides all knowledge into 21 classes, and each of these is given a single letter code. Within these classes, there is a further breakdown and letters are again assigned, e.g. N represents Fine Arts but NA refers to architecture, NB refers to sculpture and so on. Numbers and more letters are then used to divide these classes further.

Activity 2.5

With others in your group, visit your local library or school library and see what system is used.

★ Check that you understand how the Dewey decimal system works so that, when you are researching your activity, you can identify books that may be useful to your investigation.

★ Use the Dewey decimal system to find all relevant GNVQ ICT publications.

Write a user guide to explain how the system may be used to find information. Use ICT to produce the user guide and include graphics where appropriate.

Paper files

Paper files are useful when you want to store more information than can be kept on a small card index. Files can be stored in lockable filing cabinets for increased security. Often personnel details are stored on paper files.

A Birmingham school

In a school, all the students' details are stored in several large filing cabinets. Each year group is allocated a separate filing cabinet, from Year 7 through to Year 13. Within these filing cabinets, each student has one folder which contains information about SAT test results, parental emergency contact information, yearly reports, medical history and any other information regarding the student. The students' folders for each year group are sorted in order of the student's surname

When a student is not feeling well, the school nurse retrieves the folder from the filing cabinet and checks all relevant medical details. The student's parents are called using the contact sheet from within the folder and the student is sent home. A note is entered in to the student's folder that the nurse has sent the student home ill.

Exercise 2.5

What other types of information do you think are kept on a paper-based filing system in your school?

Activity 2.6

Ask members of your family if they know whether their personal details are kept on any paper-based filing systems. If so, what type of information is kept in their files?

Make notes and compare what you found with others in your group.

Did You Know?

Paper-based information is not covered by the DPA. See Good Working Practice Guide on page 389 for more details.

PAPER-BASED SOURCES OF INFORMATION

ICT-based sources of information

To access the wide range of ICT-based sources of information, first you need a computer with a telephone link, or access via your television or mobile telephone to the Internet.

Floppy disks and CD-ROMs

Disks and CD-ROMs hold massive amounts of data. Floppy disks may hold 1.44Mb of information while a typical CD-ROM can hold 650Mb. CD-ROMs both store and retrieve information more quickly than floppy disks.

Activity 2.7

- ★ Using the same computer system, save the same file, once on to floppy disk and once on to CD-ROM or the hard disk drive. Time the process. Which is quicker?
- ★ Repeat the activity, but retrieving the same file. Which is quicker? By how much?
- ★ Repeat the activity using much larger files.
- ★ Compare your results with those of others in your group. Present your combined findings graphically, using a suitable choice of chart or graph.

DVD stands for digital versatile disc.

DVDs are the latest form of removable storage. They can hold up to 17Gb of information, using both sides of the disc.

Activity 2.8

Using the Internet, find out the cheapest price of these storage types:

★ Floppy disk 1.44Mb
★ CD-ROM 64Mb
★ DVD 7Gb

Make a note of the suppliers. Compare your findings with others in your group. Present your findings graphically, using a suitable choice of chart or graph.

> If you can find trade journals for the computer industry of many years ago, compare today's prices with those charged in the past.

Activity 2.9

★ In groups of three or four, research the topic of 'disks, CD-ROMs and DVDs'.
★ Make notes on the benefits and limitations of using these methods to store and retrieve information as opposed to using paper-based resources.
★ Provide arguments for and against using ICT methods to store and retrieve information.
★ Discuss with the rest of the class.

Teletext

Teletext is a system that uses part of the broadcast TV picture, otherwise unseen to the viewer, to supply a variety of information, such as news items, weather forecasts and travel information.

> **Did You Know?**
>
> All TV channels in the UK offer this service; the BBC version is called **Ceefax**. The commercial channels were originally known as **Oracle** until the name Teletext was adopted as a brand name.

Viewers with a specially equipped TV set can replace the TV picture by text pages, simply by pressing buttons on a remote control handset.

Each page of information is numbered and all pages are transmitted in numerical sequence. A particular choice of page is made by entering the page number. There is a slight delay (until that page is next transmitted) before it appears on the screen.

The viewer cannot talk back to the provider of the pages of information, since this is only a one-way information service. Also, the waiting time limits the number of pages that can realistically be provided.

However, some pages are linked. Fastext – which uses coloured buttons – allows viewers to pass from one page to another more rapidly.

Activity 2.10

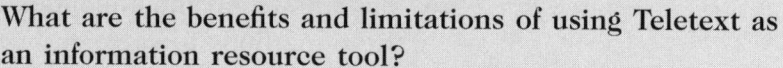

Use Teletext to find out this information, timing how long it takes for the information to appear on the screen:

★ The latest headlines
★ The exchange rate for Spain
★ The weather forecast for Malta
★ The travel situation in your local area

What are the benefits and limitations of using Teletext as an information resource tool?
Does the time taken vary at different times of the day?

Bulletin boards

A bulletin board can be likened to a computerised notice board. A bulletin board can be very useful when information needs to be disseminated across a network, or when ideas need to be shared.

Vanessa is selling a sofa!

Vanessa works for a company called Punch. She has a sofa for sale. To target as many potential buyers as possible, she puts a notice up on the department notice board and also posts the notice on the company's electronic bulletin board. While she is in the bulletin board, she sees a dog cage for sale. She prints out the information, calls the contact number and arranges a time to see the cage. Within two hours, Vanessa has had several calls about the sofa and she sells the sofa the next day. Vanessa forgets to delete the notice from the bulletin board, but does remember to take down the notice from the department notice board. After a few more hours of calls, she realises her mistake and deletes the notice.

Activity 2.11

- ★ Make a list of the benefits and limitations of using a bulletin board.
- ★ Find a bulletin board on the Internet, and read the notices.
- ★ In groups, discuss the types of information that you would *not* allow on a school bulletin board.
- ★ Individually design a leaflet, which can be given to students who register an interest in using a bulletin board. The leaflet should inform them of the rules and regulations of using the bulletin board.

Use Vanessa's case study to help you.

The Internet

The Internet and the world wide web now offer an almost unlimited amount of information. Like the Teletext system, 'pages' of textual and graphical information are displayed either on a TV screen or on the screen of a PC. Unlike Teletext, the Internet can use regular telephone lines, rather than a broadcast TV signal, to transmit information. This makes it possible for the user to interact with the system, for instance by requesting searches of valuable information, supplying information for other users to access, and ordering goods and services by credit card. Only those pages requested are transmitted, so (unlike Teletext) very large amounts of data are accessible, with no penalty to other users on the system.

An **Internet browser** is the software which allows you to navigate your way around the Internet, looking at the pages you want to see. It allows you to jump from page to page using hot links, or to move back through pages you have just looked at.

Search engines are essential tools for finding information on the Internet. The search engine is software which allows you to specify key words; it then searches the web for sites which include these key words and presents the results of the search as a list of web sites. You can then select whichever site seems suitable and this site is downloaded to your computer.

Exercise 2.6

Find out the name of the Internet browser available to you. List as many different search engines as you can.

Activity 2.12

Test as many different search engines as you can.

★ Which do you find the easiest to use?
★ Which do you think is the most reliable?
★ Which gives the quickest respose?

Explain your answers, including evidence of timings and search results.
Compare your results with others in your group. Which was the most popular search engine?

2 INFORMATION RESOURCES

Depending on your route to information, you will need some equipment and software to access different sources.

Activity 2.13

Use a graphics application to create a diagram which matches equipment type to purpose.

Include these purposes:

★ Input device, output device, storage device, software, method of access

Include these equipment types:

★ Keypad, TV, CD-ROM drive, floppy disk drive, printer, VDU, keyboard, communications, search engine, computer, web browser

Use arrows to match equipment type to purpose, and then add four more pieces of equipment for each purpose to your diagram.

How you can access the information, once at your source, depends on how the data is stored. Some data may be stored in a record-structured database using tables, records and fields. Other data may be stored as pages. **Viewdata** simply presents one page after another, although you do select the number of the next page you want to see. **Hypertext** – as used on web pages – allows you to move from page to page using **hot links**.

Activity 2.14

Using the Internet find a site which uses a hot link.

★ How easy is it to use hot links?
★ How does it aid navigation?

Write notes to explain how hot links work, and how to use them.

▼▼▼▼▼▼▼▼▼
Navigation is the movement between different pages and sites on the Internet.
▲▲▲▲▲▲▲▲▲

ICT-BASED SOURCES OF INFORMATION

Some information may be sensitive and organisations and the individual must ensure that security and confidentiality when required are maintained.

User identities are assigned to users of a computer system to allow them to log on and use the system. User identities are often called **logon IDs**. A user identity is unique to one user; it promotes security and personalisation. User identities also allow system administrators to set access rights to the system being used. Figures 2.1 and 2.2 show examples of ID cards which include ID numbers.

Figure 2.1 *Staff ID card*

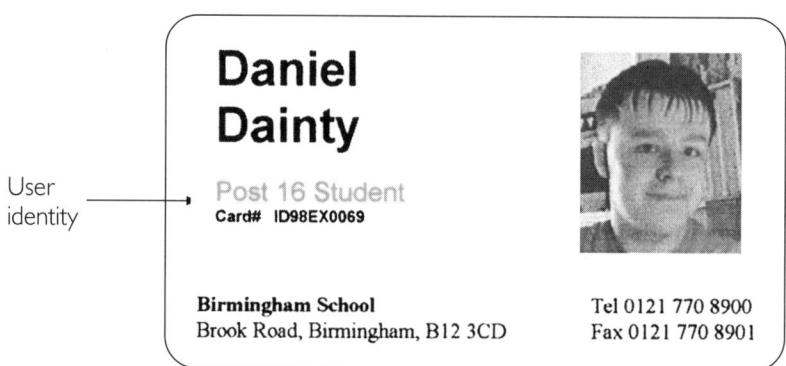

Figure 2.2 *Student ID card*

Once a user ID has been set up, a password is also created. **Passwords** allow the user to ensure that they have total control over their own user area. Alphanumeric passwords are the best form – this means they are created using both letters and numbers, e.g. GTB1802. Passwords should never be given to anyone else and should remain confidential. Passwords should be changed periodically to maintain security.

A Birmingham school

Each year new staff join the school. They are each assigned a user identification number, which is printed on a security card. The card has several functions: opening doors, printing and photocopying. On the card, the user's ID is printed.

This user ID is then used to assign a user name and a password on the computer system. Figure 2.1 shows the user ID as IDTEA00019. Assigned to this user ID is the user name DUFFA. The password is set as staff and the user will change it on their first logon. Having a user ID allows the system administrator to assign staff/student rights. When deciding on a password, the user should avoid using words that others may guess, such as pets, family or friends names.

The students' ID cards are very similar (Figure 2.2).

Exercise 2.7

What are the main difference between the two ID cards shown in Figures 2.1 and 2.2?

What system of user identities do you have in your school?

How are passwords set?

Activity 2.15

Use desktop publishing to design a leaflet for the new intake of Year 7 students, which explains what a user identity is and the importance of passwords.

Encryption is the use of a key to scramble data which can only be unscrambled using this unique key. Encryption is often used when zipping a file. The password assigned to the zip file by the user is used to encrypt the

ICT-BASED SOURCES OF INFORMATION

data and decrypt the data when opened. This is most commonly used when transferring data over the Internet to improve file security.

Figure 2.3 shows a simple method of encryption. The plain text is substituted with random encryption text when sent and on opening the file is converted back to plain text.

Figure 2.3 *A simple method of encryption*

Virus checking enables files to be checked before they are opened or transferred on to a computer system. The main reason for virus checking is so that system security can be maintained.

Mr Bickle's Home Computer

Mr Bickle is a Design Technology teacher. He does a lot of computer work at both school and home. Mr Bickle does not have access to the Internet. When he wants to transfer data between either home or school, he saves this data on to disk. As part of good working practice, before Mr Bickle opens any file from disk, he checks the file for viruses to ensure that the data has not been contaminated.

Viruses can be fatal to a computer. Some viruses can actually bring the computer to a standstill. It is even more important when the computers are networked. If a file is opened on a network which has a virus on it, depending on the nature of the virus, it may affect all the computers on the same network.

Exercise 2.8

Find out if anyone in your class has ever experienced a computer virus and what happened to their computer system. What actions should they have taken to prevent this from happening?

Activity 2.16

Use the Internet to do this research.

★ Find out what different types of virus can be found and the common effects that this may have on a computer system.

★ Find out what virus checking software is available on the market today and the cost.

Restricting physical access: sometimes, especially in a public environment, it is necessary to restrict access to a computer or its peripherals for the system to be kept in good working order. Restricting physical access simply means preventing anyone from damaging the computer or physically removing it by various methods.

Information boards at motorway service stations are positioned behind glass or very high up. Another way to restrict access is to lock the computer room!

Exercise 2.9

List as many different ways of physically restricting access as you can think of.

Computers are in use throughout society – collecting, storing and distributing information (processing). Much of that information is about living people (personal data). The **Data Protection Act** (DPA) places obligations on those who record and use personal data (data users). They must be open about the use (through the data protection register) and follow sound and proper practices (the Data Protection Principles).

The DPA also gives rights to individuals about whom information is recorded (data subjects). They may request information about themselves, challenge it, have it corrected or erased if appropriate, and claim compensation in certain circumstances. When it was first passed in 1984, the DPA also allowed the UK to ratify the Council of Europe Convention on Data Protection, allowing information to flow freely between the UK and other European countries with similar laws.

The DPA only applies to automatically processed information. It does not cover information, which is held and processed manually – for example, in

> **Did You Know?**
>
> The term 'computer' is never used in the DPA. Instead, it uses the terms data and data user.

ordinary paper files. Not all computerised information is covered by the DPA, only that which relates to living individuals. So, for example, it does not cover information, which relates only to a company or organisation.

Anyone who holds personal information about living individuals on computer must register unless covered by one of the exemptions provided by the DPA. To register as a data user, information has to be supplied for inclusion in the register:

- The name and address of the data user
- A description of the purposes for which personal data are used
- The type of personal data held
- Where the personal data are obtained
- To whom they will be disclosed
- A list of any countries outside the UK to which they may be transferred

Once a data user has registered, he or she must only act within the terms of the register entry. Not to do so is an offence. A data user can apply to the Registrar to alter his or her register entry at any time. It is an offence to fail to register or to provide false information to the Registrar.

Once registered, data users must comply with the Principles in relation to the personal data held:

- To collect and process the data fairly and lawfully
- To hold the data only for specified and lawful purposes
- To use the data only for those purposes and only disclose it to those people described in the register entry
- To ensure the data is adequate, relevant and not excessive in relation to the purposes for which they are held
- To keep the data accurate and, where necessary, up to date
- To hold the data no longer than is necessary for the registered purpose
- To protect the data by proper security

However, the Registrar cannot enforce the Principles against unregistered data users.

The Principles also provide for individuals to have access to data held about themselves and, where appropriate, to have the data corrected or deleted.

Activity 2.17

Use the Internet to find out when the Data Protection Act was updated. In groups of five, read and summarise the Data Protection Act. Include in your notes the rights of the individual and details of exemptions.

★ Create a 5-minute presentation about the Data Protection Act, using presentation software.

★ Create handouts if you think it is appropriate and will aid understanding.

How do you think that the Data Protection Act affects the way an organisation manages its information?

More information about the DPA is given in the Good Working Practice guide on page 389.

Exercise 2.10

Within your school, find out what types of information should be kept confidential. What measures has the school in place to ensure that this information is secure?

Intranets

Intranet is a localised version of the Internet.

The services on an Intranet are usually not available to the public as they host private printing facilities and internal e-mail.

A Birmingham school

A Birmingham school has its own Intranet, including localised e-mail services and the option to print to a variety of printers within the building. The web server allows users to retrieve information such as the names and e-mail addressees of fellow students and staff.

Activity 2.18

In small groups, have a brainstorming session to generate a list of the advantages and disadvantages of using an Intranet. Discuss your ideas with other groups.

On-line databases

Before you can start looking for information on any electronic database, you must decide what information you need! From this, you can decide on suitable words – called **key words** – that you will use for searching. You can then decide what sources are most likely to contain what you want. You must also be prepared to record what information you find. This might include printing it out, copying from a screen display or saving the information to a disk file.

Many on-line databases can be accessed via the Internet to query information and organisations use these on-line databases to sell products, services, etc. When accessing some on-line databases, you may be asked for some form of payment as not all the information on on-line databases are free of charge.

The Meteorological Office provide some free information but other pages are charged for.

On-line databases can also be divided into public and private.

Activity 2.19

- ★ Establish the difference between a public and private on-line database, giving two examples of each.
- ★ Using the Internet, find five free on-line databases, five pay on-line databases and three government maintained on-line databases. What are the benefits and limitations of these?
- ★ Share your findings with others in your group.

Searching
involves matching data against given criteria.

Sorting
involves reordering the data usually for a printout.

Relational operators
'less than' (<)
'greater than' (>)
'is equal to' (=)

Logical operators
AND, OR and NOT

Sometimes, even when you locate the information you need, it is not available just how you want it. There may be more information than you need, and you may need to **search** for what you really need, from all that is available to you.

The information may not be in the order you want it, so you may need to **sort** the data into an order that suits you using **relational operators** or using **logical operators**.

Combining simple searches to make more complex searches can save you time.

Activity 2.20

- ★ Find out how questions can be asked, and the different ways you can access information within an on-line help database.
- ★ Using a desktop publishing (DTP) package, write a 150-word article on the use of on-line databases.

ICT-BASED SOURCES OF INFORMATION

Finding information you need

One of the most easily available sources of ICT-based information is the on-line help supplied with applications software. You should have used on-line help many times by now and other paper-based sources. The first step you should take, before writing assignments is to decide what information is required and what sources you will use to find that information.

Josie's assignment research

Josie is set an assignment called 'What impact has ICT had on society? Discuss'.

Josie decides to use a variety of paper-based and ICT-based sources to find information for this assignment. Here is Josie's checklist for tackling this assignment:

- ★ Identify exactly what information is required.
- ★ Decide where I am most likely to find the information.
- ★ Decide on the best search techniques to use – for speed, efficiency and accuracy.
- ★ Carry out any searches on structured and non-structured data using disks, CD-ROMs and viewdata systems.
- ★ Use a web browser to find information from the Internet.
- ★ Establish the validity of the information I find.
- ★ Record the information by saving it, printing it, reading it on screen, making notes.
- ★ Draw together the information found from different sources and present it.
- ★ Draw conclusions from the information.

Activity 2.21 Following a similar process to Josie's, write a report called 'Getting a job on the Internet'.

Methods of communicating information

As well as helping us find information, ICT helps us to communicate information to others. This can be done in different ways:

- Television
- Radio
- Telephone
- Fax
- E-mail

Television allows communication of information in the form of moving pictures and sound. A **camera** records a series of images (including the sound). This data is converted into electrical impulses and transmitted by radio to a receiver, which then converts them using a cathode ray tube into an image on a TV screen.

Radio involves the transmission and reception of data using electromagnetic waves of frequency between 10^4Hz and 3×10^{12}Hz, either as acoustic signals (called **radiotelephony**) or as Morse code signals (**radiotelegraphy**). **Telemetry** uses communications (usually radio) and measuring sensors as part of a system for controlling machines and instruments at a distance, e.g. satellites and space probes. In Formula 1 racing it is used to monitor and control the performance of cars; the technicians can adjust the engine control systems from the pits while the race is in progress.

With **telephone** communications, there are now two options: a landline or a mobile telephone link. Imagine calling a friend on the telephone. When you speak into the telephone receiver, your voice causes vibrations, which are converted into an electric current. With a landline, this is passed along a wire to your friend at the other end of the telephone line. With mobile phones, it is transmitted via a satellite to your friend's telephone. It is then converted back into audible sound, for your friend to hear. Their reply is sent back to you in the same way.

Activity 2.22

In small groups, devise your own methods of communication using any/all of these items:

- ★ String
- ★ Cans
- ★ Bells
- ★ Spoons
- ★ Sellotape
- ★ Paper

See how many different systems you can devise!

Explain, in the form of a user guide, how your most successful communication system works.

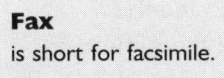

Fax is short for facsimile.

Fax transmission uses regular voice-quality telephone lines – or mobile phone networks – to send copies of documents, which may include drawings as well as text. A **fax machine** allows you to transmit and receive copies of paper document pages. To send a fax, you first dial the receiving machine, which must be available at that time, (i.e. not busy sending or receiving another fax). When you hear the continuous tone, you press the 'start' button. Your fax machine then scans the paper on a line-by-line basis. This information is transmitted along the telephone line – or broadcast via the mobile phone network – to the receiving machine, which recreates the document using photocopier technology. For this reason, many fax machines can also operate as photocopiers.

Did You Know?

To simplify the process of identifying compatibility, fax machines are classified into groups with different technical specifications.

The two fax machines must be compatible, i.e. belong to compatible groups, if they are to communicate.

If your computer is connected to the telephone line, you can send faxes directly, without the need to generate a paper copy first. This solves the problem of the receiving machine being busy; your computer can simply try again later, without human intervention.

METHODS OF COMMUNICATING INFORMATION

Activity 2.23

Find out if anyone in your group has a parent/friend who would be agreeable to you sending a fax to them. If so, send a test fax, requesting a reply. How easy is it to use a fax machine?

Explain in the form of a report, to someone who has never used a fax machine, how to send and receive a fax.

Electronic mail and networks

E-mail messages are sent from user to user on a computer network, with the message being stored in the recipient's **mailbox** or **inbox**. The next time that they use the computer, they will be told that there is a message waiting, and can read it, print it out or reply.

Because e-mail is relatively cheap, and because the sender and the recipient do not both have to be using their computers at the same time, it is becoming a popular way for people in schools, colleges and in business to communicate.

Activity 2.24

Send a mail message to a friend requesting a reply. Print out the message sent and the reply.

▼▼▼▼▼▼▼▼▼

Copying e-mails
CC stands for carbon copy.
BCC stands for blind carbon copy.

▲▲▲▲▲▲▲▲▲

If you want to send a copy message to other recipients, you have the choice to CC and BCC the message. CC means the person receives a copy of the mail message, and can also see who the message has been sent to. If you want to send a copy of a message to someone, but do not want any of the other recipients to know you have sent another copy, BCC the message.

2 INFORMATION RESOURCES

Information in organisations

Organisations range in size from a single self-employed person to giant multinational commercial companies. Types of organisation include shops, manufacturers, banks, schools and hospitals. The people in all these organisations depend on a wide range of different information to keep the organisation working well.

Every organisation holds information on its employees, its customers and its suppliers, and any regulations that must be followed, e.g. taxation rules. Some organisations may also have information on their competitors and on potential customers. Exactly what other information an organisation needs really depends on the goods or service that it sells or provides.

Generally, information used by organisations can be separated into three groups:

- That coming in from outside
- Internal or operational information
- That going out

Information coming in from outside may be obtained from many sources, e.g. telephone calls, orders from customers, regulations. Prospective employees may complete application forms, customers complete sales order forms, suppliers send product catalogues and trade magazines are published.

A Birmingham school

The reception staff are kept very busy answering incoming telephone calls: the parents of the New Year 7 call for information; parents of students within the school call and leave messages for staff and students.

Just how useful different **sources of information** are to the organisation depends on how up to date the sources are, how relevant the information is to the organisation and how easy it is to obtain the information.

Operational information is private to a company, e.g. sales and income forecasts, instructions to staff, and internal reports. This kind of information is generated by people within the company to be used by other people within the same organisation. This information is confidential to the organisation.

Activity 2.25

★ Choose one organisation that you are familiar with and make a list of all the operational information that you can think of.

★ Compare this list with others in your group. What differences are there between your lists? Suggest possible reasons for those differences.

Most organisations have a **Sales and Marketing** Department responsible for making sure the product or service is promoted well enough to have sufficient impact on the market to ensure good sales figures.

Activity 2.26

★ Think about five marketing campaigns that have had a positive impact on you and encouraged you to purchase the product/service. Write down why they were effective.

★ In contrast, list five marketing campaigns that have had a negative impact on you and discouraged you from purchasing the product/service. Write down why they were not effective.

★ Discuss your findings with others in your group. What do you think makes a marketing campaign effective?

Organisations have **Finance and Accounts** Departments who control the flow of money within a company. This department liaises with other departments to arrange for payment of goods and services. IT is also responsible for payment of wages. Each department will be allocated a budget of expenditure. The information in this area is sensitive and often confidential.

Personnel are responsible for the maintenance of staff records, personal details and pensions. The personnel department generally co-ordinate staff training sessions, recruitment campaigns and liaises with senior management. The information that is circulated in this area is also confidential and discretion is very important when working within this area.

The **Production** area is responsible for making the product and testing. Deadlines will be given and it is crucial that these are kept. Sometimes the Production area will be responsible for research and development too.

The **Purchasing** department are responsible for ordering goods/services, which tends to be done on a requisition form. Purchasing liaises closely with the Accounts department which will ultimately be responsible for the payment of the orders.

Activity 2.27

In small groups, each choose one organisation to study. Have this verified by your teacher, and then find out how each of these functions of the organisation work, giving detailed examples:

★ Operations
★ Sales and Marketing
★ Finance and Accounts
★ Personnel
★ Production
★ Purchasing

Ensure that the organisation that you choose is large enough so that all of the above functions can be covered and discussed.

Derek the Baker

Since his shop opened in 1972, Derek has not changed the quality of the bread and cakes he bakes, or the way he deals with his customers. Despite the threat of competition from nearby superstores, he still gives excellent service to the local residents and many customers who live further away but make a special trip to his bakery.

Recently, Derek has started to use a computer in the administration side of his business. He is now using word-processing and databases on a regular basis.

Derek provides a sandwich delivery service to nearby office workers. Ingredients for the sandwich fillings arrive early each morning. These come from several different suppliers so Derek uses checklists which help him to monitor what has arrived and the quality of the food. When each delivery arrives, he checks it against a delivery note. He also sample checks the quality of the delivery. If the samples are not right, the delivery will be rejected.

The sandwiches are then made and stored in a fridge. The temperature of the sandwich fridge within Derek's shop is also monitored.

For Health and Safety reasons, so that the authorities can trace all ingredients used in the many different varieties of bread, pastries and sandwiches, Derek keeps records of all recipes used in the bakery even though Derek makes bread, pastries and sandwiches every day and knows all these recipes off by heart.

There are also procedures to do with cleaning rosters, and health records of the staff who work at Derek's bakery.

All this information is word-processed. The checklist masters are photocopied. The data sheets, like the recipe sheets, are filed. Then, if any details change, it is easy to correct the document and print out a fresh version.

The information is now all in one file, instead of inside Derek's head – and it is there to be seen by any inspector who may need to check that the correct procedures are indeed being carried out.

Derek is also using databases, sometimes for special orders like weddings, but mostly in the run up to

continued

continued

Christmas, to help process orders for Christmas cakes and mince pies.

All companies, even those who employ as few as five people, have to follow Health and Safety rules. This includes assessing the risks in the workplace and drawing up procedures to minimise risks and remove potential hazards. All companies will have fire regulations, and written information about what to do when the fire alarm sounds. If you contact any small company, they should already have this documentation in place. If they don't, you would be helping them if your project involved setting up the necessary documents for them.

Activity 2.28

★ Identify all the different types of information that Derek the Baker uses.

★ Discuss in groups how ICT aids the process of handling this information.

Information overload is having too much information.

Organisations feed on information. Sometimes there is so much information – called **information overload** – that there are problems. Some workers feel left out if the organisation keeps information to itself, while others feel swamped by masses of information they think is irrelevant.

It is not just organisations that can suffer from information overload. Individuals can also sometimes be faced with so much information that they are not sure which way to turn.

INFORMATION IN ORGANISATIONS 53

While Ron's on holiday the e-mails keep coming

Ron has been on holiday for a week. When he returns there are 83 e-mails waiting for him. Facilities within Microsoft Outlook allow him to sort these on date of arrival (deal with oldest first), sender (deal with most important people first) or topic (deal with most important projects first).

Ron has a strategy to help him cope. He has a good filing system and note taking means that he can find things later. What Ron cannot deal with straight away, he adds to his 'to do' list. He also leaves himself messages. There is a moral to Ron's story: Don't hoard info!

Activity 2.29

- ★ As a group, brainstorm ideas for how to cope with information overload.
- ★ Individually, produce a poster to illustrate one or two of the main ideas.

All organisations need to send information to people outside the organisation, e.g. customers, suppliers and regulatory bodies. These communications may be in the form of written documents, e.g. letters, invoices and advertisements. Many communications use telephone links. Some organisations have a web page and may use e-mail to communicate with other organisations. E-commerce may be used to place and accept orders, and payments may be made electronically by BACS.

Organisations as well as individuals make use of a wide range of information sources and means of communication. The success of their business may depend on how well they communicate with customers, suppliers, and even how well the departments within that organisation communicate with each other.

Exercise 2.11

Distinguish between internal and external modes of communication.

Activity 2.30

Imagine you have entered a time warp and you have landed in the year 2999. Within a group of 5–8 brainstorm ideas about how businesses might communicate between themselves, their customers and their suppliers.

★ What methods of communication might have been developed?

★ Explain the advantages of your newfound technologies. Are there any disadvantages?

Revision questions

1. List as many different paper-based sources of information as you can.

2. What is the Dewey decimal system and when was it invented?

3. What are the most commonly used floppy disk and CD-ROM sizes?

4. Name two examples of Teletext.

5. What is a bulletin board and where is it used?

6. What are the differences between a public and a private on-line database?

7. What is the difference between a relational and logical operator?

8. What is the difference between an Internet and an Intranet?

9. Explain what a hyperlink is.

10. What is encryption?

11. Explain ways in which you can restrict physical access to a computer area.

12. What is telemetry?

13. What type of information is operational information?

14. What does the Production department do?

15. What is information overload?

INFORMATION IN ORGANISATIONS

Communicating with multimedia

3

- The component parts of a multimedia presentation
- What makes a good multimedia presentation
- How to plan, create and present a multimedia presentation to meet a given specification

Multimedia involves combining a range of media such as text, graphics, sound and video into a presentation, which might be used, for example, to advertise a product or a service.

Investigating multimedia presentations

The aim of a multimedia presentation is to communicate a message. The message is often aimed at a particular group of people, called the **target audience**. Commercially produced multimedia presentations are used to communicate a variety of messages: education, entertainment, advertising and so on. Those used for advertising are often given away as free CDs with many computer magazines or on the Internet. Your school or college library will probably have some interactive learning multimedia presentations on CD.

Activity 3.1

Working with others in a group, make a list of all the different multimedia presentations that you have seen in the last 6 months. For each one, make notes on where it was obtained, what is was about and who the target audience was.

Since the purpose of a multimedia presentation is to communicate a message, it is important that the message is communicated as effectively as possible.

Exercise 3.1

For each multimedia presentation listed in Activity 3.1, note the different messages that each one was used to communicate. Are there any messages that are repeated?

You will need to investigate and understand what makes a presentation effective in communicating its message.

Activity 3.2

As a class group, collect as many multimedia presentations as possible.

★ As well as magazine CDs and Internet based presentations, you may also find adverts in magazines where you can send off for a free CD.

★ Look in your school or college library for educational multimedia CDs.

★ Check Pearsons web site for this book for links to multimedia web sites.

Most people are able to say whether a multimedia presentation is good or bad, though any two people may not necessarily agree.

Activity 3.3

In groups of six, select six different multimedia presentations from your collection.

★ Conduct a survey within your group to find out which presentation is the 'best'.

★ Present your results using appropriate software techniques.

Discuss your group's findings with other groups in your class.

You need to be able to go beyond a simple subjective judgement like this and identify *why* you consider one presentation to be less good and why another is better. To investigate the effectiveness of a presentation, you need to identify a number of things about the presentation:

- The **purpose** of the presentation
- The **intended audience**
- The **components** of the presentation
- The **impact** on the audience
- The **appropriateness and effectiveness** of the presentation

What is the purpose of the presentation?

The aim or purpose of the presentation will have an important bearing on how your material is best presented. If the purpose is to educate, then you must clearly and accurately present your material in detail. If your aim is entertainment, you will concentrate on presenting material in a eye-catching and amusing way. However, for educational presentations, to be successful you might need to present the information in a way that is both easily understood and interesting.

Who is the intended audience?

Some presentations are aimed at adults, others at children. You may also need to consider whether the users will be familiar with the topic being presented and whether they will understand the language and terms you use.

What components make up a multimedia presentation?

Different elements make up the presentation; text, graphics, animation and sound – you need to consider when one type of component is more suitable than another.

Exercise 3.2

A multimedia training CD called 'Building your own computer' needs a section on installing the hard disk drive. What would be more effective: a picture and a text description of how to install the disk drive or a video showing the drive being installed?

What is the impact on the audience?

There are a number of ways to communicate a message. The most straightforward is simply to explain the information you are trying to get across. This technique suits educational or training multimedia presentations. However, there are a number of other techniques, often used in advertising, which you can broadly divide into what is called **hard sell** where the advantages of the product, or service are described in simple terms (it's the cheapest, fastest, most powerful, etc.) and **soft sell** where the audience is encouraged to believe that by purchasing this product it will improve their lifestyle or 'make all their dreams come true' (e.g. people who buy this product are rich, stylish or in-fashion, etc.).

A number of tactics can be used to communicate a message using the 'soft sell' method:

- Shock your audience

    If your message is about the dangers of smoking or drink driving, you might decide to adopt the shock tactic approach. By showing the effects of these things (dying cancer patients or terrible car accidents), you may shock the audience into taking these dangers more seriously.

- Amuse your audience

    Amusement is commonly found in TV adverts. By amusing your audience, they might look on your product in a favourable light.

- Appeal to a particular audience

    TV adverts are often targeted to appeal to a particular group of people. Adverts for soft drinks are usually targeted to appeal to young people, whereas soap powder adverts – rightly or wrongly – are targeted at women.

    If you want to produce a presentation about the problems of teenage pregnancy you might decide to use video clips of interviews with teenagers about the problem, thereby appealing to your target audience, rather than video clips of older people (doctors or parents perhaps) to whom your target audience might not relate so well.

Is the presentation appropriate and effective?

You need to decide if a particular presentation gets its message across, and give reasons why it does or does not succeed. This knowledge will help you to create effective presentations of your own. There are a number of factors which you will want to consider:

- **Quantity of information**
  Too much information may confuse or bore the audience, not enough will leave the audience dissatisfied.

- **Pace** – the pace at which information is presented.
  If information is presented too rapidly for the user to take in, the message will not get across effectively. On the other hand, if the pace of the presentation is slow the audience may lose interest.

- **User interaction** – does the user have opportunities to interact with the presentation?
  Interaction between the presentation and the user (e.g. requiring the user to click buttons or answer questions) is more likely to engage the attention of the user and therefore communicate more effectively. If the information is presented in a passive way, without requiring any response from the viewers they are less likely to remember the message.

- **Layout** – is the presentation laid out in a pleasing and professional manner?
  Messy, inconsistent layout will leave the user with a negative impression of the presentation.

- **Ease of use** – was the presentation easy to use? Were user instructions provided?
  A complex or confusing presentation may frustrate the user, they may give up trying to use the presentation or be left with a negative impression.

Activity 3.4

Choose a couple of the multimedia presentations from Activity 3.2.

> It is probably a good idea to choose two presentations that are completely different. For example, one might be an advertising presentation and another might be a training presentation.

Next produce a checklist listing the points explained above. Then, working in small groups (although you could do this on your own if you prefer) watch the two presentations. After you have watched them both, go through your checklist and write comments for each point.

> Try to explain your comments, i.e. rather than just saying some aspect of the presentation was good or bad, say why it was good or bad.

INVESTIGATING MULTIMEDIA PRESENTATIONS

Interpreting multimedia presentation specifications

Although there may be times when you produce a multimedia presentation for your own use, in your future career as an IT professional, you are more likely to be in the situation where you are producing the presentation for a client of the company you are working for.

You may be working for an Internet web page design company. Commercial organisations come to that company and ask them to produce multimedia web sites to promote their products or services. As an employee of the web page design company, you may be asked to design and produce the page for the client.

The client would provide you with a **brief**, that is a description of what the client wants you to achieve with the web site. Figure 3.1 shows an example of a brief.

The key information you need to extract from this brief is:

- Who are the **audience**? What sort of people is the presentation aimed at? You must ensure that whatever you produce will appeal to this target audience.

Memo

to: Tony Davies
from: Anita Welsh
cc:
date: 17/4/2000
subject: College Presentation

As agreed at yesterday's marketing meeting, we need you to produce a multimedia presentation about the college. The presentation will be used at college open and interview days, and will be shown to prospective students while they wait to speak to members of staff or to be interviewed. It should give some details of the facilities available to students studying at the college, as well as some information about the different courses available.

The presentation must allow students to choose which area they are interested in studying. Perhaps we could meet next week to discuss a suitable format and content for the presentation.

Thanks

Anita

Figure 3.1   *A design brief: the memo Anita sent to Tony*

✪ What is the **message**? What is the presentation attempting to communicate to its audience?

Passive audience just watches the presentation.

✪ What kind of **interaction** is required? Is the audience **passive** or do they control or respond to the presentation, perhaps for example, using buttons to select a particular path through the material?

Northgate College

Tony works in the IT support department at Northgate College. He has received a memo from Anita, the college's marketing manageress, asking him to produce a multimedia presentation about the college. Figure 3.1 shows the design brief that Anita sent to Tony. From this design brief, Tony can identify some key information about the presentation:

★ The audience are the prospective students of the college.

★ The message isn't quite so obvious from the memo, but Tony can see that since the presentation is aimed at students who are thinking of coming to the college, it should try to impress them with the range of facilities available to students and the different courses available.

★ What interaction is required? The audience need to be able to choose which area of study they are interested in.

Activity 3.5

★ Select a multimedia presentation that you consider to be good. Write a design brief for this presentation that describes the three key points listed above.

★ Swap design briefs with a friend and comment on improvements that might be made to these design briefs.

INTERPRETING MULTIMEDIA PRESENTATION SPECIFICATIONS

Planning a multimedia presentation

Once you have identified the key details from the client's brief you need to plan how you are going to achieve what is required.

Brainstorming

Deciding on the structure and content of the presentation can be the most difficult part of creating the presentation. You need to make a choice that will get the required message across to the target audience as effectively as possible. The ideas you come up with at this stage shouldn't be detailed but should identify how the user will interact with the presentation and navigate through it, and what sort of 'story' the presentation should tell. One method that can be effective in producing good ideas is **brainstorming**. This process works best with a small group of people, all of whom have studied the client's brief. The group meets together and attempts to come up with as many ideas for the presentation as possible. As each person comes up with an idea, a brief description of the idea is written on a flip chart or white board. At this point, ideas are written up without any comment. Encouragement should be given to come up with as many ideas as possible. No idea should be rejected at this stage even if it seems 'wacky' or unworkable. The idea behind brainstorming is that free thinking produces original ideas.

Northgate College

Tony and Anita have a meeting and brainstorm some ideas. Here is the list of ideas they produced:

★ Interviews with existing students
★ Some examples of how students have progressed from the college to jobs or university
★ Introduction to some of the staff at the college
★ A guided tour around the college

Activity 3.6

A local sports centre wants a short multimedia presentation, encouraging people to use all its different facilities. The presentation will be shown in reception and in the café. Create a brief for this presentation and then, with one or two others, brainstorm ideas for its structure and content.

> You might find it helpful to talk to some students on a Leisure and Tourism course about what sort of facilities a sports centre might offer.

Selecting and justifying ideas

When the brainstorming session is complete, you should have a list of ideas. The next stage is to look at each idea in turn and evaluate it to see if it could be suitable. The challenge here is to choose the best idea: something that is achievable *and* meets the client brief.

Exercise 3.3

From the ideas raised in your brainstorming session in Activity 3.6, choose the best. Give reasons for your choice.

> Look back at your evaluation of commercial multimedia presentations to remind yourself what you thought made a good presentation.

The idea is not to copy existing presentations but to use them as inspiration for your own work. Once you have chosen the idea you will need to justify your choice. In other words you will need to be able to say why you think this idea is better than the others.

PLANNING A MULTIMEDIA PRESENTATION

Northgate College

Having brainstormed a list of ideas Tony and Anita now look at each one in turn and make their selection of the most suitable:

- ★ They both agree that having interviews with existing students is a good idea. However, arranging and videoing interviews would be complex and take a lot of organising. They have a simpler idea of making audio-only recordings of brief interviews with students, accompanied with a couple of photographs of each student taken with a digital camera.

- ★ They agree that some examples of how students have progressed from the college to jobs or university is also a good idea but it would be difficult to contact ex-students and arrange the interviews.

- ★ They feel that an introduction to some of the staff at the college is not such a good idea because students might not relate as well to the staff as they would to other students.

- ★ They both agree that a guided tour around the college is a good idea. Anita suggests the guide for the tour could be a student. However, Tony points out the difficulties associated with recording a lot of video clips. He suggests the idea of using a 'virtual' student in the form of an animated cartoon, rather like the Office Assistant found in Microsoft Office products.

Tony and Anita discuss the various ideas and decide to combine ideas 1 and 4: a guided tour of the college with an animated guide, along with some brief interviews with students. The interviews will be audio-only recordings together with photographs of the students.

Using story boards and flowcharts

Once you have settled on the idea, you need to flesh it out and design the structure and content in detail. Two main tools can be used to design the presentation.

- **Story boards** are used to design the content of individual frames or slides of your presentation.
- **Flowcharts** are used to design the paths through your presentation and are particularly useful if your presentation has multiple paths that the user can follow.

A **story board** combines a diagram or picture of the slide with written details of the content. The diagram of the slide should show the individual elements and their approximate layout. The written description should provide details of the source and the content. In the case of sound and video clips, it should describe the content and should identify what the buttons or hot spots on the slide do.

Figure 3.2 shows a story board for the opening slide of a multimedia presentation on the countries of Europe.

Figure 3.3 shows one slide from the Northgate College presentation.

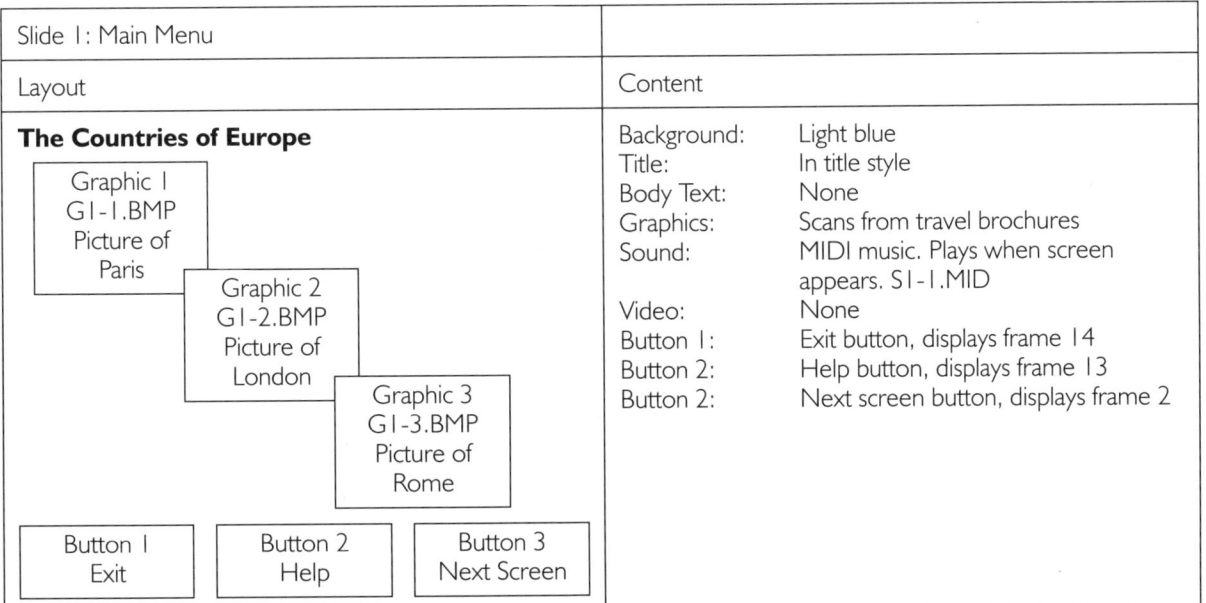

Figure 3.2 *Story board for a slide*

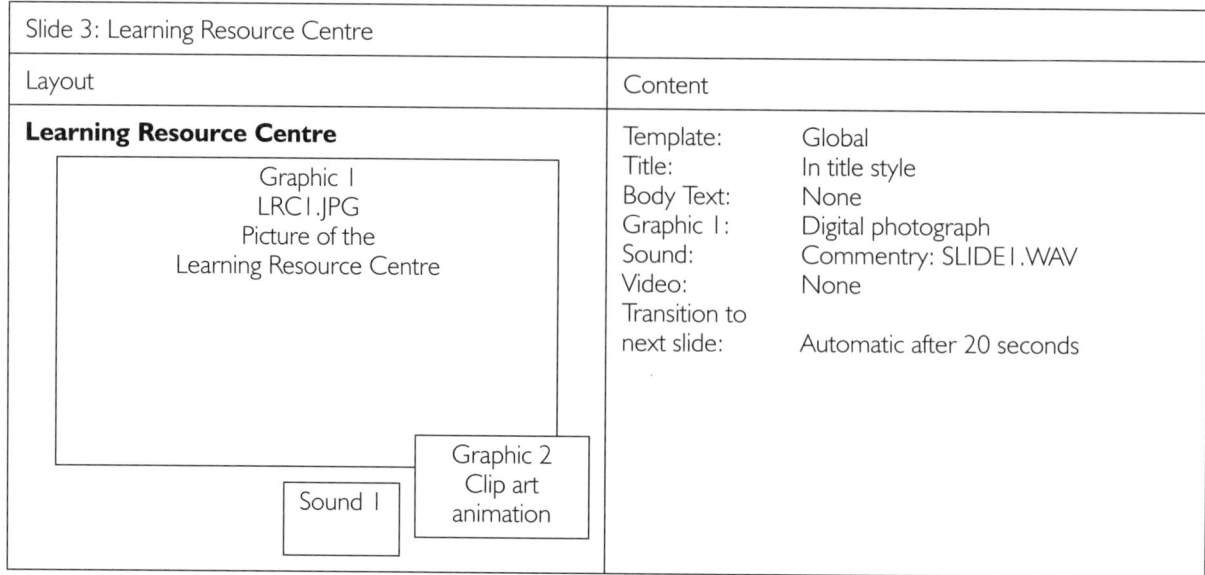

Figure 3.3 *Story board for Learning Resource Centre slide*

Flowcharts provide a simple, graphical way to design the different paths through a presentation and the choices the audience will need to make. A flowchart for a multimedia presentation consists of a series of boxes, one for each slide in the presentation. An example flowchart is shown in Figure 3.4.

Each box contains a short text description of the slide. The boxes are joined by arrows showing the route that the viewer may take through the presentation. If the viewer is to be given a choice of routes through parts of the presentation, the box representing the slide where the user makes that choice has several arrows coming from it to the other boxes that can be selected. A more detailed description of flowcharting techniques can be found in Chapter 10: *Programming*.

Northgate College

Tony's flowchart for the presentation he is designing (Figure 3.4) shows that the user can choose one of three routes through the flowchart at slide 7, and that all three routes meet again at slide 17. Tony's next step is to produce a storyboard for each slide, like the one shown for slide 3 in Figure 3.3.

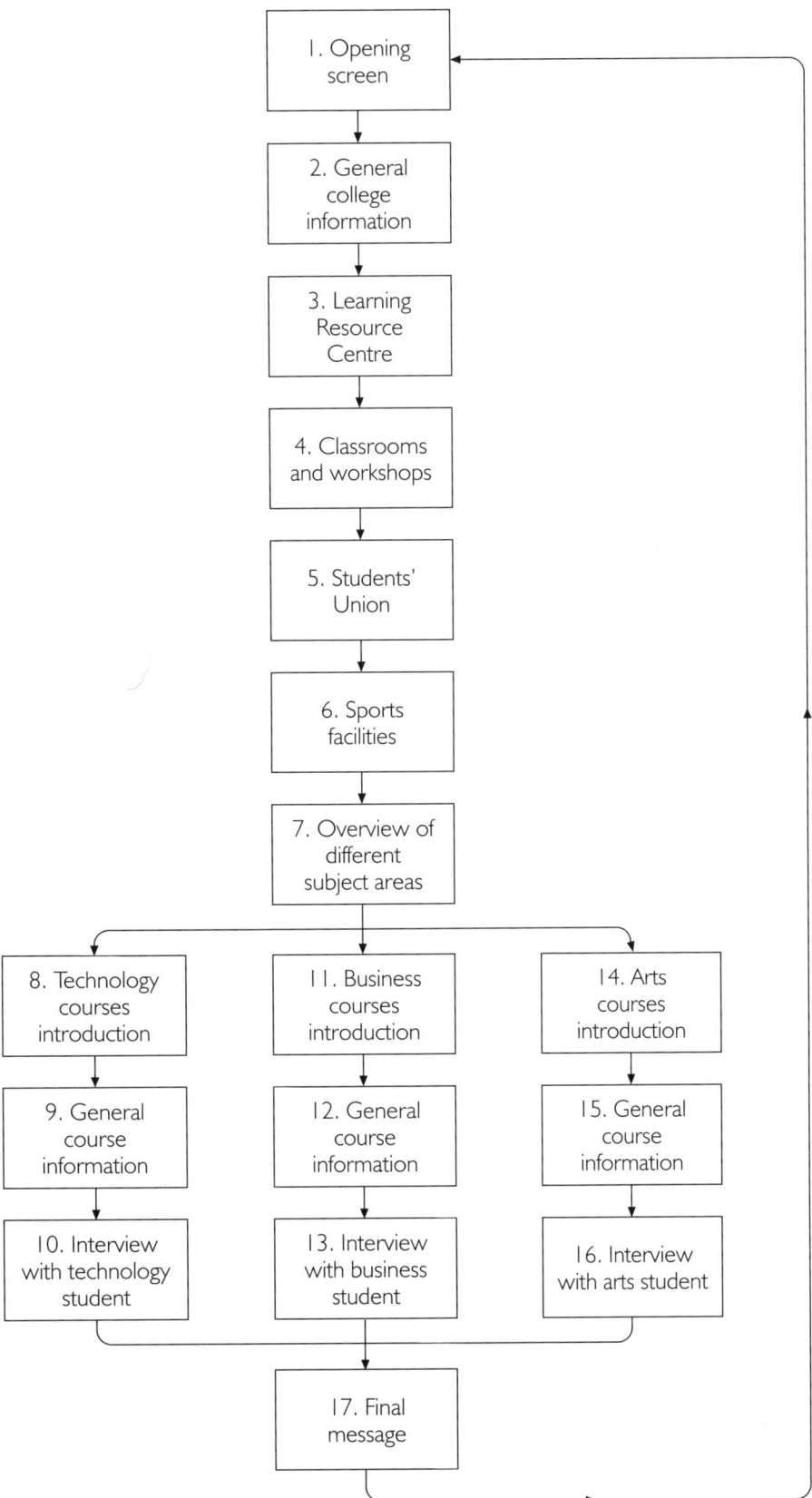

Figure 3.4 *Flowchart*

Activity 3.7

Using the brief produced in Activity 3.6 for the sports centre, working on your own, create a flowchart for the presentation, and then create storyboards for each slide.

Compare what you have produced with others in your group, and discuss how each of you can improve your own presentation.

Identifying sources

The story boards you create should identify the content of your presentation, but you also need to decide where each piece of material will come from.

Some of it you will be able to create yourself. In other cases, you will need to obtain the material from other sources. You may be able to find suitable pictures and backgrounds from the clip art that comes with software such as Microsoft Office.

There are many other places you can find pictures, video clips and music as well as on the Internet. However, you must be aware of **copyright** restrictions. Almost all commercially produced videos and music cannot legally be used in your presentation without the permission of the copyright holder. In most cases, this will only be given on payment of a royalty charge. Clip art, including Microsoft Clip Gallery Live is copyright free, although there are some restrictions to the use of these materials (for example you cannot sell them). Table 3.1 shows the different types of content you may want to include in your presentation.

> **Did You Know?**
>
> Microsoft Office users, who also have access to the Internet can use the Microsoft Clip Gallery Live, which contains over 100,000 pictures, animations and sounds. To find this site just click the Clips Online button in the clip art gallery.

Writing a script

If your multimedia presentation is to have a spoken commentary you need to write a script for that commentary. You will need to decide whether the spoken commentary will start automatically as each slide is displayed, or if it will only play if a button is clicked or a hyperlink is followed (or a combination of the two). The script needs to be written in conjunction with the story boards. That way you will know, when you come to record the commentary, which recording goes with which slide.

Content	Source
Text	You will probably need to create this yourself
Background pictures	Widely available (and copyright free) in clip art
Clip art pictures	Available as part of many software packages
Photographs	You can create these yourself if you have access to a digital camera (or a standard camera and a scanner)
Spoken commentary	You will need to record this yourself
Background music	Music CDs are copyright and you cannot use them; you may find some copyright free music you can download from the Internet
Video clips	If you have access to suitable equipment you may be able to record these yourself

Table 3.1 *Sources of content for multimedia presentations*

Figure 3.5 shows the script that accompanies the slide about the Learning Resource Centre.

Script
Slide 3: Learning Resource Centre

This is our recently built learning resource centre. It's a great place to go and study. Not only does it have thousands of books and hundreds of magazines like a traditional library, but it also has over 50 computers.

You can book up to two hours time on these computers so it's a great place to go and complete coursework.

As well as all the latest software all the computers are connected to the Internet so you can use them for research as well.

There is also a range of computer CD-ROMs available, including interactive encyclopaedias like Microsoft Encarta.

Figure 3.5 *Script for Learning Resource centre slide*

As you write the script, you will need to bear in mind your target audience – they must be able to understand the terms and language you use. You should also need to consider who is going to record the script.

> **Did You Know?**
> People with a good 'radio voice' can earn money recording so called 'talkovers' for radio and TV adverts. This is also a very lucrative side line for well known actors.

Here are some points to consider:

- **Choosing the right voice**
  Some people's voices sound better when recorded than others. You may want to make some test recordings of different people and choose the one with the best sounding voice.

- **Target audience**
  Choose a person whose voice is most likely to appeal to the target audience.

Exercise 3.4

You are creating a presentation about the latest teenage fashion trends. Whose voice would be more suitable for the commentary: your 47-year-old male teacher or one of your female teenage friends?

Northgate College

For Tony's script (Figure 3.5 on page 73), he and Anita agreed to use the animated 'virtual student' who will act as the guide to the tour around the college facilities, rather than a real student.

Activity 3.8

★ Write a script for one of the slides for your Sports Centre presentation.

★ Ask someone in your group to read it aloud for you, so that you can check how long it will take to say, and ask them to make suggestions about how to improve the script.

★ Offer to help them with their own script.

3 COMMUNICATING WITH MULTIMEDIA

Creating multimedia presentations

To create a multimedia presentation, you will need an **authoring package**. Many different packages are available and the one you choose will depend on a number of things, including how the presentation will be delivered to the audience.

> **Did You Know?**
>
> Microsoft PowerPoint is especially designed for creating slide-show presentations.

- To create a **web-based presentation**, you will need to use an HTML editor program that includes multimedia capabilities, Microsoft Front Page for example.
- For a **slide-show presentation**, like the one in the case study, you will need to use a program such as Microsoft PowerPoint.

The process of creating a multimedia presentation has a lot in common with the software development process. The analysis and design stages have already been covered, creating and testing is explained here. You might find it helpful to read the section in Chapter 10 that covers analysis, design and testing: pages 309–49.

Text

Most presentations contain some text, and all multimedia authoring software has facilities for typing, editing and formatting text. In most cases, these are similar to those found in word-processing software. If you are including a lot of text, or if there is a team of people working on a project, it may be better to prepare the text using word-processing software.

Because different programs store their data files in different formats, you cannot open word-processing files directly in a multimedia authoring program. However, most authoring software provides **import facilities** so you can import the word-processed file into the multimedia program. As part of the process, the file is converted into the correct format. Then it can be edited and formatted just the same as text created directly in the authoring software.

Authoring programs often include a variety of pre-set styles or **design templates** you can use for your presentation.

> *Microsoft PowerPoint includes a range of templates which provide co-ordinated text styles (including fonts, colours, sizes, etc.) and background graphics. See Figures 3.6 and 3.7.*

Figure 3.6 *Creating a new presentation using a design template*

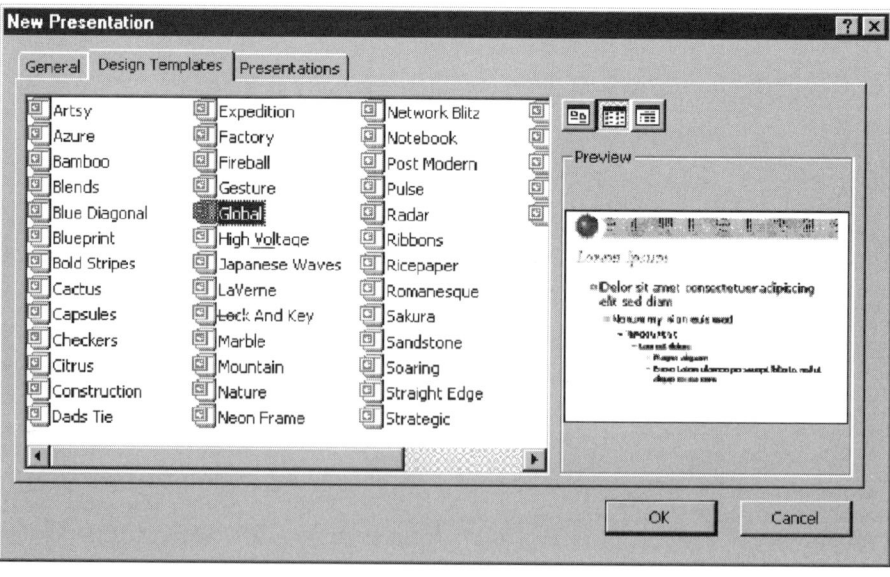

Figure 3.7 *Choosing a suitable design template*

These templates give your presentation a professional look and make it easy for you to keep your text styles consistent.

Northgate College

Tony has decided to use one of the pre-set design templates provided with Microsoft PowerPoint. He uses the option that is displayed when he runs the PowerPoint program (Figure 3.6) and then chooses a template called Global from the list provided (Figure 3.7).

Note that a preview of each template is shown on the right of the dialogue box as each template name is selected. Once the template has been chosen, the layout for the first slide can be selected (a title slide), as shown in Figure 3.8.

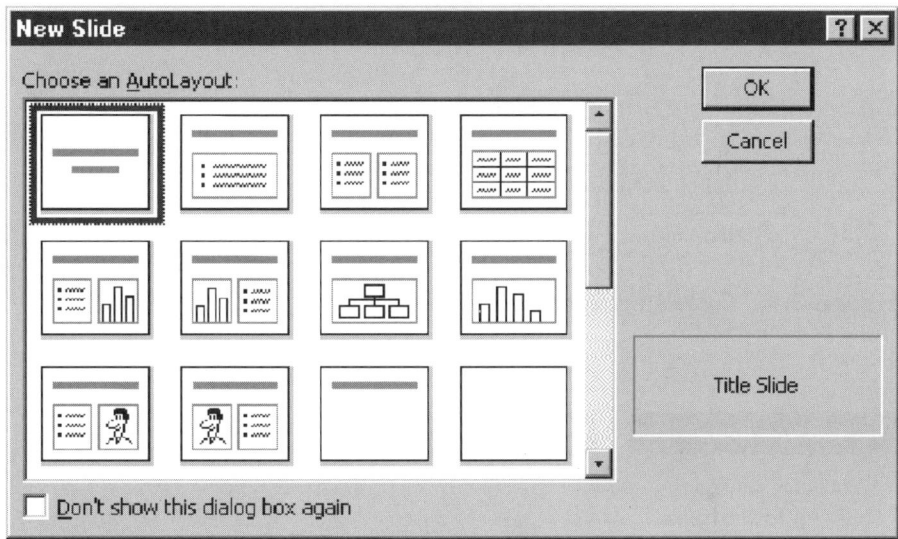

Figure 3.8 *Selecting the layout for the slide*

Activity 3.9

Select a suitable design template for your sports centre presentation. Then create each of the required slides (use your flowchart and story board to guide you) and add the text to each slide.

When text is typed into the text boxes that the title slide layout provides, it automatically appears with the formatting settings (size, font, colour, etc.) that the design template specifies (Figure 3.9).

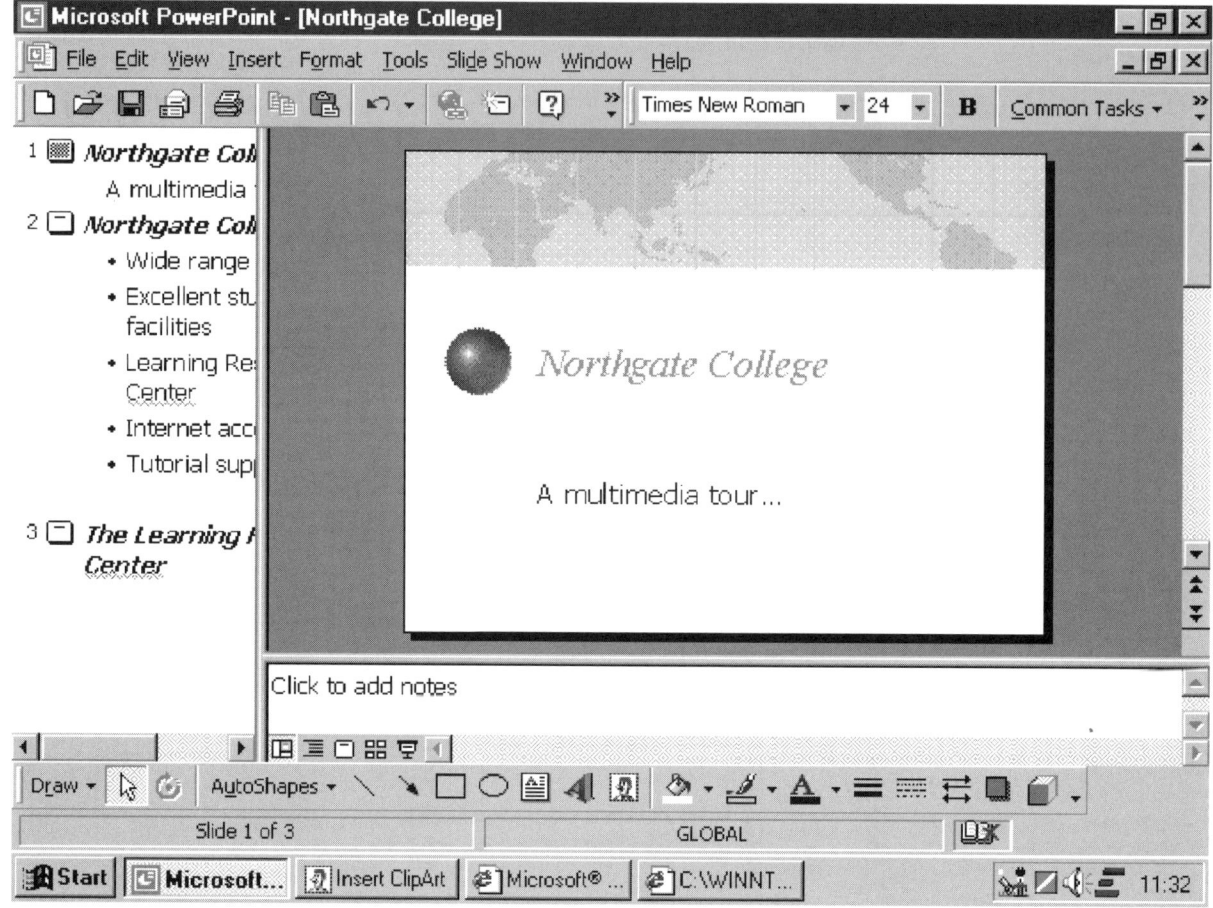

Figure 3.9 *Completed first slide*

Graphics

There are a number of different types of graphics you can include in the presentation:

> **Did You Know?**
> You can normally tell the format of a file by looking at its file extension.

> **JPG (or JPEG)** stands for Joint Photographic Experts Group, after the name of the group of developers who invented it.
>
> **GIF** stands for Graphic Interchange Format.

- **Bitmap graphics** are generally used for scanned or digital photographs. They use file formats such as BMP, GIF and JPG.

  A JPG file called MYPIC would have a full file name of MYPIC.JPG — in most cases the format name is an acronym.

- **Animations** are a special type of bitmap in which series of bitmaps are linked together to create a moving animation, rather like a simple cartoon. These are usually in GIF format.

- **Vector graphics** are used for diagrams and clip art pictures. There is a wide variety of formats, and these can be converted to a bitmap.

Graphics programs such as Photoshop allow you to convert between a wide range of formats.

To create vector graphics, you need a drawing program such as Corel DRAW. However, some authoring programs have simple drawing facilities built into them.

If you are completing the whole project yourself, you can create the drawing in the appropriate program, and then copy and paste it into the correct frame in the authoring program. However, you should always save an original copy of the drawing, in case you need to modify it later.

If you are working on the project as a team, you may have allocated tasks such that the drawings are created at a different time and on a different machine from the authoring process. In this case, you will need to save the file in the drawing program, and then import it into the authoring program at a later date. You will need to check that the file format you saved the drawing in can be imported by the authoring program.

In most cases, the native format of the drawing program (i.e. the standard format used to save the file in the drawing program) will not be supported by the authoring program. So, for example, if you save a drawing in Corel DRAW, it will be saved in .CDR format. If you try to import that drawing into an authoring program such as PowerPoint the .CDR format is not supported. The way around this problem is, as well as saving the Corel DRAW file in native format, you will need to export it using a common file format. Windows Metafile (.WMF) is a good choice as it is widely supported by other programs. However, you will need to check with the particular authoring program you are using.

Exercise 3.5

What drawing packages do you have available to you? Investigate what file formats they can import and export.

Similarly, investigate what import facilities your authoring programs provide.

File import and export options are usually found under the File or the Insert menu.

CREATING MULTIMEDIA PRESENTATIONS

If you intend to produce your presentation as an Internet web page, you will need to use either JPG or GIF file formats, because these are the only ones supported by web browser programs such as Netscape Navigator and Microsoft Explorer.

Scanning images

Did You Know?

Items that actually exist are called 'realia' – they are real – whereas items such as a digital photograph only exist in the 'virtual' world inside a computer.

If the images you want to use already exist, such as a photograph for example, you can use a scanner to convert them into a bitmap graphics file.

Remember that almost all of the pictures and diagrams you find in books are subject to copyright restrictions. When scanning an item, you need to make sure that you have a good quality original. Although, with bitmap editing software you can cut out parts of the original, you cannot significantly improve the quality of the original. So, for example, an out-of-focus photograph would not be suitable. Remember also that you cannot enlarge a bitmap picture without significant loss of quality.

Activity 3.10

- ★ Scan in a small image such as a passport size photograph.
- ★ Import the image into a program. Microsoft Word will do fine. Print a copy of the image.
- ★ Leave the image at its original size, and copy and paste it to produce another copy.
- ★ Enlarge this second copy to about twice the size. Print this second copy.
- ★ Inspect the two images and compare them with your original photograph.
- ★ What has happened to the enlarged copy?

Northgate College

Tony needs a number of pictures of the college for the presentation he is preparing, as well as some pictures of the students he will interview. He uses a digital camera to take these pictures.

The advantage of a **digital camera** is that the photos do not need to be scanned as they would with a traditional camera. Once the photos are taken, the camera is connected to the computer and the photos can be downloaded off the camera. The software the comes with the camera saves the files in a standard graphics format (in this case JPG files). These can be easily imported into PowerPoint using the Insert menu, Picture option and From file sub-option. This brings up the dialogue box shown in Figure 3.10.

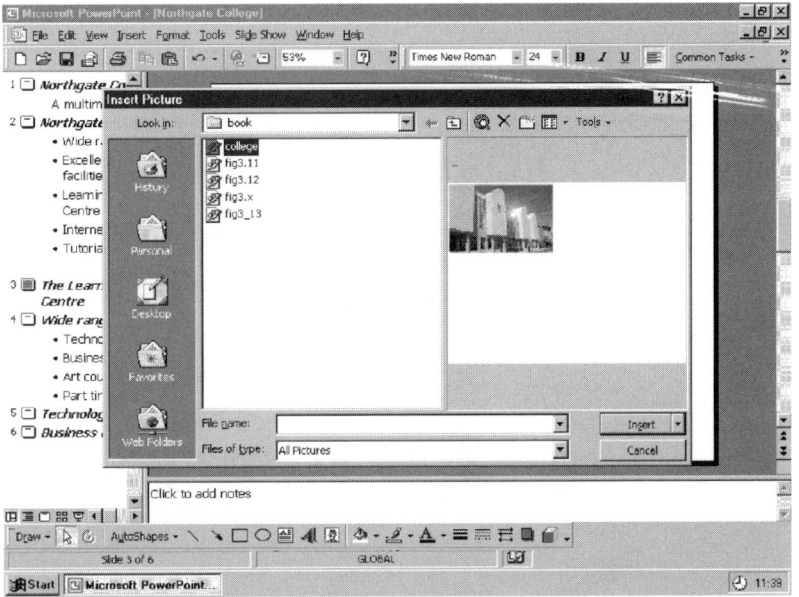

Figure 3.10 *Inserting a graphic file*

The file name of the required digital photograph is selected and the Insert button is clicked. The picture is then inserted in the current frame and can be moved or resized as required. This is shown in Figure 3.11.

Another option is to use **clip art**. Figure 3.12 shows a selection from the Microsoft Clip Gallery Live.

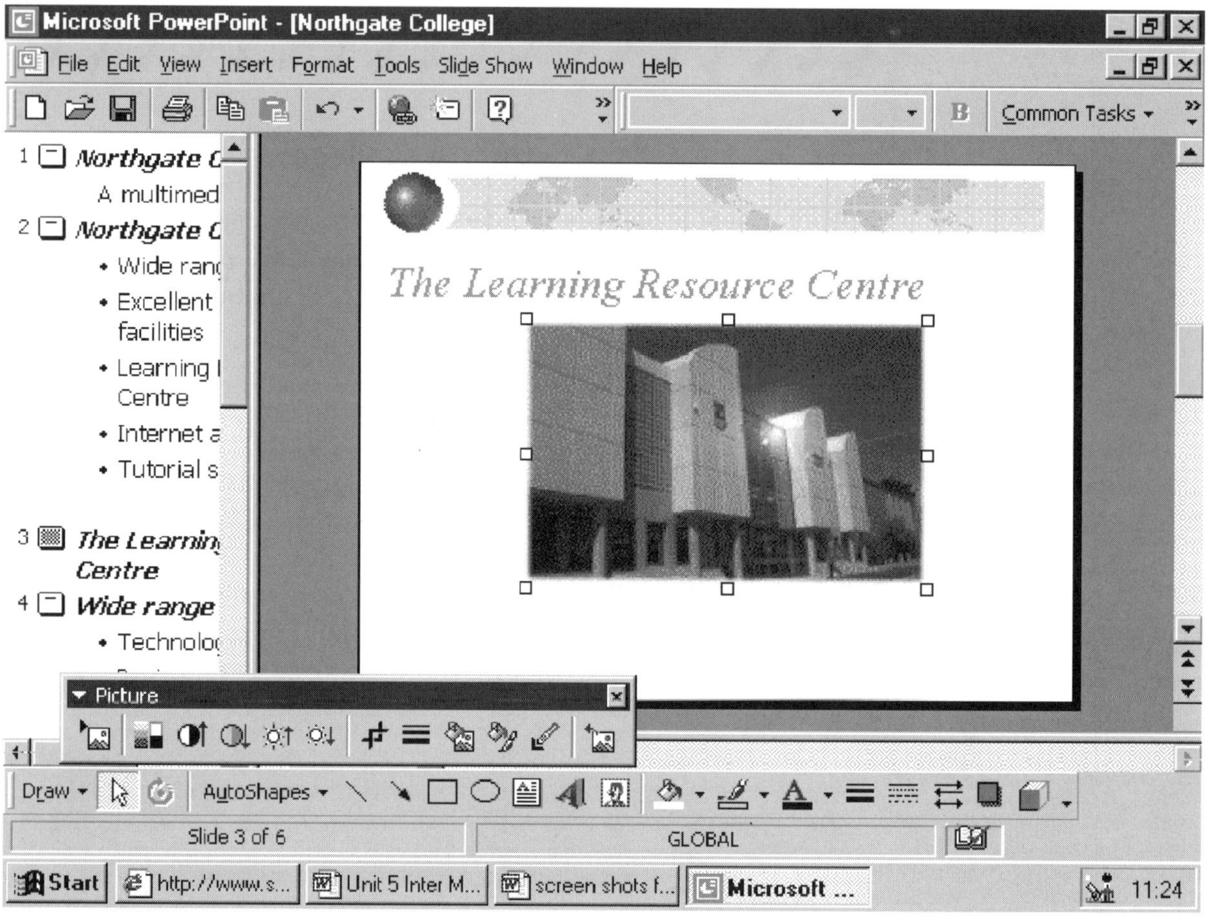

Figure 3.11 *A graphic inserted into a PowerPoint slide*

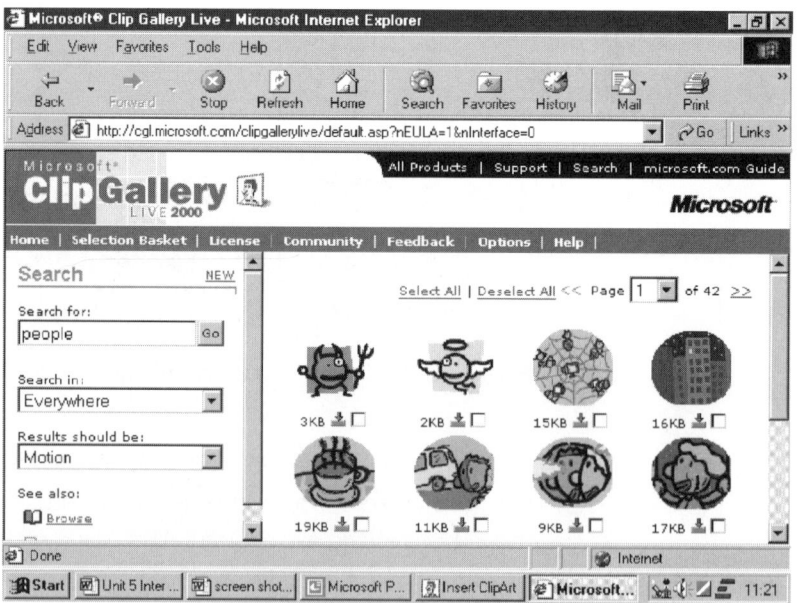

Figure 3.12 *Microsoft Clip Gallery Live – animated graphics*

3 COMMUNICATING WITH MULTIMEDIA

Northgate College

Tony also needs to find some animations for the 'virtual student' who will be the guide for the tour around the college. He decides to use the Microsoft Clip Gallery Live to search for suitable clips and finds a good selection (Figure 3.12). The animation files he downloads from the Internet are added to the clip art gallery on his computer. They are inserted into the presentation in the same way as any other clip art file, using the insert clip art button.

Activity 3.11

Collect together the images you need for your Sports Centre presentation, and insert them into the slides you created in Activity 3.9.

Remember to keep a note of which clip art images you have used on each slide, and where you found them.

Recording/editing sound files

Recorded sounds come in two categories: a commentary and background music.

First, you may wish to record a **commentary** for parts of your presentation. This will involve writing a script and then recording the commentary, either yourself or ask someone else to speak the script for you. In terms of hardware, you will need a computer equipped with a sound card, a microphone and sufficient disk space. Windows 95 comes with a simple sound recorder which will be adequate for most purposes. When using the sound recorder you may need to adjust the quality of the recording made.

Remember that the higher the quality, the more disk space is required. The quality of a digital record depends on three main factors:

- The **sampling rate**
- The number of **bits** used
- Whether you use **mono** or **stereo**

The **sampling rate** controls how often the incoming sound is measured and converted to a binary number. The more often it is measured, the better the quality of the result, but more regular samples mean more data needs to be saved onto disk. Sampling rates of 44Khz (44,000 times per second) are used for CD quality recording.

The **number of bits used** – each sample is converted to a binary number, and the more bits in the binary number, the greater the detail that can be recorded. However, using more bits for each sample means more disk space is required. CD quality recordings use 16 bits per sample.

Mono recording only uses one track (one source of incoming data).
Stereo recording uses two tracks and so takes twice as much disk space to store.

To save disk space, a setting of 22Khz, 8-bit mono is quite adequate for a spoken commentary.

Second, you may want to add **background music**, in which case you have two options:

- MIDI music
- digital recording

MIDI music is not a recording of live music such as you might find on a music CD. Instead, it is instructions to play notes on an electronic instrument (i.e. the instrument, the note, the duration of the note, etc.). All PC sound cards include a MIDI chip which allows them to play MIDI files. The advantage of MIDI files is that because they are not digitised recordings, they take up much less disk space than digital audio files. Another advantage is that a large number of copyright-free MIDI files are available on the Internet, so you can use these in your presentation.

MIDI stands for Musical Instrument Digital Interface.

Did You Know?

Some authoring packages include MIDI samples (and sometimes video clips too) just as drawing programs include clip art.

Exercise 3.6

Find out what MIDI samples and video clips come with the authoring software you are using. If you are using Microsoft PowerPoint and you have access to the Internet try accessing Microsoft Clip Gallery Live and see what clips you can find and download.

The disadvantage of MIDI files is that they sound like electronic music, especially if your sound card has a low-quality FM synthesis MIDI chip (where instrument sounds are electronically synthesised). However, if your sound card has a Wavetable chip (where actual samples of real instrument sounds are stored), MIDI music can sound quite acceptable.

With **digital recordings**, you take a music CD or cassette tape and make a digital recording of a piece of music using the Windows 95 sound recorder (Figure 3.13) as with the spoken commentary.

Figure 3.13 *The Windows sound recorder*

Did You Know?

Copyright is protected under the Designs, Patents and Copyright Act.

The advantage of this method is that the end result is a good quality recording of 'real' music. There are two disadvantages though: file size and copyright restrictions.

CREATING MULTIMEDIA PRESENTATIONS 85

Northgate College

Tony is using a spoken commentary to accompany the animated 'guide' for the tour of the college. He has already written the script for the commentary (part of it is shown in Figure 3.5 on page 73). Now he needs to record the commentary. He approaches the media department in the college who find a student with a good voice who can record the commentary. With the help of the student and a lecturer in the media department, they use the college's recording studio to record the commentary onto an ordinary cassette tape. As a separate piece of commentary will accompany each slide in the presentation each piece on the cassette tape needs to be re-recorded into a separate digital audio file on the computer. To do this, Tony connects up a cassette player to the sound card on his PC and uses the Windows sound recorder to record each file.

To save file space, Tony uses the Properties option under the File menu of the sound recorder to display the properties box, then by clicking the Convert now button he can select a suitable sample rate and number of bits. He chooses 11KHz 8-bit recording.

He also needs to record some short interviews with current students. Once again, the media department help him by lending him a portable tape recorder so he can interview students around the college. They also edit the resulting tape for him so he can easily re-record the best parts of the interviews onto his computer.

Having recorded the sound files needed, the next step is to insert them into the presentation in the appropriate place. To do that, you need to go to the slide where the sound file will be played, then select the Insert option, the Movies and Sounds option and the Sound from the file sub-option (Figure 3.14).

You can then select the name of the sound file that is to be played with this slide from the file list and click OK. A dialogue box will then ask if the sound should be played automatically when the slide loads or only when the viewer clicks the icon.

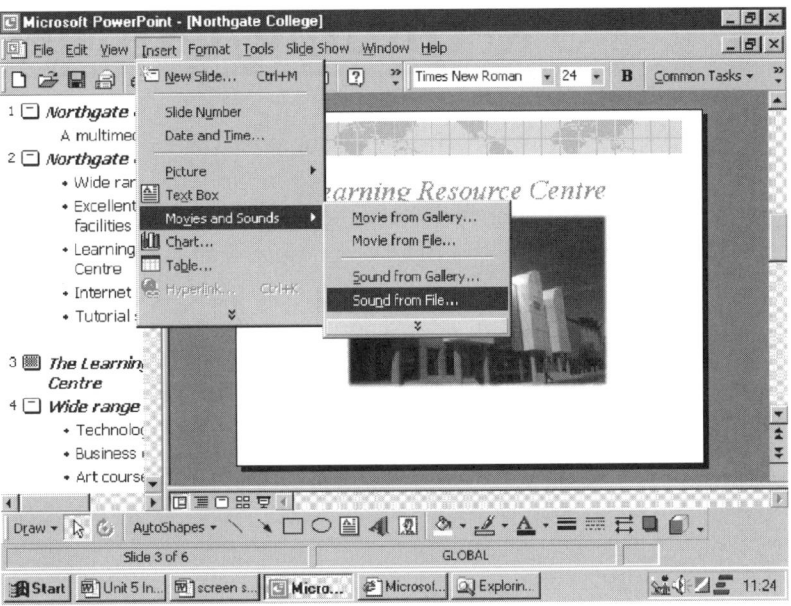

Figure 3.14 *Adding a sound file to the slide*

Northgate College

In Tony's case, he wants the sound to play automatically.

Notice that the sound file is represented by a small icon, with a picture of a loudspeaker, on the slide.

Activity 3.12

Using the script you wrote in Activity 3.8, record the commentary for one of your slides for the Sports Centre presentation and attach the resulting sound files to the appropriate slides.

If your school or college has a media department they may be able to help you with recording both audio and video for your own presentations.

CREATING MULTIMEDIA PRESENTATIONS

Recording/editing video files

Recording and editing your own video is an involved process, about which whole books have been written. Given the complexity and the restrictions imposed by disk space, you should probably aim to record only a short clip. You will need a computer that is specially equipped:

- A video capture card
- Video recording and editing software
- A video camera

It is probably sensible to record your video clip on to a camcorder video cassette *before* you attempt to make a digital recording of the video clip. This will give you greater flexibility in location, because you can take a portable camcorder almost anywhere. Also, it will avoid you making digital recordings of all your out-takes. As you did with the sound clip, it is wise to write a script first. Once you have the completed video clip, you can then plug the camcorder into your computer's video capture card and capture the final result in digital form.

Activity 3.13

If you have the equipment available, attempt to record a short video clip to be included in the Sports Centre presentation.

Creating buttons, hyperlinks

Three main methods are used to allow the user to interact with a multimedia presentation:

- Buttons
- Hot spots
- Hypertext links

Buttons offer probably the simplest method, since they can be easily seen and labelled.

If your intention is to provide an easy-to-use user interface then you may want to consider providing the same buttons, in the same place, on every frame. If you are using a slide-show type structure these may be buttons for go forward, go back, exit and help.

Hot spots, are invisible buttons but, when you move your mouse pointer over them, the mouse icon changes shape to indicate interaction is possible. Less intuitive than buttons (because they are invisible), they do nonetheless provide a neat way of allowing user interaction that gives the impression of exploring the presentation.

If your presentation was about the countries of the Europe, your initial menu frame could be a map of Europe. To select which country the user wanted to find out about, they would move their mouse over the country in question, activating a hot spot which, when they clicked their mouse button, would take them to the part of the presentation that gave information about that country.

Hypertext links are increasingly popular, and are extensively used on the web. Text contains visible hot spots (usually underlined or in a different colour) and when the user clicks on the hot spot they are taken to more detailed or related information about the text they have clicked on. These are most suitable for educational information where you want to allow a user to look up definitions of terms or related topics.

Inserting a **hyperlink** to other slides in PowerPoint is easy: select the text that the user will click on to jump to the link, then click the hyperlink button in the tool bar (or choose the Insert menu, Hyperlink option). This causes the Insert Hyperlink dialogue box to appear, as shown in Figure 3.15.

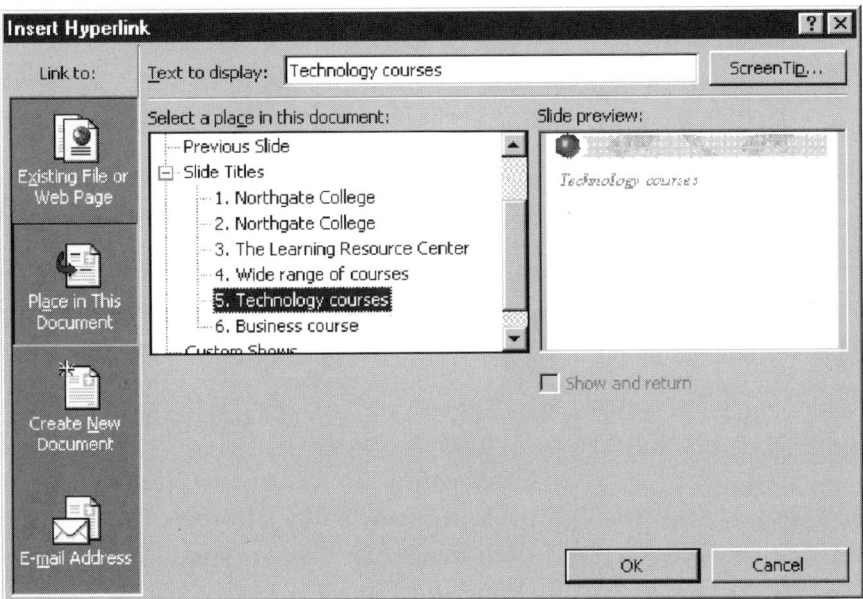

Figure 3.15 *The Insert Hyperlink dialogue box*

Northgate College

Tony has the option of using either hyperlinks or buttons to allow the users of the presentation to select which subject area they would like information on. The flowchart in Figure 3.4 on page 71 describes the different options users will have. In both cases, the slide that the link or button will jump to should already exist. Tony experiments with both buttons and hyperlinks in his presentation.

To create a link to another slide in the same presentation, click the 'Place in this document' button on the left of the box. Then scroll down the central box until the name of the slide you want to link to appears. Click on the slide name (a preview of it appears in the window on the left) and click OK. The text selected on the slide now changes colour and becomes underlined, just like an Internet hyperlink. You can check to see if the hyperlink works by clicking the slide show button to display the current slide in viewing (rather than editing) mode, click the hyperlink and the slide that you have linked to is displayed.

The same effect can be achieved, but using a button instead of a hyperlink. From the Slide show menu, choose the Action buttons option. A pop-out menu appears allowing you to choose buttons with different icons on them, such as next slide, previous slide, etc.

Northgate College

Tony wants his button to jump to a particular place in the presentation, so he chooses the blank button (first one), then drags the button shape to a suitable place on the slide. See Figure 3.16.

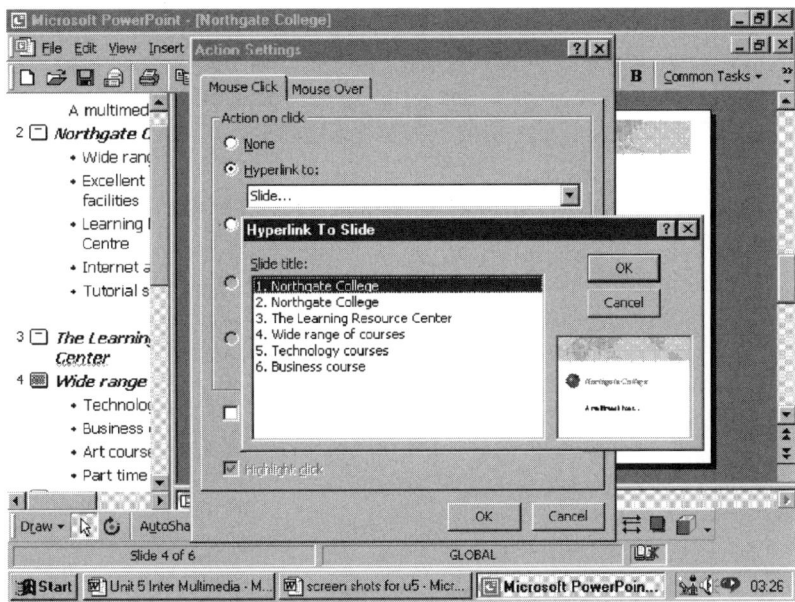

Figure 3.16 *Adding an action button*

Once a button has been created, the action settings dialogue box appears. By selecting the Hyperlink to: option and the Slide... option, another dialogue box appears allowing you to choose the particular slide you want to link to.

To add text to the button, right click on it, then choose the Add text option from the pop-out menu that appears. The text cursor will then appear in the button and you can type the appropriate text.

Activity 3.14

Using the flowchart you created in Activity 3.7 as a guide, create buttons or hyperlinks to provide the required paths through your Sports Centre presentation.

Slide transitions

If you are using a slide-show presentation, your authoring software may allow you to control how the slides change. There are two basic options:

- Self running
- User controlled

With **self running control**, the slides change after a certain amount of time and you will need to decide how much time each slide needs to be displayed. With **user controlled** slide shows, the slides only change when the viewer clicks a button or hyperlink.

You can, of course, combine the two methods with some slides changing automatically and others waiting for the viewer to click a button – perhaps where they need to make a choice, such as choosing which part of the presentation they want to view.

Some authoring software also allows you to choose a variety of effects which control how one slide changes to another, and how parts of a slide are built up.

> *A new slide may slide in from the side of the screen over the existing slide. Where a slide has a number of text bullet points on it, these may be added to the slide one at a time.*

Such effects can make the presentation more interesting to watch and can add to the visual impact of the message you are trying to get across.

Layout and design

You need to be careful about how you put these various elements together. Just sticking the different parts of the presentation together in a haphazard fashion will create a disjointed, messy looking series of frames which don't appear to belong to each other. Although your presentation will be made up of a series of frames, you will probably want to give the user the impression of a flowing, consistent presentation. To achieve this you need to obey a few rules:

- **Have a consistent background**
  Choose a colour or picture for your background and stick to it, at least until the topic changes. Features like the design templates in PowerPoint makes this easy to achieve.

- **Design a hierarchy of text styles**
  So, for example, have all your frame titles in a particular location, colour, font, size, etc. All your subtitles, body text, captions, etc. should also have their own consistent style. Most authoring packages, like word processing packages, simplify this process by providing the facility to create text styles. Use it! The usual DTP rule of normally no more than two different fonts per page should also be applied here.

- **Use consistent design elements**
  Be consistent in the way design elements such as images are presented. Only change the layout when the topic changes.

  If many of your frames contain a photograph and some accompanying text, stick to the same layout for these two elements, e.g. always have the picture on the left of the frame and the text on the right. If you use a border for one picture, use the same border for all the pictures, and so on.

Testing

Before your presentation is complete, it must be thoroughly tested to make sure every part of it works properly. This is particularly important where your presentation has several different paths through it. You must test every possible route that the users of the presentation can take, to make sure all the buttons, hot spots and hyperlinks work correctly. You should also carefully check the text in your presentation for spelling and grammatical errors. Most multimedia authoring software includes a spell checker, so make sure you use it. Don't forget to proofread your text as well, as spell checkers cannot spot every error. It is often helpful to ask someone else to test the presentation for you – they may spot errors you have missed.

If you have decided to use the Internet to deliver your presentation, your testing will need to be even more thorough. There are two different web browsers that are in common use: Microsoft Internet Explorer and Netscape Navigator. You need to check that your presentation will work properly with both browsers as they work in slightly different ways and some features in your presentation may work fine in one browser but not in the other.

Activity 3.15

Once your Sports Centre presentation is complete, spell check and proofread it carefully. Then check every possible path through the presentation (all buttons, hyperlinks, etc.) work as expected.

Presenting and evaluating multimedia presentations

Once you have completed your presentation, it is time to evaluate it. It is important your evaluation is positive and that you identify the strengths of the presentation as well as its weaknesses. You are probably not the best person to evaluate your own work, you have been closely involved in its creation. An outsider will have a fresh view of it and may be willing to be more critical. If possible therefore, ask someone else to help you to evaluate your work, preferably someone from your target audience. You may want to consider asking a whole group of people to view your presentation and then complete a questionnaire you have produced asking them to identify its strengths and weaknesses. You could use the checklist your created in Activity 3.4. There are a number of questions you need to ask:

- **Does your presentation meet the brief?**
  Go back and look at your original brief. If someone else is evaluating your work make sure they understand what your brief was.

- **Is the quality high enough?**
  Look at each of the elements of the presentation (text, sound, graphics, etc.) and decide if these elements are of high quality or not. For example, does the text contain spelling errors or layout inconsistencies? Is the commentary clear?

- **Does your presentation show good authoring techniques?**
  Do the techniques that have been used (such as hyperlinks or buttons) work correctly? Are they clear and easy to use? You should also consider whether the various techniques you have used help to get the message across, or have they just been used for their own sake?

- **Can you make any improvements?**
  No presentation is perfect, so identifying where the presentation could be improved is an important part of evaluating it.

Northgate College

Having carefully checked and tested his presentation, Tony is now ready to evaluate it. He is very pleased with the all the hard work he has done, but decides that for objective feedback he needs to ask someone else to evaluate his work. He shows the presentation to Anita, who is also impressed with it. However, she does suggest some improvements and spots a couple of minor typing errors that Tony has missed. They both agree that, since neither of them are from the target audience for the presentation, they should ask a small group of existing students from the college to view and evaluate the presentation. They do this and based on the feedback from the students, Tony makes some modifications to the presentation before the college begins to use it, happy in the knowledge that it is as good as they can make it.

Activity 3.16

- ★ Having produced your own Sports Centre multimedia presentation, ask someone else to evaluate it.
- ★ Offer to evaluate someone else's presentation.
- ★ Compare notes. Decide how best to improve your own presentation.

Revision questions

1. When considering how effective a multimedia presentation is, what factors might you want to consider?

2. What is the difference between hard sell and soft sell techniques?

3. What are the three key pieces of information that should be contained in a brief for a presentation?

4. What is the purpose of brainstorming?

5. What is a story board and how is it used?

6. What sources might you use to obtain pictures for a multimedia presentation?

7. What two file formats should you use if your presentation is to be delivered using the Internet?

8. What is an animation?

9. What is the purpose of a scanner?

10. What happens if you enlarge a bitmap image?

11. What hardware is required to record a sound file?

12. What three factors govern the quality and size of a digital sound file?

13. What is the difference between a digital sound recording and a MIDI file?

14. What is the difference between a button and a hot spot?

15. What feature of multimedia authoring software can you use to ensure a consistent style is used throughout your presentation?

Graphics and desktop publishing

4

- **Understand the uses and features of graphics software and desktop publishing (DTP) packages**
- **Use ICT to create and edit graphical images, and to produce documents including these images**
- **Use graphics software to create and edit graphic images**
- **Use DTP to construct and edit documents**
- **Research, plan, produce, edit and present a document to meet a given design brief**

This chapter looks in detail at four topics:

- The uses and features of DTP software
- The uses and features of graphics software
- Hardware requirements: scanners and digital cameras
- Working to a design brief

When you have learned about these topics, you should be able to produce these four different types of graphic image.

- An accurate scale drawing
- An edited scanned image

- A graphic which incorporates clip art
- A graphic which combines text with an image

Depending on your awarding body, this unit may be assessed through your portfolio (Edexcel) or an end-of-unit test (AQA and OCR). Prior to any test, you will be given a design brief that requires you to produce a DTP document which includes text, bitmap and vector graphics. You must interpret the design brief, sketch your initial design ideas, and obtain appropriate information to include in your document. Clip art, digital cameras and scanners can be used to obtain images. You may use graphics software to improve the suitability of your image. You will then be required to take your prepared work into the test. Your design brief will include details about the product, the **target market** and the time-scale for production. Here are some possible products:

Target market refers to a particular group of people that a product is aimed at. It is usually possible to identify general features of your target market, e.g. age, sex, social class, etc.

- Video or CD covers
- A school newsletter
- A sports magazine
- A children's book

Two case studies are used in this chapter:

- St Joseph's Infant & Junior School
- Chris Lane Family Leisure Club

Both case studies use DTP. See Figures 4.1 and 4.2 for examples of what they produce.

Chris Lane Family Leisure Club

Chris Lane uses DTP to produce their magazine for members.

Figure 4.1 *Extract from Chris Lane magazine*
Courtesy of Chris Lane Family Leisure Club

St Joseph's Infant & Junior School, Pudsey

The secretary at St Joseph's Infant & Junior School uses DTP to produce the monthly newsletter to parents.

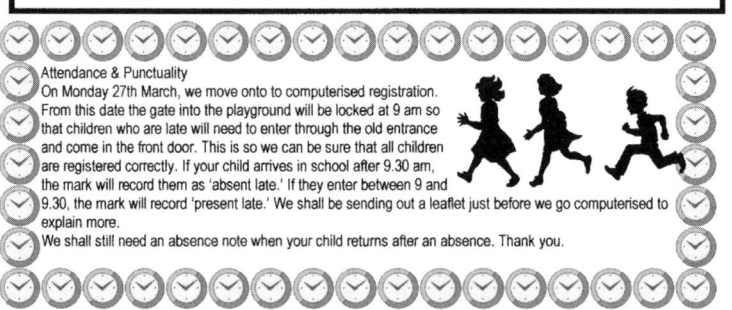

Figure 4.2 *St Joseph's newsletter*

The uses and features of DTP software

Businesses make extensive use of DTP. It can be used to produce literature with a high quality of presentation and this serves as an important marketing tool. DTP is used by businesses to produce newsletters, invitations, promotional materials (leaflets, posters, banners) and stationery.

DTP allows you to combine words and pictures to create a variety of different documents. It is particularly useful for column work, and is extremely effective in producing newspaper-style documents.

The text is usually input using word-processing software because it is easier to spell check and edit in a WP package. Also some DTP files are very large and this can slow down processing. It is better to finalise text in a WP package and then copy it into a DTP package.

DTP has various features which make it different from WP, but many are very similar. For more information, refer to Chapter 1 in the Intermediate GNVQ ICT text book in this series.

Activity 4.1

- ★ Use computer magazines or specialist text books to investigate the WP software available on the market. What DTP features are available?
- ★ Use computer magazines or specialist text books to investigate DTP software available on the market. What DTP software is available to you?
- ★ Write a report that compares the features of your DTP software with WP software. Try to include an image in your report.

Style sheets allow you to determine what fonts and sizes can be used through your document. For example, different levels of headings can be created (Figure 4.3).

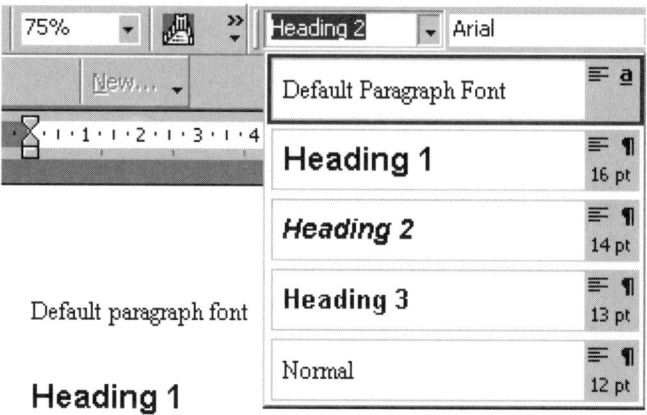

Figure 4.3 *List of styles*

Any amendments made to the style sheet results in all text in that style being altered.

Some software allows automatic text formatting, where styles are applied automatically and the user is able to accept or reject the changes.

Activity 4.2

★ Choose an assignment that you are undertaking for your GNVQ work. Word-process the work and then apply suitable styles to the text.

★ Format this as a new style and save the style so that you may apply it again in the future.

★ Check your work for accuracy, save and print.

▼▼▼▼▼▼▼▼
Paper sizes
A3 is double A4
A4 is double A5
▲▲▲▲▲▲▲▲▲

Standard paper sizes include A5, A4 and A3; see Figure 4.4. Most documents are printed on A4 paper, although an A4 size magazine, will actually be printed on A3 paper.

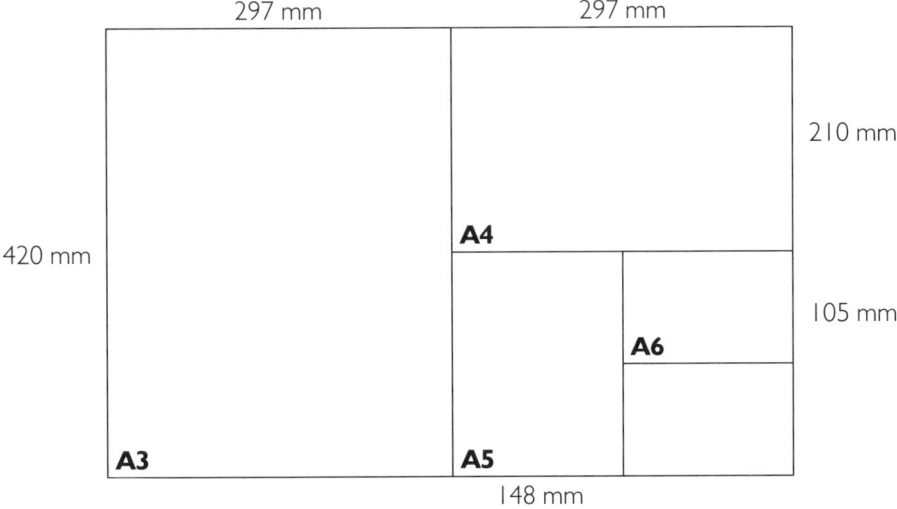

Figure 4.4 *Standard paper sizes*

Paper orientation refers to the orientation of the text on the paper. **Portrait** prints across the width of the paper. **Landscape** prints across the length of the paper. Sometimes, it is necessary to change the orientation to suit the type of document you are printing. Figure 4.5 shows a banner heading in various orientations.

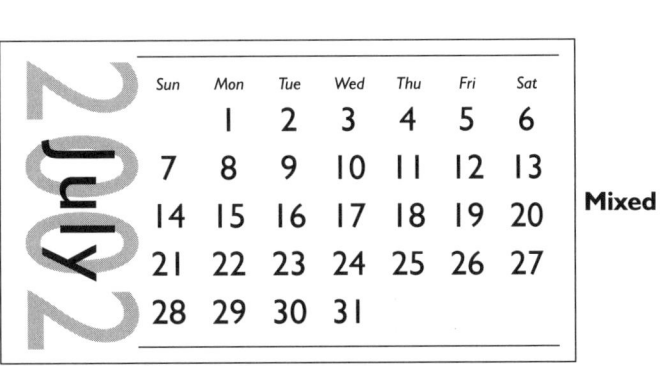
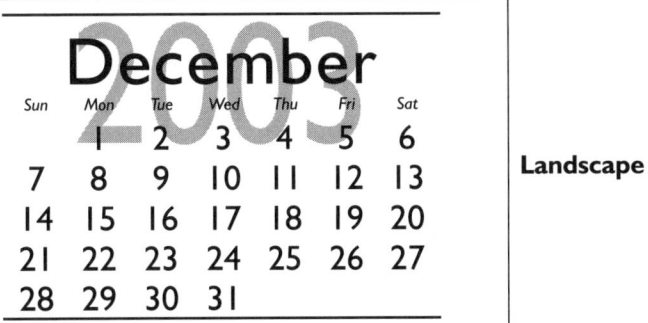

Figure 4.5 *Three orientations*

Page layout includes use of headers and footers, alignment of text, and use of columns and borders. See Figure 4.6.

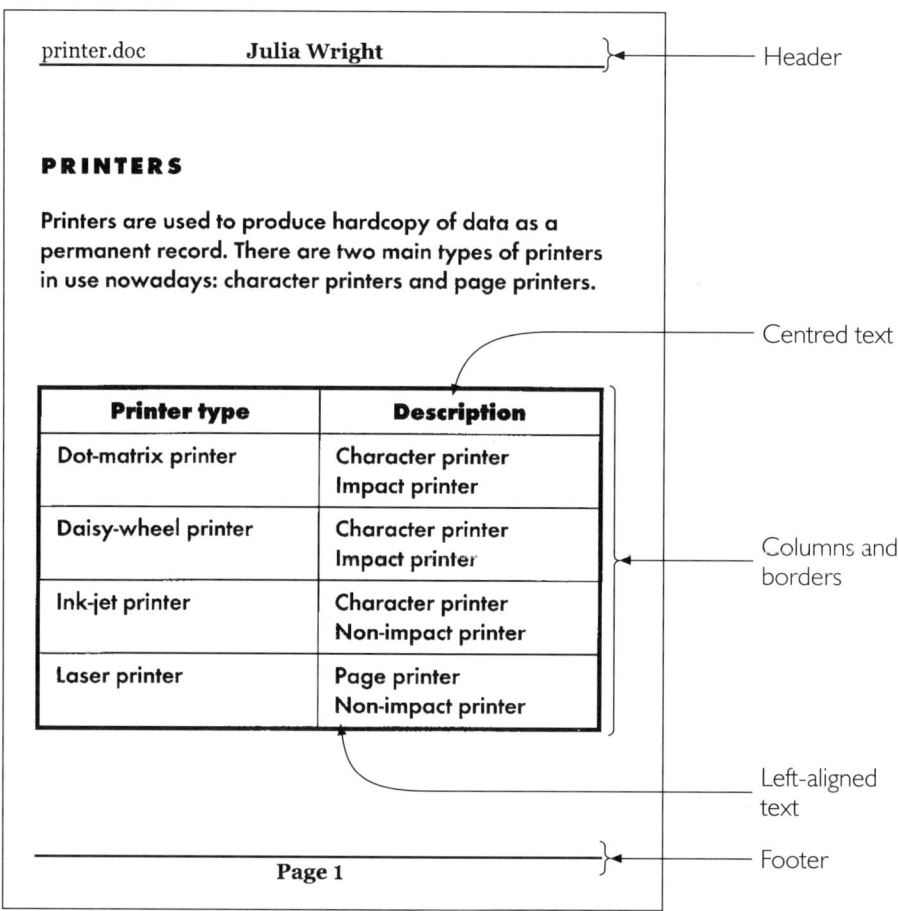

Figure 4.6 *Page layout with header and footer*

Headers and footers are used for labelling purposes, e.g. title of report, author's name, and filename. In a multi-page document, the same information appears on each page, although page numbers would differ, and the front page (and possibly the back page) would not usually show the full information. Most packages have the facility to insert variable information such as the date. This will automatically change each time you open and edit the document. They are often used to incorporate page numbers.

Activity 4.3

Use the help menu on your word-processing or DTP software to find out how to insert headers and footers. Create a document and insert your name, the date and the page number.

Ensure all your future printouts contain this information.

Alignment of text and **justification** describe how the text is arranged on the page. Figure 4.7 shows examples of left alignment, and right alignment, plus full justification and centring. Centring is often used for menus, as shown in Figure 4.8.

Left alignment is with a straight left-hand margin. This is the default alignment used in most word-processing packages.

Right alignment is with a straight right-hand margin. This is often used where graphics are placed on the left-hand side, for example in a letterhead.

Full justification is where both the right and left margins are straight and proportional spacing is automatically introduced between the words. Most text books and newspapers use full justification. The spaces keyed in by the writer are **hard** spaces and those inserted by the software are **soft** spaces.

Centred is where the text is placed exactly in the middle of each line. This is often used for menus and programmes.

Figure 4.7 *Examples of different alignment of text*

Borders can be used to surround pictures and text and thereby enhance them. These can be of different thickness and DTP packages will allow you to use decorative borders. Borders may also be shaded to give added impact. See Figure 4.9.

Activity 4.4

Investigate the borders available on your DTP software. Create your own menu, similar to that in Figure 4.8 and place a fancy border around it.

THE USES AND FEATURES OF DTP SOFTWARE

Figure 4.8 *Menu with centred text*

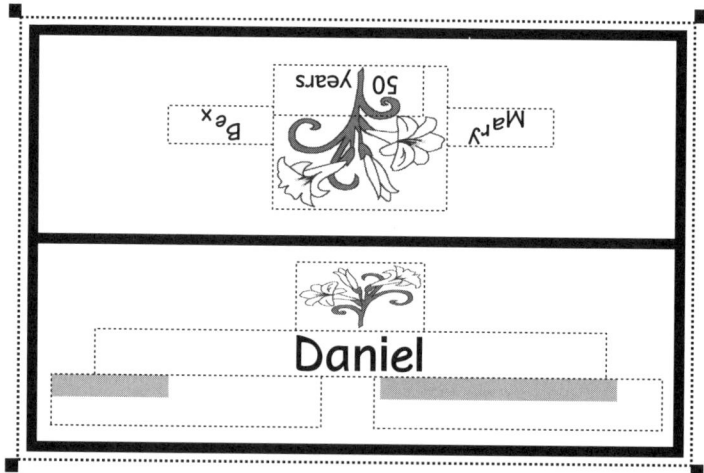

Figure 4.9 *Borders on a place card for a golden wedding anniversary party*

▼▼▼▼▼▼▼▼▼
Fonts
you can choose different **typeface styles** and **point sizes**.
▲▲▲▲▲▲▲▲▲

Fonts can be chosen to create a suitable impact on the reader.

- ✪ **Serif fonts** have small strokes attached to the upper and lower end of characters. These fonts create the impression of being joined up and encourage the reader to move from letter to letter.

- ✪ **Sanserif fonts** do not have serifs. They have a 'cleaner' look.

Times New Roman, Century Schoolbook   Arial, Century Gothic
Times New Roman, Century Schoolbook   Arial, Century Gothic
Times New Roman, Century Schoolbook   Arial, Century Gothic
Times New Roman, Century Schoolbook   Arial, Century Gothic
Times New Roman, Century Schoolbook   Arial, Century Gothic

Serif fonts   Sanserif fonts

Figure 4.10 *Different fonts (in different sizes)*

Font size (the **point size**) can also be altered to increase the impact. A smaller point size can be used in footnotes, while larger ones are more suitable for headings.

Drawing tools include line, shape, text, brush, colour, spray, arrows, eraser and node edit. See page 109 for a detailed description of each of these.

Some tools allow you to change the **attributes of text and graphic frames**. These include size, alignment, borders and shading. Shading is described in more detail on page 113.

Size of text can be altered by changing the size on the toolbar. Graphic frames can be enlarged and made smaller by using the resizing handles. See page 114 for a more detailed explanation of these.

It is possible to use **alignment** to ensure that your graphics and text are exactly lined up so that your publication appears unified and consistent. DTP packages have **layout guides**, or gridlines that help you position your graphics and text frames. These lines appear in the background of your document, but do not print. You can also adjust your **ruler guides**: for instance if you want your title to be 5cm from the top of the page. Some DTP packages also allow you to align objects together.

The uses and features of graphics software

Graphics packages are used to produce images. They can be produced using **painting and drawing packages** which allow you to create your own image and edit it.

Computer-aided design (CAD) software allows the user to produce scale drawings with different elevations or views of the design, e.g. layout of kitchen/bedroom furniture.

Activity 4.5

★ Working in a small group, investigate graphics software available on the market. What graphics software is available to you?

★ Consider the advantages and disadvantage of using graphics software with producing graphics by hand, and discuss these within your group.

★ Prepare a short talk to present your findings. Use an example of a graphic to illustrate your talk.

There are many different software packages available to produce graphics. There are two main ways of storing graphics:

- Bitmap
- Vector

Each graphics application will save images in a particular file format, such as BMP and CDR. Most applications will have their own file name extensions.

Exercise 4.1

Investigate the file formats used by your graphics software.

> The best way to do this is to try saving a graphics file. The file extension will automatically show what file format it is.

▼▼▼▼▼▼▼▼▼▼

Graphics filter
a piece of software that allows a graphics file to be understood by a different programs.

▲▲▲▲▲▲▲▲▲▲

It is possible to import bitmap and vector files into other documents, provided that there is an appropriate **graphics filter**.

Bitmap graphics consist of a number of different dots or pixels. Compared with vector graphic files, bitmap files take up a lot of storage space. Bitmap images lose their clarity or resolution if they are enlarged. Bitmap images are created with paint programs. Scanned images are always bitmap.

Vector graphics are based on co-ordinate points. These give instructions to the computer to draw lines. Graphics software – with the word 'draw' in the name – often incorporates a facility to do vector graphics. Individual components of a vector graphic can be resized and this does not result in loss of clarity.

Graphics software includes tools that allow you to draw, alter attributes, manipulate images and include clip art materials.

Drawing tools include line, shape, text, brush, colour, spray, arrows, eraser and node edit. Figure 4.11 shows the tools available on Paint and CorelDraw.

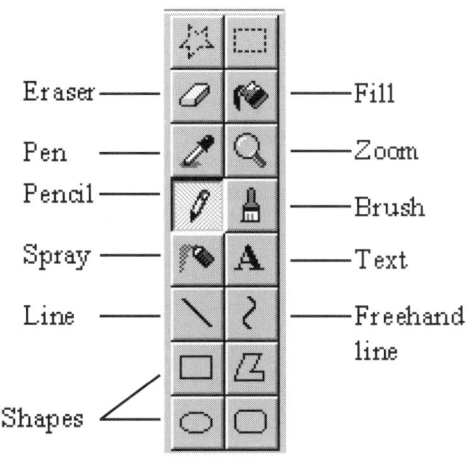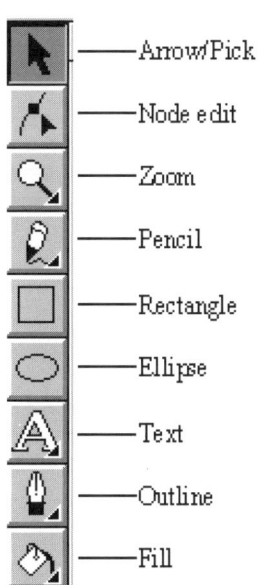

Figure 4.11   *Tools available on Paint and CorelDraw*

THE USES AND FEATURES OF GRAPHICS SOFTWARE

The **line** tool allows you to draw different types of lines on drawing objects:

- Exact straight lines, joining one point to another
- Straight lines, joining several different points
- Freehand lines

You can also have different styles of line, e.g. dotted lines or arrows as shown in Figure 4.12.

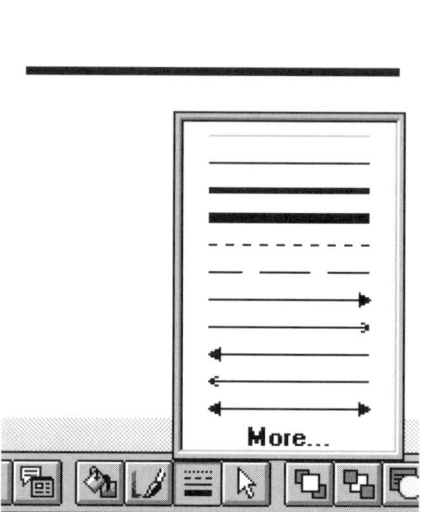

Figure 4.12 *Different line styles*

Line thickness can also be controlled. A pre-set line thickness can be selected or you may prefer to define your own width. In Figure 4.13, the thickness of the line has been increased to 6 pt.

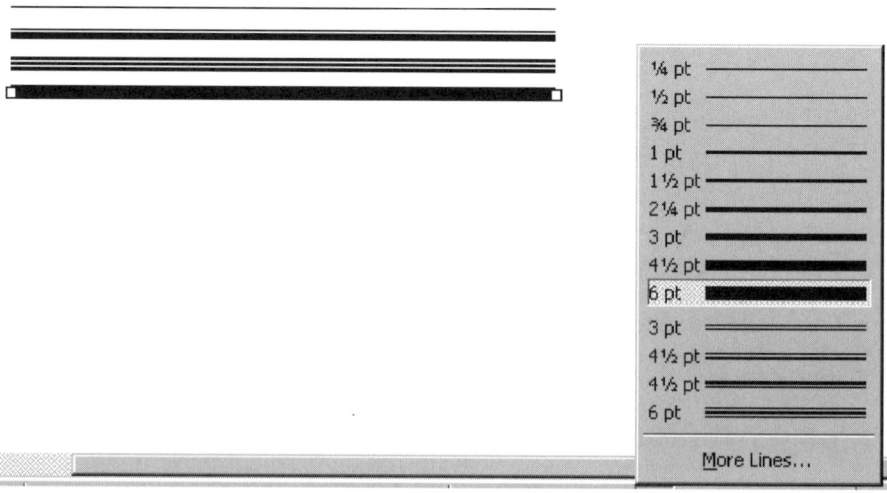

Figure 4.13 *Different line thicknesses*

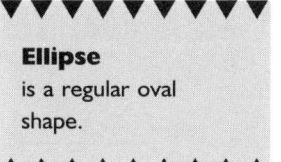

Ellipse
is a regular oval shape.

There may be several **shape** tools, so that you can accurately draw shapes such as a rectangle or an ellipse. The **ellipse** tool can be used to draw accurate circles. In some graphics software, this can be done by holding down the control key while dragging the ellipse out.

Some packages feature a small library of different shapes, e.g. a star, an arrow or a speech bubble. Figure 4.14 shows a selection of shapes.

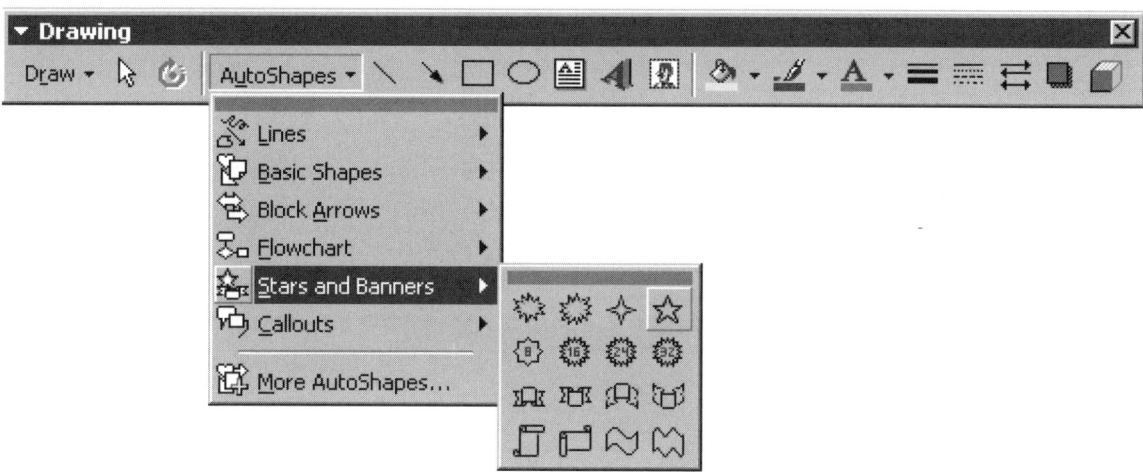

Figure 4.14 *Library of shapes*

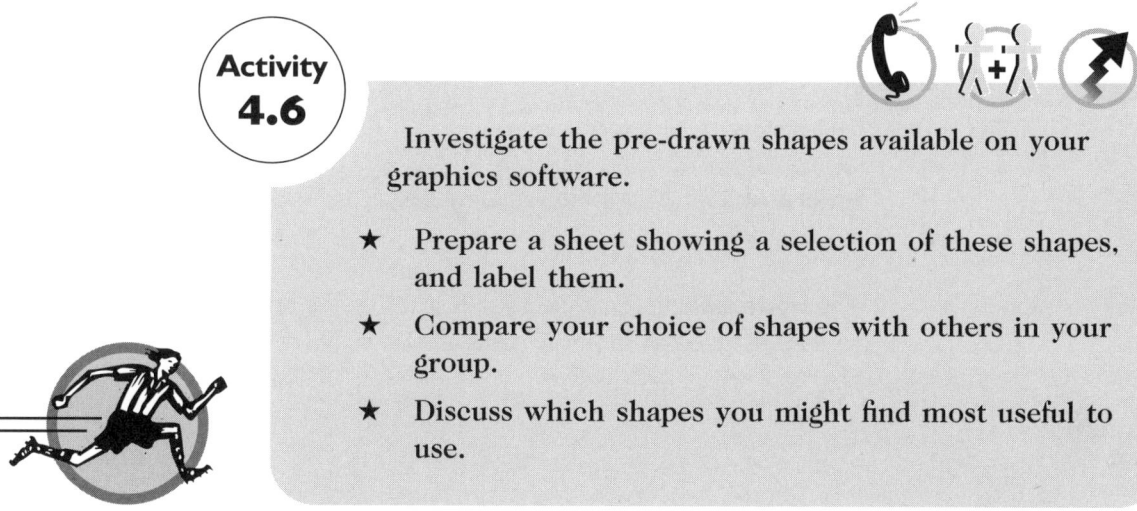

Activity 4.6

Investigate the pre-drawn shapes available on your graphics software.

★ Prepare a sheet showing a selection of these shapes, and label them.
★ Compare your choice of shapes with others in your group.
★ Discuss which shapes you might find most useful to use.

The **text** tool is used to place text on the page. This text can be edited to incorporate different fonts.

The **brush** tool is used for freehand painting. Different thicknesses and colours may be selected.

A **colour palette** is available to change the colour of an image, a shape, a line or its background. Some software features patterns and gradients as in Figure 4.15.

THE USES AND FEATURES OF GRAPHICS SOFTWARE

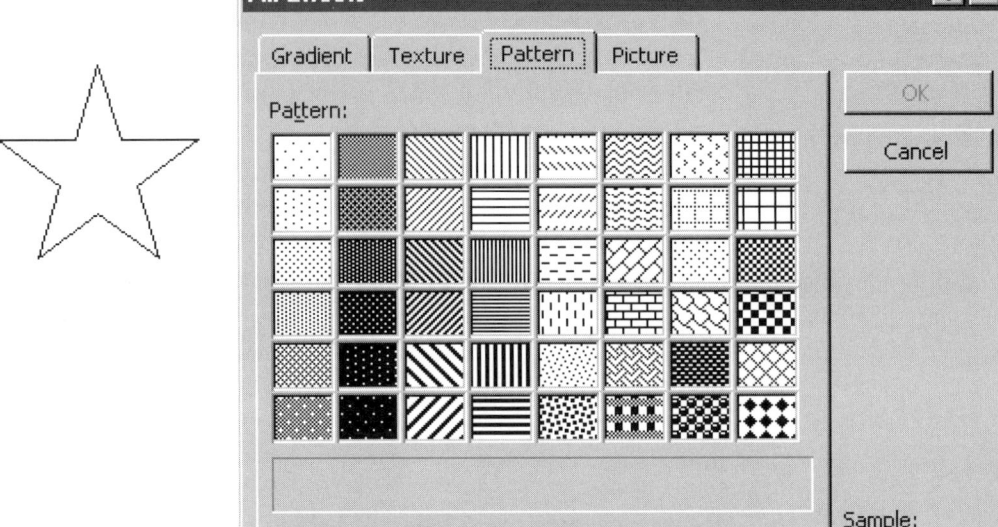

Figure 4.15 *Fill patterns and shading*

The **spray** tool is available with some graphics software and provides an effect similar to paint spray.

The **arrow** or pick tool is used to select objects for editing.

An **eraser** tool is available on some packages. This allows you to 'rub out' any mistakes.

The **node edit** tool can be used to alter details on whole lines or curves, so that a shape can be changed as shown in Figure 4.16.

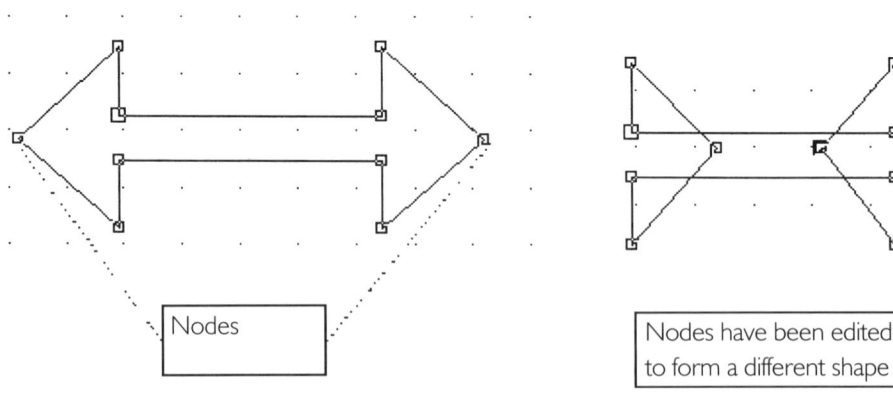

Figure 4.16 *Node editing*

Did You Know

A gradient or **fountain fill** allows you to fill an object with two colours that gradually merge into each other. **Texture fills** look like natural materials. Both types of fill use up a lot of memory.

▼▼▼▼▼▼▼▼▼

Tints
A 10% tint will have black dots covering 10% of the area (leaving 90% white).

▲▲▲▲▲▲▲▲▲

Some tools allow you to change the **attributes** of an image. These include fills, styles, line thickness, shade, width and height.

Fills are used to fill any closed object or its background with a specific colour, pattern, gradient or texture.

Shading can be used to fill a closed object or the background of an object with different combinations of black and white lines or dots. This gives the appearance of a grey shade. It is very useful for highlighting headings in tables.

Item	Cost per disk	Total
Packaging	£1.00	£100.00
Floppy disks	£1.00	£100.00
TOTAL COST	£2.00	£200.00

Figure 4.17 *Using shade for emphasis*

Exercise 4.2

What happens if you choose fill/shade for an object which is not 'closed'?

Styles are fonts that are attributed to text.

An image's **width** or **height** can be altered by using the resizing handles on the picture frame. In the cube in Figure 4.18, the width has been resized using the resizing handles. In some graphics software, you can specify the exact dimensions of your image.

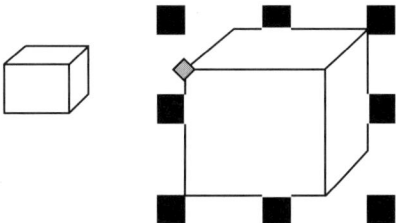

Figure 4.18 *A resized object*

Manipulation tools allow you to alter a graphic image by move, cut, copy, paste, size, mirror, rotate, and zoom. Some of the manipulation tools are shown in Figure 4.19.

THE USES AND FEATURES OF GRAPHICS SOFTWARE

A **move** can be carried out by selecting the picture frame and dragging it to a new place.

Cut, **copy** and **paste** tools allow you to select a graphic, cut (or delete) it and paste (put) it elsewhere. This facility may also be used for copying.

Size: this allows you to enlarge an image to 'scale'.

The **crop** tool allows you to cut off part of your image. In Figure 4.20, the second image is the same as the first one but has been cropped.

The **mirror** tool (Figure 4.21) allows you to produce a mirror image of the graphic.

The **rotate** tool allows you to select an object and rotate it freehand or rotate it a specified number of degrees. A document with everything aligned vertically and horizontally is quite formal. A 'jaunty angle' is effective but should match on either side as in Figure 4.22. This can be achieved by using the mirror tool.

The **zoom** tool allows you to obtain a close-up of an area you are working on. You may also 'zoom out' using a similar procedure. Figure 4.23 shows an enlargement of part of the image in Figure 4.22.

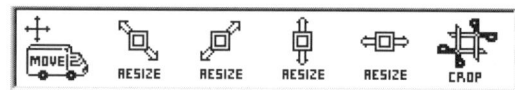

Figure 4.19 *Manipulation tools*

Figure 4.20 *An example of cropping*

Figure 4.21 *Using the mirror tool*

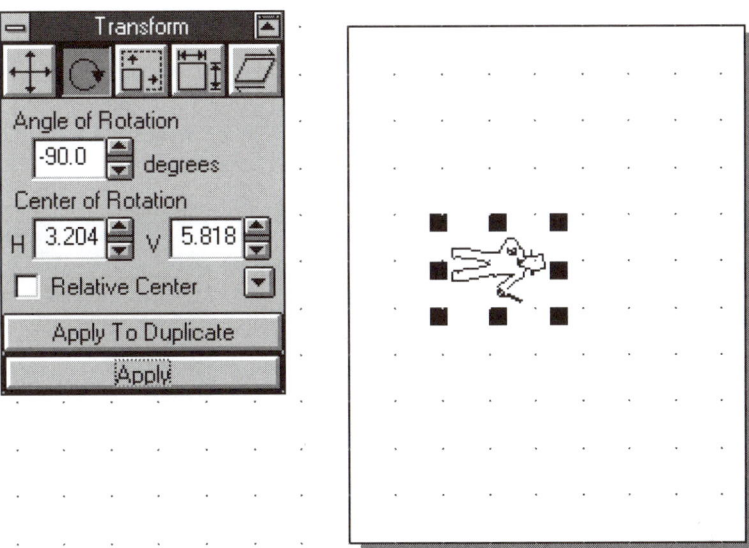

Figure 4.22 *Using the rotate tool*

Figure 4.23 *An enlargement of part of Figure 4.22*

THE USES AND FEATURES OF GRAPHICS SOFTWARE

Activity 4.7

Produce a logo that reflects your personality. Compare and discuss your logo with other members of your group.

You could incorporate some text (e.g. your initials) into your logo.

Clip art materials are often provided with DTP and graphics software as a library of pictures. They are usually free to use in any document produced using that software. It is also possible to purchase separate, more extensive, clip art libraries. Clip art offers a very useful method of adding a high quality finish to any document. Clip art images are bitmap- or vector-based images which may be edited as shown in Figure 4.24. However, it may be necessary to use different graphics software to edit the image.

Figure 4.24 *Editing a clip art image*

Activity 4.8

★ Choose your own clip art picture and edit it.
★ Annotate your two versions (before and after editing) to show what you have done and the tools you have used.

In accurate scale drawings, **vector-based graphics software** must be used. It is then possible to scale the drawing up or down without loss of clarity.

Coordinates pinpoint the exact position on the page. This is expressed as in a graph: with x and y coordinates.

A **grid** can be set up to show an arrangement of lines. This can be used with a ruler so that an object may be drawn with accurate measurements.

The **grid snap** feature allows objects to be aligned exactly to the grid lines.

Scale is used to show how large measurements have been converted into smaller ones.

A classroom that is 19m × 10m could be shown as 190mm × 100mm on a scale drawing. The scale would be 1mm = 1m.

> **Did You Know?**
>
> Orthographic drawings contain all the information needed to make an object.

Orthographic drawings can be adapted using graphics software to create perspective drawings and isometric drawings.

Orthographic drawings show three views of an object: **plan view**, **front** and **side elevations** (Figure 4.25).

Perspective drawings give an impression of how an object will actually look so features that are further away will be smaller. **Isometric drawings** are drawn on an isometric grid, with the scale in all three dimensions kept the same, so the measurements remain accurate. Distant features are the same size as those close to the viewer (see Figure 4.26).

▼▼▼▼▼▼▼▼▼

Orthographic views
A **plan view** shows a bird's eye view.
Elevation views show a diagram from the front and sides.

▲▲▲▲▲▲▲▲▲

THE USES AND FEATURES OF GRAPHICS SOFTWARE

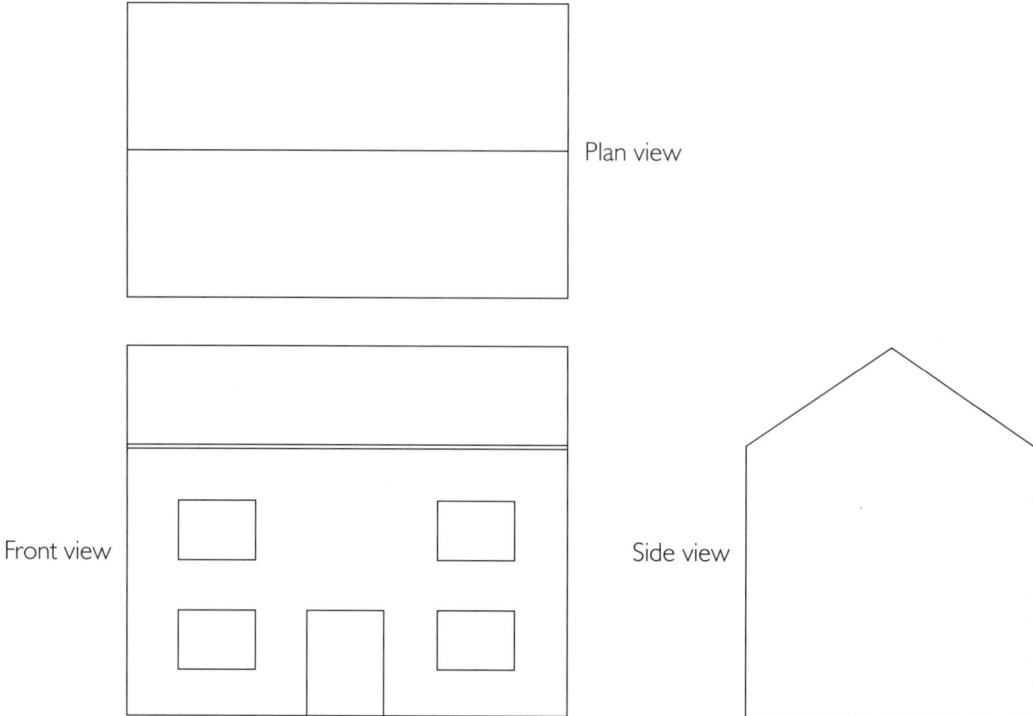

Figure 4.25 *Plan, front and side elevation views of a house*

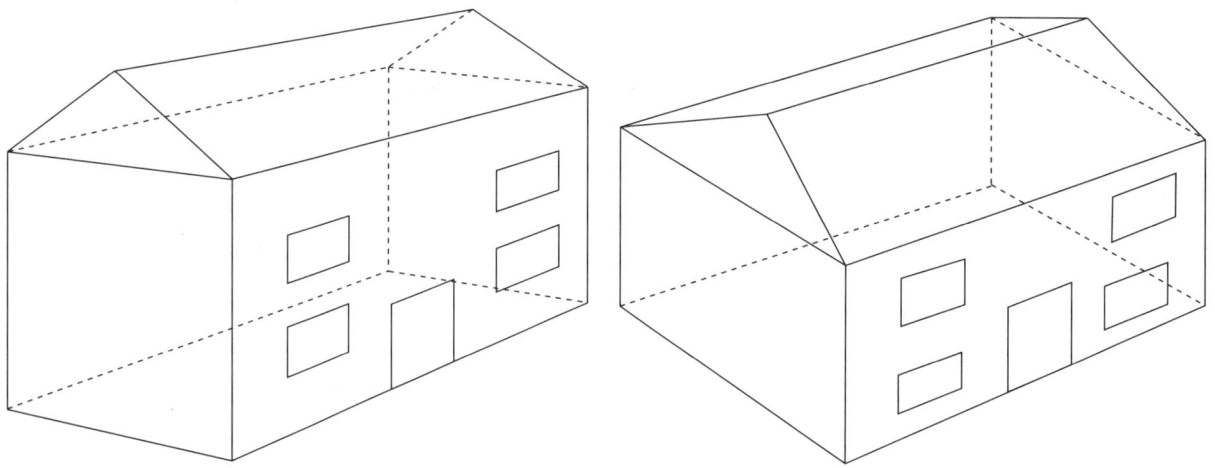

Figure 4.26 *Perspective and isometric houses*

Activity 4.9

★ Use vector-based graphics software to produce a scale drawing of your classroom.
★ Show a plan view.

4 GRAPHICS AND DESKTOP PUBLISHING

Hardware requirements: scanners and digital cameras

The hardware needed for a DTP system is similar to any other system:

- Maximum storage
- Best speed
- Keyboard, screen and printer

In addition, scanners and digital cameras are very useful.

A **scanner** uses light to sense marks on a printed page and converts them into a bitmap file that can be stored by computer. Flatbed scanners are the most common and look similar to photocopiers. Once scanned, images can be edited using specialist graphics software. It is also possible to select a small area of the original image and edit this.

A scanned photograph of a model could be edited to reduce wrinkles and skin imperfections.

A **digital camera** stores digital images for transfer to a computer and/or printing out at home. Most digital cameras allow you to preview your photo so that you can decide whether you want to store the image. Software is usually provided with the camera that allows you to upload the images to a computer and separate graphics software is available for editing the photos. Connecting cables are also required to connect your digital camera to your computer.

Activity 4.10

★ Scan a photo of yourself.
★ Experiment with your scanner software by changing your features.
★ Printout before and after images and annotate them to show what you have done.

You may want to enhance your image, or alternatively you can completely distort your facial features.

Working to a design brief

If you want to produce a design for yourself, you might think through a few ideas and then set about creating your first draft. If you want someone else to create the design, you need to explain what you want. This is called a **design brief**. The brief may be scribbled on a piece of paper or given verbally. Some are more prescriptive than others. Sometimes, the designer is given a lot of scope by a wide brief. At other times, it is necessary to do some research to find out what the user really needs.

Exercise 4.3

Consider this design brief. Design a logo for a shop that could be used on their stationery, carrier bags, etc.

What other information would you require to ensure that you produce a design that matches the user's requirements?

Activity 4.11

Design a year book for your GNVQ ICT group, working to this brief:

★ Each student should provide information about themselves which will fit on half an A4 page.
★ Ensure that all the information is accurate.
★ You may scan in photographs if you wish.

Document your year book so that it is clear how you produced it.

Activity 4.12

Design a web page for your family, working to this brief:

★ This is a wedding gift for a bride and groom.
★ Show the family tree of both families.
★ Incorporate both text and graphics.

Document a printout of your web page so it is clear where you sourced your data, and how you created the web page.

Activity 4.13

Design an information sheet about your favourite hobby, working to this brief:

★ Use desktop publishing software.
★ Include text and graphics, and use colour.
★ Present your information on a single side of A4 paper.

Document your information sheet explaining how you sourced your data and how you created the sheet.

Activity 4.14

Design material based on your favourite group's recent album, working to this brief:

★ Produce an alternative CD cover for your favourite group's recent album.
★ Produce a poster, a press release and a newspaper article advertising their forthcoming tour which is planned to promote this album. Use appropriate software and layouts for each.

Document your material showing the original album cover, and explaining how you produced the alternative CD cover, the poster, the press release and the newspaper article.

WORKING TO A DESIGN BRIEF

Revision questions

1. What are the advantages and disadvantages of using manual systems rather than computer systems for graphics and DTP?

2. What is a style sheet?

3. Explain the terms: landscape and portrait orientation.

4. What is the difference between serif and sanserif fonts?

5. What does CAD stand for?

6. What is the difference between bitmap and vector graphics?

7. When should bitmap graphics *not* be used?

8. What is the node edit tool used for?

9. Name four other editing tools.

10. What is cropping an image?

11. What are the three different orthographic projections?

12. What is the difference between a perspective drawing and an isometric drawing?

13. How does a scanner work?

14. What does a digital camera do?

15. What is a design brief?

Computer-aided design

5

- **When computer-aided design is used**
- **Why computer-aided design is used**
- **3D models**

This chapter has a practical focus throughout with many activities and case studies. You will look at computer-aided design (CAD) packages and how they can be used to produce plans, 3D models and illustrations.

This chapter looks in detail at five topics.

- Computer-aided drafting
- Image manipulation
- 3D models
- Illustration
- Plans

Throughout all the work you do during the course you should be demonstrating good practice. This involves using standard ways of working, which is described in more detail in the *Good Working Practice guide* on page 389.

Computer-aided drafting

A draughtsperson produces drawings, e.g. technical plans. Computer-aided drafting is drawing using a computer rather than by hand. Software packages specifically designed for computer-aided drafting are called computer-aided design (CAD) packages.

Exercise 5.1

Using the Internet, search for as many different CAD packages you can find.

Make a note of the suppliers of at least five different CAD packages. What is the price range for these packages?

Did You Know?

Packages that are designed for a specific purpose are called **bespoke** *packages.*

Some businesses – especially those which design or manufacture products – make extensive use of CAD packages to produce a variety of different drawings, from kitchen designs to car engine designs to printed circuits.

Exercise 5.2

Using information from the Internet search of Exercise 5.1, write to or e-mail five companies who supply CAD packages and ask for further details of their software.

CAD packages provide many different tools to enable the user to create drawings. However, there are four basic drawing tools:

- Lines
- Basic objects
- Construction objects
- Precision commands

Images created on CAD packages use vector graphics. Vector graphics are based on co-ordinate points, and give instructions to the computer to draw lines, or shapes, and hence enable the creation of 2D and 3D graphics.

For more information about vector graphics (and how they are different from bitmap graphics) see Chapter 4.

Lines

The **line tool** allows you to draw different types of lines of varying length and to scale. A line is an entity with a start point and an end point. Between these two points many different types of line can be drawn – including straight, curved, dotted or dashed, as shown in Figure 5.1.

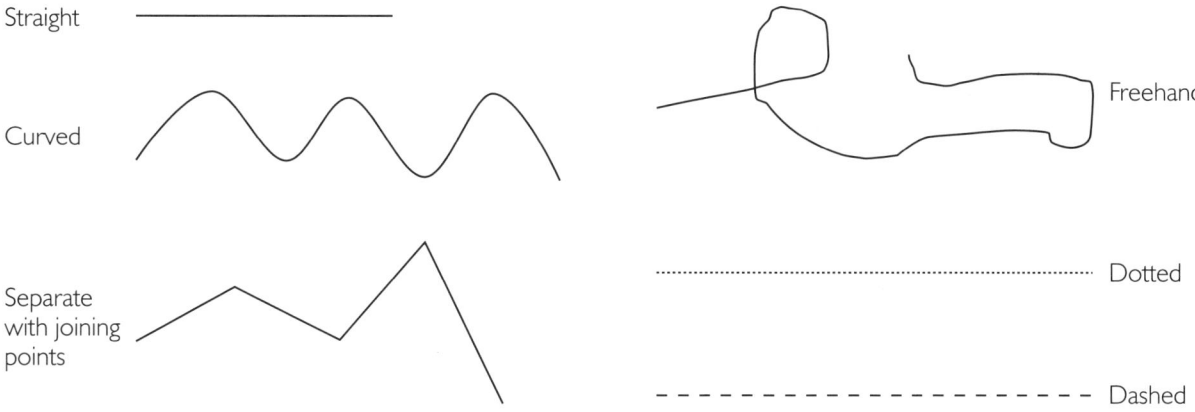

Figure 5.1 *Different types of line*

Did You Know?
Colour may also be used to highlight recent changes.

Lines may have different **line thickness** to depict different component parts; see Figure 5.2. **Colour** may also be used. Different tones and shades can be used to represent different components, and/or the user can assign colours to line types. Some CAD packages have set colours for certain components.

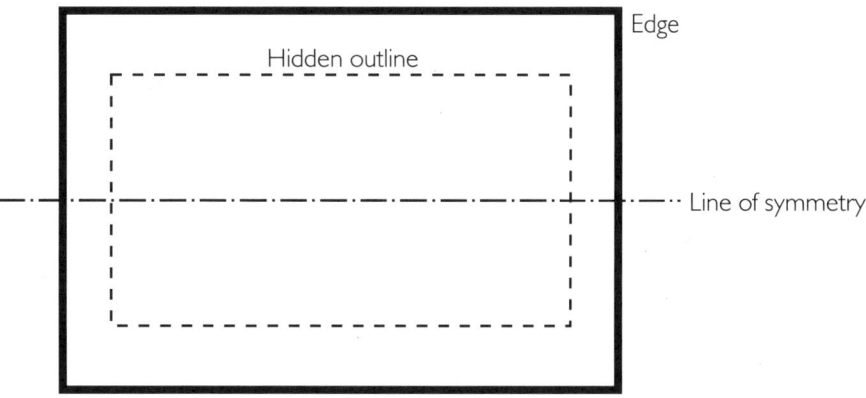

Figure 5.2 *Line thickness*

A company **house style** may specify a **gallery of colours**. Palettes are used to change the colour of an image, line, shape or background.

An engineering drawing has different line thicknesses to represent different things as shown in Figure 5.2. A thick continuous line is used for visible outlines and edges, and thin/thick short dashes represent hidden outlines and edges. A thin chain represents centre lines and lines of symmetry.

Activity 5.1

Search the Internet, and other sources of information, to find more examples of the use of different line thicknesses to represent different things. Compare your findings with others in your group.

Designers may customise their own pens, each with a different thickness, within the drawing packages and these may be saved for their own future use.

Exercise 5.3

Using a CAD package, experiment with all the different types of lines that you can find. How many different line types can you find?

Activity 5.2

★ Using a CAD package, draw a square of sides 10cm in length using a solid line of 5mm thickness.

★ Copy this square and change the line type and colour.

★ Write notes on how to do this, for someone who has never used a CAD package before.

Basic objects

To create the images that designers require some basic shapes – called **objects** – are pre-programmed into the CAD packages (see Figure 5.3):

- **Points** are marks on the drawing where lines can be drawn to and from.

- **Continuous lines** – i.e. lines with no segments – may be used to represent boundaries.

- **Rectangles** are closed figures with four sides with all four angles right angles (each one equal to 90°).

- **Polygons** – closed figures made by joining line segments – are used to draw free form shapes.

- **Curves** are simply lines, which can bend. There are many different curve types: **spline curve** is one example.

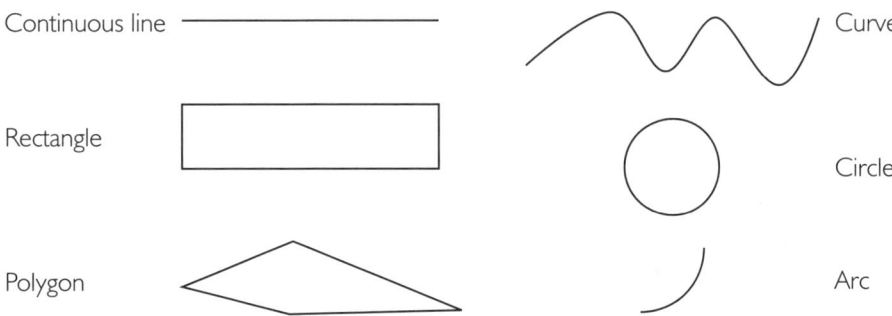

Figure 5.3 *Basic objects: continuous line, rectangle, polygon, curve, circle and arc*

Activity 5.3

★ How many different types of curve does your CAD package support?

★ Draw examples of each and print out your results using arrows and text boxes to label what the images represent.

- A **circle** is a curved line with every point equally distant from the centre. These are used to represent holes and round objects.

- An **arc** is part of a circle and can be used to show the direction a door swings or a rounded wall.

Activity 5.4

Using the basic objects, draw a simple layout of the computer room you use for this course. Use objects to symbolise furniture:

- ★ Circles – chairs
- ★ Arcs – door opening
- ★ Arc – cupboard
- ★ Continuous lines – perimeter of room
- ★ Polygons – computers
- ★ Rectangles – tables

Compare your layout diagram with others in your group. Identify ways in which you could improve your diagram.

Construction objects

As well as the basic objects, CAD packages can be used to draw more complex objects. For a bathroom designer, objects such as a bath, shower, sink, taps will appear in most bathrooms, so the CAD system may be set up to construct these automatically. Similarly, a kitchen designer would need objects for cupboards, sink units, and so on.

For 3D images, more construction objects are available (see page 142). Construction plans include walls, windows and ducts for water, gas and electrical cabling. Architects therefore need these basic construction objects.

Exercise 5.4

Refer to a book on architecture and find out what symbols are used to represent walls, windows and doors.

Activity 5.5

★ In small groups, find out what construction objects are available within your CAD software and how they are used. Word-process your findings.

★ Individually, create a simple diagram using construction objects.

Start with construction lines.

Precision commands

Scale is applied to diagrams to represent the exact measurements of the components. The manufacturers of the item will need these measurements for the manufacturing process. Very large diagrams are usually drawn at a reduced scale and small components are drawn at an enlarged scale. Whenever a drawing is to scale, the scale that has been used should appear somewhere on the drawing. This will be expressed as a ratio. In Figure 5.4, the full size diagram is expressed as 1:1, twice the original size is expressed as 2:1 and half the original size is expressed as 1:2.

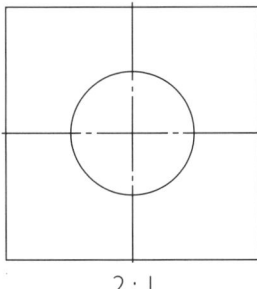
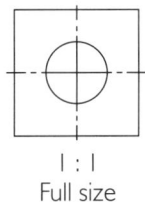

Figure 5.4 *Sample of different scale ratios*

Exercise 5.5

Which of these scales are reductions? Which are enlargements?

1:25   25:1   1:100   100:1

COMPUTER-AIDED DRAFTING

> **Activity 5.6**
>
> Using a CAD package, draw an image of your choice and then apply these scales to the original (1:1):
>
> ★ 1:3 (reduction)
> ★ 4:1 (enlargement)
>
> Produce a printout showing all three images, suitably labelled.
>
> Choose your original image so that all three images will fit onto a single page of A4.

To produce accurate scale drawings, **precision commands** are used. **Coordinate systems** use numbers to explain exactly where one point is, i.e. its **position in space** in relation to another. Co-ordinates can be either **relative** or **absolute**.

- **Relative coordinates** are based from the last point plotted.
- **Absolute coordinates** are based from the same point each time, e.g. a grid origin.

There are three ways of expressing co-ordinates: Cartesian, polar and isometric.

- **Cartesian coordinates** of 2D points are expressed using two numbers: x and y (horizontal plane and vertical plane). In 3D, three numbers are needed: x, y and z, as shown in Figure 5.5. 3D figures drawn using the xyz axis show the **perspective** of an image; things that are further away look smaller.

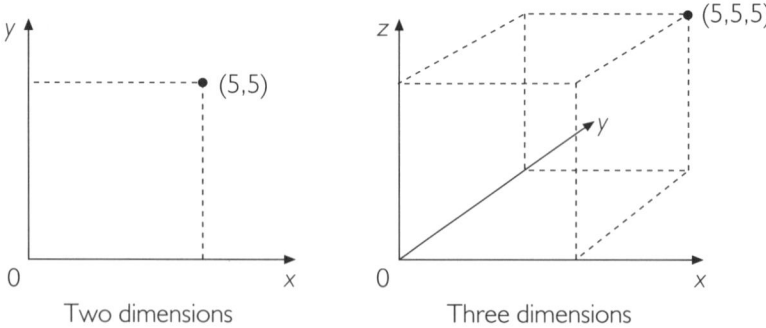

Figure 5.5 *Axes in two and three dimensions*

5 COMPUTER-AIDED DESIGN

> **Did You Know?**
>
> Using polar coordinates to describe the position of a point in 3D, a distance from the centre and two angles are needed, similar to longitude and latitude.

- **Polar coordinates** are used to describe 2D shapes as two numbers – both distances: the radius from a centre point and the angle anticlockwise from the horizontal.

- **Isometric coordinates** are based around three axes, which make angles 30, 90 and 150 degrees with the horizontal as shown in Figure 5.6. They are only used when drawing 3D objects on 2D paper/screen, and then only because they maintain length. So, for example, a cuboid drawn isometrically has parallel sides everywhere. Because length is maintained, isometric drawings do not show any **perspective**. Isometric drawings are most easily drawn on triangular grid.

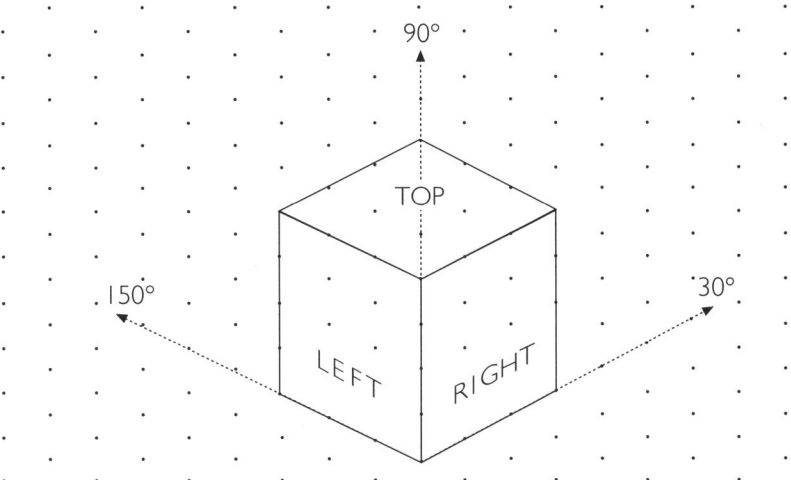

Figure 5.6 *Sample isometric cube*

 **Activity 5.7**

Use a CAD package for this activity.

★ Draw a rectangle with sides 10cm by 5cm using Cartesian co-ordinates.
★ Draw a circle using polar co-ordinates.
★ Draw an isometric cube similar to the one shown in Figure 5.6.
★ Write notes explaining how you did this, for someone who has never used a CAD package before.

A **grid** can be useful and can be set to a user's own specifications, e.g. at 1mm intervals or 10cm intervals. The user can also choose to either see the grid on screen, or have it present but invisible to the eye.

Having set up a grid the user has the option to snap on to the grid. Then any point that the user draws 'snaps' to an intersection point of the grid. To place a point in the middle of a grid section, the user has two options: turn the **snap to grid option** off, or reduce the size of the grid intervals.

Exercise 5.6

Using a CAD package, experiment drawing a shape with the grid on/off and snap on/off. What are the benefits/limitations of the grid and snap options?

Data entry of a drawing may be by direct entry or tracking:

- **Direct entry** is used when the user knows the co-ordinates or important points in the drawing. The user keys the co-ordinates directly into the data entry field and this becomes the start point for the line/object.

- **Tracking** involves tracing the mouse over an original drawing and clicking at intersection points. Tracking is used extensively in the production of Ordnance Survey maps.

Users of CAD must be able to use a range of symbols and abbreviations to enhance drawing clarity. As a result of this, a library of graphics has been created which meet industry standards:

- Mechanical symbols
- Electrical symbols
- Dataflow symbols

Many symbols and abbreviations are recommended by the British Standards Institution.

Exercise 5.7

Find out what British Standards relate to mechanical symbols.

5 COMPUTER-AIDED DESIGN

Mechanical symbols

Did You Know?

Welding is the process of uniting two pieces of metal by fusing them together to form a permanent joint.

Bearings are difficult to represent diagrammatically, so they are represented by a conventional symbol (Figure 5.7). The symbol does not imply a particular bearing type.

There is also an industry standard for representing welding requirements on drawings. These symbols are specified in the British Standard BS 499.

Figure 5.7 *Bearing symbol*

Activity 5.8

Find and make notes on the symbolic representation for these types of weld:

★ Spot weld
★ Plug weld
★ Square butt weld

Obtain a copy of the British Standard BS 499 or try to find this information on the Internet.

Using CAD, draw one of the symbolic representations.

Exercise 5.8

Explain in the form of a report what surface finish is and how CAD designers use it when constructing their drawings.

▼▼▼▼▼▼▼▼▼
Tolerance
is an acceptable margin of error, e.g. the maximum and the minimum size permitted.
▲▲▲▲▲▲▲▲▲

Tolerance is stated on diagrams where accuracy is essential. Tolerance may also be shown as a range, e.g. 3mm +/− 0.1mm of component size as shown in Figure 5.8.

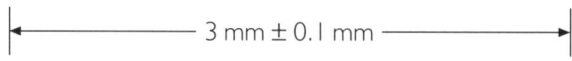

Figure 5.8 *Tolerance*

Electrical symbols

Electrical circuit drawing also uses symbols which are industry standard, as shown in Figure 5.9.

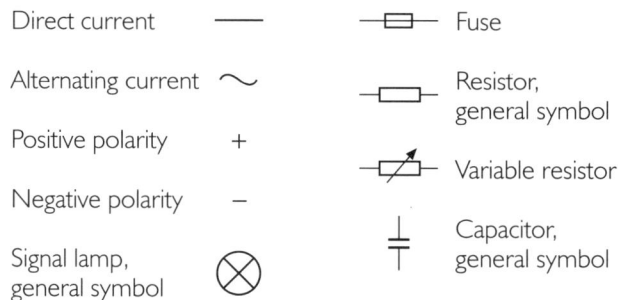

Figure 5.9 *Electrical symbols, including resistors, capacitors and fuses*

Exercise 5.9

Find out what British Standards relate to electrical symbols.

Dataflow symbols

Dataflow symbols are used to show how data is processed within an ICT system. For example, special symbols are used in flowcharts to show the different kinds of actions that might take place. Figure 5.10 shows five of the symbols used in flowcharts.

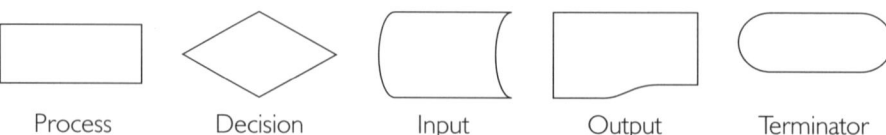

Figure 5.10 *Flowcharting symbols*

Activity 5.9

Other dataflow symbols are used in other types of charts in ICT.

★ Working with others in your group, find examples of other symbols.

★ Individually, prepare a one-page spread of sample symbols, suitably labelled.

You may need to look in text books for an Advanced Vocational course in ICT.

Annotating diagrams

All drawings using CAD can be annotated with text and dimension features:

- Text style
- Dimension
- Dimension style

All CAD packages have a standard **default text style**, in which all annotations on the drawing appear. However, the user can change the default style of text. The user may also want to create their own styles of text and save them for future use. A company may set up its own house style to be applied to all drawings.

Exercise 5.10

What is the default style of text on your school CAD package?

Dimensions are the way the distance and angle variables are shown. Dimension variables can be turned on/off as required. For distance variables, the user sets how the variables are to be displayed, e.g. to 1 or 2 decimal places, in centimetres or metres. Each CAD package has its own set of dimension variables.

COMPUTER-AIDED DRAFTING

Activity 5.10

* Using the CAD package in your school, experiment with the following dimension styles and try to change them:

Arrow types	Linear	Aligned
Angular	Diameter	Radius

* How easy is it to create your own and save them? Why would you want to do this?

* Write notes on how to control the dimension style for someone who is new to CAD.

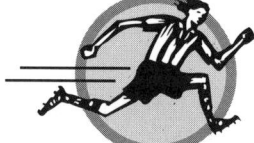

Plotting

CAD users tend to use plotters as opposed to printers to produce hardcopies of work. This is mainly because CAD drawings are often too large to print on A4 paper. There are several different types of plotter. With some, the paper moves in one direction while 'pens' move perpendicular to it. With others, the paper stays still while the pen moves across the surface.

Exercise 5.11

Research different types of plotters, and write notes to explain the main differences between plotter types.

When choosing the size of paper to plot on to, the user will also be asked for the orientation: **landscape** or **portrait**.

Activity 5.11

Using a CAD package, look at the plotting options. List the sizes of paper that your plotter can print on, starting with the smallest. Present your results as a table.

Image manipulation

Image manipulation is used to change an original drawing in some way. There are different types of source material that could be used:

- Lens-based
- Paper-based
- Electronic-based
- Resolution

Lens-based image manipulation

Lens-based image manipulation is concerned with photography and photocopies. Photographs can be taken to aid the designing process and they can be developed using many different techniques. Many years ago, only black and white photographs were available and in one size only and with one finish, but now photographs can be developed in different finishes, matt, gloss and different sizes. Photocopying is also now readily available and this can help with increasing the sizes of drawings and changing the tone, perhaps to darken lines.

Paper-based image manipulation

Paper-based drawings include initial sketches and design ideas, or hardcopy printouts of latest versions. Designs evolve and so drawings may be modified many times, at each stage of the design cycle. Each time a drawing is modified, it should be assigned a new **version number** so that the designer, and others, can keep track of how many alterations the drawing has undergone and whether they are referring to the most up-to-date version The designer can write notes on the drawings to aid understanding and these can be incorporated next time the electronic version is updated.

Activity 5.12

Using the Internet, or other sources of information, find the answers to these questions:

★ When was the first colour photograph produced?

★ How many different types of finish can be put on a photograph?

★ What are the three most common sizes of photographs?

★ Who invented the photocopier and when?

★ What is the largest size drawing a photocopier can reproduce?

★ List ten features of a photocopier and explain how these might be useful for a designer.

Make notes on what you find and compare these with others in your group.

> Keep a record of the sources of your information. You or others in your group may want to return to the web site to find out more detail at a later date.

Electronic-based images

Scanning constitutes electronic manipulation. Drawings are scanned in and the designer can then modify them on the computer. Often, when drawings are scanned in, the quality degrades. The designer will use features on the software to counteract this. These features include **despeckling**, **deskewing** and **erasing**.

Activity 5.13

Use the Internet, and other sources of information, to find out about different types of software which can be used for image manipulation and scanning.

★ List the features which are common to these applications that help to improve the quality of scanned drawings.

★ Find out, in particular, all that you can about despeckling, deskewing and erasing.

★ Compare notes with others in your group.

Resolution

dpi stands for dots per inch.

Resolution is a measure of the quality of printing, calculated in **dpi**: the higher the dpi, the better the quality of the print.

One of a printer's most saleable features is how many dpi it will print to. Obviously, the better printers will print to a higher dpi.

Exercise 5.12

Research five different styles of printers from the same manufacturer. Find out what the printing facilities are and how many dpi they will print to.

Techniques available

Many techniques can be used to manipulate graphics images: colours and palettes; cut, copy and paste; distort; filters; rotate; scale; sizing and layers.

> **Did You Know?**
>
> For one cut, you can paste many times!

Copy is a tool used to replicate an image. **Cut and paste** can be used to remove an image from one position and place it in a different position within a file or in a completely different file. When the image is cut it is placed in the pasteboard, ready for pasting.

> **Did You Know?**
>
> You can specify the angle by which the object should be rotated, or you can rotate the object freehand.

Rotate can be useful for any image but is usually done extensively in 3D solid modelling. It turns the image around a specific point so that it can be viewed from different angles.

Objects can be rotated around the origin axis, or around a set of co-ordinates as shown in Figure 5.11.

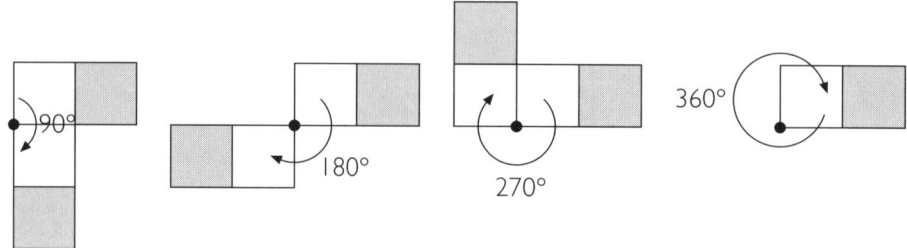

Figure 5.11 *Examples of rotation using the absolute method*

Activity 5.14

Objects can be rotated using the absolute or relative method. Find out how relative rotation works.

> Your on-line help may provide some useful information on the difference between absolute and relative methods.

Sizing is used to resize the drawing. It can be used to reduce the size of the whole drawing for printing or increase the size to look at parts in more detail. To look at a drawing in more detail, there is the **zoom** facility, which allows you to increase the magnification.

Exercise 5.13

Using your CAD package, find out what different zooming options are available.

Did You Know?

When designing a house, the plans are built up in layers, floor plan, electrical wiring and plumbing.

Layers are applied to drawings so that the component can be built up and easily viewed. You can assign as many layers as required. This is like putting transparent overlays one on top of another. **Colours** are generally assigned to layers for ease of identification. **Locking** is used to safeguard work that has been done. The user has the option to lock areas or layers. Those layers still remain visible, but you can not alter them in any way, while they remain locked.

Activity 5.15

Two techniques are not discussed above: distort and filters.

★ Find out what these techniques are and practice using them.

★ Print out examples of them being used.

★ Write notes on how to use them, for someone who has not used a CAD package before.

Activity 5.16

Using your school CAD package, use the line and shape tool to experiment with the techniques available. If there is another CAD package available to you, experiment with the alternative package. What are the benefits and limitations of each package?

IMAGE MANIPULATION

3D models

Images can be 2D or 3D. 2D images are 'flat' images. Those that are in 3D appear to be 'jumping out' from the page. Apart from the 2D tools, there are special tools for 3D imaging:

- Cubes and cones and spheres
- Shading, surface textures and texture mapping
- Views, wire frame and perspective
- Cross-sections, isometric and axonometric

Isometric
Having a plane of projection equally inclined to the three perpendicular axes.

Axonometric
A method of projection in which a drawing of 3D object has all lines to exact scale, and appears to be distorted.

Cubes, cones and **spheres** are the basic building blocks or construction objects for a 3D model. See Figure 5.12.

 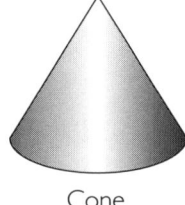 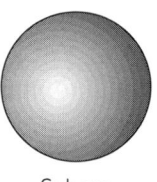

Cube   Cone   Sphere

Figure 5.12 *Sample cube, cone and sphere*

Shading can be used to add an extra dimension to the drawing. On systems with fewer than 256 colours, the shade command removes all the hidden lines and displays the shade in one colour. On systems with more than 256 colours, the shade effect takes light into consideration and alters the shade colour accordingly.

Surface textures allow the user to add a fill texture to a drawing. This can give the image a 3D effect which allows it to stand out from the rest of the drawing. Textures can be customised to a particular organisation's needs.

A kitchen designer may apply different surface textures to represent different styles of kitchen furniture or different effects on doors or other surfaces.

Activity 5.17

★ Draw each of these objects and apply shading and surface texture: cube, cone and sphere.

★ Print all three on a single sheet of A4 and annotate your diagrams with details of how you created the shading and surface texture effects.

Wire frame is the basic outline drawing but with no detail such as filling, texture, etc. This is useful because it allows you to see if any objects are completely obscured by those in front.

Activity 5.18

Convert the objects that you drew in Activity 5.17 to wire frame objects.
Print the images out again and compare them with others in your group.

Did You Know?

Turning on a lathe is done to make a shape such as a screw fitting or a shape with a particular cross-section, e.g. a table leg. **Extruding** a shape is done, for example, by forcing metal or plastic through a 'die' to make a rod or tube.

Cross-sections enable the user to take a slice out of their drawing and see all the inside bits! It would be the same as cutting a piece of chocolate cake and seeing the filling.

Like rotation, **reflection** is useful when viewing 3D objects. See Figure 5.13.

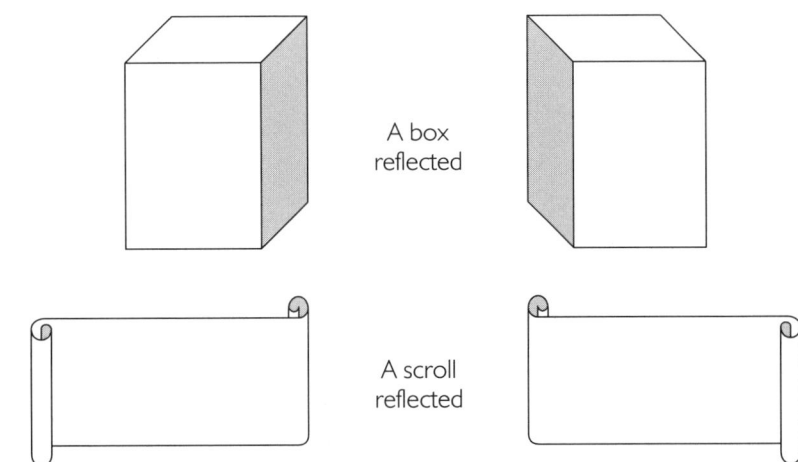

Figure 5.13 *Reflected images*

3D MODELS

Perspective viewing allows the user to view the object in 3D space. It enables the user to visualise how the drawing will actually look when built. You can look at the drawing from different viewpoints. Perspective gives you the feeling that you can actually walk all the way around what you have drawn.

Grouping of objects is done when the user wants to select various objects as one entity. Objects can then be moved, with ease. Objects can also be ungrouped.

Activity **5.19**

★ Using the objects you created in Activity 5.17, copy the cone three times and rotate anticlockwise through 90°, 180°, 270°.

★ Group all the cones and copy all four cones twice.

★ Write notes on how you did this, for someone who is familiar with CAD but has not used these features before.

Exercise 5.14

Find out what is meant by the term 'hierarchical objects'.

Illustration

Graphical images are often used as illustrations, e.g. for a book or a CD.

A **book illustration** used for the front cover of a book has to be eye-catching so that people notice it and are tempted to pick it up and maybe buy it. The GNVQ series of books shown in Figure 5.14, for example, has similar designs on the front of each book, so that the user can identify and, hopefully, remember the book.

Activity 5.20

Think about some books you have read recently.

★ Are there any book covers that stick in your mind? If so why?

★ Choose an author who has the same style of book cover for all books and scan in three of the book covers. Explain how the book covers are the same.

★ Do you think that keeping the same style promotes or hinders the sales of the book? Discuss this with the rest of your class.

Within books, illustration are also used to explain a point being made within the text. For any book, or series of books, it is important that the figures follow a style.

Exercise 5.15

Look at the illustrations in this book. Comment on the style used, e.g. for the captions, labels and icons. What are the advantages of using the same style throughout?

Advertisements always – or nearly always – include graphical images so that they are eye-catching. Posters are a very good source of advertisements. These may be on large billboards or in the format of flyers which are distributed by hand or sent with mailshots.

ILLUSTRATION 145

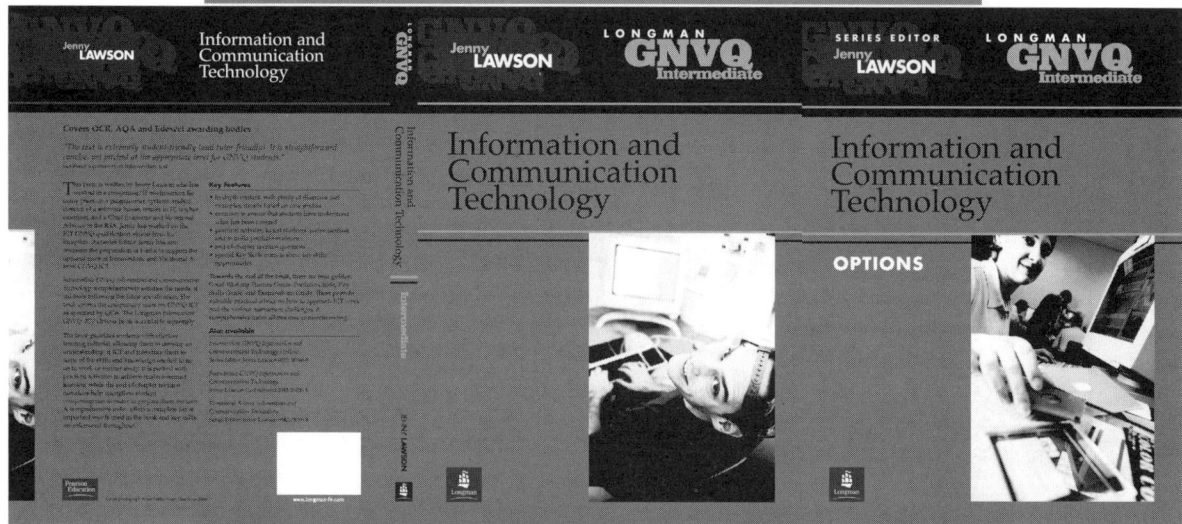

Figure 5.14 *The GNVQ/Vocational A-level ICT series' book covers*

Exercise 5.16

Find an example of an advert, which has no graphical image, only text.
Find another advert that has only graphics and no or very little text.
How do these two types of advert convey their message?

A CD cover must be eye catching. The most important features are the artist's name and album title and these must be easily visible. CD covers must be very carefully designed. When on a shelf in a shop, they must stand out from the rest!

Activity 5.21

From your own or a friend's collection choose four CD covers, two which you think are good examples of product marketing and two which you think are poor examples.

★ Scan or photocopy them and incorporate them into a word-processing document, which lists ten reasons why you think the CD covers are good/poor.

★ Compare your reasons with those of others in your group.

During the design stage of a product, before manufacturing starts, the designer will use **product visualisation** to show how he/she expects the product to look. Packaging is an important part of marketing. Having the most attractive box or jar is just as important as having an eye-catching cover for a book or CD.

Activity 5.22

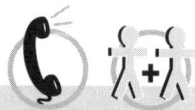

Visit a supermarket and look at a range of products, e.g. shampoos or soap powders.

> Alternatively, as a group, you could collect together a selection of products from home – preferably empty bottles or boxes!

- ★ What different shapes are used? Look especially at the labels on the bottles and the boxes. What is the most eye-catching design?
- ★ What would make someone want to buy the product?
- ★ Produce your findings in a word-processed report.

> Where possible, take photographs to supplement your report.

Did You Know?

Artist impressions of criminals, called Identifit photos are used on TV programs such as Crimewatch UK. They have proved to be very successful in jogging the memory of the public.

Artist impressions are used to visualise how something will look, e.g. a new housing state. It is difficult to visualise 3D objects, so an artist impression is helpful.

Companies who build conservatories often use artist's impressions when trying to sell their products. The Police force also uses artist impressions when searching for criminals. The artist bases their drawing on descriptions of criminals given by witnesses.

Activity 5.23

- ★ List two other programmes on TV that include artist impressions.
- ★ List two other organisations that use artist impressions to help to sell their product.
- ★ In each case, explain why artist's impressions are used rather than photographs.

5 COMPUTER-AIDED DESIGN

All organisations tend to have a **corporate image**, some form of identity, that people remember them by and associate with the product or service being offered.

Activity 5.24

Choose three companies and describe their corporate image. How are their corporate images different? Present your findings to the rest of your group.

★ How do the companies promote themselves?
★ What other modes of advertising are used?
★ Are computers used to project a better corporate image?

Logos are one way of projecting a corporate image. They are usually identifiable with the product or service, or name of organisation and should be easily recognisable.

Activity 5.25

★ Individually, search the Internet and find five different company logos. Print these out, keeping a note of the web site addresses.

★ Discuss with others in your group, the relevance of the company logos and how any of them could be improved.

★ Design your own logo and explain why you have chosen this design. This could now be incorporated into the header/footer of all the work that you produce, to act as your signature mark!

ILLUSTRATION

Activity 5.26

For this activity, the class should be split into several small groups. Each group is to form a design team, bidding for the marketing plan of a company which will be trading on the Internet. Each team needs to produce a design for a new product on a web site to advertise the company.

- ★ First a new corporate image including a logo for the company is to be discussed and designed. Artist impressions and other visual material should be produced.
- ★ Detailed designs should then be produced and promotional material such as flyers or posters created.
- ★ Each team should then present a portfolio of its marketing plan to the other groups. Members of staff and other groups should conduct judging, and give constructive advice to each team.

Each member of the team should contribute at all stages in the project and each of the members of the group should have a specific responsibility.

Areas for group responsibility could include: Chairperson, Secretary, Finance, Design and Marketing.

Plans

Plans are 2D representations of a 3D object, e.g. a house, used to view the house in a predetermined scale.

Plan view show objects viewed from above. **Elevation** shows the view from the front. **Side view** shows the view from the side. See Figure 5.15.

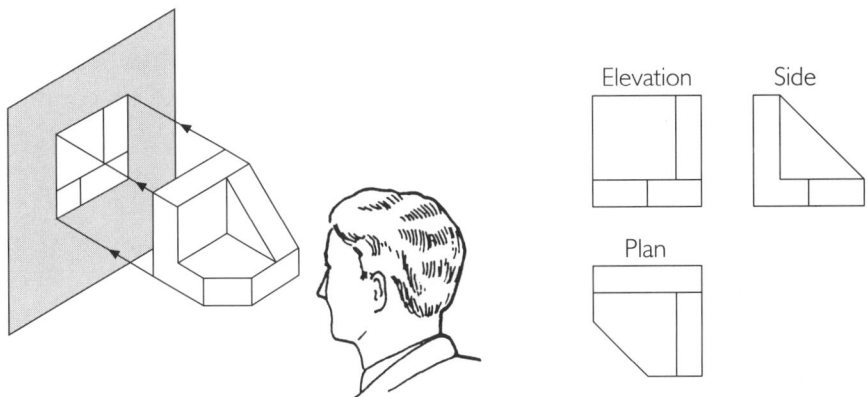

Figure 5.15 *Example of plan, side and elevation*

Wiring or plumbing plans are used by electricians, engineers, builders to see the layout of where the cables/pipes must run. Builders and architects produce **interior plans of buildings** to show how a building will be constructed. The drawings are usually layered for ease of viewing.

Garden plans are used to show how a garden will be laid out. They often use artistic impressions in conjunction with the plans so that the full 3D appearance can be appreciated.

Activity 5.27

★ Measure and sketch your own or a family member's garden.

★ Using CAD, the tools and features discussed in this chapter, replicate your sketch.

Use different colours for lines and shapes. Remember to use a scale. Group objects for ease of movement.

Activity 5.28

★ Choose a three-dimensional object, like a table or a chair. Measure all relevant dimensions and angles.

★ Using CAD, draw the image to scale and show it from three views: plan, side and elevation.

★ Why would a designer need to plan and view the object from all three perspectives?

★ Evaluate your drawing, explaining the problems you had in creating the image. List five improvements that you would make to your drawing.

Revision questions

1. What is the benefit of lines having different thicknesses?

2. Give five examples of construction objects and explain who might use them.

3. What is the difference between relative and absolute co-ordinates?

4. What do Cartesian, polar and isometric describe?

5. What does the term tolerance mean when using CAD?

6. What does text style mean?

7. What do arrow types, linear, angular and radius all have in common?

8. What is lens-based image manipulation?

9. What does dpi stand for?

10. Is 13:1 an enlargement, or a reduction?

11. What are layers? How can they be used?

12. What is a surface texture?

13. What is a wire frame used for?

14. How can locking be a useful tool when using CAD software?

15. Why is it important that advertisements are eye-catching?

Numerical modelling using spreadsheets

- Understand the variety of ways in which numerical data may be modelled using spreadsheets

- Produce a spreadsheet model to meet a given brief

- Use a spreadsheet model to make predictions from data collected

- Explore the use of spreadsheet modelling to make predictions from data collected

- Solve numerical modelling problems using mathematical, statistical and logical functions on a spreadsheet

This unit extends the work done in Intermediate Unit 1: *Presenting Information*, and Unit 2: *Handling Information*.

This unit is assessed through the work presented in your portfolio to meet the requirements of the assessment evidence grid. Details of how to prepare your portfolio for assessment are given in the *Portfolio guide* on page 393.

This chapter looks in detail at six topics.

- Data collection methods
- Designing models for numerical data using a spreadsheet
- Using spreadsheet models for numerical modelling

▼▼▼▼▼▼▼▼▼

Spreadsheet
is a set of data stored on a grid. The grid is divided up into rows usually numbered 1, 2, 3..., and columns usually lettered A, B, C...

Cell
is the smallest area that can contain data on a spreadsheet.

Cell reference
gives a cell's column and row, e.g. cell B5 is in column B and row 5.

▲▲▲▲▲▲▲▲▲

- Producing reports
- Using spreadsheet models for prediction
- Documenting your solution

Two case studies are used to introduce and illustrate the ideas of this chapter:

Inner Whorl Stained Glass

Inner Whorl is a small business making stained glass windows, jewellery and ornamental objects. Most of the windows are made to order. Smaller pieces are made in bulk and sold through craft shops and fairs.

The business uses numerical models on a spreadsheet for cash flow forecasting, budgeting and estimates for customers.

Davina Brown

Davina Brown is a researcher. She has to survey groups of people on their opinions and provide data for commercial clients who use this information in devising new marketing campaigns and in designing new products and services.

You will look at the ways that spreadsheets are used to organise, analyse and present data. You will see how calculations can be performed on the data and how information based on the data can be presented in different ways. You will look at the ways that spreadsheets can be used to predict results and trends.

For your portfolio, you will need to design a similar spreadsheet to meet the specification given to you by your teacher or someone else. You will need to research the needs of a user of your system, enter data into a spreadsheet and use it to present the information gained by analysing the data.

You should try to identify the information needs of some local organisations, like the ones used in the case studies, who might be able to help with the specification and use of spreadsheets.

Finally you will need to produce documentation for your spreadsheet. This should consist of two parts – a guide for the users of your spreadsheet and a technical guide that explains how you created the spreadsheet.

Data collection methods

You must be able to identify an appropriate collection method for a given data situation and know about the **data collection methods** available. These methods are either **primary** or **secondary research**.

Primary research methods

> **Did You Know?**
>
> Collecting your data yourself is called **primary research**.

There are three methods of primary research:

- Observation
- Interviews
- Questionnaires

Exercise 6.1

Copy Table 6.1 and match the type of primary research to the circumstance described.

Situation being researched	Type of primary research
Counting traffic passing a fixed point	Observation
Obtaining staff opinions in a shop employing six people	Interview
Asking 100 customers in the shop their opinions	Questionnaire
Finding profit made by a young enterprise company by examining receipts and other paperwork	
Taking a straw poll of 12 students to find their opinions on a new course	
Asking all 300 students on a course their views on library opening hours	

Table 6.1 *Sources of primary research*

Did You Know?

A count of vehicles, and their speeds, is often collected by sensors that are connected to rubber strips across the road. When a vehicle passes over them air is pushed out. This triggers the sensor. They can't be used spotting speeding vehicles though . . . why not?

Observation

A traffic census could be carried out by **observing** the traffic passing a chosen point on a road. Each vehicle that passes is noted down. It is possible to use a tally chart for this (Figure 6.1).

Holiday destination	Number of people	Total
UK	ⅧⅠ IIII	9
Spain	ⅧⅠ ⅧⅠ III	13
Greece	II	2
Turkey	IIII	4
France	ⅧⅠ III	8
Other	III	3

Figure 6.1 Tally chart

Exercise 6.2

Sometimes it is possible for the data to be automatically collected. What data can be collected by a person observing vehicles passing a chosen point that cannot easily be collected by a sensor?

Did You Know?

Data collection is sometimes called **data capture**.

Point-of-sale terminals in a shop also collect data about products purchased as they are scanned.

Exercise 6.3

Shops also collect data about their customers. What data can they collect, and how is it collected?

DATA COLLECTION METHODS 157

Face-to-face interviewing

▼▼▼▼▼▼▼▼▼
Responses are answers to questions, respondents are the people who are giving the answers – the people you are interviewing or who are filling in questionnaires.
▲▲▲▲▲▲▲▲▲

Market research is finding out people's views on a particular topic. **Interviewing** them and recording their answers can do this.

Davina Brown

Davina collects information from members of the public. The questions and type of interview are decided by the organisation she is collecting data for. She is also told how many people she must interview and how many in each age range, etc. She interviews them, either face-to-face or over the telephone, and enters their responses onto forms.

Davina then transfers the responses from the forms to a spreadsheet so that it may be processed and analysed.

Exercise 6.4

Why does Davina Brown enter the responses onto a form, rather than keying it directly into a spreadsheet?

If there are a large number of questions, or if you need responses from people who you cannot meet, then a **questionnaire** may be more appropriate.

Questionnaires

The design of a questionnaire is very important. A poorly designed questionnaire may confuse the person who is filling it in; see Figure 6.2. Well-designed questionnaires are straightforward to complete and are easy to read.

When you design a questionnaire consider the following points:

- Before deciding on the questions, think carefully about what analysis is to be done on the answers. If a question doesn't help with this analysis, it is probably not worth including.

- Include an introduction and thank the person who is to fill in the questionnaire.

- Is the data being collected confidential? Do you need to ask respondents their names?

- Leave plenty of space for responses.

- If questions are to be filled in by someone else then the layout must be clear. Avoid too many words and different fonts. Make all tick boxes the same size if possible, and certainly the same height.

- Use closed rather than open questions wherever possible.

Question types
A **closed**, or multiple-choice, question has a fixed number of responses e.g. 'Have you visited a supermarket in the last month?' (answers: Yes or No.)
An **open** question can have any answer e.g. 'What is your favourite holiday destination?'

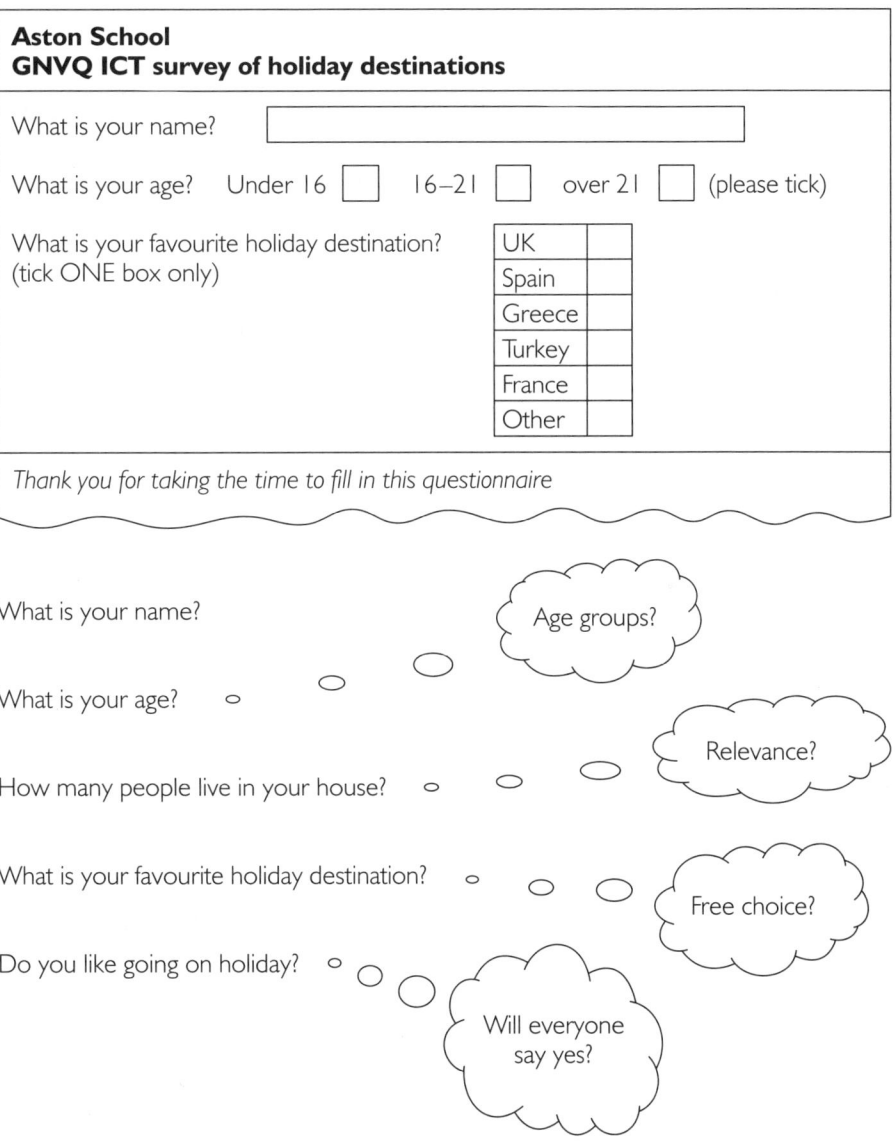

Figure 6.2 *Example of good and bad questionnaire design*

- Closed questions should list the possible answers with tick boxes and should have an option for 'Other answers'. When data is transferred from the answers to closed questions, consider numbering the options or using codes such as M/F for male/female.

You must be able to identify the types of data that can be collected using questionnaires and how this data can be stored in a spreadsheet for analysis purposes. For example, will the answers to questions always be text or always numeric? If an answer is sometimes text and sometimes numeric then it will be necessary to treat that answer as text. If a calculation has to be carried out on an answer then that answer must be numeric.

The way in which data is to be analysed, and results presented, also affects the design of questions.

- If your answer needs to be a number so that it can be included in a calculation, this must be made clear in the question so that invalid answers are not given.

    For example 'How many people live in your house?'

- With numeric data, it is possible to ask for a precise answer or a range.

    For example the question 'What is your age?' can be answered with a number (e.g. 16) or a range (e.g. 15–20).

    If the answer is to be included in a calculation it is better to ask for a precise answer. If a chart is to be drawn, with no calculations, then a range may be appropriate.

- If answers to a question are to be analysed using a chart, then it is better if the question has a fixed number of multiple choice answers, rather than allowing any response. This is because a chart will be difficult to interpret if there are many different answers.

- Charts are sometimes difficult to read if one answer is given by the overwhelming majority of respondents.

    For example 'Do you like ice cream?'
    (Yes/No/Don't know)

- A pie chart should only be used if there are a few different answers.

For example 'Where did you go on your last holiday?'
(United Kingdom/Europe/USA/Other)

A pie chart is difficult to read if there are too many different answers or for an open question.

For example 'What model of car does your family have?'

Exercise 6.5

Copy and complete Table 6.2 to show whether a question is open or closed and whether a bar chart and a pie chart can be expected to show the answers sensibly.

Question	Open or closed?	Chart used to display answers	
		Bar/pie	Reason for choice
What is your favourite holiday destination?	Open	Bar	Too many different choices
What is your age?	Closed	Bar	Too many different choices; may be better to ask 'which age group?'
Are you under 16?	Closed	Either	Only two choices
How many people live in your house?	Closed	Bar	Difficult to draw very small segments for houses with, say, seven people in
Do you eat meat?			
How will you vote in the next election?			
What is your favourite TV soap?			
What month were you born in?			
What do you think about school uniform?			

Table 6.2 *Open and closed questions and charts*

DATA COLLECTION METHODS

Activity 6.1

Design a questionnaire to collect data about students in your class. Analyse the data collected to produce these results:

* A bar chart showing how far students travel each day
* Average heights of boys, of girls and overall
* A chart showing people's favourite football team

Activity 6.2

Design a questionnaire to collect data of your own choice. Decide on a reasonable number of people to collect data from. Keep the collected data to build a spreadsheet in Activity 6.4.

Secondary research methods

Referring to a previously published source such as a book, web site or a computerised database is called **secondary research**. One of the main sources for secondary research is *Social Trends*, published each year by the Government and containing data on the UK.

Secondary research methods are used when it is impossible, or unreasonable, to collect the information by direct interview, questionnaire or observation. Secondary research relies on the use of data that has already been collected. Care should be taken when doing secondary research.

- Is the data up to date?
- Is the data relevant to the task it is being collected for?

> *In collecting data about people's wages, it is important to ensure that statistics used are as recent as possible and refer to the correct type of work and part of the UK that is being researched. For a study of wages in Scotland it would not be helpful to consult statistics for Wales.*

Exercise 6.6

Find secondary sources that provide data for each of these.

- ★ World records in athletics
- ★ Examination performance
- ★ Employment statistics for your town, city or county
- ★ Distances people travel to work
- ★ Hospital admissions

Activity 6.3

Collect data of your own choice from secondary sources. Decide on a reasonable quantity of data to collect. Keep the collected data to build a spreadsheet in Activity 6.4.

Exercise 6.7

Give primary and secondary methods of collecting each of the following items of data:

- ★ The number of people who go to the a cinema in a week
- ★ The average amount of money spent by customers of a supermarket
- ★ The cost of a holiday in Spain

Designing models for numerical data

Data may be modelled in a number of ways:

- The data can be put into a table or spreadsheet, using formulae to perform calculations on the data.
- The data can be presented as a chart or line graph.
- The data can be written as a general rule or formula.

Spreadsheets

Spreadsheets may be used to analyse numerical data collected. There are several standard applications for their use. Spreadsheet **models** of the application contain formulae and data values. By changing the values of data, 'what-if?' questions may be asked and the spreadsheet will recalculate the results.

> **Did You Know?**
>
> The standard rate of VAT (currently 17.5%) is applied to most items but not all. For example some things are zero-rated and have no VAT, e.g. books. Other things have a reduced rate of VAT, e.g. domestic fuel has a VAT rate of 5%.

Inner Whorl Stained Glass

When a customer asks Inner Whorl to produce a window, an estimate of its cost is calculated. The cost includes the number of hours work involved in creating the window and the cost of materials. To calculate the cost, the height and width of the window must be measured and the type of glass to be used agreed upon. A spreadsheet can then be used to calculate the total cost. Inner Whorl is not registered for value-added tax (VAT) but it must pay VAT on glass and lead purchased. The spreadsheet model includes this in the estimate.

Job costing

Customers often require estimates of the cost of jobs from traders. The actual cost of the job will also need calculating. By collecting data about the job, a spreadsheet may be used to provide the costing; see Figure 6.3. The use of a spreadsheet allows changes to be made and costs to be recalculated quickly.

	A	B
1	Type of Glass	English Muffle
2	Cost per sq m	36
3	Length	1.2
4	Width	1.4
5	Glass cost	£ 60.48
6	Lead etc	£ 8.40
7	Hours	10
8	Rate	£ 15.00
9	Labour	£ 150.00
10	Total cost	£ 218.88

Figure 6.3 *Spreadsheet showing the costing for a new window*

Exercise 6.8

What other trades can provide estimates of costs for a job that are based on a fixed calculation? What data does the tradesperson need to collect in each case?

Budgeting

A spreadsheet can be used to record the expected income and expenses for an individual person, a family or a business; see Figure 6.4. By changing the values of data, it is possible to see whether enough money is coming in to cover future expenses.

DESIGNING MODELS FOR NUMERICAL DATA

	A	B	C	D
1	TWO PEOPLE SPENDING SEVEN DAYS IN GERMANY			
2				Total
3	Flight per person		£ 68.00	£ 136.00
4	Hotel per night per person DM	70	–	
5	£		£ 22.22	£ 311.11
6	Spending money per day		£ 50.00	£ 350.00
7	Airport Parking per day		£ 5.80	£ 40.60
8	Train fare from airport per person DM	24		
9	£		£ 7.62	£ 15.24
10	Overall Total			£ 852.95
11	Exchange rate (DM to £)	3.15		

Figure 6.4 *Spreadsheet showing the costs of a holiday*

Statistics and survey analysis

The data collected from a survey can be manipulated and the results analysed. The data is manipulated in two ways:

- **Charts** and **graphs** may be drawn up from the data to show trends, frequency of responses, etc.

- **Statistics** may be calculated such as averages (mean, mode and median), minimum, maximum.

Davina Brown

Once Davina Brown has collected data, she either sends it to the organisation who commissioned the research to be analysed, or carries out some analysis herself to be sent with the data. This includes producing charts and calculating statistics.

For example, she has asked people's opinions on whether the pound should be replaced by the euro. The results were displayed as a pie chart showing the three answers (yes, no and don't know!).

In the same survey she asked people how much money they spent on holidays each year. An average (mean) was calculated for different age groups.

Spreadsheets have built-in functions to calculate statistics.

For example AVERAGE and RANGE. These are dealt with later in this chapter, from page 177.

They also have facilities to produce charts and graphs; see Figure 6.5.

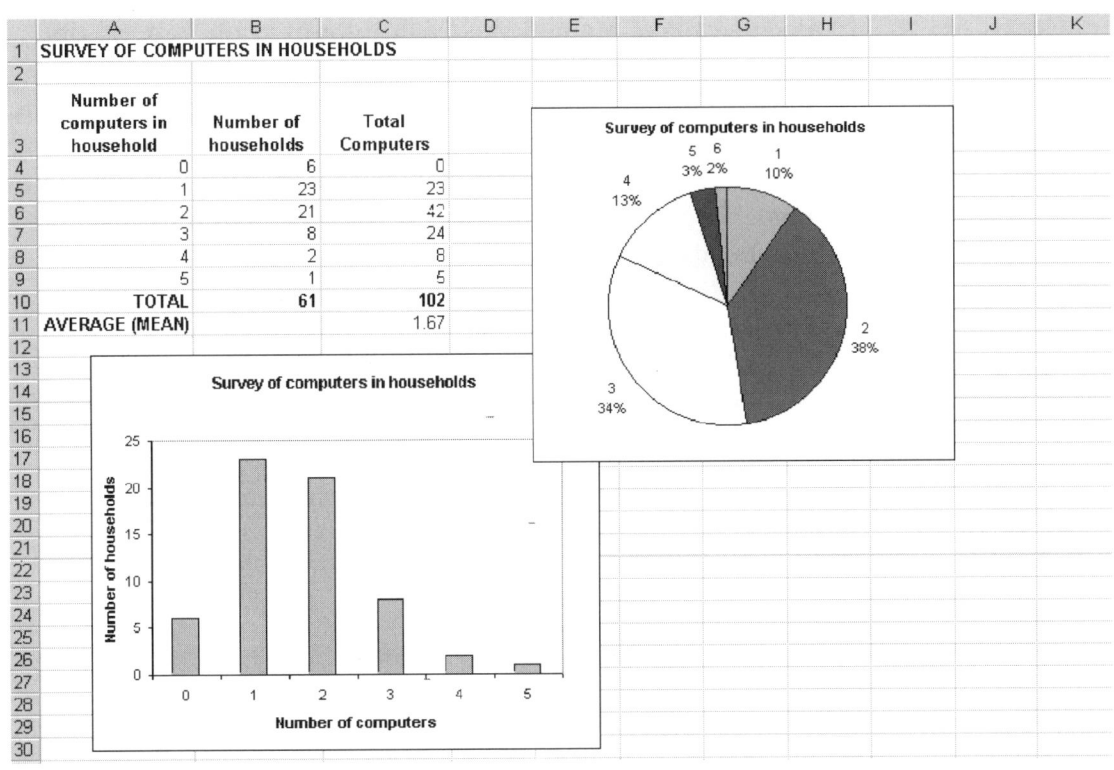

Figure 6.5 *Statistics and charts*

These may be created from scratch each time or a **wizard** or **macro** may be used. (See Unit 3 for more details on macros.)

Wizard
is a program that takes the user through a process, step-by-step.

Macro
is a program to carry out a process. It may be provided with the software or may be created or recorded by the user.

Break-even analysis

Data on income and costs can be entered onto a spreadsheet. It is possible to vary either the income or the costs until a profit (or surplus) is made. The point at which an overall loss becomes an overall profit is called the **break-even point**; see Figure 6.6. In a manufacturing or retailing business break-even analysis can be used to determine the minimum quantity of products to make or sell, and the price to sell them for, so that a profit is made. In calculating the break-even point, all income and expenditure **overheads** need to be considered.

Inner Whorl Stained Glass

Inner Whorl Stained Glass was asked to make souvenirs for sale in the Heritage Centre in a coastal resort. It was decided make stained glass fish, mounted on a metal pin. Making several identical items is cheaper than making individual ones because the same pattern is reused and the time taken to make them is reduced. To calculate the price, Inner Whorl had to calculate how many fish could be made in each hour, the cost of the raw materials and overheads.

Initially these types of calculations are done on a spreadsheet as part of the annual business plan. Once a price for a similar item has been calculated Inner Whorl can make a good estimate of the best price without reusing the spreadsheet. See Figure 6.6.

	A	B	C	D	E	F	G	H	I	J	K	L
1	BREAK EVEN ANALYSIS											
2												
3	Income											
4												
5	Price per fish	£2.50			£2.50			£2.50			£2.98	
6	Quantity sold	70			100			84			70	
7	Total Income		£175.00			£250.00			£210.00			£208.60
8												
9	Expenditure											
10												
11	Glass per fish	£0.60			£0.60			£0.60			£0.60	
12	Pin	£0.18			£0.18			£0.18			£0.18	
13	Time (hours per fish)	0.1			0.1			0.1			0.1	
14	Hourly rate	£10.00			£10.00			£10.00			£10.00	
15	Total cost per fish	£1.78			£1.78			£1.78			£1.78	
16	Quantity made	100			100			100			100	
17	Overheads	£30.00			£30.00			£30.00			£30.00	
18	Total Expenditure		£208.00			£208.00			£208.00			£208.00
19												
20	Profit/loss		-£33.00			£42.00			£2.00			£0.60

- Loss if 100 made and 70 sold
- Profit if 100 made and 100 sold
- Minimum 'break even' - make 100, sell 84
- Minimum 'break even' price if only 70 sold

Figure 6.6 *Profit and loss, break-even and profit*

Payroll

A spreadsheet can be used to calculate the pay owing to employees. This can take into account hours worked, tax and other deductions. If the rate of pay or the rate of tax changes, the payroll model can be altered so that correct calculations are made for the next pay day. It also allows a company to see what the effect of changes such as an increase in the minimum wage, or National Insurance rates, would have on their budget.

> **Inner Whorl Stained Glass**
>
> As part of their annual budgeting Inner Whorl produce a cash flow forecast. Sales of stained glass windows and souvenirs tends to be seasonal with most income in the summer months as a result of craft fairs. The cash flow forecast allows Inner Whorl to see how much deficit will be built up in the early part of the year. This needs to be balanced by surplus from the previous year.

Cash flow

A spreadsheet can show the income and expenditure for each day, week or month over a period of time; see Figure 6.7. This allows the individual or business to predict when they will be 'in the red' and to anticipate when to borrow or draw on reserves. It may also be necessary to have more frequent invoicing so that money flows into a business sooner if a shortfall is anticipated.

Mathematical investigations

Many mathematical problems involve formulae. A spreadsheet allows the formulae and data values to be altered to see the effect.

> *A piece of A4 paper can be folded to make a box. If the paper is folded at different places the volume of the box varies. A spreadsheet can be used to calculate the volume of the box for different folds; see Figure 6.8.*

	A	B	C	D	E	F	G
1	CASHFLOW FORECAST						
2							
3	Month	April	May	June	July	August	Sept
4							
5	Total Income	1200	1500	1800	2000	2000	1200
6							
7	Glass etc	300	600	600	600	0	0
8	Electricity etc	30	30	30	30	30	30
9	Telephone	10	10	10	10	10	10
10	Advertising	100	50	0	0	0	0
11	Rent	200	200	200	200	200	200
12	Craft fairs	100	200	300	250	250	0
13	Transport	50	50	50	50	50	50
14	Wages	800	800	800	800	800	800
15	Total Expenditure	1590	1940	1990	1940	1340	1090
16							
17	Surplus/deficit	-390	-440	-190	60	660	110
18	Balance B/F	1000	610	170	-20	40	700
19	Balance C/F	610	170	-20	40	700	810

Figure 6.7 *Cashflow forecast*

	A	B	C	D	E	F	G	H	I	J
1	Volume of box made from single sheet of paper									
2										
3	Paper									
4	Size	A4								
5	Height	297								
6	Width	210								
7										
8	Box									
9	Height	10	20	25	30	35	40	45	50	55
10	Width	190	170	160	150	140	130	120	110	100
11	Length	277	257	247	237	227	217	207	197	187
12	Volume	526300	873800	988000	1066500	1112300	1128400	1117800	1083500	1028500

Maximum volume achieved between heights of 40 and 45 mm

Figure 6.8 *A mathematical investigation*

Activity 6.4

Build spreadsheets to hold the data collected in Activities 6.2 and 6.3.

The appearance and layout of a worksheet

Worksheet
is the area on a spreadsheet into which data is entered.

A **worksheet** is formatted in a similar way to a word-processed document or database report. Figure 6.9 shows some of the common formatting attributes.

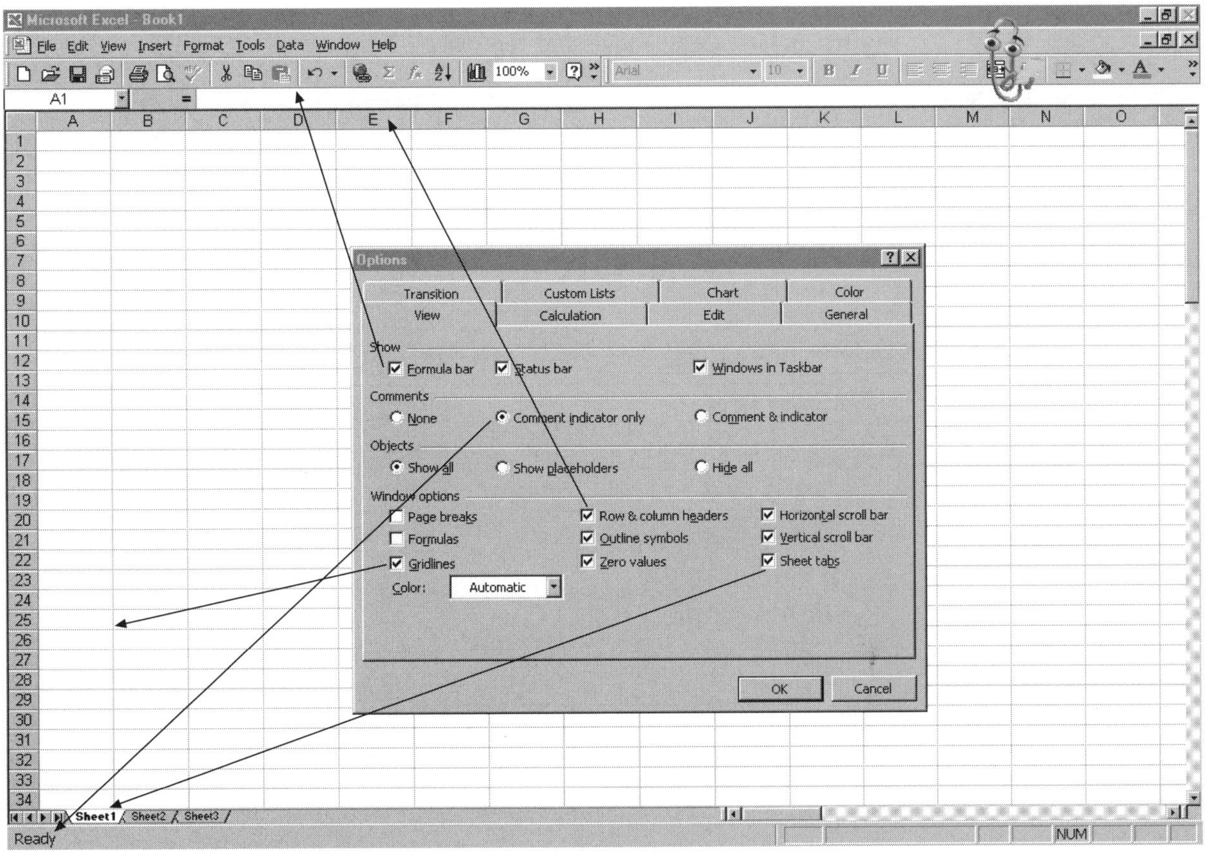

Figure 6.9 *Worksheet format attributes*

DESIGNING MODELS FOR NUMERICAL DATA

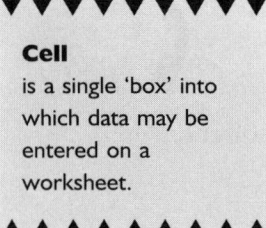

Cell
is a single 'box' into which data may be entered on a worksheet.

Each **cell** has its own unique reference containing its row and column; see Figure 6.10.

![Figure 6.10 spreadsheet showing cells B2 through B11 with values and formulas, and =SUM(B2:B11) in B13]

Figure 6.10 *Cells, range and reference*

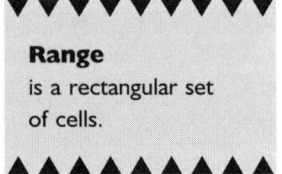

Range
is a rectangular set of cells.

The data contained in individual cells and **ranges** may be formatted in a similar way to text in a word-processed document. Some of these effects are shown in Figure 6.11. These effects may be the same or different to those used when the data is printed in a report (see page 182).

	A	B	C	D
1	Text formats		Number formats	
2	Bold text		Number keyed in	2
3	Coloured text		Decimal places	2.0000
4	*Italic text*		Currency format	£2.00
5	Shading		Date format	2-Jan-1900
6	Text wrapped into a single cell			
7				
8		Use of a text box to overlay text onto the grid		
9				
10				

Figure 6.11 *Data format attributes*

172   **6 NUMERICAL MODELLING USING SPREADSHEETS**

Activity 6.5

Using on-line help or other information sources, make sure you can use spreadsheet facilities, and produce printouts to show examples of your work.

- ★ Modify the character style (font and size).
- ★ Modify the display format, for example to currency, or to date.
- ★ Modify the alignment of data (left, right, centre, decimal).
- ★ Use text boxes to display text data overlaid on the row/column grid.

Activity 6.6

Using the spreadsheet software, produce annotated printouts that show that you know how to modify the presentation of a spreadsheet:

- ★ Border(s)
- ★ Shading
- ★ Row height and column width

> You can annotate your spreadsheet by using text boxes overlaid on the row/column grid.

Once the data has been entered into a range of cells it may be protected so that it cannot be accidentally erased. It may be desirable to hide rows and columns to improve the display. This is useful if calculations have several stages and only the end result is to be seen.

Often the top rows need to be repeated as headings on each page printed. Rows and columns may have labels in them that need to remain fixed on screen so that they do not scroll out of sight. This is known as **freezing** part of the worksheet. It helps the user with data entry because the row and column labels are always visible. See Figure 6.12.

DESIGNING MODELS FOR NUMERICAL DATA

	A	B	C	D	E	F	G	H	I
1	Date	Creditor	cheque	cash	grants	Debtor	materials	capital eqpt	stationery
2	27-Oct-98					Glass Studio		£75.00	
3	15-Feb-99					Purbeck Press			£17.59
4	15-Feb-99					Purbeck Press		£17.59	
5	2-Mar-99					Kansa Craft	£100.68		
6	22-Mar-99					Staples			£18.75
7	4-May-99					Season Master	£8.83		
8	10-Aug-99					CopyHut			£4.10
9	13-Aug-99					Swanage Angling	£9.97		
10	19-Aug-99					Kansa Craft	£267.27		

	A	B	C	D	E	F	G	H	I
1	Date	Creditor	cheque	cash	grants	Debtor	materials	capital eqpt	stationery
44	18-Mar-00					Merlins	£2.50		
45	18-Mar-00					G&T's	£4.07		
46	18-Mar-00					Merlins	£16.82		
47	18-Mar-00					B and Q Poole Warehouse		£62.28	
48	20-Mar-00					Hobbycraft	£24.53		
49	27-Mar-00					Craft Depot	£58.00		

The first row on each page is the same – it is row 1 that has been frozen

Figure 6.12 *Freezing rows and columns*

Activity 6.7

Using the spreadsheet software, produce annotated printouts that show that you know how to control cells:

★ Protect/unprotect a cell and a range of cells.

★ Hide/unhide rows and columns.

★ Name cells and attach cell notes to a cell to explain its content.

▼▼▼▼▼▼▼▼▼

Formula
is a calculation defined by the user.

Function
is a calculation provided by the spreadsheet application program.

▲▲▲▲▲▲▲▲▲

Formulae and functions

Formulae and **functions** may be entered into cells to calculate results from data entered in other cells (Figure 6.13). By the use of formulae and functions, calculations can be carried out to see the effect of changing data values.

A formula (or function) may be copied, or **replicated**, into a range of cells. In doing so, references to cells either change (**relative**) or are fixed (**absolute**).

6 NUMERICAL MODELLING USING SPREADSHEETS

	A	B	C	D	E
1	VAT rate	17.5			
2					
3	Item	Price	VAT		Formula
4	A	4.56	=B4*$B$1/100	=C4+B4	
5	B	5.64	=B5*$B$1/100	=C5+B5	
6	C	3.54	=B6*$B$1/100	=C6+B6	
7	D	2.2	=B7*$B$1/100	=C7+B7	
8					
9			Total	=SUM(D4:D8)	
10					
11					Function

Figure 6.13 *A formula and a function entered on a worksheet*

When the formula is replicated all relative references are automatically changed. This is a very powerful feature of a spreadsheet. Figures 6.14 and 6.15 show examples of absolute and relative referencing.

Formulae usually use relative referencing as the default because it is the most commonly used. If relative referencing is used when absolute referencing is needed an error will be generated in the formulae because cell references will have changed when they should have been fixed.

Inner Whorl Stained Glass

In calculating the cost of a window a fixed amount is charged per hour for labour. If several windows are to be produced then the calculation for each window will have the same charge per hour included. A formula is used that includes the size of the window, the type of glass and the labour cost per hour.

The formula is then replicated for each window. In the replication the references to the size of window and type of glass is a relative reference because it will change for each window. The reference to the labour cost is absolute because it is the same for each window.

See Figure 6.15.

DESIGNING MODELS FOR NUMERICAL DATA

	A	B	C	D	E
1	VAT rate	17.5			
2					
3	Item	Price	VAT		Relative references
4	A	4.56	=B4*$B$1/100	=C4+B4	
5	B	5.64	=B5*$B$1/100	=C5+B5	
6	C	3.54	=B6*$B$1/100	=C6+B6	
7	D	2.2	=B7*$B$1/100	=C7+B7	
8					
9			Total	=SUM(D4:D8)	
10					
11					
12					
13			Absolute reference		

Figure 6.14 *Absolute and relative referencing, showing changing formulae*

	A	B	C
1	Type of Glass	English Muffle	Water glass
2	Cost per sq m	36	45
3	Length	1.2	
4	Width	1.4	
5	Glass cost	=B2*$B$3*$B$4	=C2*$B$3*$B$4
6	Lead etc	=B3*B4*5	
7	Hours	10	
8	Rate	15	
9	Labour	=B7*B8	
10	Total cost	=B5+$B$6+$B$9	=C5+$B$6+$B$9

Figure 6.15 *Absolute and relative references on a window estimate*

Exercise 6.9

Why does Inner Whorl use a reference to the labour cost per hour rather than use the actual amount in the formula? Should this be an absolute or a relative cell reference?

Activity 6.8

Using the spreadsheet software available to you, produce annotated printouts that show that you know how to use functions and formulae:

★ Enter formulae into a spreadsheet (either by keying in or by using the mouse to select the cells to be used in the formula).

★ Enter functions into a spreadsheet (either by keying in or selecting from a list of available functions).

★ Replicate formulae and functions (either by use of menus or by highlighting and using a keyboard shortcut).

★ Use relative and absolute references.

Statistical functions

There are very many functions that provide statistics about data entered into a spreadsheet:

- **SUM** calculates the total of data in a range of cells.
- **MIN/MAX** finds the maximum or minimum data value in a range of cells.
- **RANGE** finds the difference between the maximum and minimum data values in a range of cells.
- **AVERAGE** finds the arithmetic mean average of data values in a range of cells.
- **MEDIAN/MODE** finds the median or mode average of data values in a range of cells.

Davina Brown

Davina Brown is part of a team of researchers. Between them they usually interview over 1000 people in any survey. One survey asked the number of computers in each person's house. Statistical functions could be used to find the total number of computers used (SUM), average number (MEDIAN, MODE, AVERAGE) and quickly display the maximum number (MAX).

DESIGNING MODELS FOR NUMERICAL DATA

Exercise 6.10

A survey is carried out to find the average number of telephones in people's homes. The average may be given as the mean, median or mode. 1008 people were surveyed and the total number of telephones was found to be 2634. Which is the most useful average to use?

- ★ Mode: 2 telephones in each house
- ★ Median: 3 telephones
- ★ Mean: 2.6 (to one decimal place)

Explain what each average is describing.

Activity 6.9

Include some statistical functions on the spreadsheets created in Activity 6.4, checking the results displayed for reasonableness and usefulness. Produce annotated printouts to show your understanding of statistical functions.

Logical functions and operators

Logical functions and operators allow the contents of a cell to be determined by the values in other cells:

- ✪ **IF** is a function that selects one formula or another depending on whether a condition is true or false (see Figure 6.16).

- ✪ **AND** is an operator that gives a true result only if *both* of two conditions are true.

- ✪ **OR** is an operator that gives a true result if *either* one or *both* of two conditions are true.

	A	B	C	D
1	Age	Software	Books	Over65 and Software twice Books?
2	66	20	50	=IF(A2>65 AND B2>=2*C2 "Yes", "No")
3	46	200	30	=IF(A3>65 AND B3>=2*C3, "Yes", "No")
4	20	100	110	=IF(A4>65 AND B4>=2*C4,"Yes", "No")

Figure 6.16 *Use of the IF function*

Davina Brown

Davina carried out a survey which asked people how much money they had spent on each of books/magazines and computer software in the last year. People were then categorised according to their expenditure. One category was all people over 65 who had spent at least twice as much on computer software as on books/magazines. Davina entered the data into a spreadsheet. Some of the cells contents are shown in Table 6.3.

Cell	*Contents*	*Condition*	*Logical operators*
A1	Age	Is age greater than 16?	=(IF A1>16 . . .)
A1	Age	Is age between 16 and 18 inclusive?	=IF((A1>=16 AND A1<=18) . . .
B6	Price	Is price less than 5.00?	
B6	Price	Is price between 5.00 and 10.00 inclusive?	
C8	Colour	Is colour blue?	
C8	Colour	Is colour blue or green?	
D6 D7	Price1 Price2	Is Price1 greater than Price2?	
D6 D7	Price1 Price2	Is Price1 at least 10.00 and at least twice as much as Price2?	

Table 6.3 *Logical operators exercise table*

Exercise 6.11

Refer to Table 6.3. What values would be displayed in each of cells D2, D3 and D4?

Copy and complete Table 6.3 to show the use of logical operators.

Activity 6.10

Include some logical functions and operators on the spreadsheets created in Activity 6.4, checking the results displayed for reasonableness. Produce annotated printouts to show your understanding of statistical functions.

Exercise 6.12

Did You Know?

The AND operator always narrows down results. The OR operator widens results.

Four statements are shown to 100 people and they are asked if they agree or disagree with each. The total numbers of people who agree with each statement are found. Which of these totals will be highest?

★ Number of people agreeing with statement A

★ Number of people agreeing with statement A AND statement B

★ Number of people agreeing with statement A AND statement B AND statement C

★ Number of people agreeing with statement A OR statement B

★ Number of people agreeing with statement A OR statement B OR statement C

Functions applied to tables of data

A spreadsheet may also be used to store tables of data. These may be treated as single tables in a database (see Chapter 8 for discussion of relational databases with several tables). There are several functions that may be used:

- **LOOKUP** enables data to be looked up in a table; see Figure 6.17.
- **INDEX** allows data to be referenced by its position in a table.

> **Inner Whorl Stained Glass**
>
> Inner Whorl Stained Glass provides estimates for windows that include a variable cost depending on the type of glass. A code is entered for the type of glass, e.g. M for 'Muffled' and the price charged for this type can then be looked up by using a function such as LOOKUP(B1,C2:C4,D2:D4).
>
> The text in cell B1 is matched against the content of column C and the price looked up in column D (Figure 6.17).

	A	B	C	D
1	Type of Glass	English Muffle	Glass type	Cost
2	Cost per sq m	36	English Muffle	36
3	Length	1.2	Patterned Glass	55
4	Width	1.4	Water Glass	45
5	Glass cost	£60.48		
6	Lead etc	£8.40		
7	Hours	10		
8	Rate	£15.00		
9	Labour	£150.00		
10	Total cost	£218.88		

B2 = =LOOKUP(B1,C2:C4,D2:D4)

Value displayed — LOOKUP function

Figure 6.17 *LOOKUP function*

DESIGNING MODELS FOR NUMERICAL DATA

Producing reports

For a professional report, it is important to present information in a spreadsheet in the most effective way. Often, the results of collecting and analysing data are best shown on a chart or a graph. This section covers presentation of spreadsheet data, and the production of charts and graphs from that data.

Modifying the format of output from a spreadsheet model

The output from a spreadsheet may be formatted to make it easy to read. This formatting control over the page layout and the layout of the tables containing the data. Many of the formatting options are similar to those used in word-processing applications but some are specific to spreadsheets.

Exercise 6.13

★ List three formatting processes that can be done on both a word processor and a spreadsheet.

★ List three formatting processes that can only be done on a spreadsheet.

Activity 6.11

Make sure that you remember how to carry out each of these tasks using spreadsheet software. Produce annotated printouts to show your understanding of each of them.

★ Modify the page size and orientation.
★ Show/hide gridlines and row/column headings on a worksheet.
★ Set up a custom header/footer including variables such as date, time, file name, user ID.
★ Set up worksheet templates.
★ Display the formulae contained in cells.
★ Use buttons and macros to allow the user to move from one worksheet to another.
★ Display drawing and picture objects on a worksheet.

If unsure, use the software's in-built 'Help' function and examples.

Charts and graphs

It is important that you choose the most appropriate type of chart or graph. See Figure 6.18 for the chart types offered.

Figure 6.18 *Graphs and charts*

PRODUCING REPORTS 183

A **pie chart** (Figure 6.19) is only useful with a small number of **categories**. It is not useful if one data value is much larger or smaller than the others. It shows the relative percentage of data in each category.

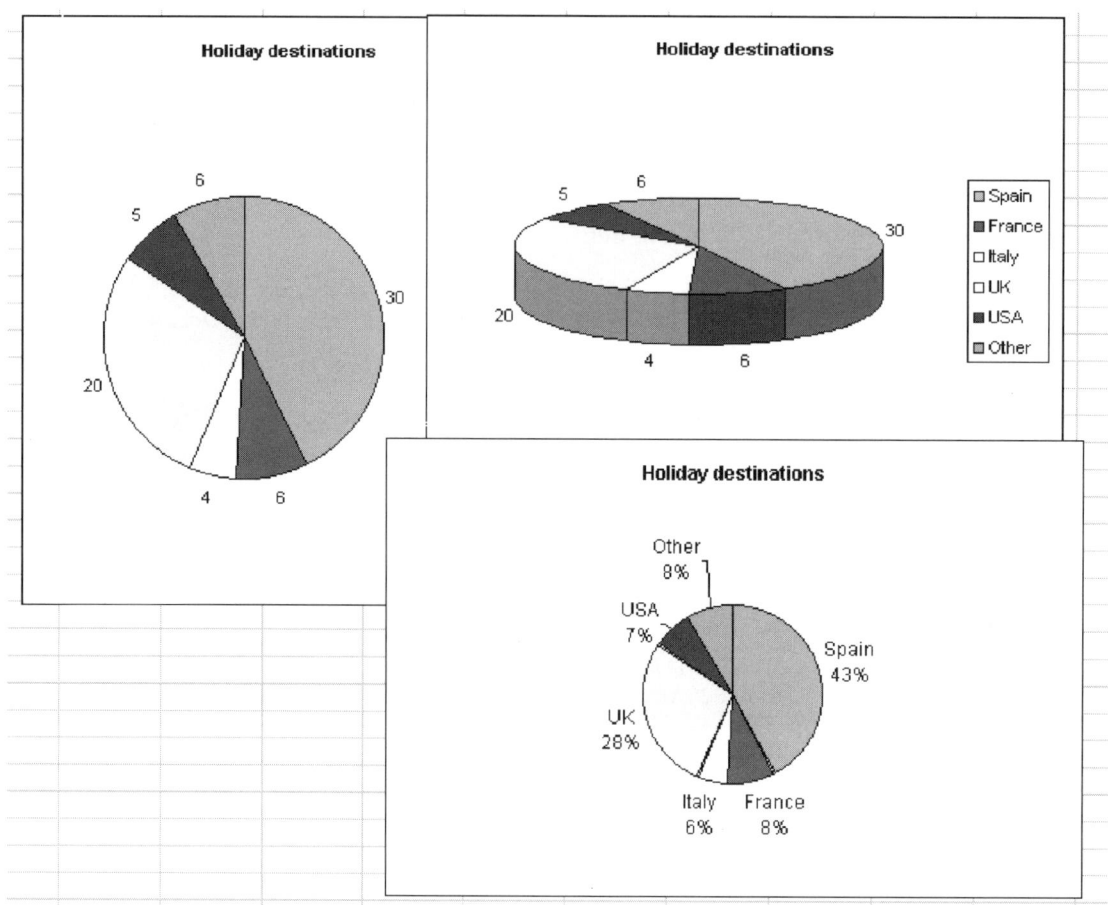

Figure 6.19 *Pie charts*

A **bar chart** (Figure 6.20) may be used to show tables of data with the height of each column representing the frequency or percentage of data in each category. It is not useful if one frequency is very much larger or smaller than the others. Axes should be labelled and a legend included if appropriate.

Data on a bar chart is said to be **discrete** when there are distinct categories. When data is continuous a **histogram** may be drawn, where the area of the bars indicates the frequency.

A **pictogram** shows discrete data by representing the value of the data as a set of symbols.

A **line graph** (Figure 6.21) can be used for continuous numeric data. Be careful to check a line graph to ensure that it is a fair representation of data.

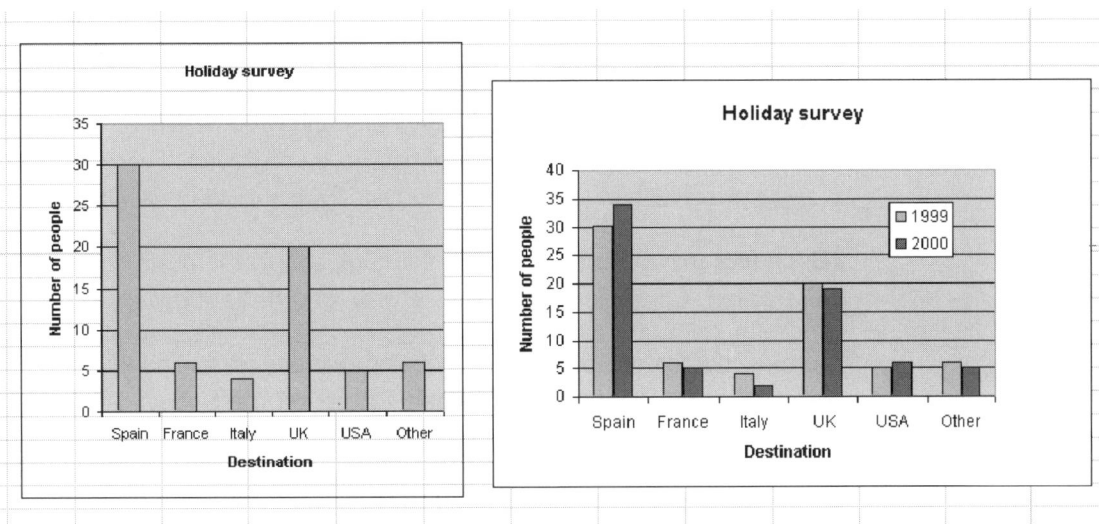

Figure 6.20 *Bar charts*

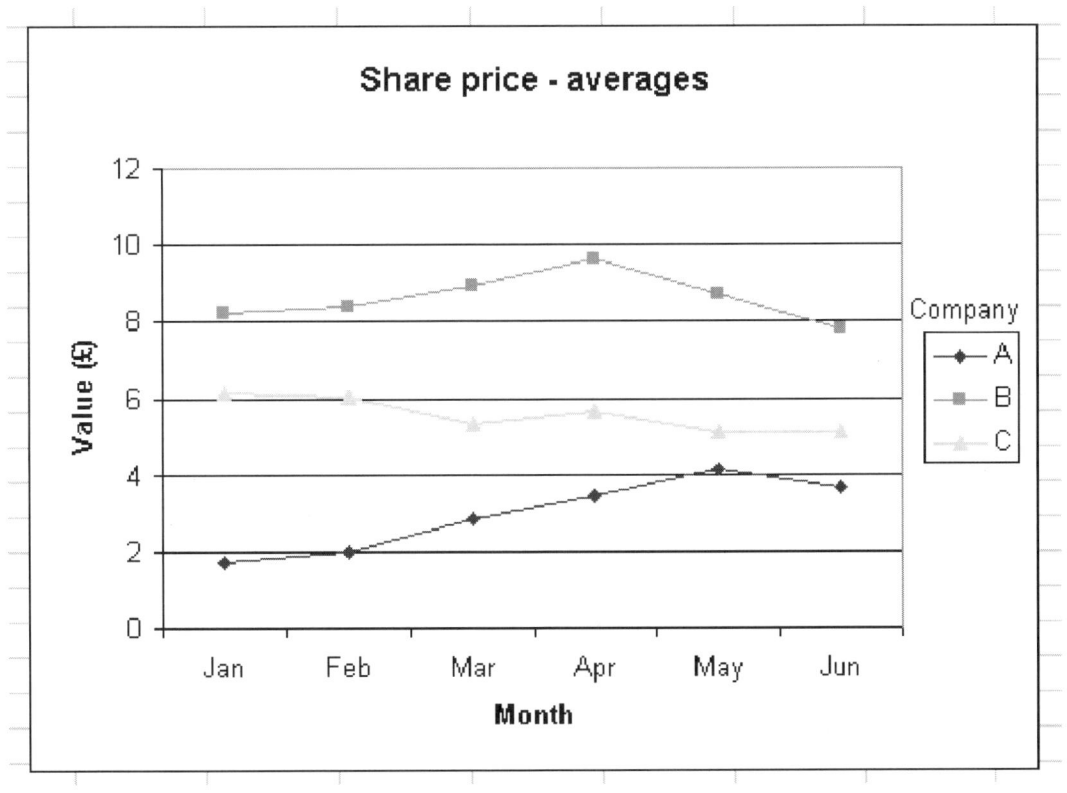

Figure 6.21 *Line graphs*

PRODUCING REPORTS

Some spreadsheet packages will require you to draw an **x–y scatter graph** to show a trend in data.

A **composite chart/graph** shows a line graph on a bar chart. It is used when there are two different sets of data to be displayed. There are three axes – horizontal and left and right vertical. Each should be labelled.

3D charts may be used if it is felt that they add to the quality of presentation. Care should be taken as they are often difficult to read.

You must be able to identify data as being discrete or continuous. In your presentation of data, you must be able to respect the type of data being portrayed:

- Use pie charts for categorised data
- Use pictograms or bar charts for discrete data
- Use graphs or histograms for continuous data

In presentation of spreadsheet data, you are expected to use good practice:

- Clear and concise labelling, for example of axes, and legends if appropriate
- Appropriate and informative choice of scales
- Appropriate use of shading without distorting the information portrayed
- Appropriately set ranges on each axis, to give a complete picture of the data

Exercise 6.14

Collect sets of data from secondary sources that may be best displayed in each of a bar chart, pie chart and line graph. Try displaying each set in each way. Share your results and discuss which charts are meaningless representations of the data.

Activity 6.12

Display the data on the spreadsheets created in Activity 6.4 in the most appropriate way as a chart, checking the results displayed for reasonableness.

Using spreadsheet models for prediction

Once a spreadsheet model has been built a very powerful feature is to answer 'what-if?' questions. This process is summarised in Figure 6.22.

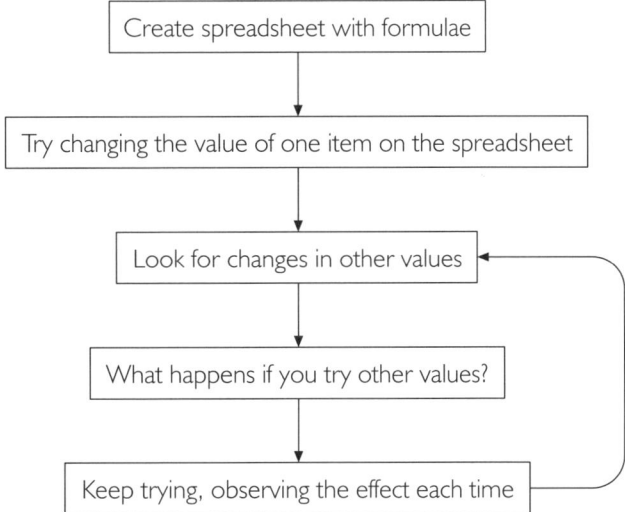

Figure 6.22 *'What-if?' process*

By changing the data in one set of cells changes can be caused in data values in other cells. This allows the spreadsheet to be used to predict the effect of varying data.

Inner Whorl Stained Glass

Inner Whorl Stained Glass currently operate from a small craft workshop. They are considering expansion. One option would be to move into larger premises that they would rent on a monthly basis, another option is to share premises with other craftspeople.

The effects of these increased costs can be entered into their annual budget sheet. The question being asked is 'What if we increase our overheads by £100 per month? £200? £300?' By entering different values into the spreadsheet the effect on the annual budget may be seen.

Predictions can also be made by interpreting graphs. Data values may be read from the graph or the graph may be extended. This can be done using pencil and ruler on a printout of the graph or by using formulae to calculate values.

Activity 6.13

Draw a graph to show the conversion between degrees Celsius and degrees Fahrenheit using the formula $F = 32 + (1.8 \times C)$. Use the range 0–50 degrees Celsius on the horizontal axis.

★ Use both the graph and the formula to find how many degrees Fahrenheit are equal to 30 degrees Celsius.

★ Use the graph to find how many degrees Celsius are equal to 60 degrees Fahrenheit. Check your answer with the formula.

Activity 6.14

A family borrows £5000. At the end of each month, they pay off £500 and interest of 1% is added to the balance remaining.

★ Use a spreadsheet and a graph to predict how long it will take them to pay off the loan (in the final month, when the balance is less than £500 they pay off the balance in full).

★ How would the amount of time taken to pay off the loan change if they paid £250 per month?

★ What if they had to pay off the loan in 24 months? How much would they have to pay each month?

> You will need to find the answer to this by trial and refinement.

▼▼▼▼▼▼▼▼▼▼
Trial and refinement is guessing the solution to a numerical problem and seeing how close it is to the correct answer by putting it into a spreadsheet and seeing the effect. Another solution is then chosen to try to get closer to the desired result.
▲▲▲▲▲▲▲▲▲▲

Documenting your solution

Once a spreadsheet model is completed, it must be documented. There are two main types of documentation:

- Technical documentation
- A user guide

> **Technical documentation** is written to explain how the spreadsheet was designed.

Technical documentation should be written so that bugs that are found in the system can be corrected. Similarly, it should be helpful when changed user requirements mean changes need to be made to the spreadsheet. This documentation needs to include all information needed to maintain the spreadsheet:

- Explanation of the **design** of all of the worksheets – which cells contain which data
- Explanation of all **formulae** and **functions** used
- Explanation of all **testing** carried out

> **User guide** is a document which shows users how to use the spreadsheet.

A **user guide** should be a self-contained document, suitably structured for ease of use and including everything the user may need to know:

- A front cover
- Contents page
- Samples of questionnaires, data collection forms, spreadsheets and results
- An index

To explain how to carry out tasks, a user guide should contain screen shots in between the text. It should also include information to show a user how to make the best use of the data:

- How to add, delete and amend data and formulae
- How to produce charts and graphs
- How to use any macros contained in the spreadsheet

Exercise 6.15

Why is technical documentation not included in a user guide?

Activity 6.15

Find examples of user guides.

★ Look at their contents, layout and style. Which ones are easy to use? Which are not well designed?

★ Write a list of features that make a *good* user guide and another of those which make a *poor* user guide.

The spreadsheet must be tested to ensure that data can be **added, deleted** and **amended** and that correct results are obtained. The tests should be supported by printouts to show that the spreadsheet is working correctly. Test data values must be designed to include representative values of all possible data:

- Relevant valid data
- Data in/out of range
- Incorrect data
- Boundary data

Activity 6.16

For this activity, use the spreadsheet that you created in Activity 6.4, or another spreadsheet of your choice.

★ Carry out tests to show that the spreadsheet is working correctly.

★ Produce a user guide and technical documentation for the spreadsheets you created.

Revision questions

1. Explain the differences between use of questionnaires and interviews.

2. What is the difference between a closed and an open question?

3. List seven features of a well-designed questionnaire.

4. List three examples of secondary sources of data.

5. Describe the stages involved in carrying out a 'what-if?' question on a spreadsheet model.

6. What do these words mean – cell, range, reference?

7. Explain the difference between spreadsheet formulae and functions.

8. Explain the difference between absolute and relative references, and give an example of the use of each.

9. Give two examples of statistical functions.

10. Give an example of a logical operator and show its use in a function.

11. Describe the characteristics of data for which a pie chart would *not* be a suitable method of display.

12. What is meant by a composite chart?

13. List the contents of a user guide.

14. List the contents of technical documentation.

15. Describe test strategies for a spreadsheet model.

Databases

- Develop your understanding of the use of databases and database management systems
- Research the information needs of a user
- Design and create a relational DBMS to meet those needs
- Produce a user guide for the database

▼▼▼▼▼▼▼▼▼

DBMS
stands for database management system – it is a computer program to manipulate the data held in a database.

▲▲▲▲▲▲▲▲▲

▼▼▼▼▼▼▼▼▼

Database
is a set of stored data.

▲▲▲▲▲▲▲▲▲

Did You Know?

The word 'database' usually refers to data stored on a computer, but it can be used to describe data stored on paper, or more usually, card.

This unit develops the work done in Intermediate Unit 1: *Presenting information* and Unit 2: *Handling information* and is assessed through the work presented in your portfolio. You need to meet the requirements of the assessment evidence grid given in the unit's specification. Details of how to prepare your portfolio for assessment are given in the *Portfolio guide* on page 393.

In this chapter, the term **database system** is used to mean a **database** *and* the DBMS taken together.

This chapter looks in detail at seven topics:

- Researching a user's requirements for a DBMS
- Designing the database structure
- Creating screen forms
- Generating reports on screen and on paper
- Queries
- Customising the database
- User guides and technical documentation

DATABASES

Two case studies are used to introduce and illustrate the ideas of this chapter:

Goodwood Hotel

The Goodwood Hotel has 68 bedrooms – singles, doubles and suites. These three types of room cost different amounts and this 'tariff' is also varied during the winter and for regular customers who are eligible for a discount.

The hotel uses a computerised DBMS to keep track of its bookings and the amount owed by each customer. While in the hotel, customers may make use of the restaurant and bar facilities and their expenditure is recorded through the same DBMS. When they incur any expense, customers must sign to confirm that the payment should be added to the bill.

When a customer leaves, the hotel produces an invoice showing the amount owing and details of each item of expenditure.

Did You Know?

An invoice is the document given to a customer showing the amount to be paid for goods or services.

The College

The College is a further education establishment with about 2000 full-time students and another 6000 part-time. These include people attending evening classes and using the drop-in ICT facilities.

Each student has an identity card which is used in the library where it can be read by a bar code reader. The code on the card uniquely identifies the student. The codes are stored on a computerised DBMS that also holds personal details of each student (name, address, etc.) and of the courses the student is following. The system is also used by the examinations office in The College, and by college managers for storing information on teaching and other staff, and the college budget.

> **Did You Know?**
>
> Often it is not necessary to use a DBMS to store data. If the data can be stored in a single table, a spreadsheet is often sufficient. Spreadsheet software has many database functions. These allow the user to sort data into order or to extract parts of the list by using searches or filters. It is only when the data becomes complex, or the needs of the user cannot be met by the spreadsheet, that a database management system must be used.

This chapter looks at the ways in which databases are used by these organisations to organise their data. You will see how forms are designed to make the input of data as straightforward as possible (e.g. Figure 7.1 on page 198). Similarly, reports are designed to present information in formats that help in the efficient running of the organisations (e.g. Figure 7.3 on page 202).

For your portfolio you will need to design a similar DBMS to meet the specification given to you by your teacher or someone else. You will need to research the needs of a user of your system and design a database with forms and reports to meet these needs.

You should try to identify the information needs of some local organisations, like the ones used in the case studies, who might be able to help with the specification of a DBMS.

Finally, you will need to produce documentation for your DBMS. This should consist of a guide for the users of your DBMS.

Researching a user's requirements for a DBMS

Data is stored in a database to meet the needs of a user. It is important to find out and understand what these needs are, *before* the database is constructed. Needs can be researched in several ways:

- By **interviewing** the user face-to-face
- By **observing** the user at work
- By using **questionnaires**

Exercise 7.1

What are the advantages of using each of these methods of research? What are the disadvantages?

Did You Know?

When a DBMS fails it is usually because the research has not been done properly. Maybe the designers did not identify exactly what data had to be input to the system. Or maybe the information output from the system was not quite what was needed.

The face-to-face interviews, observations or questionnaires must identify the requirements of the system:

- The **purpose** of the proposed DBMS
- The data that is to be **input** into the system
- The information that is to be **output** from the system
- The **processing** that has to be done to the input to obtain the output

Exercise 7.2

What would happen if an air traffic control system used a database to track details of all flights and that database was not designed properly?
Try to find examples of a real-life DBMS that went wrong. What were the consequences?

7 DATABASES

The purpose of a database

In researching the purpose of using a database, you are attempting to find answers to three questions:

- What tasks is the database helping the user to perform?
- How are these tasks carried out at present?
- What advantages would a database bring to the work of the user?

Goodwood Hotel

At the hotel, a DBMS is used to keep records on all of the bookings made by its customers. These include bookings for overnight stays, meeting rooms, leisure club facilities and the restaurant.

Before a computerised database was used, the hotel had to rely on many pieces of paper. These became messy and difficult to read when changes were made. This caused errors if staff misread them. The computer enables bills to be updated more easily, especially when the same customer uses many facilities in different parts of the hotel, because each customer has a unique identity code.

Customers who use the hotel regularly are able to pay their accounts monthly. The database keeps a record of the amount owing. The customers' names and addresses are kept on the database so the hotel can use it to send out publicity to its existing customers to advertise special events or new facilities. In any business, it is more efficient to encourage customers to come back again, rather than looking for new ones.

Figure 7.1 shows the form completed by customers when they book into the hotel. Figure 7.2 shows a bill. Notice how the bill is itemised to show customers exactly how it has been calculated. This is done automatically, and very quickly, by the DBMS. Notice also that every item has its own unique reference so that, if the customer queries the bill, the management can track each item back to check that it had been signed for.

Goodwood Hotel

12 Burlington Road, Knollsea, BH19 7RD
Tel 01929 334321   Fax 01929 334622
email: reception@goodwoodhotel.co.uk

BOOKING REFERENCE
SURNAME
OTHER NAMES
ADDRESS

TELEPHONE NUMBER
ARRIVAL DATE
NO. OF NIGHTS
ROOM TYPE
OTHER FACILITIES REQUIRED
ACCOUNT NUMBER

Figure 7.1 *The form filled in when a customer books into the Goodwood Hotel*

Goodwood Hotel

12 Burlington Road, Knollsea, BH19 7RD
Tel 01929 334321   Fax 01929 334622
email: reception@goodwoodhotel.co.uk

BOOKING REFERENCE   00/02389
CUSTOMER NAME   A Burdett

DATE	REF	DESCRIPTION	AMOUNT
17/11/00	DR307	Bed & Breakfast	67.00
17/11/00	T307001	Telephone	1.20
17/11/00	R307001	Restaurant	23.50
17/11/00	T307002	Telephone	2.70
17/11/00	B307001	Bar	6.90
18/11/00	DR307	Bed & breakfast	67.00
18/11/00	T307001	Telephone	0.60
		TOTAL TO PAY	168.90

Figure 7.2 *A customer's bill from the hotel*

The College

The College uses a DBMS to store details of all the students and the courses being offered. There are 8000 students at The College on a variety of full-time and part-time courses. Keeping track of them all is very difficult to do efficiently with a paper-based system.

Using a computerised system, enables the college staff to have up-to-date lists of students enrolled on courses, to keep track of grades and qualifications obtained and to handle examination entries efficiently. It is also used to produce staff and student timetables, and to process loans in the library and in the learning resource centre.

Did You Know?

*Users of database systems that store confidential data are often required to sign a **non-disclosure agreement**. In doing so they are agreeing not to share the data with anyone who is not authorised to see it. Examples of confidential data include that relating to government, personal data, copyrights and patents and companies' financial information.*

Using a DBMS has many advantages for the user:

- The avoidance of **data duplication** – if data is stored more than once it is likely that one version will not be updated which may cause errors and ambiguities.

    A person's address or name may be spelt differently if held in two separate files. In a database the name and address will only be stored once

- **Consistency of data** – once the data has been entered, it may be accessed many times and is the same wherever it is accessed. On a network, this also includes access from several terminals simultaneously.

- **Security** – each user, or type of user, may be given a different 'view' of the data, so managers may see more of the data than those entering the data.

- **Updating** of data is easy to control. When one user updates data, all other users see the new data. This is connected to the avoidance of data duplication.

Did You Know?

The Data Protection Act requires that any data describing people can only be stored on a computer system if it has be registered.

Exercise 7.3

A doctor uses a DBMS to manage patient records.
What are the benefits in computerising the database compared to using a paper-based system?

RESEARCHING A USER'S REQUIREMENTS FOR A DBMS

Data requirements

When researching a system, the database designer must identify what data needs collecting and how it is to be collected. (See for example Table 7.1.) This will involve looking at any existing forms used for data collection. The research should identify what changes could be made to make existing data collection systems more efficient.

Forms may be redesigned when the computer system is implemented.

Manual data entry may be replaced by automatic data entry.

Goodwood Hotel

When a customer books into the hotel a booking form is completed. See Figure 7.1 on page 198. The data requirements for this form are summarised in Table 7.1.

Exercise 7.4

The hotel keeps its records on computer for three years. How much disk storage is needed to store all of the bookings on the computer?

Activity 7.1

Consider the data requirements for a database that holds information on students and their examination entries at your school or college.

★ Complete a table similar to Table 7.1 to show the data requirements.

★ Estimate the disk storage required.

Data	How collected	Comments
Booking reference number	On booking sheet, preprinted	Manual system: staff keep a record of the next available reference number
		Computerised system: number automatically generated
Customer surname, other names, address and telephone number	On booking sheet or taken over the telephone	Care needed with spellings; validation not possible with proper names
Number of nights and other facilities required	On booking sheet or taken over the telephone	Computerised system can automatically check availability and in/out dates against number of nights
Room type required	On booking sheet or taken over the telephone	Coded: DB, SG or ST
		Can be entered as codes or by ticking box
Date of arrival	On booking sheet or taken over the telephone	
Account number, if a regular customer	On booking sheet or taken over the telephone	Computerised system: can check that an account exists and, if it does, notice any discounts allowed or any debts outstanding
General data requirements for bookings		
Number of bookings 'open' on any one day		Max. 500
Number of bookings taken each year		15 000–30 000
Number of customers in any three year period		20 000–50 000
Number of characters entered on each booking		Max. 170

Table 7.1 *Data requirements – customer booking at Goodwood Hotel*

Activity 7.2

What are the data requirements for a database that holds information on the patients at your doctor's surgery? Complete a table similar to Table 7.1.

Output needs

When researching a new DBMS, it is often easiest to start by first identifying the output required. Once you understand what is needed from a system, it makes the task of identifying the other requirements that much easier. On the other hand, if you are uncertain what is to be output from a database system, it is very difficult to identify the input requirements.

When existing DBMSs are being studied, it is also usually easier to find examples of output reports. See, for example, Figures 7.2, 7.3 and 7.4.

> **Goodwood Hotel**
>
> The hotel uses its DBMS to produce reports: the bills given to customers (Figure 7.2 on page 198), and room availability lists (Figure 7.3).

Room availability for **18/11/00**

Room number	Available?	Room number	Available?	Room number	Available?
101	Y	210	Y	312	N
102	Y	211	Y	313	N
103	Y	212	Y	314	N
104	Y	213	N	315	Y
105	N	214	Y	316	Y
106	Y	215	N	317	N
107	Y	216	Y	318	Y
108	N	217	N	319	N
109	Y	218	N	320	N
110	N	219	N	321	Y
111	Y	220	N	322	N
112	Y	221	N	323	N
113	Y	301	N	324	N
114	Y	302	N	325	N
201	N	303	Y	326	Y
202	Y	304	N	327	Y
203	N	305	N	328	Y
204	N	306	N	329	Y
205	N	307	N	330	Y
206	Y	308	N	331	N
207	N	309	N	332	N
208	Y	310	Y	333	Y
209	N	311	N		

Figure 7.3 *A room availability list*

The College

The College uses its DBMS to produce several reports. These include class lists, showing which students are following each course, and examination entry lists (Figure 7.4).

```
THE COLLEGE INFORMATION SYSTEM

Class      1/T6                    Course   GNVQ Advanced IT

Tutor      D Laws

Ref no.    Surname         Other names
81920      Arkle           David P
81928      Bennett         Paul
83291      Chaudhury       Dilip M
84379      Eeles           Anna D
86779      Fazal           Asif
86387      Gudmundsson     Erik J
87910      Hamil           Stefan
83109      Johansson       Karin F
93201      Le Fosse        Alice
90119      Momtaz          Roshan
72019      Neil            Andre
87260      O'Regan         Carole R F
88720      Ortiz           Danielle
81201      Phillips        Paula T
83567      Smith           Kai
82680      Thomas          David
85467      Wilson          Julia F


Printed on 06/01/01 at 15:39
```

Figure 7.4 *A class list*

Activity 7.3

Copy and complete Table 7.2 to list the output reports that are produced from each of the systems listed.

DBMS	Output reports
Hotel booking	Customer bills, list of rooms available
College enrolment	Class lists, examination entries
Doctor's patient details	
Supermarket point-of-sale (POS) terminals	
Supermarket stock control	
Railway company timetabling	
Gas company billing	
Travel agency ticketing	
Mail order company ordering	

Table 7.2 *Output reports*

Processing needs and rules

So that the correct output is produced from inputted data, usually some processing is carried out. Typical processes are sorting data into sequence, and filtering (so that only part of the data is output). Each process is defined as a small program or as a set of rules.

Goodwood Hotel

When a customer checks out of the hotel, processing is carried out, resulting in a bill being printed:

★ Enter customer room or account number.
★ Read customer record to obtain list of all facilities used by the customer.
★ Read records of each of the facilities to find how much is to be charged to the customer.
★ Calculate total owing.
★ Print itemised bill showing facilities used and total owing.

The College

When The College DBMS is used to print examination entry lists, this processing is carried out:

- ★ Input examination code.
- ★ Read examination data.
- ★ Read student data.
- ★ Select those students entered for the examination code.
- ★ Print examination details (code, title, date, time, room).
- ★ For each student entered for that examination, print student details (candidate number, name).

Activity 7.4

At the beginning of each day, each doctor in a surgery is given a list of the patients to be seen that day. What steps are required in the processing to produce this list?

Input design

So that the DBMS can process data to produce the required outputs, the data must be collected and input into the system. There are three main ways in which data may be input:

- ✪ **Keyed directly** into the computer through a screen-based form (see page 216)
- ✪ **Collected** on paper and later keyed into the computer
- ✪ **Input directly** into the computer from a computer-readable input device

RESEARCHING A USER'S REQUIREMENTS FOR A DBMS

The design of any documents (on paper or on screen) used to collect this data is important. A poorly designed document may not collect the correct data, may not match the requirements of the screen-based forms (see page 216) or may not collect the data in an easy-to-use format.

Each output or processing requirement will have its associated input requirements.

Goodwood Hotel

The customer's bill is calculated from all of their expenses. This includes room and meal costs, and any extra purchases made in the bar.

When a customer has a meal in the hotel restaurant, the staff record the details on a form. The data is then input into the DBMS. When a customer makes a purchase at the bar, the staff enter the customer's room number into the EPOS terminal and the data is immediately input into the DBMS.

The College

When a student borrows a book from the college library, the details of the loan are entered into the DBMS. The student has a card with a bar code on. Each bar code uniquely identifies a student. The card is read by a bar code reader. If this fails, the library staff can key the student number in directly. A similar process is used for the book being borrowed.

Bar codes are not the only way of providing unique identification cards. Many systems use magnetic stripes, as on credit cards. One development of these is the **smart card,** a card with a small processor on it that can hold much more data. Security systems in companies often have door locks which require staff use a smart card for access. For even greater security, systems exist that recognise people by their fingerprints or patterns in their retinas (the area at the back of the eye).

Activity 7.5

Copy and complete Table 7.3 showing the data input into each DBMS and how it is collected.

System	Input data	Data collection method
Hotel	Customer bar costs Restaurant costs	Keyed into EPOS terminal Data collection form
College	Student ID	Read from bar code on card
Doctor's patient details		
Supermarket point-of-sale (POS) terminals		
Supermarket stock control		
Railway company timetabling		
Electricity/gas company billing		
Travel agency ticketing		
Mail order company ordering		

Table 7.3 *Data collection methods*

Designing the database structure

After researching the needs of the user, the next stage is to design all of the parts of the DBMS.

Tables and entities

▼▼▼▼▼▼▼▼▼
Entity
is simply something which can be described by data.
▲▲▲▲▲▲▲▲▲

Each **entity** has a **table** of data. In this section, we look at how the tables are related to each other and how they are designed.

Entities are described by a word written in capital letters. The word usually describes one thing. Hence STUDENT, rather than STUDENTS or Student.

Goodwood Hotel

In the hotel DBMS, the entities include CUSTOMER and ROOM.

The College

In The College the entities include STUDENT, TEACHER and EXAMINATION.

Activity 7.6

Copy and complete Table 7.4 showing some of the entities in each application's database.

DBMS	Entities
Hotel booking	CUSTOMER, ROOM
College enrolment	STUDENT, TEACHER, EXAMINATION
Doctor's patient details	
Supermarket point-of-sale (POS) terminals	
Supermarket stock control	
Railway company timetabling	
Electricity/gas company billing	
Travel agency ticketing	
Mail order company ordering	

Table 7.4 *Entities*

Relationships between tables

Entities can be linked by **relationships**. When describing a relationship, it is necessary to state which two tables are involved, and what it is that causes the relationship. It is also necessary to give the **scope** of the relationship. There are four possible scopes:

- one-to-one

    ONE man is married to ONE woman

- one-to-many

    ONE person owns MANY cars

- many-to-one

    MANY cars are owned by ONE person

- many-to-many

    In a car pool, any car may be driven by any employee and any employee may drive any car so MANY employees drive MANY cars

Each scope of relationship is shown on a diagram, using a line with **crow's feet** to represent 'many' (Figures 7.5, 7.6, 7.7 and 7.8).

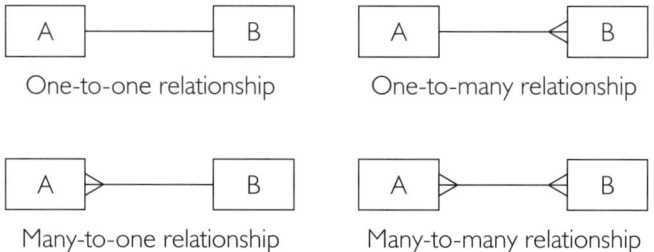

Figure 7.5 *Crow's feet used to describe relationships*

Goodwood Hotel

In the hotel DBMS, the entity BOOKING is related to the entity CUSTOMER. The relationship is:

BOOKING 'made by' CUSTOMER

It is a many-to-one relationship because many bookings can be made by each customer but each booking is made by only one customer. See Figure 7.6.

Figure 7.6 *The relationship between BOOKING and CUSTOMER*

The College

In The College DBMS, the entity STUDENT is related to the entity TEACHER. The relationship is:

STUDENT 'taught by' TEACHER

This is a many-to-many relationship because each student is taught many teachers and each teacher teaches many students. See Figure 7.7.

Figure 7.7 *The relationship between STUDENT and TEACHER*

Did You Know?

If entities have many-to-many relationships, there can be problems in processing the data. To cope with this another 'link' table is drawn up.

A 'link' table between two entities that have a many-to-many relationship is called an **intersection table** (see Figure 7.8).

The College

The many-to-many relationship between STUDENT and TEACHER is broken by use of another table called LESSON as shown in Figure 7.8.

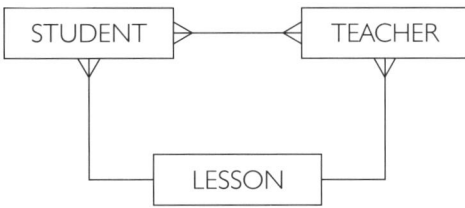

Figure 7.8 *The relationship between STUDENT and TEACHER showing the link table: LESSON*

Activity 7.7

Using the applications listed in Table 7.4, identify six examples of relationships:

★ For each one, write the relationship out as a sentence.

★ Draw a diagram to show the scope of each relationship.

Activity 7.8

Choose a company or organisation that may hold data on a database. Research the information stored in the company or organisation. This may be done by face-to-face interview, questionnaire or observation.

★ List the entities used to describe the data.

★ Describe the relationships, and their scope, between the entities.

Design of record (row) and field (column) structure in tables

Each entity's table contains **rows** and **columns** (Figure 7.9). Each row contains a **record** and describes a single example of the entity. The record is made up of several items of data. These items are called **fields** and a separate column in the table represents each field. In designing the table for an entity, it is important to include an appropriate number of fields (columns) but to avoid duplication.

CUSTOMER							
REF	SURNAME	OTHER NAMES	ADDRESS1	ADDRESS2	ADDRESS3	ADDRESS4	TELEPHONE NUMBER
4850	Burdett	Anna G	13 The Square	Wildrington	Oxford	OX42 5ER	01865 76182
4852	Smith	Phillip F T R	36 Green Avenue	Coldslack	Lancashire	LA4 4WW	01282 65189
4866	Jones	Marion	8 High Road	Gloss Green	Bucks	HP5 6TR	01442 54179

Figure 7.9 *The table for CUSTOMER in Goodwood Hotel's DBMS*

Exercise 7.5

If a field can contain either 'Male' or 'Female', why is it better to enter these as 'M' and 'F'?

Each table must have a **primary key**. This is the field, or combination of fields, that contains a unique reference to each record. It is often a number such as a reference number. If a table does not have a unique field then one must be generated.

Exercise 7.6

What is the primary key for CUSTOMER?

If two tables are linked by a relationship then the primary key of the first table may be shown as a field in the second table. It is called a **foreign key** in the second table.

> ### Goodwood Hotel
>
> In the hotel DBMS, the primary keys for each entity are:
>
> ★ CUSTOMER – Customer Reference Number
> ★ ROOM – Room Number
> ★ BOOKING – Booking Reference Number
>
> In the table that holds details of each BOOKING, the customer who made the booking is identified by a Customer Reference Number. This is a foreign key in the table BOOKING. See Figure 7.10.

BOOKING				
REF	DATE FROM	NIGHTS	ROOM NUMBER	CUSTOMER REFERENCE
300291	17/11/00	2	307	4850
300292	17/11/00	1	109	4852
300293	18/11/00	3	109	1209

Figure 7.10 *The table for the entity BOOKING showing foreign key*

There are several other things to consider when designing the fields within tables:

- Choose a **field name** to reflect the content in a meaningful way.
- Include a **description**. This will be useful documentation.
- Set a **data type** to match data it will hold, for example, alphanumeric/text or numeric.
- Set a **field width** large enough to contain data, but without wasting space.
- Set a suitable **data-entry format**, for example date, time, or currency.
- Set simple **validation requirements**, for example within a number range, of a data type, or a choice such as M or F.

The College

The design for the fields in the table for the entity STUDENT is shown in Figure 7.11.

The primary key is Reference. Each student is given a unique reference number when starting at The College.

The foreign key is Course. This field describes a course and does not actually describe a student. It is a link to the COURSE table and shows which course a student is following.

STUDENT		
Field	Data type	Format, examples, comments
REFERENCE	Text	5 numeric characters, e.g. 86219, primary key no need to store as number as no calculation required
SURNAME	Text	25 characters
OTHER NAMES	Text	30 characters
ADDRESS1	Text	30 characters
ADDRESS1	Text	30 characters
ADDRESS3	Text	30 characters
ADDRESS4	Text	30 characters
TELEPHONE	Text	12 characters
COURSE	Text	6 characters, e.g. CLAIT, foreign key

Figure 7.11 *The entity STUDENT – design of fields*

Exercise 7.7

Why is Student Number used as a primary key and not Surname?

Activity 7.9

Choose two of the entities for the applications listed in Table 7.4. For each entity, design the fields that describe it.

Activity 7.10

Find out how to set up a new database using the software available to you.

★ Create a database to include at least three entities for one of the applications listed in Table 7.4.

★ Include the relationships between the tables and the design of the fields in each table.

> Take care to identify the primary key and foreign keys in each table.

DESIGNING THE DATABASE STRUCTURE

Creating screen forms

These are known as screen forms because the data is often written on paper forms and then keyed into a similar layout on screen. Screen forms are also known as **data-entry forms**. Good screen-based form design is important.

- The form should allow **easy entry of data** without confusing the user through difficult layout, etc.

- The form should be similar in layout to existing paper-based forms.

- The form should make **appropriate use of display formats** such as number of decimal places or DD/MM/YY format for dates.

- The form should validate data on entry.

  *A range check can be applied to numeric data, data may be restricted to certain values such as Yes/No or an **input mask** may be applied.*

- There should be **menus** or **buttons** to help the user to move around the form, and between forms.

  Make sure you show your form design to other people including the users of the form. Ask them to comment on the design, and then improve it to reflect their comments.

▼▼▼▼▼▼▼▼▼

Input mask validates data entered by ensuring that it conforms to a given 'picture'. For example a National Insurance (NI) number is always 2 letters, 6 digits and 1 letter. The mask for this is 'AA999999A'.

▲▲▲▲▲▲▲▲▲

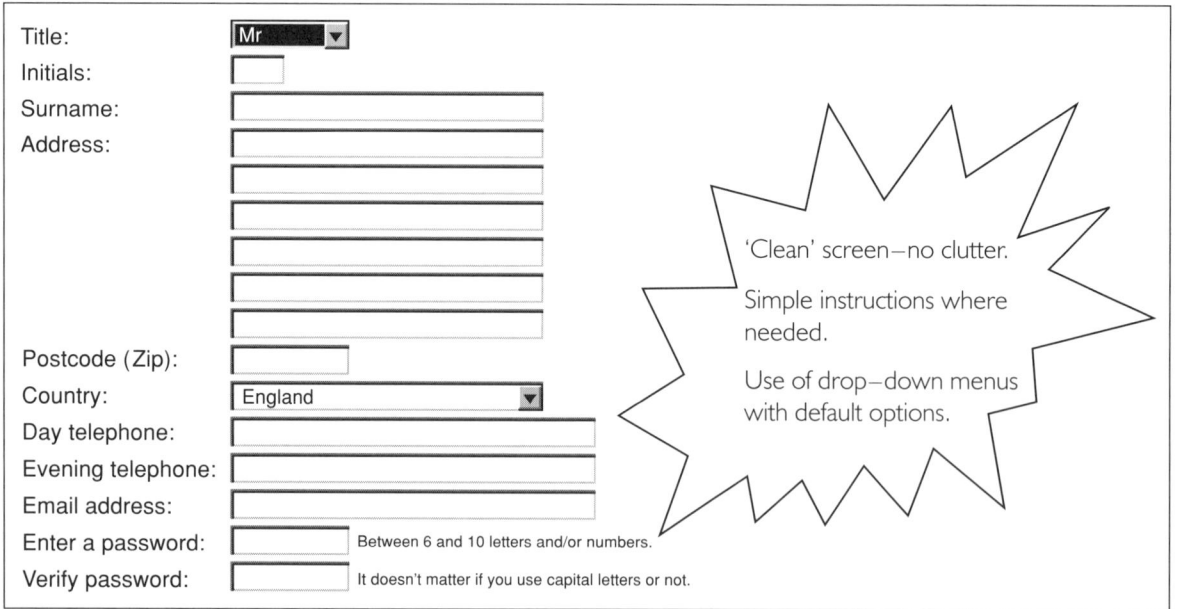

Figure 7.12 *Examples of good screen form design*

7 DATABASES

The software used to create the forms will provide some features to enhance design (see Figure 7.13):

- Drawing objects (lines, shapes)
- Borders
- Appropriate use of font, shading and colour
- On-screen field descriptions, often at the bottom of the screen on a status bar

Figure 7.13 *Screen form used by receptionists*

Exercise 7.8

Compare Figure 7.13 with Figure 7.1.

★ How closely does the screen-based form match the paper-based one?

★ Why are they not exactly the same?

Exercise 7.9

Figure 7.14 shows a screen-based form used on the Internet for customers to make a booking with a hotel. There is more use of colour, and the hotel's logo appears on this form.

Why are these good design features on this form, whereas they are less important on the form used by the receptionists, Figure 7.13?

Welcome to the Goodwood Hotel Booking system. Please enter your details in the boxes below.

Surname [   ]
Other names [   ]
If you have an account number please enter it here [   ]

Date of arrival (day 1-31) [ ] Month [January ▼] Year [2000 ▼]

Type of room required   [Double room ▼]
Second room required?   [No ▼]
Third room required?   [No ▼]

For bookings requiring more than three rooms - please telephone or e-mail us by clicking here.

We have a range of conference and sporting facilities. Please enter a description of those facilities required
[   ]

Figure 7.14 *A screen-based form for hotel booking on the Internet*

Activity 7.11

Design a screen-based form for each of these:

★ A doctor's receptionist entering details for a new patient

★ A travel agent booking an airline ticket for a customer

★ A point-of-sale (POS) terminal operator keying in item codes and quantities at a checkout

Activity 7.12

Find out how to create a screen-based form using the DBMS available to you.

★ Create two data-entry forms to input new records into the database you created in Activity 7.10.

★ Input a sample set of data of at least 20 records.

Generating reports on screen and on paper

A **database report** shows data extracted from a database. The layout of information may be **tabular**, or in a similar layout to a form. Care should be given to user-friendly positioning of fields. It is possible to display information from a single table or, by use of relationships, combined information from related tables.

Activity 7.13

Find out how to produce reports using the DBMS available to you.

★ Design and produce a report that displays data from one table only.

★ Design and produce a report that displays data from two tables.

The appearance of the report can be enhanced by using features similar to those used in word-processing.

- Paper size and orientation
- Colours, fonts and shading
- Headers and footers

Examples of these features are shown in Figure 7.15.

Reports may be printed out but need not be. Sometimes, it is more appropriate to have the output displayed on screen only. Sometimes, it is essential to have a printed copy of a report:

- Hard copy to be taken away, perhaps for further processing
- Too much information to be read on screen
- Too much information displayed to remember

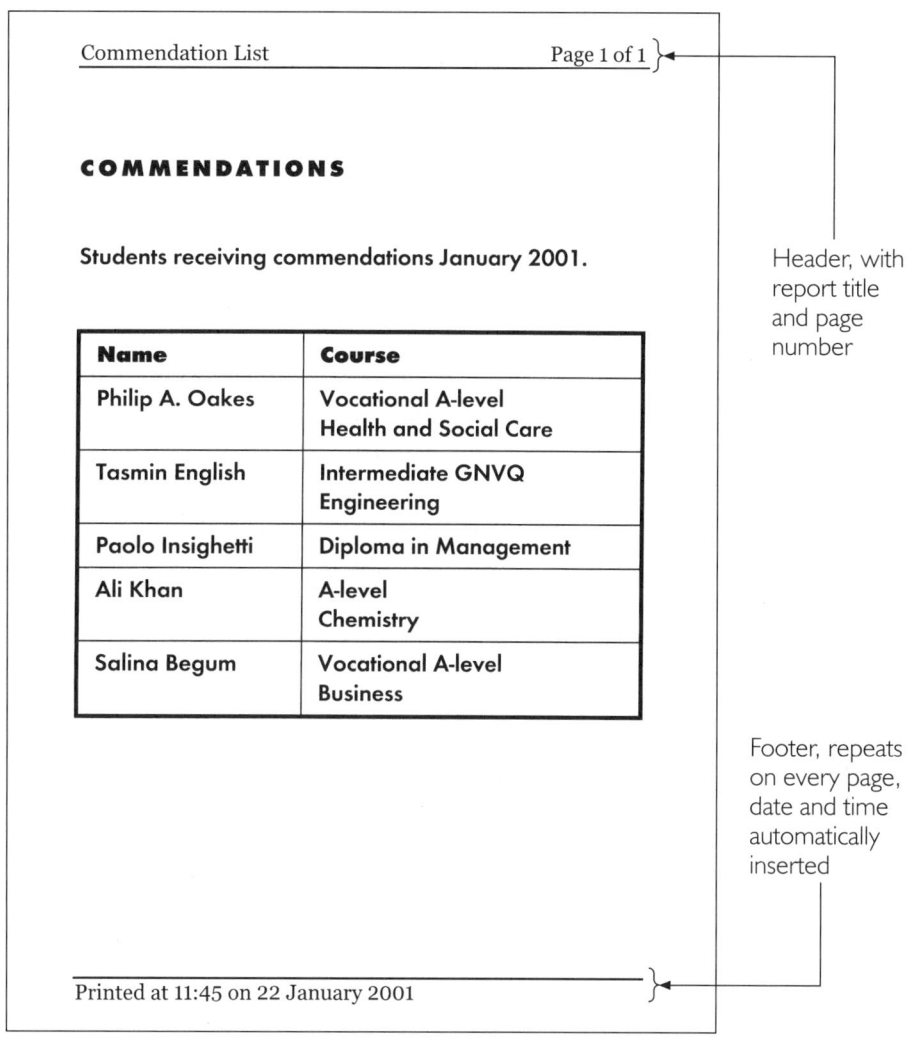

Figure 7.15 *Enhancing the appearance of a report*

Sometimes, a screen-based report is sufficient:

- A small amount of information displayed
- No time to wait for the printout
- No permanent record of the information required

Goodwood Hotel

The hotel uses a screen-based report to identify which rooms are available. There is no requirement to print this out and, as the customer requires a response immediately, there is no time to wait for the printout. The receptionist can read the screen-based report and tell the customer which rooms are available. See Figure 7.16.

The hotel uses a printed report to list the rooms that are being vacated each day. When a customer vacates a room it needs to be prepared ready for the next occupants. The printed list is given to the cleaners so that they know which rooms to prepare. A printed report is needed so that the cleaners can take it away from the computer. There would be too many rooms to remember and so a hard copy is needed. See Figure 7.17.

```
Goodwood Hotel

Room availability as at 18:30 on 29/09/00 (S=single room)

First Floor        Second Floor       Third Floor

101                205                301
102                212                302
108                213 S              305
109 S
```

Figure 7.16 *A screen-based report showing available rooms*

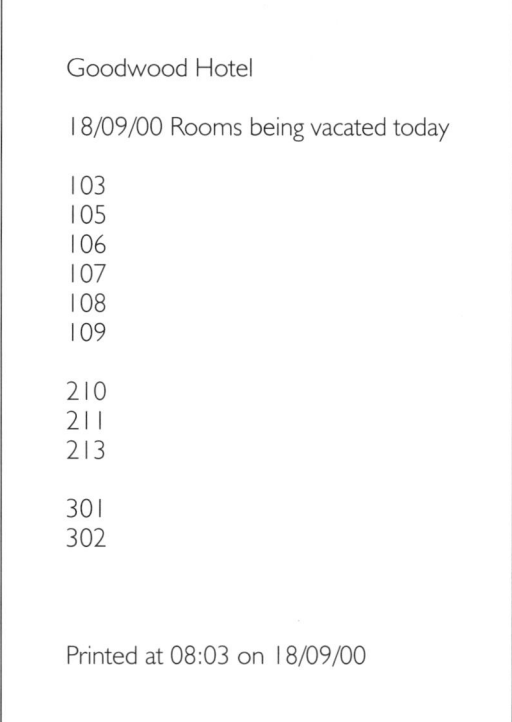

Figure 7.17 *A paper-based report showing rooms to be prepared for new occupants*

Exercise 7.10

In what way do design considerations for printed reports differ from those for screen-based reports?

Give examples of screen-based reports and printed reports for one of the applications listed in Table 7.4.

Explain why the report is either screen-based or printed in each case.

Activity 7.14

Find out how to produce reports using the DBMS available to you. Create a screen-based report to list the data entered into your database in Activity 7.12.

Grouping and sorting data

In a report, it is often helpful to group sets of data. Each group can be identified by a **group header** above, or a **group footer** below, the data items. **Summaries** such as totals, averages may be printed at the end of the report.

Information may also be **sorted** into order. The order is either alphabetical or numerical; it can be ascending (A to Z, 000 to 999) or descending (Z to A, 999 to 000). Sorting may also be done on a single field or on more than one field.

A sort by surname and then by first name is used in a telephone directory.

It is usual to sort data when there are more than a few records.

The College

Figure 7.18 shows an examination entry report. The data is grouped into students taking each examination. Each group of data is sorted and has a header showing the name of the examination. The footer has a total to show the number of students entered for the examination.

The College

Examination entries report

Printed on 12/01/01 at 15:54

EXAMINATION NAME   GNVQ (ADVANCED) BUSINESS UNIT 2
EXAMINATION CODE   5410
DATE & TIME   23/01/01 0930–1130
ROOM NUMBER   A14

Candidate number   Name

Candidate number	Name
55125879	Annis, Simon G
55125998	Edwards, Paulette T
55126003	Franks, Rachel
55126007	Patel, Indira
55126009	Shek, Kai Fee
55126012	Thomas, David
55126013	Thomas, Paul
55126014	Tranik, Stefan

Number of candidates sitting = 8

EXAMINATION NAME   GNVQ (ADVANCED) BUSINESS UNIT 4
EXAMINATION CODE   5412
DATE & TIME   24/01/01 0930–1130
ROOM NUMBER   A18

Candidate number   Name

Candidate number	Name
55125882	Ashurst, James
55125998	Edwards, Paulette T
55126000	Farwig, Eduard T
55126003	Franks, Rachel
55126005	Lippiatt, Ruth R
55126007	Patel, Indira
55126009	Shek, Kai Fee
55126010	Tamplin, Helen K
55126012	Thomas, David
55126013	Thomas, Paul
55126014	Tranik, Stefan

Number of candidates sitting = 11

Figure 7.18 *A report showing grouping and sorting of data*

Activity 7.15

Find out how to produce grouped and sorted data using the DBMS available to you.

★ Group and sort data output on the reports you created in Activities 7.13 and 7.14.

★ Include appropriate group headers and summary footers.

Queries

It is not always necessary, or useful, to print out all of the data in a database each time a report is produced. It would be wasteful of paper too!

Often, only a restricted set of data is needed – either only certain records or certain fields are displayed. Search criteria are used to identify which records are included. The required fields must be specified as well. See Figure 7.18 on page 225.

In Figure 7.18, only the student's candidate number and names have been printed, not their address or course details. The search criteria has selected only those candidates entered for each examination.

Did You Know?

Often managers need to have summary information only.

Summary reports have just totals and counts on – no records are displayed. For example: a summary of hotel bookings made in each month.

Another type of report is an **exception report** which shows those records which do *not* meet a particular criteria. Exception reports are often generated periodically so that managers may investigate the data further, e.g. students who had *not* attended examinations.

A **query** is used to extract part of the data from the database for inclusion on a report. The rules by which this is done will be designed to meet the **needs of the user**. A query may require the user to enter these rules, or criteria, via a form.

▼▼▼▼▼▼▼▼▼

Criteria
are rules that narrow down which records are to be included in a report.

▲▲▲▲▲▲▲▲▲

A criterion could be to display information about only those students who are under the age of 18.

Simple queries

A query is written in three parts: FIELD condition CRITERION

Table 7.5 shows some examples of criteria that could be applied to data in a student database to narrow down the records to be included on a report. This process is sometimes known as **filtering** the data.

Criterion	Explanation
NAME = 'Smith'	All records for students named Smith
AGE < 18	All records of students under 18
CLASS ≠ '4GT' CLASS <> '4GT'	All records of students not in class 4GT
NAME includes 'Smith'	All records for students named Smith, Smithson, Naismith, etc.
NAME = 'S*'	All records for students whose names begin with S (the * is a **wild card**)
AGE between 16 and 18	All records for students aged 16 to 18

Table 7.5 Criteria that can be applied to narrow down selection

▼▼▼▼▼▼▼▼▼
Wild card is a symbol that indicates that any value can be included in place of that symbol:
* indicates one or more characters
? indicates a single character.
▲▲▲▲▲▲▲▲▲

Activity 7.16

Find out how to apply queries to the data in the database you created in Activity 7.10.

★ Carefully consider the needs of the user of the database and design some appropriate queries.

★ Produce reports to show the results of these queries.

Exercise 7.11

A database is used in a doctor's surgery to store details of patients. Assume that the database contains the fields Age, Sex, Clinic, Last Appointment.

Write down the criteria that apply for each of these queries.

★ All patients under 18
★ All female patients
★ All patients that have attended a clinic

Complex queries

Two, or more, queries can be combined to make the selection more precise. They are connected using logical operators (AND, OR).

Table 7.6 shows some examples for a student database including use of the negative logical operator NOT.

Complex criterion	Explanation
(AGE=16) OR (AGE=17)	All records for students aged 16 or 17
(AGE=16) AND (NAME='Smith')	All records for students aged 16 named Smith
NOT (AGE=16) (this is the same as AGE<>16)	All records for students not aged 16

Table 7.6 *Complex criteria*

In general, use of AND narrows down a search and use of OR widens the search. However, care needs to be taken when using the logical criterion AND in the same field.

The criterion (AGE > 18) AND (AGE < 11) will give no matches because a person cannot both be over 18 AND under 11.

Exercise 7.12

A database is used in a doctor's surgery to store details of patients.
Assume that the database contains the fields Age, Sex, Clinic, Last Appointment.
Write down the criteria that apply for each of these queries.

- ★ All patients under 18
- ★ All female patients
- ★ All patients that have attended a clinic
- ★ All male patients that have attended a clinic
- ★ All female patients that have not had an appointment for over six months

Queries that require the user to enter the value of a variable

If a query is to be used several times, it is a good idea to save the query and to give it a name. Each time the query is used the criterion may be either kept the same or varied.

> *A query to find a student named 'Smith' could be reused to find a student named 'Khan'.*

The user uses a data-entry form to enter the value they need to find. The criterion then becomes NAME=name_entered.

The value of name_entered is taken from a data-entry form or dialogue box. When the query is run the user must supply its value. Sometimes this value is called a **parameter**.

Customising the database

Once the parts of a database have been designed – tables, queries, forms, and reports – they need to be presented in a user-friendly way. This can be done through providing a menu of options. Menus may be full screen, pull down or in the form of a dialogue box

The users of a database system are normally issued with user identities (IDs) and passwords. A user's ID determines which menus and data are accessible. The use of IDs and passwords helps maintain the security of the data as do regular back up procedures.

Selecting an item from a menu, or clicking on a button will cause an action to be carried out. This action is controlled by a small program or **macro**. Macros can be used to automate any action. They can be made to carry out the action when a particular event occurs:

- When a button is pressed
- When an option is selected from a menu
- When a form is opened
- When the mouse is moved to a particular part of a form

Goodwood Hotel

When a receptionist has to produce a bill for a customer a menu of options is called up on the screen. One of these options produces the bill. The processing that is carried out is explained on page 204. This processing is activated by the use of a macro that is executed when the menu item is selected.

Find out how to do each of these using the DBMS available to you.

★ Create a user menu to lead the user through available options.

★ Automate a process by using an existing macro or creating a new one.

★ Attach a macro to a menu choice or to a button.

User guides and technical documentation

Once a DBMS is completed, it must be documented. There are two main types of documentation:

- Technical documentation
- A user guide

> **Technical documentation** is written to explain how the database was designed.

Technical documentation should be written so that bugs that are found in the system can be corrected. Similarly it should be helpful when changed user requirements mean changes need to be made to the DBMS. This documentation should contain all information needed to maintain the database:

- Explanation of the **design** of all of the tables, forms, reports and queries
- Explanation of the design of all of the fields showing **key fields**
- Explanation of the **testing** carried out

> **User guide** is a document which shows users how to use the database.

The user guide should be a self-contained document, suitably structured for ease of use and including everything the user may need to know:

- A front cover
- A contents page
- Samples of screen-based forms and reports
- An index

To explain how to carry out tasks, a user guide should contain screen shots in between the text. It should also include information to show a user how to make the best use of the data:

- How to add, delete and amend data
- How to search for data
- How to use any menus contained in the DBMS
- How to use any macros contained in the DBMS

Activity 7.18

Find examples of user guides.

★ Look at their contents, layout and style. Which ones are easy to use? Which are not well designed?

★ Write down a list of features that make a *good* user guide and another which make a *bad* user guide.

Activity 7.19

Produce a user guide and technical documentation for the database you created in Activity 7.10.

The database must be tested to ensure that data can be **added**, **deleted** and **amended**. The tests should be supported by printouts to show that the DBMS is working correctly. Data values must be designed to include representative values of all possible data:

- Relevant valid data
- Data in/out of range
- Incorrect data
- Boundary data

Goodwood Hotel

When a customer books into the hotel, the number of nights that they wish to stay is entered onto the screen form. This value must be between 1 and 28. Anyone who wishes to stay over 28 nights is booked in again.

To test the data entry for this field the following values could be used:

- ★ 1 boundary
- ★ 28 boundary
- ★ 0 too small
- ★ 29 too large
- ★ XX wrong type

Here are more tests to apply to the DBMS:

- ★ Enter a new booking – run a report to check that the booking has been added correctly.
- ★ Delete a booking – run a report to check that the booking has been removed correctly.
- ★ Add expenses to a customer account – print a bill to check that the bill is correctly calculated.
- ★ Run through all of the menus to ensure that the links from one menu to the next are working correctly.

Activity 7.20

- ★ Design tests for your database.
- ★ Carry out these tests to ensure that the database system is functioning correctly.

Revision questions

1. What are the advantages of using a DBMS compared to other ways of managing information?

2. Why is it often easier to consider output needs of a system before input needs?

3. What is the purpose of 'processing' in a DBMS?

4. What is the difference between 'sorting' and 'searching'?

5. Give three ways in which data may be collected and input into a database.

6. What is meant by an entity?

7. List the different possible scopes a relationship may have, and give examples.

8. What does one row in an entity's table represent?

9. What does one column in an entity's table represent?

10. What must be considered when designing a field?

11. What is the difference between a primary key and a foreign key?

12. What are good design considerations when design on screen forms and reports?

13. What is meant by 'grouping data'?

14. What is the purpose of a query in a DBMS?

15. What should be included in a user guide for a DBMS?

Monitoring and control systems

8

- Explore the use of IT in data logging and monitoring systems, and control systems
- Understand the need for the many types of control system currently in use
- Design and construct a working control system
- Recognise the components of a control system
- Know where to find and how to select appropriate input and output components for a control system
- Write a control program

This unit is assessed through an external assessment. Details of how to prepare for this assessment are given in the *Examination guide* on page 401.

This chapter looks at six topics:

- What is a control system?
- Where are control systems used?
- Designing a control system
- Input and output components
- Controllers
- Implementation and testing

Three case studies are used to illustrate the points of this chapter:

- Central heating system
- Metal casting
- Swipe card entry system

What is a control system?

▼▼▼▼▼▼▼▼▼▼
Control system
is a system that has a decision making component, which tells the system how to act.
▲▲▲▲▲▲▲▲▲▲

You will have come across many different control systems but you may not have realised it at the time.

Control systems can be found everywhere, from traffic lights to video recorders, car engines to aeroplane cockpits.

Control systems have a **function**; they are used to carry out a task automatically. They make use of decision-making parts that receive input information and decide what action to take.

▼▼▼▼▼▼▼▼▼▼
Function
The task that a control system is designed to perform. A control system may have one or many functions.
▲▲▲▲▲▲▲▲▲▲

Control systems are sometimes used for tasks that are too dangerous or too fast for a human to do, but are also used when the task is repetitive or too expensive to use a human operator.

Control systems are a part of ICT because they work with information. This information is passed around the control system as a signal. As with many other ICT systems, this information is received, processed and then output in a continual loop.

In this section, you will learn what a control system is and how to recognise one.

Control system components

▼▼▼▼▼▼▼▼▼▼
Automation
Designing and building systems that perform automatic functions
▲▲▲▲▲▲▲▲▲▲

A control system is a collection of components that all work together to perform an automatic function.

The components that are used to build a control system fall into one of three categories:

- Input
- Decision
- Output

WHAT IS A CONTROL SYSTEM?

A human being is a natural control system.
Input components are the body parts that provide the senses: eyes, ears and noses.
The decision component is the brain, making the decisions for the body.
The output components are body parts that then carry out an action: arms, legs and hands.

All information flows in a control system by following the path shown in Figure 8.1.

Figure 8.1 *Information flow in a control system*

▼▼▼▼▼▼▼▼▼▼
Input components give information to the control system.
▲▲▲▲▲▲▲▲▲▲

Input components are the eyes and ears of the control system. They collect information about the world around the control system. This information is what the control system needs to calculate its actions.

A control system is used to control the temperature in a room. The input component in this system would be a temperature sensor that measures the room temperature.

Input components are also called **sensors**. Most control systems have more than one sensor.

You can find out more about input components on page 259.

▼▼▼▼▼▼▼▼▼▼
Decision components process the data from the input components.
▲▲▲▲▲▲▲▲▲▲

Decision components take information from the input components and decide what action needs to be taken by following a program.

A control system is designed to control the speed of a motor. The decision component in this system would take information from a speed sensor and then decide if the motor is going too fast or too slow.

Decision components are also called **controllers**. Most controls systems have only one controller.

You can find out more about decision components on page 263.

▼▼▼▼▼▼▼▼▼▼
Output components carry out the instructions from the decision components.
▲▲▲▲▲▲▲▲▲▲

Output components take instructions from the decision component and enable it to carry out its actions.

A control system is designed to control traffic lights. The output component in this system would be the red, amber and green lights, which the controller can turn on in sequence.

Some output components are also called **actuators**, they allow the control system to carry out a physical movement.

You can find out more about output components on page 259.

One everyday example of input, decision and output components is found at traffic lights; see Figure 8.2.

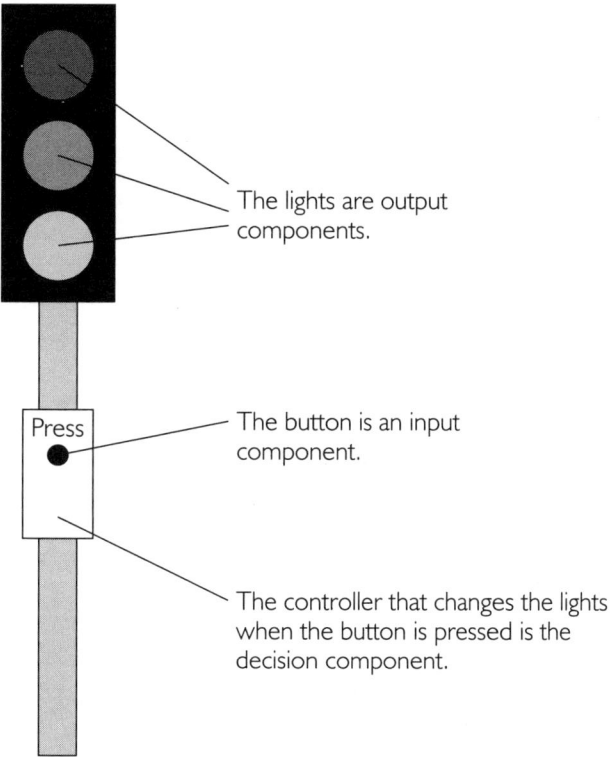

Figure 8.2 *Traffic light control system*

Applications of control systems

There are many examples of control systems that you can find in everyday life. They range from large complex systems that control aircraft to small simple systems used to control electrical appliances.

The following are examples of control systems found in a home. Within each of these, a control system is being used:

> **Did You Know?**
> The biggest use of control systems is found in the manufacturing industry. In fact, the book you are reading now will have been made by a machine, controlled by one or more control systems. The pages have been printed, cut and bound, all under the watchful eye of a control system.

- **Central heating system** – Controller is used to turn heating on at pre-set times.
- **Refrigerator** – Controller is used to keep the correct temperature inside the refrigerator.
- **Automatic timer for lights** – Controller is used to turn lighting on at pre-set times.
- **Oven** – Controller is used to keep the correct temperature inside the oven.
- **Alarm clock radio** – Controller is used to turn alarm/radio on at pre-set times.

Exercise 8.1

Write down six other control systems that you have used. What is the function of each control system?

> Look around where you are at the moment. You will probably be able to see at least one control system.

Advantages and limitations of control systems

> ▼▼▼▼▼▼▼▼▼
> **Advantages** are how the control system can be used to help us.
> ▲▲▲▲▲▲▲▲▲

It is important to know that there are both advantages and limitations of using a control system. These must be considered before starting to design a control system.

These are some of the **advantages of using a control system** instead of using a human operator.

- **Speed**
  A control system can operate much faster than a human operator. This is why they are used for assembly and production.

- **Accuracy**
  Control systems don't make mistakes. They will always do the same thing, time after time.

- **Convenience**
  Just think how nice it is that a control system turns the heating on before you wake up and before you return home. Control systems are sometimes used just to make life easier.

- **Safety**
  A control system can be used where it is too dangerous for a human.

  Control systems are used for the cleaning robots inside a nuclear reactor or the Mars Rover expedition.

Exercise 8.2

Write down two more advantages of using a control system instead of a human operator.

> Think of an example of a control system. How exactly is this control system better at doing its job than a human operator?

All of these advantages mean that control systems are being used in more and more applications every day, but control systems can also have their limitations.

▼▼▼▼▼▼▼▼▼▼
Limitations
are reasons for not using a control system.
▲▲▲▲▲▲▲▲▲▲

These are some of the **limitations of using a control system** instead of using a human operator.

- **Inflexibility**
  A control system can only do the function it was designed for. It can be very expensive to change a control system to do a different task or have different components.

- **Cost**
  Control systems are expensive to design and build. Sometimes, the cost of using a control system may be more than using a human operator.

- **Malfunction**
  If part of a control system breaks or there is an error in its design, the control system cannot fix itself. This can be dangerous, so care needs to be taken to maintain control systems that are used for dangerous functions.

- **Experience**
  A control system never improves, it is only as good as its original design. A human operator can learn from experience and improve over time.

Exercise 8.3

Write down two more disadvantages of using a control system instead of a human operator.

> Think of an example of a control system. What problems could this control system face and what would the effect be?

Activity 8.1

Find an example of a control system. Produce a written report of the control system:

★ The function the control system is designed to do
★ A brief description of the input and output components
★ The advantage of using this control system instead of a human operator
★ The limitations of this control system

> The control system could be used in the home or in a place of work. You will be able to find examples in magazines or books on the subject.

Where are control systems used?

This section considers looks at three different case studies, all examples of real control systems.

Environment control

▼▼▼▼▼▼▼▼▼
Environment control
is the control of heating, cooling and air conditioning in a building.
▲▲▲▲▲▲▲▲▲

Most buildings have some form of environment control, helping to maintain comfortable surroundings.

This section looks at an example of environment control based on a central heating system (Figure 8.3).

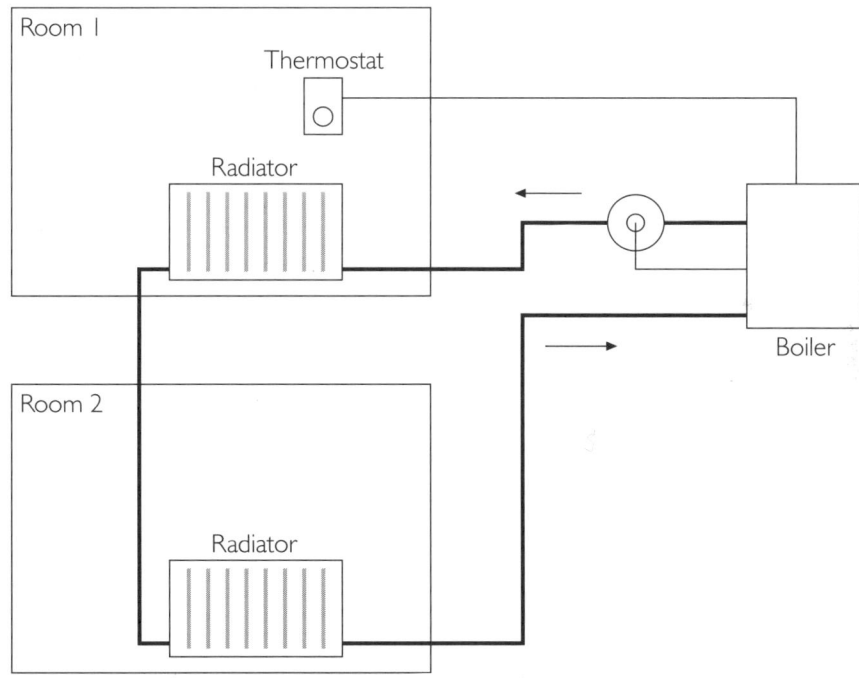

Figure 8.3 *Central heating system*

Central heating system

Central heating systems supply heat from a single source to a number of rooms in a building. This is a much more efficient method than having a heat source in each room, but such a system must be controlled so that the temperature of each room is correct.

A system like this measures the heat in the room and, based on the desired temperature, turns the boiler on and off; see Figure 8.3.

In a central heating system, the controller is called a thermostat. The user can pre-set the thermostat to the desired temperature.

Within the thermostat is a control system. If the room temperature is below the desired temperature, the control system sends a signal to turn the boiler on. If the room temperature is above the desired temperature, the control system turns the boiler off.

While the boiler is turned on, it heats the water in the system. Whenever the boiler is on, the pump is also switched on to push the water around the water pipes. Once the heated water reaches the radiator, the room starts to warm up.

Electrical wires are used to connect the thermostat to the boiler and the boiler to the pump. These wires will carry the information around the system.

> **Thermostat** is a device that measures room temperature and has an input dial so that the required temperature can be set.

The **information flow** in this central heating can be shown as a **flow diagram** (Figure 8.4).

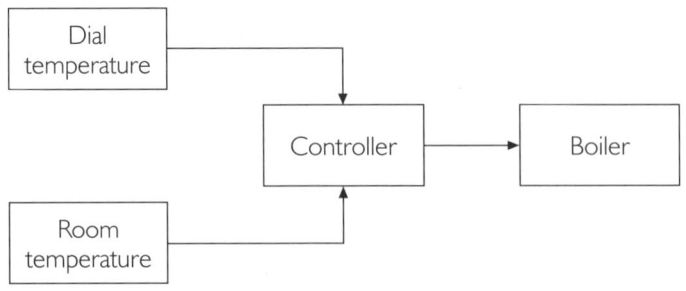

Figure 8.4 *Information flow in a central heating system*

Notice that the central heating system controller has two inputs: room temperature and dial temperature. The controller decides whether to turn the boiler on based on these inputs. The system is summarised in Table 8.1.

Component	Type
Room temperature	Input
Dial temperature	Input
Thermostat	Controller
Boiler	Output
Pump	Output

Table 8.1 *Components in the central heating system*

The processing involved is most easily explained by a single cycle of information flow around the control system. Table 8.2 shows a single cycle of information flow around the central heating control system when the actual room temperature is 18°C and the required room temperature is 22°C.

Step	Action	Value
1	Measure room temperature	18 °C
2	Measure dial temperature	22 °C
3	Is room temperature > dial temperature?	No
4	If No then turn boiler ON	Boiler ON
5	If boiler ON then turn pump ON	Pump ON
6	Repeat cycle	

Table 8.2 *Single cycle of information flow around the central heating system*

Exercise 8.4

Copy Table 8.2 and complete the Value column for the following case: actual room temperature = 23°C; required room temperature = 22°C.

What are the **advantages** and **limitations** of the central heating system?

- **Advantages**
  The central heating system is controlled by a thermostat and therefore the room temperature can be automatically controlled. By setting the dial temperature, the thermostat can regulate the room temperature.

- **Limitations**
  This system is limited by only having one thermostat. If you want the temperature of each room to be different, the system would need extra inputs. Thermostats can also malfunction, failing to measure the temperature correctly. If the thermostat fails, the boiler will either stay on or stay off.

Production automation

Casting
is where metal is heated to melting point and poured into a mould, then cooled to form a moulded shape of metal.

Control systems that are used in production automation are used to carry out repetitive manufacturing tasks. This next case study looks at a metal casting control system that is used to produce over 10,000 small metal parts per day.

Metal casting

In this application, a control system is used to make small metal parts using a process known as **casting**.

The metal casting control system is used to control the following components:

- ★ Heating elements
- ★ Blast cooler
- ★ Reject arm

The heating elements need to be controlled to keep the metal at a temperature just above melting point. If the metal temperature is too low, the metal will set before it is poured. If the metal temperature is too high, the metal will be too hot and it will not set before the mould is removed.

When the metal has been poured, a controller operates the switch which cools the metal with a blast of cold air: the blast cooler. The cooling metal becomes solid again, formed in the mould.

A **reject arm**, a mechanical arm, then shoots out from above to break the metal unit away from the cast. When it breaks away, the cast unit then falls into a collection bin.

In the **heating elements system**, the temperature of the metal is measured by a temperature sensor called a **thermocouple**. This temperature is fed back to the valve controller, which works out how much gas to allow into the furnace. If more gas is needed, the controller can open the **servo valve** to allow more gas in. Table 8.3 lists the components for this part of the system, and Figure 8.5 illustrates the system.

Component	Type
Thermocouple	Input
Melting temperature	Input
Valve controller	Controller
Valve	Output

Table 8.3 *Heating elements components*

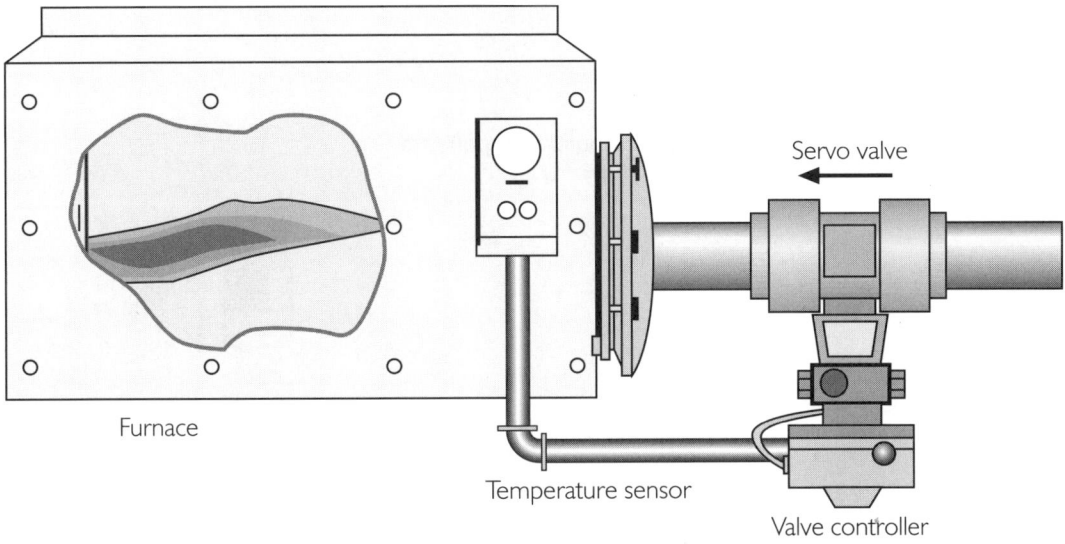

Figure 8.5 *Controlling the heating elements in a furnace*

- The **blast cooler**, shown in Figure 8.6, is started by a switch operated from a controller. The system works by opening a valve, which allows cold air to flow out of a pipe, onto the metal. Table 8.4 lists the components needed for the blast cooler.

- The **reject arm**, shown in Figure 8.7, is also operated from a switch. The components needed for the reject arm are listed in Table 8.5.

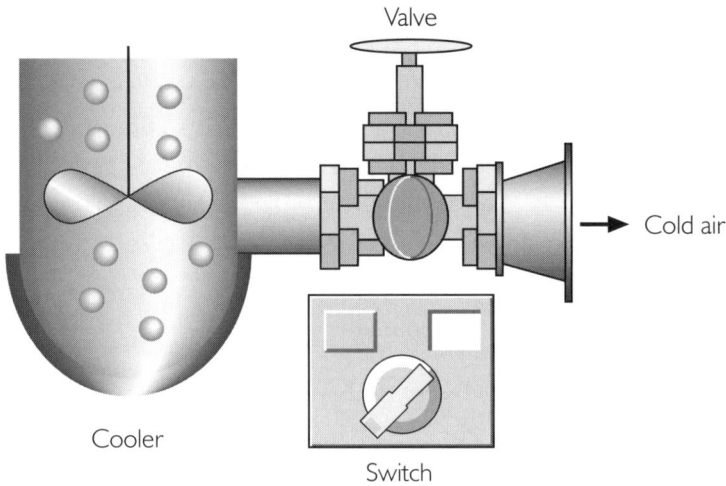

Figure 8.6 *Blast cooler*

Component	Type
Switch	Input
Controller	Controller
Valve	Output

Table 8.4 *Blast cooler components*

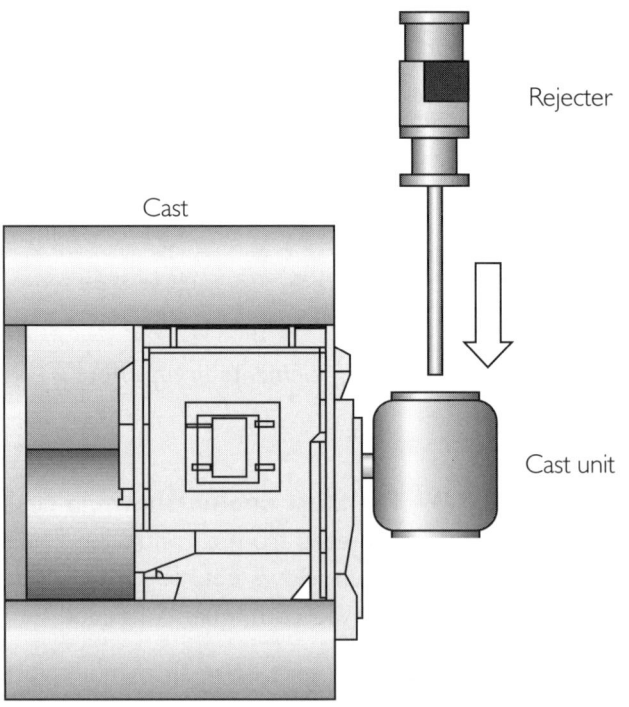

Figure 8.7 *Reject arm*

Component	Type
Unit sensor	Input
Switch	Input
Reject controller	Controller
Reject arm	Output

Table 8.5 *Reject arm components*

▼▼▼▼▼▼▼▼▼
Electrical cabinet is a locked metal box where dangerous electrical components can be safely protected.
▲▲▲▲▲▲▲▲▲

These systems work together to produce cast units many hundred times an hour. The whole system is controlled by a single controller that is mounted in an **electrical cabinet** on the side of the system.

Table 8.6 shows a single cycle of information flow around the metal casting system.

Step	Action	Value
1	Measure metal temperature	3060 °C
2	Measure melting temperature	3500 °C
3	Is metal temperature > melting temperature?	No
4	If No then OPEN servo valve	Servo OPEN
5	Is switch ON	Yes
6	Open blast cooler valve	Blast OPEN
7	Is switch ON	No
8	Close blast cooler valve	Blast CLOSED
9	Is unit complete?	Yes
10	If unit complete, operate reject arm	Arm OUT
11	Is unit rejected?	Yes
12	If unit rejected, return reject arm	Arm RETURN

Table 8.6 *A single cycle of information flow around the metal casting system*

Exercise 8.5

Copy Table 8.6 and complete it for the following cases:

Metal temperature = 3600°C

Melting temperature = 3500°C

What are the **advantages** and **limitations** of the metal casting system?

- **Advantages**
  Because of the high temperatures needed to melt the metal, using a human operator to perform the same function would be unsafe, so using a control system is safer than using a human operator. Also, the system can produce parts much faster than a human operator. Another advantage is that the system can be run continuously over an eight-hour shift without needing breaks.

- **Limitations**
  The system can only cast one type of product. If the product is changed, the system will need to be redesigned.

Later sections look at how the controller code is designed. See page 263.

Security control

▼▼▼▼▼▼▼▼▼
Security control is used in many buildings to restrict the entry of personnel to certain areas by use of a control system.
▲▲▲▲▲▲▲▲▲

This section looks at an example of security control based on a swipe card entry system.

Swipe card entry system

Many buildings use a swipe card entry system to allow only certain personnel access to secure areas. This system is used in an IT company to allow only system managers to enter the room where backup files are kept.

The person wishing to enter must swipe their card through the card reader.

Within the swipe card reader, a magnetic code reader reads the identity code on each card. The identity code is sent to the controller, which compares it against a list of accepted codes. The controller searches through a database of accepted codes that is stored in the controller memory. If the identity code matches one of the accepted codes, the controller sends a signal to the magnetic door latch to release the door and allow entry.

The components used in this system are shown in Table 8.7 and the swipe card entry system is described in Figure 8.8.

Component	Type
Identity code	Input
Accepted codes	Input
Controller	Controller
Magnetic door latch	Output

Table 8.7 Components in the swipe card entry system

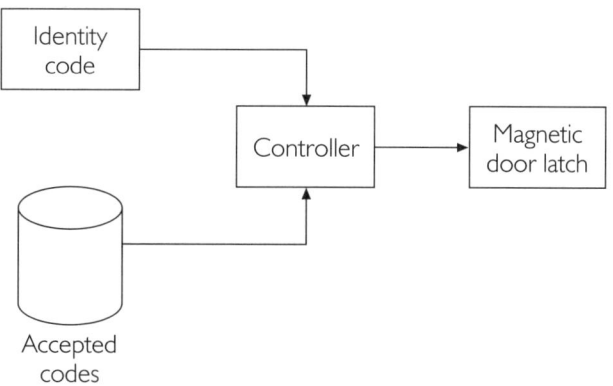

Figure 8.8 The information flow in the swipe card entry system

Notice that the controller has two inputs: the identity code from the card and the database of accepted codes.

The database of accepted codes is shown in Table 8.8. The swipe card entry system controller decides whether to open the magnetic door latch based on these inputs.

Table 8.9 shows a single cycle of the information flow around the swipe card entry system when a person arrives and wants to enter – for a person whose identity card has the code 1785.

Accepted codes
1781
1782
1785
1787
1790

Table 8.8 *Database of accepted codes for the swipe card entry system*

Step	Action	Value
1	Swipe card	1785
2	Search database for identity code	
3	Is code found in database	Yes
4	If Yes then open magnetic door latch	Latch OPEN
5	Wait 5 seconds	
6	Lock door latch	

Table 8.9 *A single cycle of information flow around swipe card entry system*

Exercise 8.6

Copy Table 8.9 and complete for the following cases:

Identity code = 1782

Identity code = 1789

What are the **advantages** and **limitations** of the swipe card entry system?

- **Advantages**

    The advantage of this swipe card security system is that the system can restrict access to certain areas without the need for a security guard to be present. It thus saves on a person's wages.

- **Limitations**

    If an identity card is lost or damaged, the system will not allow entry even if the person is a systems manager.

Designing a control system

There are many areas that need careful thought when choosing or designing a control system. A good design will produce an easily constructed and successful control system with the minimum of errors.

This section covers the basic techniques of designing a control system and the different types of documentation used in the design process.

System specification

> **Specification**
> or 'spec' is a written document, used to show what the control system is designed to do and how it works.

> **IO**
> stands for input/output.

All good control systems are first designed on paper, in a document called a **specification**. The specification tells the person who is designing, building or installing the control system, all about how the control system works.

A specification contains these details:

- A system environment definition
- A block diagram
- An IO schedule
- A process description
- Electrical wiring diagrams

System environment

> **System environment**
> is the area in which the control system is expected to work and the various input and output information that is available.

The very first thing to consider when designing a control system is the **system environment**.

If you were designing a control system for controlling the lighting in a coal mine, the system environment definition may be written as: 'This system is expected to work in a damp environment with temperature ranges from 0°C to 30°C. Input signals include operator key-switches, light intensity sensors, moisture meters and emergency safety controls.'

The system environment will show if special components need to be used or if any additional safety measures need to be taken. It is important to show these details throughout the design of the control system as it may affect the both the cost and operation of the control system.

Here is a list of safety features that you may need to include in a system environment:

- High voltage
- Damp or water (risk of electrical shock)
- Dangerous moving machinery
- High temperatures
- Remote locations
- Dangerous chemicals
- Domestic use (special safety considerations)

A further use of the system environment is to show any other control systems that are to be used together with the new control system. This is especially important if the new control system is designed to work with any existing systems.

For example, it is often too complicated to use a single control system to control a complete factory, so many smaller control systems are used to control separate parts of the manufacturing process. These controllers are then linked together by a larger controller which acts as a **supervisor**. If you were writing the system environment for a new control system in this factory, you would need to show what connections the supervisor controller requires.

Activity 8.2

Working in a group, each person must find a suitable control system and write a description of the system environment. You must clearly state the following items:

★ Location
★ Environment
★ Safety
★ Other control systems

Make a presentation of your system environment to the other members of the group.

Block diagram

> **Block diagram** shows what components are used, the signals that pass between each component and the direction of dataflow.

Block diagrams are a simple way of showing how each control system component functions with each other.

Block diagrams use blocks and lines.

- The **block** shows the name and type of the component.
- The **lines** show the direction of information flow and the type of information. The lines are also used to connect the blocks together and to show which information is required.

Input/Output schedule

> **IO schedule** is a table of the input and output signals that are to be used in the control system.

> **Tag names** are short names (6–10 letters/numbers) that uniquely identify a signal or component.

The IO schedule will show all the information within the control system. The table lists the signals, indicating name, type, and location. An example is given in Table 8.10 for the control system for the central heating system.

To make designing control systems easier, it is helpful to use **tag names** for the signals and components.

The temperature input signal from tank 67 may have a tag name of TEMP67.

Once defined in the IO schedule, these tag names are used instead of the longer name everywhere else in the system specification.

Signal	Tag	Type	Location
Room temperature	TEMP_RM	Input	Room
Dial temperature	TEMP_DL	Input	Room
Pump	PUMP_ON	Output	Boiler room

Table 8.10 *IO schedule for central heating sysem*

Tag names can be grouped to show the location of the signal, and this helps the designer to quickly know where the signal can be found.

All the signals which are associated with the pump could start with 'PUMP_'

DESIGNING A CONTROL SYSTEM

If a program is required in the control system, the IO schedule can also be used to show the controller memory location where the signal can be found.

A controller with 5 inputs and 5 outputs could be listed in the IO schedule and numbered as: Input_1 to Input_5 and Output_1 to Output_5.

Process description

The process description, describes how the control system works, showing how the control system is required to act when it receives an input signal.

When you are designing the controller software, the process description will tell you what operations the control system has to do.

A process description can be written as a number of IF . . . THEN . . . type rules.

IF the BUTTON is pressed THEN turn the LIGHT on.

These rules can be very easily programmed into the controller, to produce the correct function.

Exercise 8.7

Write a process description of the control system you have used in Activity 8.2 as IF . . . THEN . . . rules.

Electrical wiring diagrams

When the control system design is complete, it will need to be built or installed. The electrical wiring diagram shows all electrical connections that are required and where the connections are needed.

These diagrams become very important if any maintenance is needed to be done on the system. Often, if there is a fault in the control system, the wiring will need to be checked and it is these diagrams that the electrician will need to refer to.

Input and output components

Input and output components allow the control system to communicate with the outside world.

- **Input components** provide data to the controller to tell the controller of any changes.
- **Output components** allow the controller to make any actions.

There are two types of input or output component depending on the signal involved: **digital** or **analogue**.

Digital input components

▼▼▼▼▼▼▼▼▼
Digital components are parts of a control system that work with information that is only ever true or false.
▲▲▲▲▲▲▲▲▲

A digital component is used to give a true or false type input signal. The information that it provides can only ever be true or false. This is usually done with a voltage.

For example 0 volts is false, 10 volts is true.

The controller receives this information and carries out the action required. This could be to check if a switch is closed or a light is on, before starting a control sequence.

The following are examples of digital input components: switch, pushbutton, proximity sensor, contact sensor.

Exercise 8.8

Write down three more examples of digital input components.

Think of questions that the controller might ask that have a true or false answer.

Analogue input components

▼▼▼▼▼▼▼▼▼

Analogue components are parts of a control system that work with numbers.

▲▲▲▲▲▲▲▲▲

An analogue input component provides information that is a number from a range of values on a scale. They are used to give a number as an input signal. The information is usually provided as a voltage (from 0 to 10 volts) or in current (from 4 to 20 mA).

The **resolution** of the analogue component will determine the **accuracy** of the input signal. Analogue input signals are usually used for comparison or with a mathematical expression.

The following are examples of analogue input components: thermocouple, pressure gauge, speed sensor.

Central heating system

Inside the thermostat is an input component to measure the room temperature. The input component is an analogue input component called a thermocouple. A thermocouple measures room temperature and translates it into a voltage.

25°C is represented by 7.0V.

The temperature is on a range of −10°C to 40°C and the voltage is on a range of 0 to 10 volts.

Exercise 8.9

Write down three more examples of analogue input components.

Think of questions that the controller might ask that have a number as an answer.

Digital output components

Digital output components receive only true or false type information from the controller and then change into either one position or another. This could be to start a motor or to turn a light on.

The following are examples of digital output components: light bulb, buzzer, fan.

▼▼▼▼▼▼▼▼▼
Solenoid
is an electro-magnet that, when input voltage signal is high, it moves a metal rod. When the input voltage is low, the rod returns to its home position.
▲▲▲▲▲▲▲▲▲

Swipe card entry system

In the swipe card entry system, the magnetic door latch is only in the open or closed position. The digital output component that is used in this system is a linear mover called a solenoid.

Exercise 8.10

Write down three more examples of digital output components.

> Think of actions that the controller might take which have only a true or false change.

Analogue output components

Analogue output components receive analogue information, which is then used to set a position or speed or other value from a range. This can allow the controller to make small changes.

Motor and pump are examples of analogue output components.

Metal casting

In the metal casting machine, a servo valve is used to control the gas flow into the furnace. The servo valve receives an analogue signal from the valve controller to set its position. The position will determine how much gas is allowed into the furnace.

Exercise 8.11

Write down three more examples of analogue output components.

> Think of actions that the controller might take which have a value from a range.

Controllers

The controller is the brain of the control system. It gives the system its ability to make decisions. A controller takes information from its input components and decides how to alter its output components.

The two most common forms of controller are the programmable logic controller (PLC) and the personal computer (PC). Both are based on a microprocessor that can be programmed to follow a set of instructions.

Programmable logic controllers

A programmable logic controller (PLC) is a type of computer that has been designed for use in a harsh environment. It is capable of working in extreme temperatures and under conditions that would cause many desktop computers to fail.

The operating system of a PLC is specifically designed around an internal clock. By using this feature, program code can be designed to carry out processes at exact times.

A PLC does not have the normal operator devices (mouse, keyboard, monitor) that are supplied with a PC. The PLC is designed to be programmed with a special hand-held device, which is then disconnected and the PLC left to function alone. Recently, due to the ease of use of many desktop PC systems, it is now more typical to use a PC to program a PLC.

Many different PLC programming languages are available, each manufacturer having their own preferences. One of the most popular languages is based on the wiring connections found in an electrical wiring diagram. This is called **relay ladder logic (RLL)**. Programs written using this language are very similar to electrical circuits.

There are three main program commands:

- ◊ Contacts
- ◊ Coils
- ◊ Function blocks

Contact is a digital input, either from one of the controller sensors or from the controller memory.

In PLC language, a **contact** is represented by the symbol

This is the contact for input 4.3, which is the third input in memory block 4. When the sensor detects it, it changes from a false to a true voltage. This is called **closing a contact**. You can think of this as pressing a switch:

- When the contact is closed, the voltage can then travel across the ladder to the next program instruction in sequence.
- If the contact is *not* closed, that ladder cannot proceed.

In most PLC languages, a **coil** is represented by the symbol

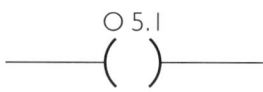

> **Coil**
> is a digital output, either to one of the controller output components or to the controller memory.

This is the coil for output 5.1, which is the first output in memory block 5. When the controller wants to turn an output on, it sends a true voltage out to the output component. This is called **energising a coil**. The output is usually the last program function of a ladder.

In most PLC languages, a **function block** is represented by the symbol

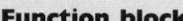

> **Function block**
> is a program subroutine, which can be used to process analogue inputs and outputs.

This example is a sum function block, which adds together the numbers at address N2 and N3 and stores the result in address N6.

Function blocks are used to perform many of the control routine structures that are found in other programming languages. Here are some of the most frequently used function blocks:

- **SUM** – used to add two numbers together
- **MULT** – used to multiply two numbers together
- **DIV** – used to divide one number by another
- **DELAY ON** – used to wait for a set time before turning an output on
- **DELAY OFF** – used to wait for a set time before turning an output off

The contacts, coils and function blocks are connected together in a **ladder**, which allows multiple inputs and multiple outputs; see the simple example in Figure 8.9 and the more detailed ladder of Figure 8.10.

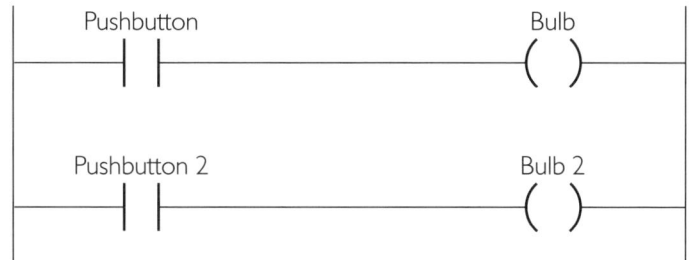

Figure 8.9 Simple RLL 'ladder' code turns the bulbs on when pushbuttons are pressed

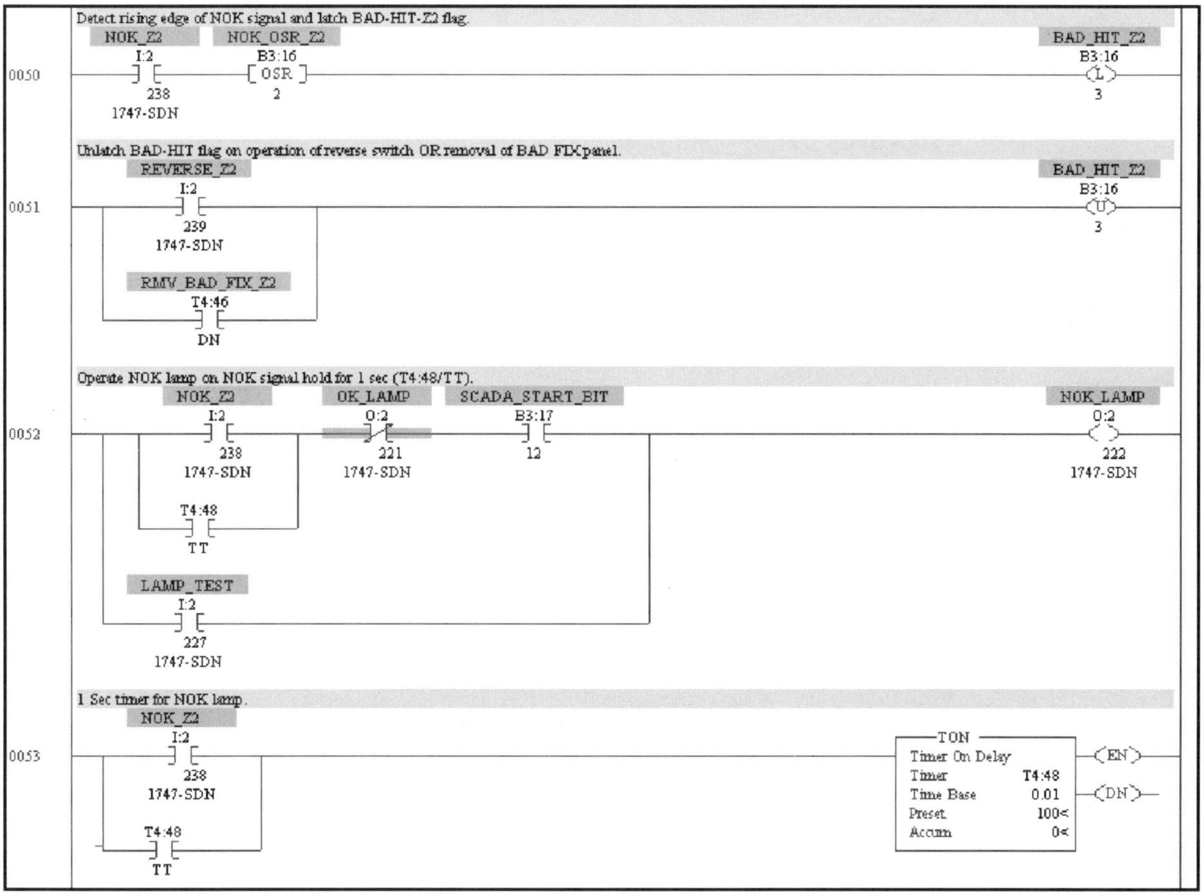

Figure 8.10 Ladder logic example

Metal casting

The casting system is controlled by an Allen-Bradley PLC. This is a compact size controller which is fitted with input cards for digital inputs and analogue inputs and output cards for digital outputs and analogue outputs.

The controller is mounted in a steel cabinet near to the casting area and is capable of withstanding the harsh environment.

Part of the ladder logic code in the controller is shown in Figure 8.10.

Personal computer controllers

As prices of personal computers fall, they are increasingly being used as controllers in many different applications. Special cards called **interface cards** can be fitted to the computer to allow sensors to be connected for input and output components for output.

The most common language that is used for control software in personal computers is BASIC. For more details about BASIC see Chapter 10: *Programming*.

Controller routine structures are used to design the sequence of a control program. Here are three of the most frequently used program routine structures that you will find in a controller program.

- **FOR NEXT**
  The FOR NEXT loop is used to perform a control action a defined number of times.

  A FOR NEXT loop may be used in an automatic alarm clock, to activate the alarm bell for 100 rings:
  FOR I = 1 TO 100
  RING(BELL)
  NEXT I

- **REPEAT UNTIL**
 The REPEAT UNTIL loop is used to perform a control action until an event happens.

 A REPEAT UNTIL loop may be used to put the heater on until the room temperature is the same as the set temperature:
 REPEAT
 OUTPUT(HEATER) = ON
 UNTIL TEMP = SET TEMP

- **IF THEN ELSE**
 The IF THEN ELSE structure is used to perform a control action when an event happens, otherwise perform an alternative action.

 IF THEN ELSE may be used to open a valve when a switch is closed:
 IF SWITCH CLOSED THEN
 OUTPUT(VALVE) = OPEN
 ELSE OUTPUT(VALVE) = SHUT

Using special instructions, such as Input and Output, to send and receive data via the interface cards, many different control system programs can be designed using BASIC. Table 8.11 shows an example of a BASIC program used in a control system.

Swipe card entry system

In the swipe card entry system, the BASIC code shown in Table 8.11 is used to input an identity code, compare it with a stored database and decide whether the person has security clearance.

Activity 8.3

Add code to that given in Table 8.11 to allow the door to be held open for a 5 second wait while the person passes through.

For safety, the output will need to be held at 10 volts for the wait time, so that the door does not trap fingers.

Line number	Instruction	Comment
100	PRINT ("Insert swipe card")	
101	FOR Count = 1 to 5000	{Wait 5 seconds}
102	NEXT Count	
103	REPEAT	
104	Card_In = Input (1,1)	{Check if card is inserted}
105	UNTIL Card_In = TRUE	
110	ID_Code = Input (1,0)	{Input the identity code}
120	FOR Count = 1 TO LEN (Database)	
130	IF ID_Code = Database (Count) THEN Clearance = TRUE ELSE Clearance = FALSE	
140	NEXT Count	
150	IF Clearance = TRUE THEN OUTPUT (1, 10) ELSE GOTO 180	{Output 10 volts to magnetic latch}
160	PRINT ("Card OK")	{Identity card is accepted}
165	PRINT ("Remove swipe card")	
170	GOTO 200	
180	PRINT ("Card Not Accepted")	{Identity card NOT accepted}
190	PRINT ("Remove swipe card")	
200		{End of check sequence}

Table 8.11 *Coding for swipe card entry system*

Implementation and testing

> ▼▼▼▼▼▼▼▼▼
> **Implementation** of a control system is the action of installing the system in its correct area and making it work.
> ▲▲▲▲▲▲▲▲▲

When a control system has been fully designed and built, it must be installed and then tested to find any mistakes or problems. This is called the **implementation** stage.

The next section looks at the requirements of implementing a control system and issues that you will need to know.

Wiring

The implementation of a control system will often require its components to be wired together and the system to be connected to the electricity supply. This is done by following the instructions given in the **electrical wiring diagrams,** as described on page 258.

There are many different types of wiring, depending on the level of electrical power that the wires will carry (Table 8.12).

Power	Voltage	Wiring
Low	Below 24 volts	Light duty
Medium	110/240 volts	Medium duty
High	Above 415 volts	Heavy duty

Table 8.12 *Wiring needed to match levels of power*

There are also many different types of wiring, dependent on the type of information that the wires will carry:

- Data
- Electrical
- Fibre-optic
- Temperature
- High power
- Audio
- Video

When the control system is implemented, it will use one or more of these types of wiring.

Safety

There are two main areas of safety that must be considered when implementing a control system:

- Safety during installation
- Safety after installation

It is important that, when installing the control system, all necessary safety precautions are taken to protect the personnel involved. Electrical wiring can be dangerous, with the risk of injury through electrical shock. This is why only a qualified electrician is allowed to connect the electrical supply and complete the wiring.

After installation of the control system, the operators of the control system must also be protected from any danger. This includes making sure that there is protection from many possible dangers:

- Electrical shock
- High temperatures
- Moving machinery
- Lasers
- Excessive noise
- Dust/pollution
- Radiation

The best way to make sure that correct safety precautions have been taken is to consult safety standards, such as British Standards or CE marking. These are available from libraries, or on the Internet.

Testing

A control system must go through many tests before it is complete.

The customer will want the control system to be tested to find any problems before the system is installed and used.

▼▼▼▼▼▼▼▼▼
Test schedule
is the document used to test the control system.
▲▲▲▲▲▲▲▲▲

A **test schedule** is written by following the process description, to show how the control system is meant to operate (Table 8.13). All of the functions of the control system are listed in the test schedule, alongside a tick box. As each of the functions of the control system are demonstrated, the test schedule is ticked off, until all of the functions have been tested.

Function	Output	Tested
Increase the dial temperature, the boiler should turn on	BOILER_ON	
Decrease the dial temperature, the boiler should turn off	BOILER_ON	
Disconnect the boiler, the pump should turn off	PUMP_OFF	

Table 8.13 *Test schedule for the central heating system case study*

Activity 8.4

★ Copy the test schedule in Table 8.13.
★ Add another function to be tested.
★ Are there any functions that need to be tested in sequence?

Improvements

▼▼▼▼▼▼▼▼▼
Effectiveness
is how well a control system performs the task that it was designed to do.
▲▲▲▲▲▲▲▲▲

When the installation of the control system is complete and fully tested, the system is ready for use. It is then important to make sure that any control system continues to work properly and achieves the task that it was designed to do. This can be done by regularly inspecting the system and re-testing its functions, using the test schedule.

This testing is done to check the **effectiveness** of the control system.

▼▼▼▼▼▼▼▼▼
Continuous improvement
is a process to make sure that systems are working at their best.
▲▲▲▲▲▲▲▲▲

If the control system is not effective, it will waste money or resources during its operation. It may need to be redesigned or modified to improve its effectiveness. Many businesses use a process called **continuous improvement** to keep a high level of effectiveness of a control system. The system is analysed every few months and a report is written to suggest the best improvements.

> **Efficiency** is a measure of how much power is needed by the control system in performing the task that it was designed to do.

The improvements to a control system may come from replacing worn or damaged parts, but often system components are replaced when better versions become available. As information technology continues to develop, components are getting faster, more accurate and more **efficient**.

By replacing components and modifying the design, a control system can be made to keep working effectively. This enables it to continue automatically performing its tasks with the minimum of errors and maximum reliability.

Revision questions

1. What is a control system? Give four examples of control systems.

2. What are the three main components of any control system?

3. Explain these terms: sensor, controller, actuator.

4. What is environmental control?

5. What is a thermostat?

6. How can the information flow in a control system be shown?

7. What is a servo valve?

8. Why is an electrical cabinet necessary?

9. What information is contained within a control system specification?

10. What is the system environment? List seven safety features that you may need to include in a system environment.

11. Explain these terms: block diagram, IO schedule, tag names.

12. Explain the difference between analogue and digital components.

13. Give four examples of digital input components, three examples of analogue input components, three examples of digital output components, and two examples of analogue output components.

14. Explain the differences between FOR NEXT, REPEAT UNTIL and IF THEN ELSE controller routine structures.

15. Explain the difference between the terms effectiveness and efficiency.

Networks and communications

9

- **Acquire an understanding of communications and networks**
- **Use computer networks to manage files**
- **Use a range of network services to send and obtain information**
- **Identify the main components of a computer network**
- **Sketch the layout of a computer network**
- **Configure a computer system to access a network**
- **Develop good practice in your use of Information and Communication Technology**

In this unit you will be assessed on your ability to use network services to communicate with others and to organise the files used in directories showing an understanding of security issues and the advantages and disadvantages of using networks. You will need to show an understanding of the purpose of the main network components and be able to attach a standalone computer system to a network.

This chapter looks at three topics:

- ✪ Networks and their uses
- ✪ Network security
- ✪ Network services and electronic communication systems

Four case studies are used to illustrate the use of networks and communications:

- American Airlines
- Eddie Stobart
- Comet
- Richmond-upon-Thames College

As with other units, you will be expected to adopt standard ways of working. See Good Working Practice guide on page 389.

Networks and their uses

In the early days of computing, a single computer with the power of a modern PC would have cost hundreds of thousands, if not millions, of pounds. Each computer would probably have had to be shared by several hundred users. The original approach was **batch processing**. Programs and data were punched on to cards or tape and then sent in batches to the computer centre. After processing, the results were sent to back to the user, usually in the form of paper listings. Because of the obvious inefficiency of this process, **interactive systems** were developed which allowed users to transmit programs and data to the computer and obtain immediate results. To do this required a means of communication between the users, who could be in numerous locations, and the computer, and led to the first computer networks.

The technology of networking has developed at an ever increasing pace and this, together with rapidly falling prices of computer hardware, has led to the situation we have today: computer networks are everywhere and affect many aspects of our daily lives.

So how are networks now being used in businesses?

There are two main types of network:

- Local area networks (LANs)
- Wide area networks (WANs)

> **LAN** stands for local area network.
>
> **WAN** stands for wide area network.

LANs are normally restricted to a single building (or perhaps a group of buildings such as a college campus). During the 1980s, many organisations installed large numbers of PCs; to enable these PCs to communicate and share data, they were connected to form a LAN. Workstations connected to the LAN can then communicate with each other at high speed.

> **PSTN** stands for public switched telephone network.

WANs cover a large geographical area (even the whole world!). Originally WANs used the telephone network (the **public switched telephone network** or **PSTN**) and generally operated at relatively low speeds.

PSDN
stands for packet switched data network.

ISDN
stands for integrated services digital network.

Did You Know?

Other countries have their own telecommunications companies known as PTTs (from the French – Poste Telegraphie et Telecommunications).

Did You Know?

The Swedish telecommunications company, Nokia has now produced a device called the Communicator, which is a combination of a mobile phone and a palm-top computer. As well as making phone calls from the bus on the way to college, students can now surf the Net and send e-mails. You can find out more at the Nokia web site www.nokia.com.

However, in recent years, high-speed networks have been built specifically for data transmission (**packet switched data networks** or **PSDNs**) or for a mixture of voice and data (**integrated services digital network** or **ISDN**). These use digital rather than analogue transmission and high-speed media such as fibre optics or satellites, and operate at very high speeds. WANs are normally operated by telecommunications companies such as British Telecom in the UK.

In recent years, other organisations (e.g. Mercury in the UK), and cable TV companies have started to offer communications services in competition with the PTTs. The introduction of digital television and the use of the Internet for sound and video transmission means that the traditional distinctions between broadcasting, telephone services, and data communications are no longer clearly defined.

Companies or other organisations who want to use WANs usually use the services of the PTT or other network provider; this is easier than laying their own cables across the world! However, there is the option to lease lines from the PTT to ensure unrestricted access. This gives organisations, in effect, their own **private WAN.**

> *Examples of private WANs are **JANET** (Joint Academic Network) linking UK universities and colleges, and most banks, which use private WANs to ensure the security of their networks.*

Some networks use **broadcast radio** signals rather than cables.

> *One example is the **Teletext** system in which information is sent along with the sound and picture signals to television receivers.*

The pages of information are stored in the receiver and accessed when required by the viewer. Data can also be sent via the **cellular radio** system used for mobile telephones or by means of **microwave** or **satellite** systems.

MAN
stands for metropolitan area network.

A third type of network is a **metropolitan area network** (**MAN**). A MAN is a WAN that covers a city or town and is put into place to increase the capacity for businesses using the internet within the area of the MAN.

American Airlines

American Airlines is one of the world's largest airlines and has always been a leading user of computerised reservations systems. In the 1960s, they developed an on-line reservations system called SABRE which is used by many airlines and enables travel agents throughout the world to check seat availability and make bookings for their clients.

Travel agents typically take 8.5% of the price of an air ticket so American Airlines have been looking for ways in which their customers could make their own reservations to enable them to reduce prices and increase profits. However, the SABRE system has a very complicated user interface. So, in 1995, American Airlines launched a system called EasySabre; this was made available through the Compuserve network but, as the number of transactions grew, the Compuserve network was unable to provide the necessary capacity. American Airlines have now built a new system which allows members of their Frequent Flyer programme to access the SABRE system directly through a new user interface on the American Airlines world wide web site. This runs on a Sun Solaris microcomputer system on the same site as the SABRE mainframe computers in Tulsa, Oklahoma. The system also holds information about customers' seating preferences and enables them to choose their seats on a graphic illustrating the layout of the aircraft's cabin. Marketing information about members' interests and favourite destinations enables the airline to send details of promotions covering the airline and its hotel and car rental partners.

Eddie Stobart

Founded in 1970, Eddie Stobart is one of the UK's leading transport and warehousing organisations, with a fleet of over 800 lorries and a network of depots throughout the country. One of their largest customers is Tesco supermarkets who use the services of Eddie Stobart to take delivery of goods from smaller suppliers and consolidate these into larger loads for delivery to Tesco's own warehouses. The smaller suppliers want to be able to make sure there are always sufficient goods in Eddie Stobart's warehouses to meet Tesco's requirements. So these suppliers now enjoy remote access to the LANs in the warehouses – via a dial-up system using a variety of modem speeds, or via an ISDN line or through the Internet. The suppliers use a device called a **remote access switch** which allows for up to 120 simultaneous remote accesses via a range of different technologies and also allows Eddie Stobart's own employees dial-out facilities to obtain access to Internet Service Providers.

Comet

Comet, the home electronics retailer, has developed a web site called eComet, to offer 2,000 electrical and new technology products for purchase online. Comet expects to sell over £1 million pounds worth of goods via eComet in its first year and recoup all the investment in the development of the system. Within 7 to 10 years, Comet predicts that a quarter or more of its business will be completed online.

Comet's online shopping system is one example of shopping through the Internet. The system was developed by IBM, using its Net.Commerce software, and runs on a server at an IBM site in Portsmouth. It is one of 450 such servers at the site managed by a team of 70 IBM staff. This type of installation is now becoming known as a **server farm**.

Activity 9.1

In small groups, find some other examples of organisations that make major use of data communications and networking.

Share your findings with others in your class, and thus build up a comprehensive list of network users.

Physical components of networks

Networks require a range of physical components to link computers together so that communication can occur between them. In this section, three main components are considered:

- Cables
- Connectors
- Network cards

Exercise 9.1

Find out the name of a device which is required to increase the distance over which communication signals can travel.

Find out the name of a device which is required to link several computers to a central point.

Data is transmitted through **cables** either as electrical signals or as optical light signals. There are several different types of cable, as shown in Figure 9.1:

- Two wire
- Twisted pair
- Coaxial
- Optical fibre

Two-wire, the most basic form of electrical cable, consists of a pair of copper wires separated by an insulator or dielectric. Two-wire cabling is

NETWORKS AND THEIR USES 279

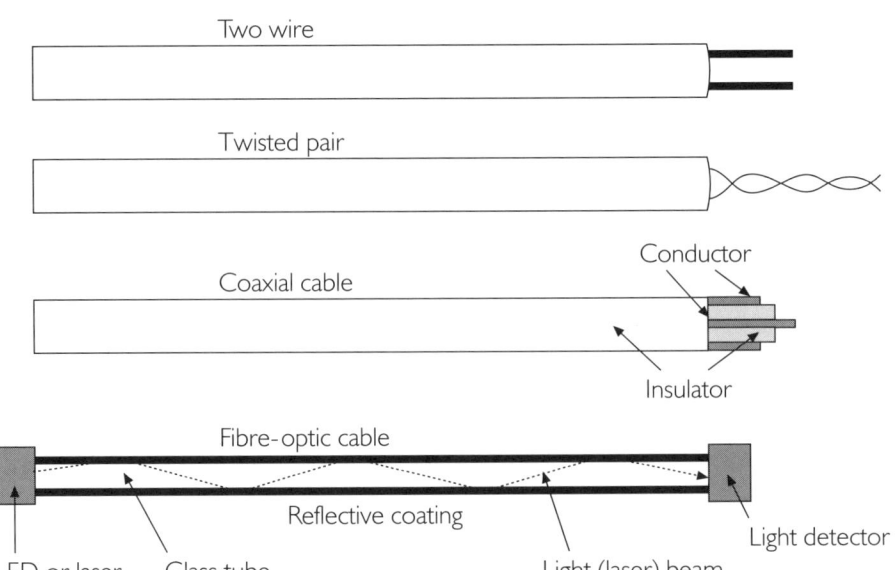

Figure 9.1 *Types of cable media used in data communication*

> **Did You Know?**
>
> Cross talk is caused when the electrical signals in one pair of wires produces a magnetic field which can, in turn, cause a signal to flow in another pair of wires. This problem sometimes occurs with the telephone system when someone else's conversation is heard on the line.

> **Did You Know?**
>
> A more effective way of eliminating cross-talk, and also **interference** (sometimes called 'noise') from outside sources such as electrical machinery and radio waves, is to use a special type of cable: **coaxial cable**.

▼▼▼▼▼▼▼▼▼▼

Optical fibres are very thin glass fibres with reflective coating.

▲▲▲▲▲▲▲▲▲▲

quite suitable for low-speed transmission, but if a number of two-wire lines are laid side by side, transmission can suffer from a problem known as **cross-talk.**

Twisted pair cabling is created by twisting the two wires in each pair around each other, and this can largely eliminate the cross-talk problem. This enables a large number of twisted pairs to be packaged together in large cables. This system is often found in telephone wiring and can also be used for high-speed data communication.

Coaxial cable consists of a copper wire surrounded by an insulator. A second conductor is wrapped around the outside, and the whole cable is enclosed in a second insulator. Coaxial cable is more expensive than twisted pair but can achieve transmission rates of up to 100 Mbps.

Coaxial cable is also found in the home. It is used to bring the signal from your television aerial to the socket on the back of your television, and is also used for cable television systems.

Fibre-optic cables use light rather than electricity to represent data. Just as different voltages can represent binary 1s and 0s in an electrical system, they can be represented by a light signal being on or off. (Just as Morse code can be transmitted by means of a flashing light.)

Light from a **light-emitting diode** (**LED**) or a **laser** is shone into the end of the cable and travels along the cable being reflected from the sides. Large numbers of fibres can be packaged in a cable, which can be laid underground

> **Transfer rates**
> **Tbps** stands for terabits per second.
> **Gbps** stands for gigabit per second.
> **Mbps** stands for megabits per second.
> 1000 Mbps = 1 Gbps
> 1000 Gbps = 1 Tbps

> **Cable connectors** are the plugs and sockets used in network systems.

> **Did You Know?**
>
> RS232 was originally designed for speeds of up to 20Kbps and distances of up to 50 feet. A newer standard, RS449, can be used for speeds of up to 2 Mbps and cable lengths up to 200 feet.

> **Workstation**
> a single-user computer used by an individual to gain access to the LAN.

or in a building in the same way as electrical cables. Because lasers and LEDs can be switched on and off very rapidly, very high transmission rates (up to 2000 Mbps) can be achieved. They also have the advantage that because they use light rather than electricity, they are not affected by electrical interference. Their disadvantages are that they are more expensive than electrical cables and are more difficult to install, as they cannot be bent around very sharp corners.

There are a number of different types of **cable connector** depending on the types of cable to be connected.

*RJ-11 connectors are the familiar plugs and sockets used for telephone connections. **RJ-45** is a similar system used in twisted pair LANs. The numbers refer to the standard that defines the exact shape and size of the plugs and sockets to ensure that an RJ-11 plug will fit into an RJ-11 socket anywhere in the world.*

Another very important standard in networks is **RS232** that defines the signals between a computer and a modem. The full RS232 standard defines 25 different lines but in practice only 9 are normally needed for computer to modem connections. RS232 is an American Standard; the European equivalent is **V.24**. The connectors used to implement these connections – **DB25**, and **DB9** for the 25 pin and 9 pin versions – are those used for the COM ports of a PC.

Coaxial cables use a system of connectors called **BNC**. Computers are often connected to LANs with BNC T connectors.

A **network interface card** (**NIC**) is a printed circuit board (PCB), sometimes called a LAN card, which is added to a PC to allow it to access the LAN. The type of board depends on the technology used on the LAN. The board has a socket on the back into which a cable with connectors such as an RJ-45 or BNC is plugged.

It is important to ensure that the NIC does not conflict with any other boards, such as a sound card, and sometimes it is necessary to make changes to the **IRQ** (**interrupt request queue**) settings on the NIC. This is done either by means of switches on older NICs or by software on most modern NICs. The documentation provided by the NIC manufacturer will explain exactly what to do.

Workstations normally use the disk resources of the file server. A variety of different types of workstation may be attached to a LAN with differing facilities, according to the needs of individual users. There are two main types:

NETWORKS AND THEIR USES

- **Intelligent terminals**: workstations that carry out all their own processing
- **Dumb terminals**: workstations in networks where all the processing is carried out by the servers

In networks today, workstations can usually work in either mode depending on whether the processing being carried out needs to be centralised on the server – such as processing data on shared database systems – or processing data for an individual user, such as word-processing a letter.

The **file server** holds software required by the workstations, including the Network Operating System. Files are downloaded from the server to the workstation and uploaded from workstation to server. Because of the heavy demands made on the file server, it usually has a fast processor, a large RAM and several high capacity disk drives. The file server will also usually include a **backup device**, such as a **tape streamer**, so that disks can be regularly backed up to protect workstation users against the loss of their files. File servers are usually located in a separate room from the workstations so that physical security can be maintained.

Many networks today use several file servers to share the workload of the network; one server is the controlling system and manages users logging on to the system, while another may be used to handle e-mails, and another the company's Intranet, and so on. This also improves the chances of the workstations continuing to work should one server break down, although some services may be lost.

The **print server** has one or more printers attached and provides a printing service to workstations. The print server maintains queues of print requests. Normally these are serviced on the basis of first in, first out (FIFO), but the network manager (or another authorised user) can decide to put important work to the head of the queue and to cancel print requests which are no longer required.

Activity 9.2

Working in small groups, identify any networks in use in your school or college.

★ Make notes on what equipment is involved: the type of equipment, make and model.
★ Find out what cabling and connectors are used.
★ Compare your findings with others in your class.

Network topologies

Topology is the way in which the various points (or nodes) in the network are connected to each other; it is the 'shape' of the network.

This section looks at the three main network topologies, as shown in Figures 9.2 to 9.5:

- Bus
- Ring
- Star

In a **bus network**, all the nodes of the network are connected to a single cable (Figure 9.2). A bus network can also have branches (Figure 9.3).

> **Ethernet** is a type of bus network that uses **coaxial cable**. Thick ethernet operates at a speed of 10 million bits per second (Mbps). Each segment of the network can be up to 500 metres long and this system is known as **10base5**. Thin ethernet operates at 10Mbps with a maximum segment length of 200 metres (**10base2**). Because thin ethernet is cheaper (it is sometimes known as 'cheapernet'!) and is easier to install, it is commonly found in schools and colleges. There is also a version of ethernet that uses twisted pair cabling (10baseT).

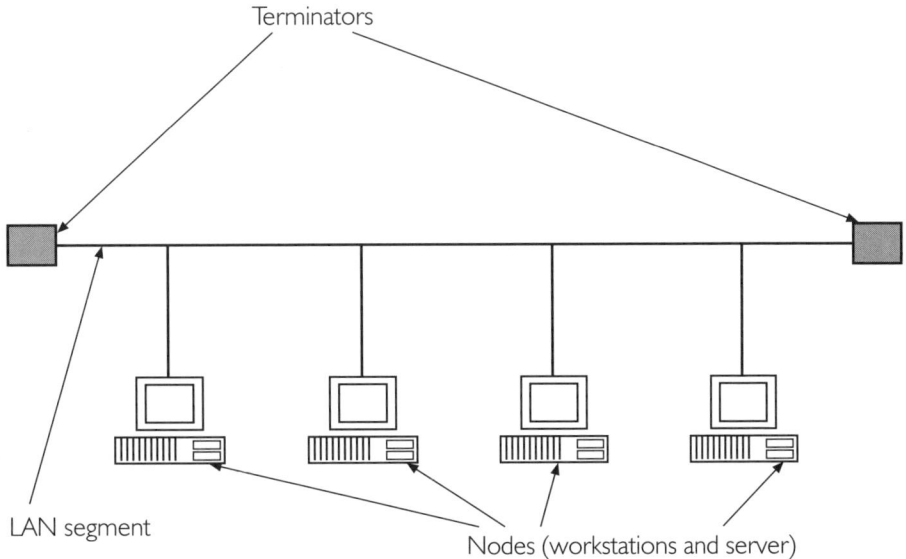

Figure 9.2 *Simple bus network*

Although they are called **ring networks**, these networks are not necessarily circular in shape! You can think of a ring network as a bus network with the ends joined up, and the ring could be any shape it needs to be to join the nodes (Figure 9.4).

NETWORKS AND THEIR USES 283

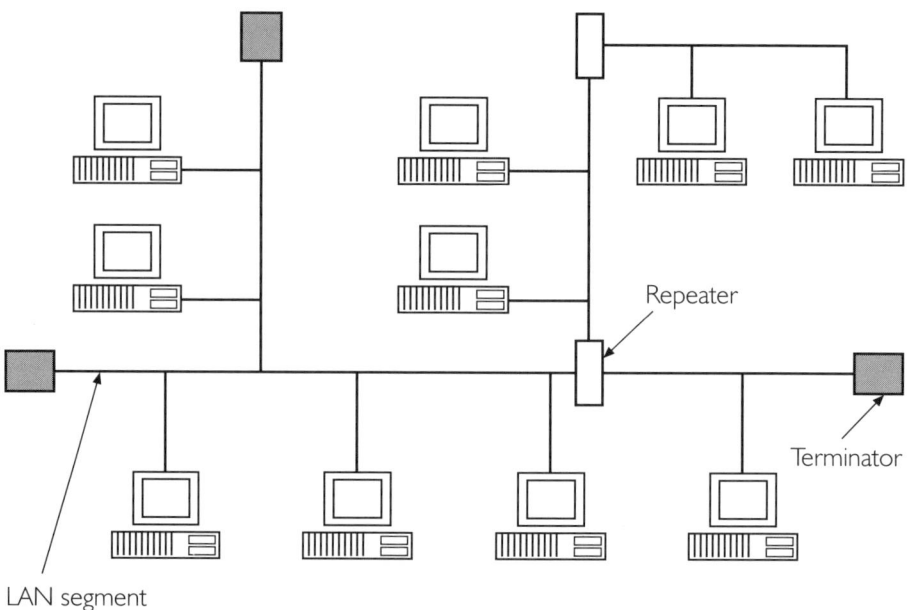

Figure 9.3 *Complex bus network*

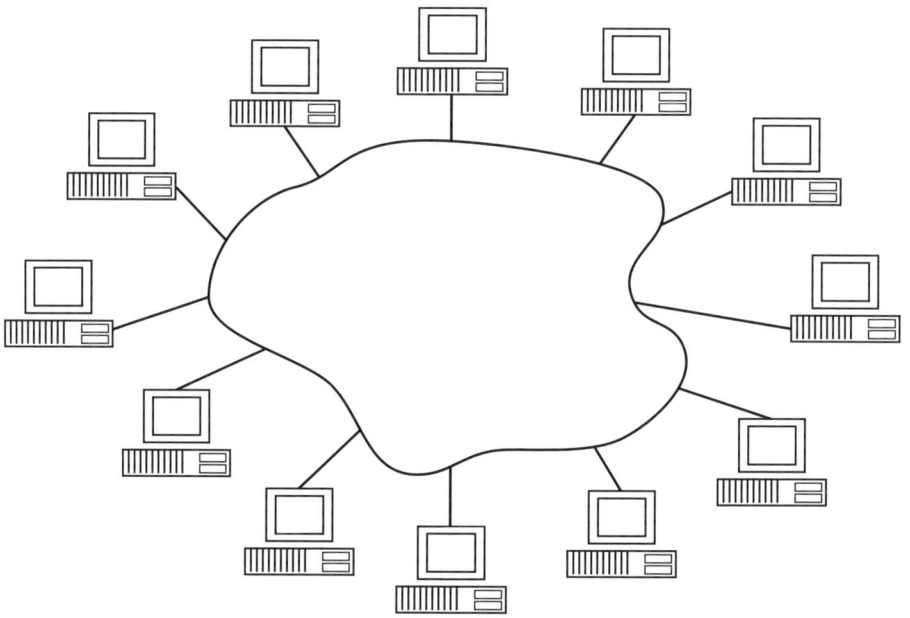

Figure 9.4 *Ring network*

Star networks have one central node with other nodes connected to it (Figure 9.5). Just as a ring network is not necessarily circular a star network is not necessarily star-shaped! It is the method of connection that is important. Early computer networks nearly always used a star topology with a number of terminals connected to one large computer.

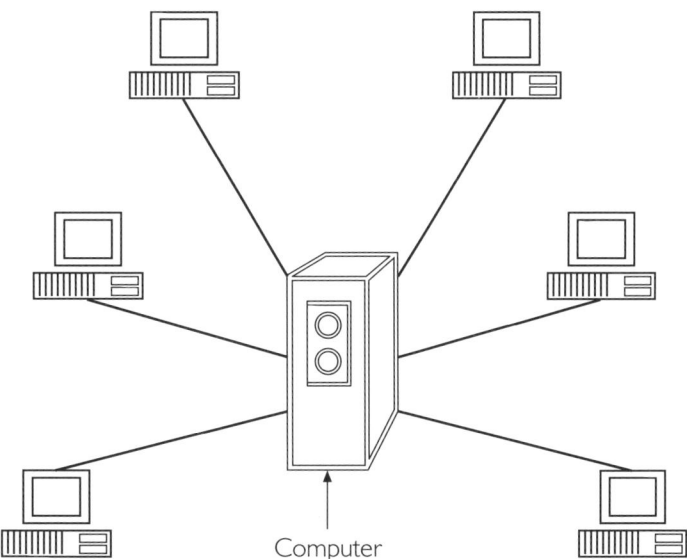

Figure 9.5 *Star network*

Activity 9.3

Working on your own, complete your investigation of the LAN in use at your school or college.

★ Draw a diagram showing the topology and the workstations and servers.

★ Is it a single-segment LAN or does it have other devices to boost the signal to different areas of the buildings?

★ Include information on the type of cabling and connectors used.

Refer back to your notes from Activity 9.2.

Connection methods without cables

Communication is often made without using cabling: **wireless media**. Just as radio can be used to transmit voice signals, it can be used to send data. There are various types of radio transmission:

- Broadcast radio
- Microwave
- Satellite communication
- Cellular radio
- Infra red

With **broadcast radio** signals are transmitted in all directions and can be received by anyone with a suitable receiver. Data transmission rates with broadcast radio are generally low and there are obvious problems of privacy and security, so it is not widely used.

Exercise 9.2

Think of two examples where broadcast radio might be used.

Microwave is a form of high frequency radio that can be used to achieve very high data transmission rates. It can be focused into beams and transmitted between special receiving dishes. Microwaves can only travel in straight lines and are blocked by buildings, hills and the curvature of the earth. To travel long distances, microwave signals must be relayed between transmitters that are within line-of-sight of each other (Figure 9.6).

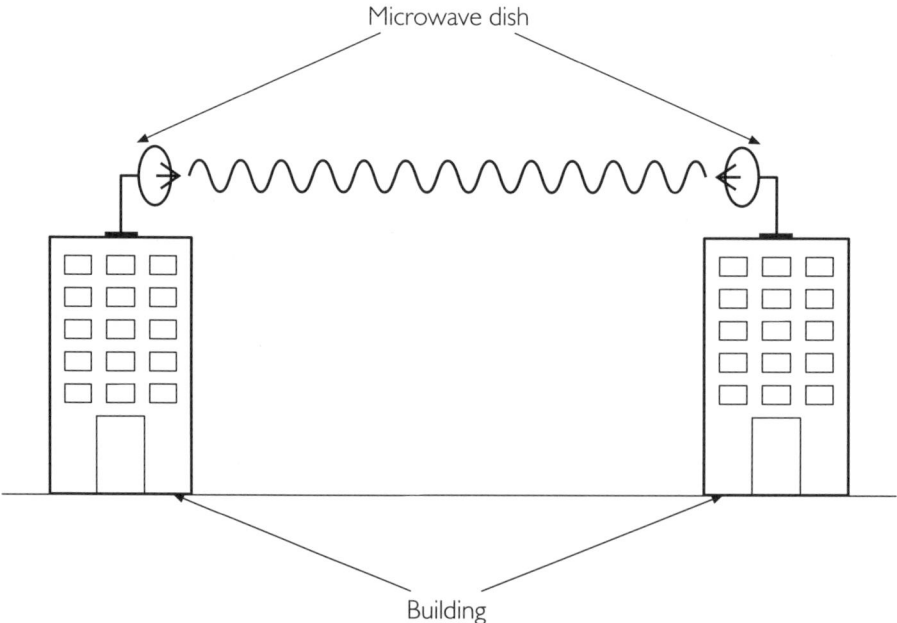

Figure 9.6 *Microwave transmission*

> ### Exercise 9.3
>
> Think of two examples where microwave transfer might be used.

Did You Know?

Communications satellites are in orbits 22,300 miles above the equator. At this height, they circle the Earth once every 24 hours, but as the Earth itself is also revolving once every 24 hours, the satellites are *geostationary*.

▼▼▼▼▼▼▼▼▼▼
Geostationary
remaining in the same position in the sky when viewed from the Earth.
▲▲▲▲▲▲▲▲▲▲

Satellite communication is often used for long distance communications. Signals are sent from earth stations to a satellite and relayed back to another earth station that may be thousands of miles away (Figure 9.7). Because the satellites are geostationary, the receiving dishes on earth can be pointed at a particular satellite and do not have to be moved. Satellite communications uses high frequency radio and can achieve very high data transmission rates.

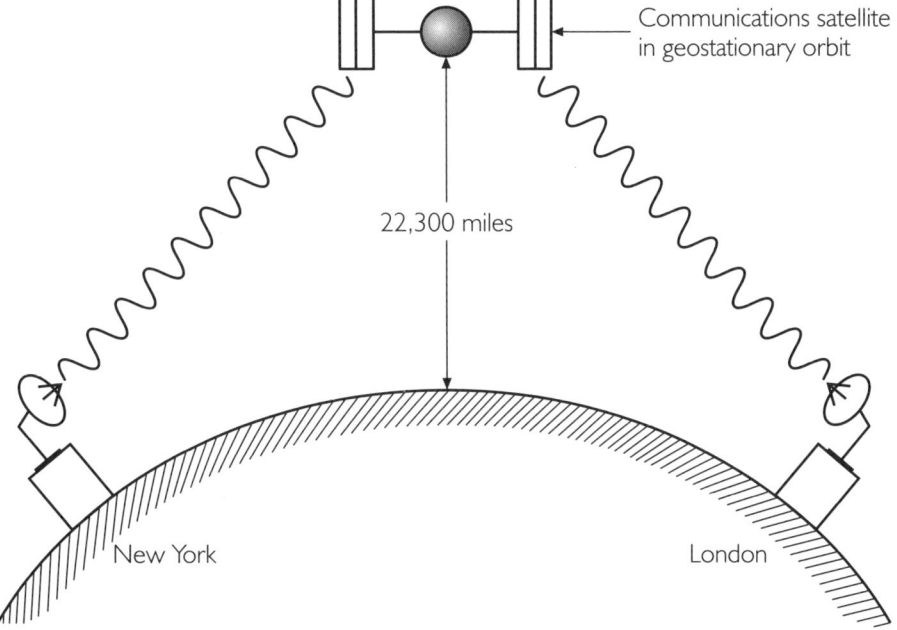

Figure 9.7 *Communications satellites*

Did You Know?

The cellular phone system can be used in the same way as the normal phone system to transmit data as well as voice.

Cellular radio has been developed over the last few years to enable the introduction of mobile telephones. With large numbers of users, it would be impossible to allocate individual radio frequencies to each phone so, with a cellular radio system, the country is divided into a number of geographical areas called **cells.** These vary in size according to the number of mobile phone users in the area. In cities, the cells are small; in rural areas they can be much larger. Within each cell, the phones can each operate on a different frequency so that privacy and security is maintained. Cells in adjacent areas use different sets of frequencies, so when a user moves from one cell to another, the transmission is automatically switched to a new frequency. Non-adjacent cells can use the same set of frequencies. The system keeps track of which cell a particular phone is in, so calls can be routed to the appropriate cell.

> **Activity 9.4**
>
> Working in small groups, investigate the coverage of mobile phones across the UK.
>
> ★ Try to find out which companies offer the best coverage.
>
> ★ Find out if there is any opposition to the placement of equipment needed to improve coverage.

Infra red is a form of light which is invisible to the human eye but can be used in the same way as laser beams to carry data. It is used in TV remote controls but can also be used to communicate between computers or between a computer and a printer over a short distance. Just like the TV remote control, the signal needs a clear 'line of sight' between the sender and the receiver.

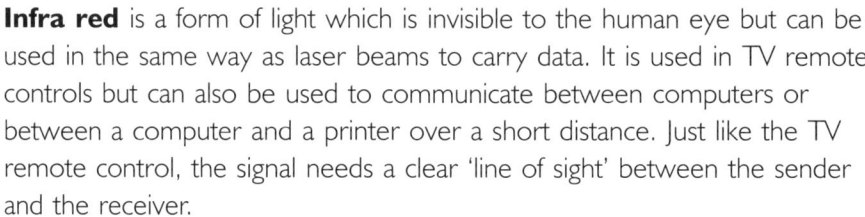

Exercise 9.4

Think of two examples where infra red communications might be used.

Advantages and disadvantages of using networks

There are many advantages of using networks:

- Shared access to centrally held data
- Shared hardware
- Shared software
- Centralised control of data, hardware and software

In any organisation, data is an important resource. Data often needs to be shared by many users but this use must be carefully controlled.

With standalone computers, data can only be shared by transferring copies on diskettes. This can lead to many different versions of files being used in an organisation.

With a LAN, shared or common data, such as a company's customer files can be held centrally on a file server.

Although PCs are now widespread, and prices continue to fall, it is often still necessary to share expensive items of equipment, such as printers. These shared devices are connected to the LAN via a **server**, which handles requests from network users. For details of **print servers**, see page 282.

> **Did You Know?**
>
> If software is used by many workstations, it is important that software copyright is not infringed and that an appropriate licence is obtained to allow network use of any software package.

In a LAN, software required by a number of users is usually held on a **file server**. This means it only has to be installed once, rather than be loaded on the hard disks of many individual workstations. File servers are generally powerful PCs with a large random access memory (RAM), and large amount of hard disk space.

Access to data, software and hardware can be more easily controlled and monitored by providing users with a **user ID** and **password** and setting the **privileges** of each user – such as the **access rights** to different sets of data or whether a user is allowed to use a specific printer or piece of software.

As well as advantages, there are also many disadvantages:

- Slow response times
- Access limitations for shared resources
- Risk of tampering by hackers

> **Did You Know?**
>
> Most network operating systems require a minimum of 1Mb per workstation attached to the server and it is now possible to buy servers with more than one processor.

The file server shares its processing time and memory equally between each user. The more users accessing a file server at the same time, the slower the server will be in handling each request. To overcome this, it is important to have enough RAM. Another solution is to add additional file servers to the network to share the work load.

Sharing printers can cause delays in the production of work due to long documents being printed by a user or by a large number of users sharing the same printer causing long print queues.

Internet access for a company will normally be through one shared line either using a modem or an ISDN line linked to the telephone network. If three or four users access the Internet at the same time, each user will notice a slowing down in the speed at which web pages are downloaded. Many larger companies use leased lines to increase the capacity for Internet access where this is an important part of the company business.

▼▼▼▼▼▼▼▼▼
Hackers
People who spend there time trying to break into networked systems.
▲▲▲▲▲▲▲▲▲

Most **hackers** are harmless and are only doing it to prove they can break a system's security! A few, however do break in to steal data or make alterations to the data.

Richmond-upon-Thames College

Richmond-upon-Thames College is a further education college near London with over 4000 full and part-time students. Like most colleges, it has a big demand from students for access to computers. The network is constantly growing and there are currently over 500 networked computers in all parts of the college. Some are in classrooms; others are in open access areas where students can make use of them outside their normal class times.

The network is also used by administrative staff to maintain records of student enrolments and attendance. Security of data is obviously a key requirement.

The older parts of the network use thin Ethernet cabling but a new building for engineering, computer studies and mathematics, opened in 1996, uses a system of twisted pair cabling. Fibre-optic cables are used for links between the buildings.

The college is connected to the Internet via a service provided by Research Machines Limited (RML), a major supplier of computer systems to education. The connection is via a British Telecom Kilostream leased line.

The network uses Novell Netware as the network operating system and the Media Access Protocol is Ethernet.

Activity 9.5

Find out what legislation exists to deter hackers. Write a report of your findings, or prepare a presentation on the topic.

Try government web sites for information about legislation.

Using a network

Most colleges and schools have their computers connected together to form a LAN, normally in the form of a client–server network. Each student workstation acts as a client and there are one or more server computers which are used to store files, manage printers and perhaps provide access to other networks. The LAN is normally set up by the network manager to make access by students as simple as possible. At the same time, security systems ensure that students only have access to their own files and others that they have been given permission to use. There are a variety of functions when using a LAN, although some of these may only be done by the network manager:

- Accessing allocated workspace with a password
- Creating and modifying the directory-folder structure of nested subdirectories
- Copying, moving, renaming and deleting files or directories
- Displaying directories in different orders
- Locating files
- Creating, editing, saving and printing on a network
- Checking access rights
- Checking for network users
- Setting directory and file access rights to other users (read/write, read only, no access, with/without password)
- Reading from, writing to, and copying files from and to another user's allocated workspace where access is granted

Activity 9.6

Create a log sheet with the list above as entries.

★ During your course, when you do any of the things listed, make notes in the log.

★ Note any special commands that you had to use, and especially about how you overcame any difficulties.

LAN users are each allocated a **user ID** and **password** by the network manager. Each user ID is set up to give its owner the necessary **access rights.** The password (which can be changed by the user) should prevent the user ID being used by any other students.

Exercise 9.5

Do this exercise with a friend. First write down ten passwords that you might choose to use. Do not show each other your lists. Then write down ten passwords that you think the other might use. Then, compare the lists.

How predictable were you, or your friend, in choosing passwords?

What advice could you give to someone when choosing a password?

Did You Know?

The password allocated by the network manager should only be used to initially log on and should then be changed to ensure confidentiality. In general, a password should normally be at least 6 characters in length and should be meaningless to avoid the risk of it being guessed by another user.

In most networks, users are allocated a **directory** on the file server.

The full directory path name may be something like SYS:\students\gnvq99a\gnvq99a013.

For convenience, a path name can be 'mapped' so that it is referred to by a single letter followed by a colon such as F: just like the 'A drive' or the 'C drive' on a standalone computer. Files can then be stored on the 'F drive' just as if it were an extra drive attached to a standalone computer. The 'mapping' is performed by a set of commands called a **login script** that is executed each time a user logs on.

The exact process of logging on may vary between networks, but the example in Figure 9.8 shows a typical login screen. This screen appears automatically after the workstation is switched on or reset.

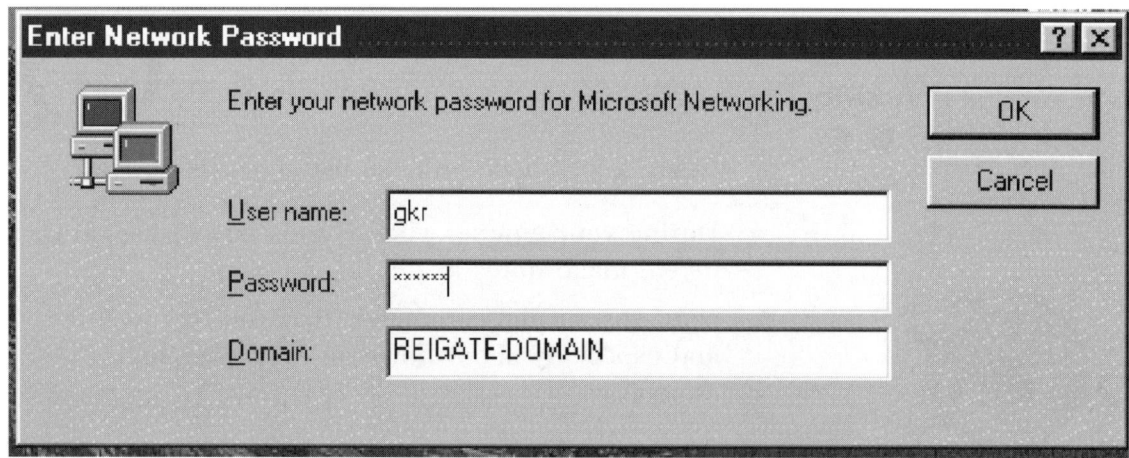

Figure 9.8 *Network login screen*

Activity 9.7

Go through the process of logging on to your workstation.

★ Make notes of every step, so that someone new could follow them.

★ Ask a friend to follow your instructions 'to the letter' to see how well you have explained the process.

★ Amend your instructions in the light of any comments received from your friend.

Creating and modifying the **directory (folder) structure** of nested subdirectories would normally be carried out using a program such as Windows Explorer. New directories (folders) can be added from the 'File' menu using the 'New Add Folder' command. It is important to think about the structure of your nested subdirectories before creating them. You will already have a main directory set up for you by the network manager at your school or college. To prevent confusion between different files saved in that directory, you should create subdirectories for each subject you study, e.g. for GNVQ IT, and then, inside this subdirectory, create further directories for each unit you study. Figure 9.9 shows Windows Explorer being used to create a new directory on a drive (C:).

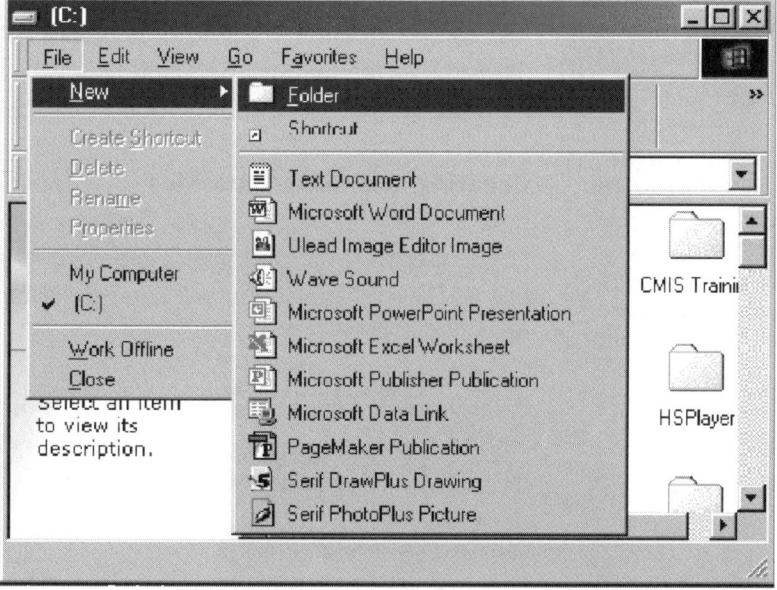

Figure 9.9 *Windows Explorer used to create a new directory*

Renaming (Figure 9.10) or **deleting** files can be done via the 'File' menu, and copying and moving files is done via the 'Copy', 'Cut' and 'Paste' functions on the Edit menu. As far as the user is concerned, these operations are done in exactly the same way for files on a file server, as they would be for files on the C drive (the hard disk) of the workstation.

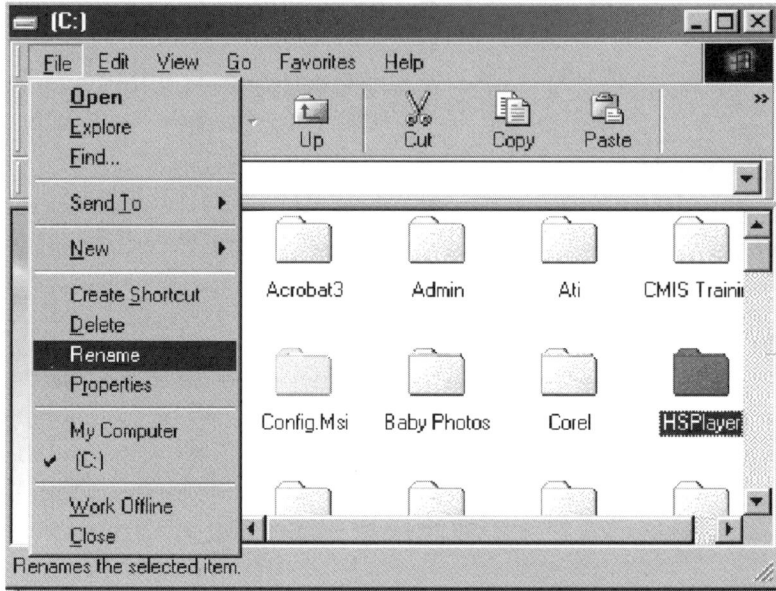

Figure 9.10 *Windows Explorer being used to rename a file*

Directories can be displayed in different ways. Options are set by using the View drop down menu and selecting List display option and then the order can be shown in any of the following orders – name, type, date or size.

> **Did You Know?**
>
> Even if you can only partly remember a file name or a piece of text, if you type 'net', all the files with these letters in would be found, e.g. 'network' and 'Internet'.

Files can be located using Find on the Start menu in Windows. As well as the name of the file, you will need to set the drive if the file is stored on the network and put a tick in the Include subfolders box.

Creating and using data files on a network is the same as using the C: drive or the A: drive. When you first save a file you need to locate your home directory with the drive letter set by the network manager. Later, to edit and save changes, you will need to locate the file again on the network drive in the same way.

Printing will be sent to a default printer for the workstation you are on. If you wish to change the printer, you can do so by using File Print and, from the drop down list of printer names available to you, by selecting the required printer.

You can check **access rights** on any directory by testing whether you can read and write files on the directory.

A network manager needs to be able to tell who is logged on to a network. This can be done from a server through the server tools for viewing properties of a server. Some networks allow users to have a similar option on their workstation but usually this is not available as it can lead to a breach in security.

Most network systems allow the network manager to set file and directory rights so that specific files and directories may be accessible by only one user or shared by a number of users.

Did You Know?

In schools and colleges, often, staff can access students' network files but students should not be able to access staff files!

Shared directories (often called **pools**) may be set up for groups of students. Staff can then distribute information to students via the pool. Staff have full access rights but students only have the ability to read and copy the information.

Further restrictions may be made to files by setting a **password** on a file when it is saved the first time or added later.

Exercise 9.6

Find out what options are available as access rights on the network that you use.

Did You Know?

Access rights can be set on individual files in Microsoft Office 2000 when saving for the first time through the Tools menu and then choosing General Options.

Once access has been granted to another user's workspace it may be used in exactly the same way as a user's private file or directory, subject to the access rights which have been granted.

Network security

The widespread use of networks brings with it the risk of security violations. Valuable information can be lost if unauthorised users are able to access an organisation's computers. This is a growing problem; every week there are new cases of computer hackers accessing supposedly secure systems, and of the havoc caused by computer **viruses**.

Activity 9.8

Investigate the market for virus protection software. Produce a table showing at least four different software products, their price and what facilities they offer in the way of virus protection.

Security methods

To protect against unauthorised access organisations employ a number of different techniques:

- Access is **restricted by logical means** through the use of user IDs and passwords. Users may have different access rights so that they can only have access to data they need to do their job.

- Access to computer systems can be **restricted by physical means** so that only authorised personnel can use the systems.

  Access can be restricted by some kind of pass system, with perhaps magnetic stripe cards to open doors. Workstations can be built with locks that need a key for them to work.

- **Virus checking software** should be used to detect and remove viruses before they can cause damage. This will usually be managed centrally with regular updates being automatically upgraded on workstations when a user next logs on to it after the update has been carried out on the server.

- Every network system needs a good **backup and recovery system**. Backing up of files on the file server may be done by the user copying to a diskette. Alternatively, backups may be left to the network manager who will regularly copy the disks of the file server on to a backup device, e.g. a tape streamer. The network manager should test the recovery system regularly to ensure tapes hold the data correctly, and replace old and faulty tapes.

Applying just one or two methods of network security may not be enough to prevent illegal access and loss of data. A combination of all methods and the careful monitoring of event logs and system messages is necessary to keep data as secure as possible from illegal tampering or loss of data.

Sophos virus checking software also detects software that is used by computer hackers to break the security of a computer system.

Activity 9.9

Working in small groups, summarise the protection methods in place at your school or college. Discuss 'gaps' in the security and produce a report outlining suggested improvements.

Role of the network manager

Networks do not look after themselves, so most organisations employ a network manager to ensure an efficient secure and safe service is provided to the users. The network manager has many responsibilities:

- Ensuring that the network is correctly designed and installed to meet the requirements of the users

- Adding users and groups allocating their **user ID** code and **password**

- Configuring the **file servers** and **print servers** so that users have access to the facilities such as disk space that they require and that appropriate **access rights** are set

- Ensuring that regular **backups** are made of files on the file servers

- Monitoring the use of the network by checking for disk space, deleting old files, setting print queues and checking user activities

- Updating **virus checking software**

- Observing **software copyright** and where necessary obtaining multi-user software licences

Did You Know?

Backups are usually stored on another site so that, in the event of a disaster such as a fire or explosion, essential data is not irretrievably lost.

Activity 9.10

Find out more about the day-to-day work of a network manager, so that you can produce a job specification for the post of network manager.

★ Prepare a questionnaire for your network manager so that you can find out more about his/her job functions.

★ Interview the network manager and ask questions from your questionnaire.

★ Make notes during the interview, to help you in the preparation of the job specification.

★ Ask the network manager to comment on how realistic your job specification is.

Network services and electronic communication systems

Modem
is a device that allows the normal voice telephone network to be used to transmit data.

To gain access to network services, a **modem** may be required, or alternatively a digital service such as **ISDN** may be used.

Network services

The technology of data communications allows the PC user to gain access to many different network services:

- Electronic mail (e-mail)
- File transfer
- On-line databases, e.g. Internet search
- Bulletin boards (or forums)
- Conferencing

E-mail allows a letter or other message to be prepared on a PC and then, rather than printing the letter and sending it through the normal mail service, it can be transmitted electronically to the computer of the recipient. The message can be read on the screen and, if necessary, printed on a local printer. e-mail may be sent between users on a LAN or via a WAN using a commercial service which provides electronic mail boxes for subscribers. Nowadays, e-mail is more usually sent via the Internet. Everyone connected to the Internet has a unique address and can send and receive mail to and from millions of people, worldwide. E-mail can arrive on the other side of the world in seconds and has the potential to replace the conventional mail system which e-mailers now refer to as 'snail mail'.

Did You Know?

Some companies offer free e-mail services. One of the most popular is *hotmail* run by Microsoft. One of the big advantages of these services is that they may be accessed by anyone with Internet access, via any Internet Service Provider. An e-mail address can be obtained by accessing the hotmail web site at www.hotmail.com.

Activity 9.11

Collect evidence of e-mail correspondence that you have made. Annotate the printouts to show features of your e-mail software.

Electronic communication is often used for **file transfer** between computers. All electronic communications is subject to occasional transmission errors; this can be caused by electrical interference so when transferring large files, the probability of an error increases. A file such as a program is useless if even one bit is changed so file transfer software must have good error detection and correction capabilities.

File compression software such as WINZIP or PKZIP may also be used to reduce the amount of data and the transmission time. The receiver of the file must then decompress the file before using it. Of course, it is important to check for the presence of computer viruses in any files transferred from other computers.

Files can also be transferred as **e-mail attachments**. This means that you can e-mail photographs taken with a digital camera or documents which have been scanned. You can even send digitised voice messages, music or video clips.

Just as you can copy files from a diskette to a hard disk on your own computer, using the Internet and File Transfer Protocol (FTP) it is possible to

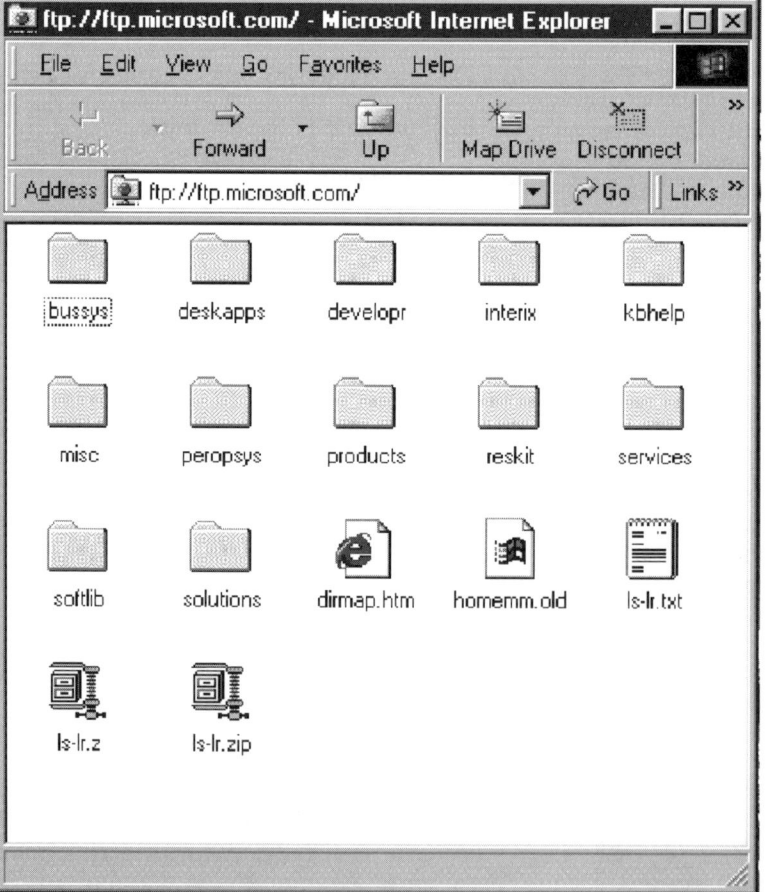

Figure 9.11 *Microsoft FTP directories*

copy files from a hard disk on a computer on the other side of the world and it is almost as simple. FTP is the system that lets you do this and many organisations have set up directories on their systems from which FTP users can list and copy files at will. To see files available from Microsoft, type the address ftp://ftp.microsoft.com (Figure 9.11). Of course, FTP users must know what they are looking for; it can prove easier to find the files via a search engine and then to use the download facility of the web browser.

With little or no technical knowledge, you can explore the web following hypertext links between documents. This is popularly known as **surfing the net**. It can be fun but can also waste a lot of time. If you are looking for something specific, you can use a **search engine** which allows you to input key words to find the information you need. A popular search engine is called **Yahoo** and its home page is shown in Figure 9.12.

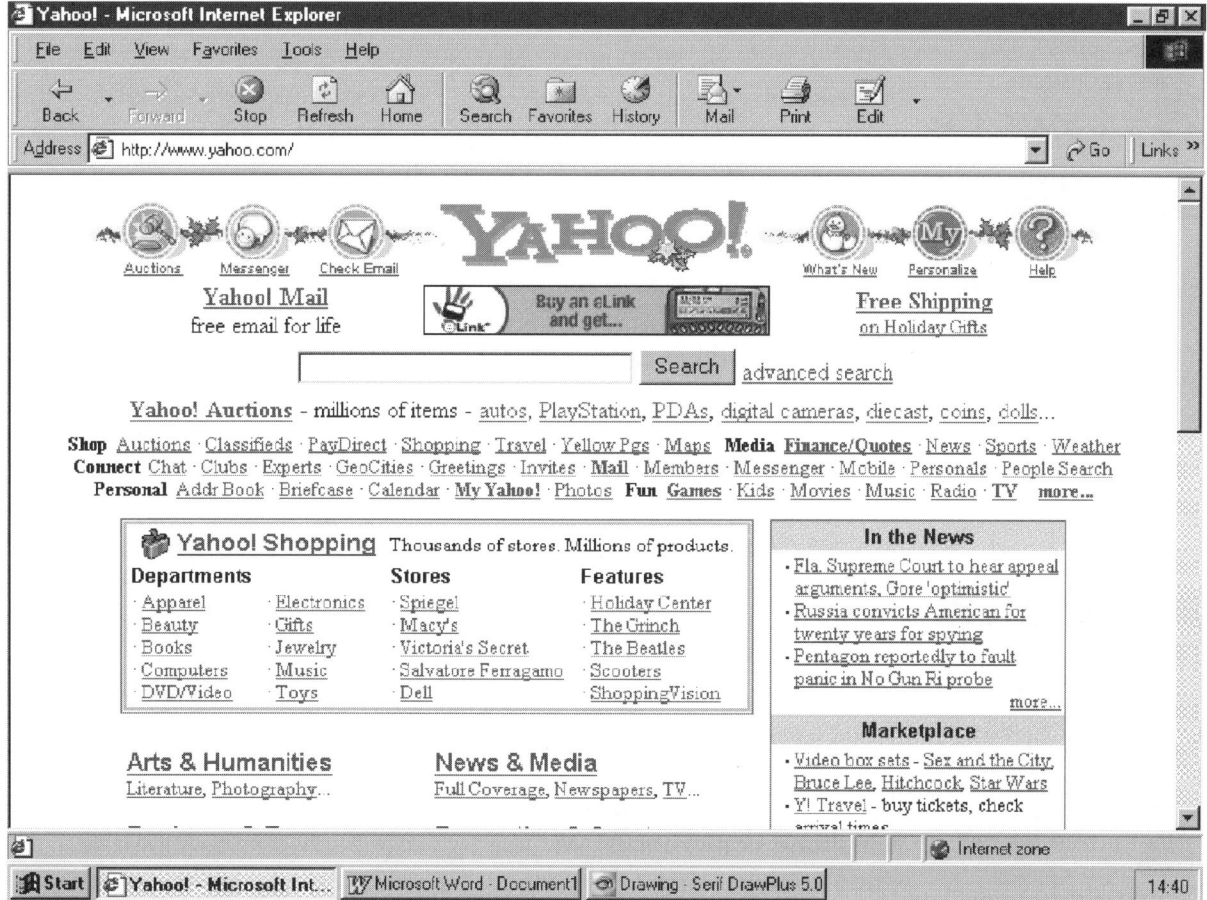

Figure 9.12 *Yahoo*

Activity 9.12

Try out a number of different search engines and compare the results you get from each of them.

★ Are they all equally user-friendly?
★ How do their speeds compare?
★ Compare your results with others in your group.
★ Write hints for someone who has not surfed on the net before.

▼▼▼▼▼▼▼▼▼

Forum is a gathering of people with a particular interest.

▲▲▲▲▲▲▲▲▲

Did You Know?

The term 'forum' originally referred to the forum in Rome, a market square where in ancient times people gathered to exchange ideas and do business.

Did You Know?

The technology of **video conferencing** is advancing rapidly. It is now possible to buy a small video camera that fits on the top of a PC to implement a very low-cost video conferencing system.

People with a common interest or hobby can exchange information or ideas via **electronic bulletin boards.** Users can post information to be read by others who share their interest. Before the Internet became widely available, bulletin boards were set up on computers which could be accessed directly by means of a dial-up connection using a modem. Telephone numbers of the bulletin boards were published in magazines. Nowadays this type of bulletin board has largely been replaced by web sites.

In the electronic age, people all over the world can 'meet' others with similar interests without leaving home. Scientists, in particular, make a great use of electronic fora (plural of forum) and there is no doubt that the use of computer networks has done much to speed up the pace of scientific progress.

It is now possible for a number of computers to be connected together so that messages may be sent and read by a number of users who wish to discuss a particular subject. They form an **electronic conference**. This type of communication is used extensively by researchers in universities who want to collaborate with colleagues worldwide via the Internet.

*So called 'chat lines' on the Internet are another example of **conferencing** and also an easy way to waste lots of time!*

Companies can avoid the need for expensive travel to meetings by holding **telephone conferences**. With the high speed networks now available, **video conferencing**, where the participants can see each other on screens, is also possible.

302   9 NETWORKS AND COMMUNICATIONS

Setting up an electronic communication system

To **set up a workstation** with a modem to a telephone line, you require a computer with a modem and connecting cables, disks for setting up the modem and a disk from an Internet service provider (ISP).

▼▼▼▼▼▼▼▼▼
Internal modem
is a card inside the computer.
▲▲▲▲▲▲▲▲▲

If you have an **internal modem** you only need to connect it to the telephone line using a cable with an RJ-11 connector. If the modem is external then you need to plug the DB9 connector from the modem into one of the COM ports on the back of the computer. You should then be ready to turn the computer on. See Figure 9.13.

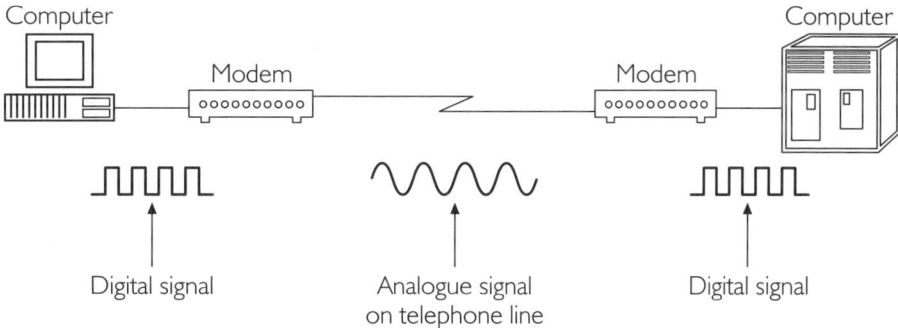

Figure 9.13 *Computers connected by modems*

When the modem is first installed you need to run the set up program from the appropriate disk following the instructions provided for the modem. You should have information ready such as telephone numbers and **modem speed of transfer**. Often this, and other **protocols**, are set automatically for you. Once the modem is set up, the ISP disk can be run, and you will need to provide a user ID and password. Running this disk should establish your link to the Internet. For future access, you should only need to open your Internet browser or your e-mail software.

Activity 9.13

On a computer with a modem installed, go to the control panel and double click on the modem icon. Click on the properties button for the modem and make a note of the protocols/settings.

> **Did You Know?**
>
> For short distances (up to 10 metres), it is possible to connect two computers without involving modems, telephone lines or NICs. This is easily done with a **null modem** cable between the COM ports. The wiring of the cable makes the signals appear as if the computer were connected to a modem and so communications software designed for use with modems can be used for communications between computers over a short distance. A null modem cable is particularly useful for connecting a laptop to a desktop computer to transfer files and software such as Laplink has been developed to make this process very simple.

To **add a workstation to a network**, you require a computer with a network card, a cable with either RJ-45 connectors or BNC Connectors, Windows operating system CD-ROM plus information about the domain name used on the network and the protocols used for communication handling. If the default settings for the protocols are not used, you also need to know what these changes are. **Communications protocols** can be quite complex, as they have to define the rules for every possible situation. These are some of the most important protocols you may come across in setting up a workstation.

- NETBIOS – Network basic input/output system
- TCP/IP – Transmission control protocol/internet protocol
- IPX/SPX – Internet packet exchange/sequenced packet exchange
- NetBEUI – NetBIOS extended user interface

The **domain name** is an identifier for all workstations and servers that have potential access to all the same facilities.

First, connect the computer to the network using the cable. Then, turn on the computer. You then need to access network set up options through the control panel to add a network client and choose the necessary protocols. When adding the network client option, you are asked for a computer name and workgroup or domain name. There is also a checkbox that should be set to enforce checking (**verification**) that users log on as a valid network user. When the system restarts, the login screen should appear with the correct domain name.

Sending and receiving e-mail is done by accessing an e-mail application on the server. The user needs to know the e-mail addresses of people to whom mail is to be sent. If the recipient of the mail is a user of the LAN, the e-mail address may be the same user ID but if the recipient is external to the LAN, the mail will be sent via the Internet and the e-mail address may be of the form jsmith@btinternet.com where the name after the @ is their internet service provider.

Figure 9.14 shows the options available in a popular e-mail application called Outlook Express. A number of other e-mail applications are available, all having similar features.

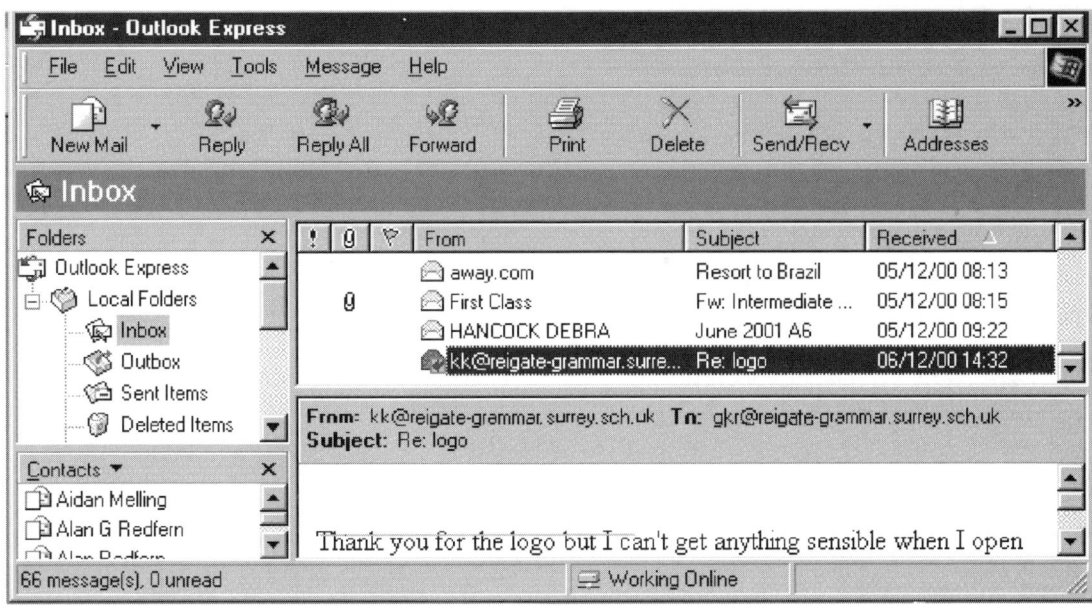

Figure 9.14 *Outlook Express mail Inbox*

> **Did You Know?**
>
> In 2000, a virus called The Love Bug spread throughout the Internet and brought many companies' e-mail systems to a halt. It worked by examining users' e-mail address books and sending e-mails to all the addressees. The person responsible for creating this virus has been caught and is awaiting prosecution in Indonesia.

As well as the ability to send, receive and reply to e-mail an e-mail application offers several other facilities:

- To send and receive attachments
- To maintain an e-mail address book
- To handle distribution lists
- To file e-mail appropriately

When using e-mail it is particularly important to ensure that any files received as e-mail attachments are checked for viruses, especially if they are executable programs (.EXE files).

Revision questions

1. State six possible benefits of the use of a network over the use of standalone computers.

2. State four possible disadvantages of using a network.

3. Why are client–server networks more common than peer-to-peer networks?

4. What is a NIC?

5. What is the main difference between a LAN and WAN?

6. State four different types of service that may be obtained on a network?

7. What is the function of an ISP?

8. What is the function of a web browser?

9. Name two popular web browsers.

10. Why might optical fibre be a suitable medium for a LAN in a car factory, which uses a lot of electrical equipment?

11. State three of the main responsibilities of a network manager.

12. What type of connector is used with twisted pair cabling?

Programming

10

- **Explore the software used to create programs**
- **Write and test programs in ways that other people can understand**
- **Write guidance for people who will use your programs**
- **Investigate what makes a well-written program**

This chapter covers five topics:

- The components of a computer program
- Program development
- Use of programming languages
- Testing programs
- Documentation

There are many different application programs available: games, word-processors, databases, etc. These application programs contain many different functions and some users may never require a specially written program. However, there are cases where users need capabilities and functions which are not present in an existing application program. In these circumstances, the user must either write a program (or programs) to provide the function or have the program written for them. In your future career as an IT professional, one area you may become involved in is writing programs to meet users requirements. Modern computer programs are complex and you need to understand how to design and write programs and what components go together to make a program.

To help you to understand the theory of computer programming, some simple example programs written in the BASIC programming languages will be used. Later in the chapter, a complete program development case study is described using the modern Windows version of the BASIC programming language, Visual Basic.

BASIC stands for beginners all-purpose symbolic instruction code.

A program is a set of instructions which tells a computer what to do. Programs are what makes computers so powerful. Unlike a calculator or a typewriter which has only a limited set of functions built into it, a computer is a general purpose device which can perform an unlimited range of different functions. All you need to do is to write the program to provide the required function!

The microprocessor at the heart of a computer can only understand instructions in the form of binary codes. Programs created using binary codes alone would be very difficult for humans to understand, so all modern programming is done using **symbolic languages**, with English-like statements being used to represent the binary codes.

Most computer programs work by accepting some kind of **input** from the user of the program, **processing** it in some way and producing some kind of **output**.

> Look at the Windows calculator in Figure 10.1. The user clicks on the buttons to **input** the numbers and what you want to do with them (add, subtract, etc.), when the user clicks the = button the calculator program does some **processing** and displays the result, which is the **output**.

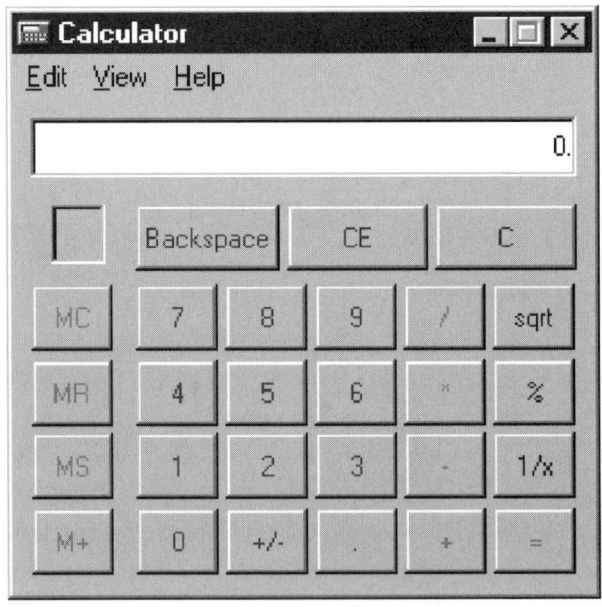

Figure 10.1 *The Windows calculator*

Program development

It is important to remember that, in most cases, professional programmers are writing a program for someone else to use. Before any programming code is written, it is important to understand what the user requires.

A programmer that works for a bank may be asked to write a program for the cashiers who work on the front desks. They need to look up customer details on their computer screens and check information like loan repayment figures while the customer waits. In this type of situation, it is important the programmer is aware of exactly what the cashier needs. It is also important to remember that while the programmer is presumably an expert in computer programming, s/he may know rather less about how a bank cashier works. On the other hand, the bank cashier knows all about working on the front desk of a bank but may know little about computers and what they can do.

Unless the programmer and the cashier are able to communicate with each other about what is needed and what is possible, the end result may be a program that does not meet the needs of the user (the cashier).

CASH-IN Bank

The CASH-IN Bank provides, along with its other banking services, a foreign exchange service. This means that customers can exchange their money for foreign currency, e.g. French Francs or Spanish Pesetas. Each currency has a different exchange rate. For example, currently the exchange rate for British Pounds to French Francs is 10.80, so you can exchange £1 for 10.80FF (although rates do change over time -- more about that later). CASH-IN wants to provide its cashiers with a simple currency converter program that will calculate the correct amount of foreign currency they should give a customer.

Modern computer programs are very complex and are often written by a team of people rather than one person. They usually contain a number of different programs that need to work together. For this reason, they need to be carefully planned and designed to make sure they will work properly when they are completed.

The process of creating a computer program has a number of steps called the **program development lifecycle** (Figure 10.2).

- Feasibility study
- Systems analysis and design
- Prototyping
- Programming
- Testing
- Implementation

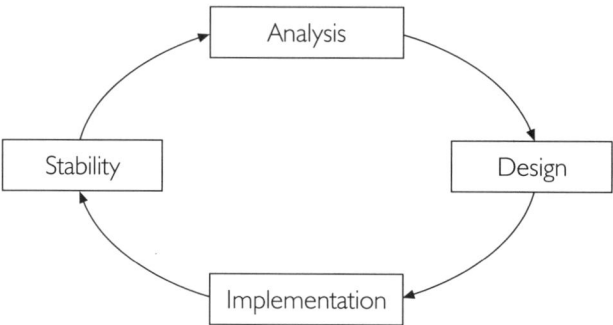

Figure 10.2 *The program development lifecycle*

A **feasibility study** answers a very important question: can the development of the software be justified? In other words: is it technically feasible and economically desirable? The feasibility study begins with a preliminary investigation which involves obtaining some general information:

- The system currently being used, its benefits and limitations
- The additional requirements of the new system

Then, from the information gathered during this preliminary investigation, a report is produced:

- A statement of the purpose of the system
- A definition of system scope
- A list of current deficiencies
- A statement of user requirements
- Cost benefits or limitations of development
- Conclusions and recommendations

The primary source of information for the feasibility study are the users of the current system.

If the feasibility study recommends that the new software be developed, then the process of **systems analysis** is started. This involves several stages:

- The first stage is an **investigation** into how the current system works and what the new system needs to provide. This is basically an extension of the feasibility study, with the systems analyst collecting more detailed information from the users of the existing system.

- **Use of structured analysis tools**: this stage involves using a number of techniques (often utilising diagrams) to model the flow of information and the interrelationships in the system.

- Finally, the systems analyst needs to draw together the information that has been gathered and analysed in the two previous stages into a document called the **systems specification**.

- Using the system specification the detailed **systems design** of individual programs in the system is carried out.

While the previous stage is still underway, **prototypes** of some of the programs may be produced. These are not fully working versions of the program, but are produced to test the theory of the system specification and design, and to give the users a 'taste' of things to come. The point being that if the users do not like what the system designers have in mind, it is easier to change the design at this stage rather than when the complete, fully working programs have been produced. Prototyping can produce programs that are well matched to the user's needs as the user is involved in the design of the program. Prototyping is also an iterative process (based on the user's comments on the first prototype, another one is produced and evaluated by the users and so on) that can continue through the development of the system, with the user's comments on each prototype helping to refine the final system.

CASH-IN Bank

The cashiers at CASH-IN are a bit vague about exactly what they want the program to do, so a series of prototypes will be developed so that the cashiers can help guide the development of the program with their suggestions.

In the **programming** stage, a programmer, or more likely, a team of programmers, write the program instructions (or code) that will make the system work.

Finally there is the **testing**. All programs need to be tested carefully to check that they work properly.

Exercise 10.1

Bugs and viruses sound like similar sorts of things, but they are not. Find out what the difference is between a bug and a virus.

> **Did You Know?**
>
> In one of the first computers, made in the 1940s, an error was caused by an insect caught in the computer. So, errors in programs are called **bugs**, and finding and correcting them is known as **debugging**.

Once the programs in the system have been tested and all the errors and problems ironed out the system needs to be given to the users. This **implementation** stage involves installing the software on their computers, giving the users training in how to use the new software and ironing out any problems which come to light at this stage. It may also include transferring data from the previous system (computerised or manual) that the new system is replacing.

Exercise 10.2

To complete this unit you will need to write some programs. Choose one of the programs you will be writing and plan how long it will take you to complete each stage of the development cycle. When you have completed the development of the program you should return to your plan and compare how long each stage actually took with how long you thought it would take when you created your plan.

Program design techniques

A wide range of program design techniques have been developed over the years to enable programmers to plan how their program will work before they begin writing the actual instructions. Many of these techniques themselves are complex and descriptions of them occupy entire books.

The importance of careful and thorough design cannot be over emphasised.

Imagine if, when building a skyscraper building, the builders just turned up on a bare piece of ground and began digging foundations and laying concrete and bricks as each one of them thought best. The resulting structure would be a chaotic mess. It would probably be dangerous and no one would want to live and work in it.

In the same way that an architect needs to carefully design a building in consultation with the people who are going to use the building, so a program must be carefully planned and designed. There are a wide range of things that need to be considered in the design of a program:

- What will the user interface look like (screens, menus, dialogue boxes, etc.)?

- If the program reads or writes data to files, what format will the files be in, and what fields and data types will be used?

- How can the program be broken down into manageable chunks, called procedures? This often needs to be done so the work can be completed by a team.

- What storage areas (variables) will be needed and what names should be used?

- How will the program flow be controlled? For example, what repeated activities will be needed and what decisions will the program need to make?

The first step in developing a program design is the written description of the program required: the **program specification**. This is developed in conjunction with the eventual users of the program as part of the system analysis process. The purpose of the program specification is to answer some of the questions listed above. The program specification will also contain a description of what processing each program in the system will carry out. To describe that processing, a number of different techniques can be used. Three simple techniques are described here:

- Structure diagrams

- Flowcharts

- Pseudo-code

Structure diagrams provide a general overview of the processing required in the system. As such they are good for understanding the main steps into which the program needs to be broken down. For example, you might use a structure diagram to help you decide how to split your program into different procedures or sections. A structure diagram breaks the processing steps in a system down into three types:

- **Sequence**: processing steps follow on one after another
- **Iteration**: a sequence of steps is repeated, in a loop
- **Selection**: a point at which there is a choice between several processing sequences

> **Did You Know?**
> *Selection* is normally achieved using an IF instruction.

These steps are represented in diagrammatic form using boxes containing the name of the processing step. Figure 10.3 shows a simple structure diagram for a calculator program (the completed program is shown later in Figure 10.5). Notice that the structure diagram shows only sequence processing steps.

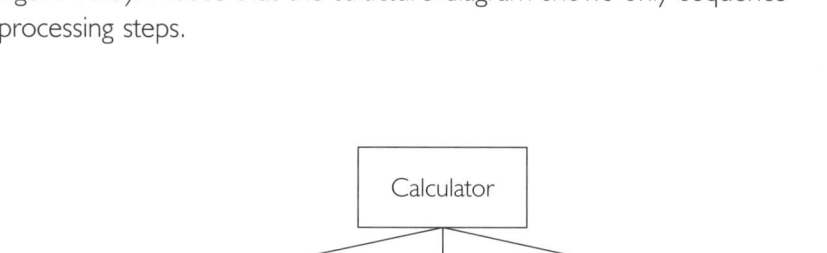

Figure 10.3 *Structure diagram for the calculator program*

However, this only allows for adding numbers. Suppose the program gave the user a choice between adding and subtracting? This is a **selection** processing step, which is shown in a structure diagram by a box with a letter O in the right corner. Figure 10.4 shows the modified structure diagram.

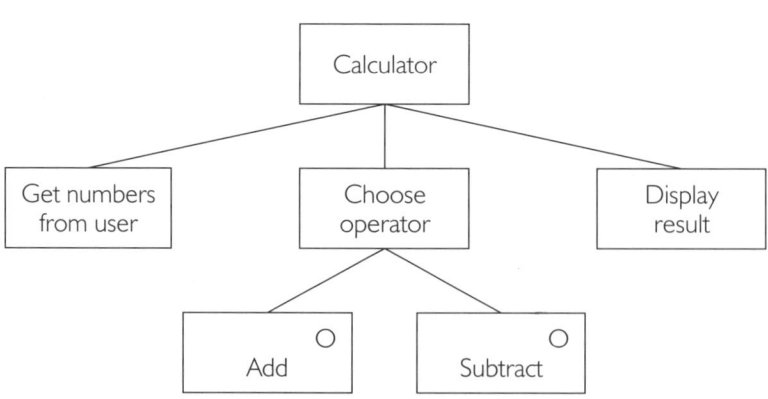

Figure 10.4 *Structure diagram for the calculator program, including selection*

This design only allows for the adding or subtracting of one number. But the user of a calculator may want to repeat the process of adding or subtracting numbers. In a structure diagram this is an **iteration** process. This is shown by a box with an asterisk in the right corner. Figure 10.5 shows the completed structure diagram with the iteration process added.

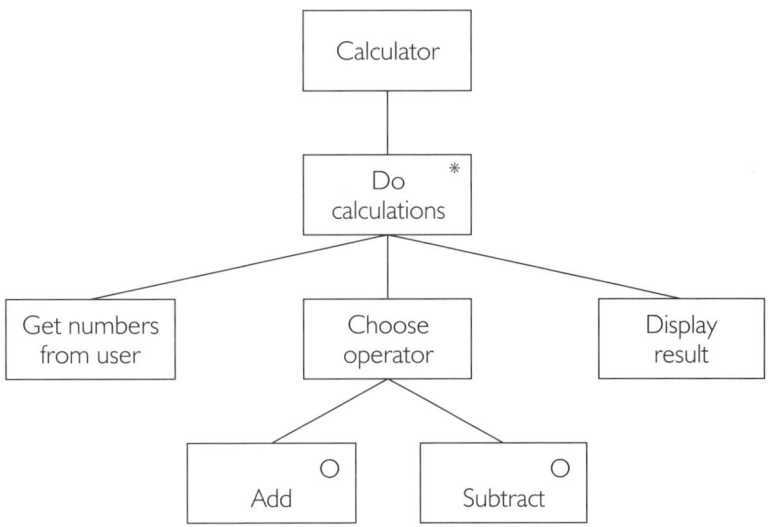

Figure 10.5 *Complete structure diagram for the calculator program*

Structure diagrams are quite simple to draw because they contain very little detail about exactly what processing is involved in each step. For example, in the iteration processing step, no information is given about how the loop is ended. For this reason, they are useful only at the early stages of system design.

Activity 10.1

Develop the structure chart shown in Figure 10.5 to show the processing steps required in a calculator that can divide and multiply as well as add and subtract.

Flow charts are another diagrammatic method that can be useful for designing programs (or indeed other non-programming procedures). They provide more detail than structure diagrams and so can help you to develop a better understanding of what program instructions are needed inside a program or procedure. They break the processing steps down into a series of actions, such as obtaining some input from the user or calculating some value. The flowchart starts with the word Start in a round cornered box, shown in Figure 10.6.

Steps which involve processing are contained in a rectangle; steps which involve input or output are contained within a skewed rectangle (Figure 10.7).

In both cases, steps are linked by arrows. Where a choice or decision needs to be made the text describing the questions being asked is contained in a diamond shape (Figure 10.8), which has two routes out of it. One route represents the route to take if the answer to the questions is 'yes'; the other is the route if the answer is 'no'.

The end of the process is represented by the word 'End' in a round cornered box (Figure 10.9).

Figure 10.6 *Flowchart start box*

Figure 10.7 *Flowchart input/output and processing boxes*

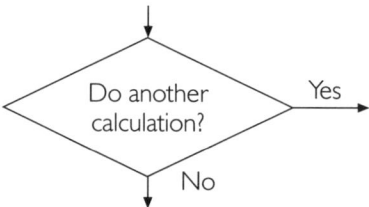

Figure 10.8 *A flowchart decision box*

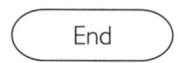

Figure 10.9 *Flowchart end box*

Flowcharts are a good introduction to program design methods. However, they do have a number of limitations. In particular they are not good for complex problems as the flowcharts themselves become too complex to follow. Also they do not always represent the sequence of commands in the actual program very well. Figure 10.10 shows the flowchart for the calculator

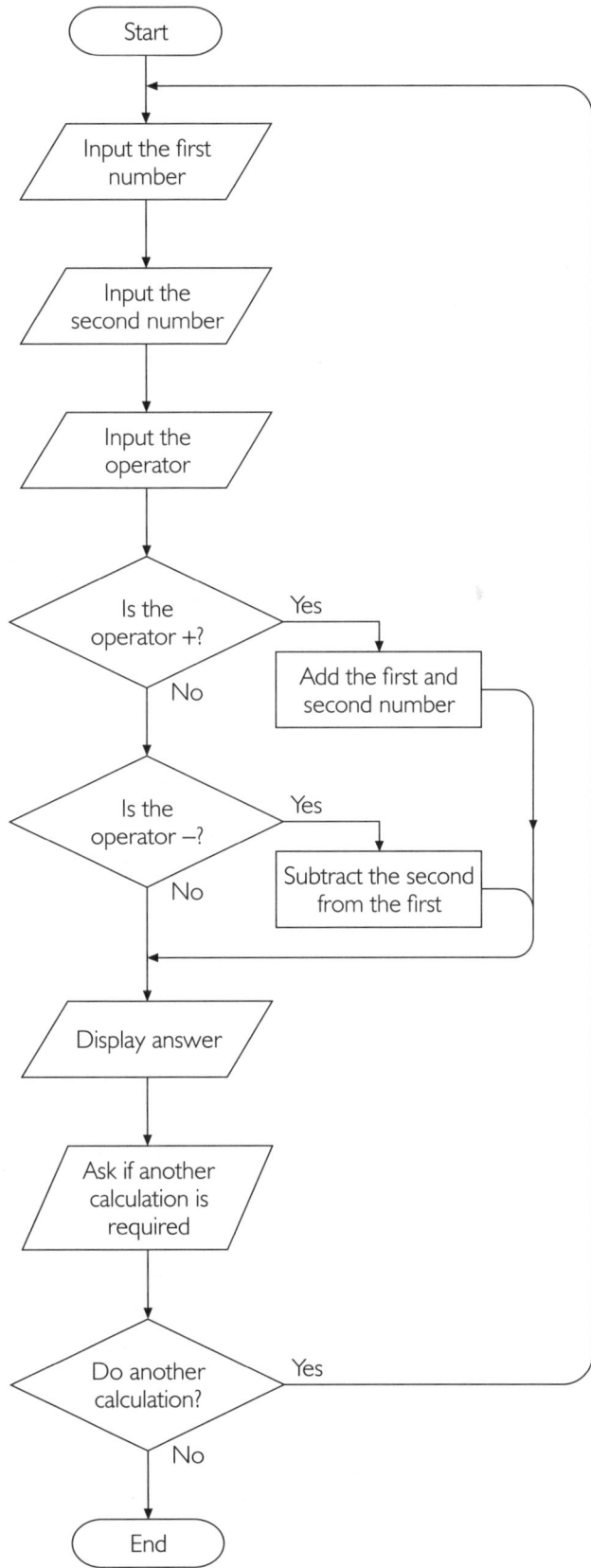

Figure 10.10 *Flowchart for the calculator program*

program and Figure 10.11 shows a simple flowchart to help to clarify the programming steps that will be needed in the currency converter.

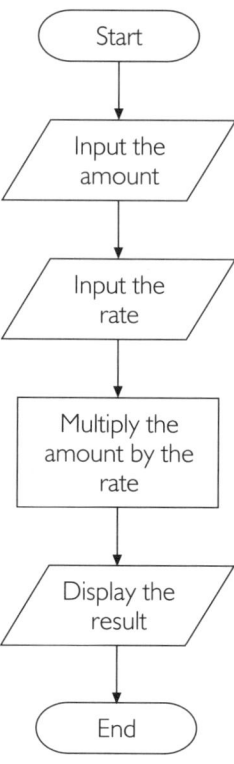

Figure 10.11 *Flowchart for currency converter*

Pseudo-code is a 'half way house' between actual program code and normal spoken English. Unlike flowcharts and structure diagrams, pseudo-code looks very much like the program instructions that will eventually be written. It also describes the program in detail, but too much detail for the early stages of program design. It uses programming-like statements (such as IF . . . THEN . . . ELSE and DO . . . WHILE). It is used to work out the sort of programming instructions required without having to worry about the exact syntax of the language involved. It is sometimes referred to as **structured English**. There are no exact rules on how to use pseudo-code, but you need to use your experience of real programming languages and keep in mind that the result should avoid any ambiguity. Vague statements like 'Process payments file' should be avoided; instead, you should try to identify exactly what processing is required.

Pseudo-code is best used to help in the development of complex programming steps. The simple programs written so far would not require designing using pseudo-code; the BASIC language looks like pseudo-code in any case.

An example of pseudo-code is shown in Figure 10.12. This processing step involves calculating the correct VAT amount, depending on one of three rates, rate 1 is 0%, rate 2 is 5% and rate 3 is 17.5%.

```
Procedure VAT-calc
   If rate = 1 then
      VAT-AMOUNT = 0
   Else if VAT-RATE = 2 then
      VAT-AMOUNT = NET-AMOUNT*5%
   Else if VAT-RATE = 3 then
      VAT-AMOUNT = NET-AMOUNT*17.5%
   End-if
Return
```

Figure 10.12 *Pseudo-code example*

Activity 10.2

Both pseudo-code and flowcharts can be used to analyse non-programming problems, as well as programming ones. Writing pseudo-code for non-programming problems is a good way to practice the technique.

★ Try to write pseudo-code for searching for a book in the library.

★ Ask someone else to test your pseudo-code, and offer to test theirs.

Activity 10.3

Many people enjoy playing computer games and, although some games are very complex indeed, you can design and write some simple computer games yourself.

Imagine a guessing game program: the program is to generate a number between 1 and 10 (called a random number) and then the user can try to guess the number. The program should tell the user if the guess was too high or too low, and allow more guessing until the correct number is found.

★ Draw a sequence diagram for this program.

★ Then go on to create the pseudo-code for it.

★ Ask someone else to test your pseudo-code, and offer to test theirs.

PROGRAM DEVELOPMENT

The components of a computer program

Having looked at how a program is designed, the next section considers how to write the program. A program for the simple calculator for which sequence diagrams and flowcharts have been drawn is now to be written.

Variables

Programs need to store data (information) while they are processing it.

A calculator program needs to store details of which keys are clicked so it knows how to process the data that is input.

This data is stored in the computer's memory. The places in the memory where the data is stored are called **variables**. Variables have names, given by the programmer, so they can be referred to within the program. It is usual to declare (list) the variables that are going to be used at the beginning of the program, and to say what type of data (e.g. text or numeric) will be stored in the variable. Variables also have a **value**, that is the value of the data stored in the variable. Consider this simple example of a variable to store a person's first name:

```
Variable name:   First_name
Type:            Text
Value:           'Alan'
```

The variable's name and data type are declared at the beginning of the program, the value will probably change as the program runs and may depend on things such as user input – hence the name variable (i.e. the value of a variable varies as the program runs).

Figure 10.13 shows an example of a very simple non-Windows calculator program, which will add two numbers. It is written using the BASIC programming language.

```
10 DIM NUMBER1 AS INTEGER
20 DIM NUMBER2 AS INTEGER
30 DIM ANSWER AS INTEGER
40 PRINT "Enter the first number"
50 INPUT NUMBER1
60 PRINT "Enter the second number"
70 INPUT NUMBER2
80 ANSWER = NUMBER1 + NUMBER2
90 PRINT "The answer is "; ANSWER
```

Figure 10.13 *Simple non-Windows calculator program*

Let us analyse the program in detail:

```
10 DIM NUMBER1 AS INTEGER
20 DIM NUMBER2 AS INTEGER
30 DIM ANSWER AS INTEGER
```

▼▼▼▼▼▼▼▼▼

DIM
is short for dimension and determines the 'size' of a variable, i.e. the storage space to be allocated in memory.

▲▲▲▲▲▲▲▲▲

The **DIM instruction** is used to define a variable. AS INTEGER instructs the program to create a variable that will hold integers (whole numbers with no fractional part). So, the first three lines define the three variables that the program uses to store the two numbers that the user types in (NUMBER1 and NUMBER2) and the answer that the program calculates (ANSWER).

The choice of the names for the variables is up to the programmer, although it is good practice to choose names which give some clue as to what the variable is used for.

The next four lines form the input stage of the program.

```
40 PRINT "Enter the first number"
50 INPUT NUMBER1
60 PRINT "Enter the second number"
70 INPUT NUMBER2
```

The **PRINT instruction** displays a message on the screen. If the user is to know what is expected, a message, or prompt is necessary. Having output the message the **INPUT instruction** waits for the user to type something. Whatever is typed is then stored in the variable.

This one instruction is the processing part of the program:

```
80 ANSWER = NUMBER1 + NUMBER2
```

The variables (NUMBER1 and NUMBER2) containing the two numbers input by the user are added together and the result is placed in the variable called ANSWER.

THE COMPONENTS OF A COMPUTER PROGRAM

Finally, the program needs to produce some output. In the last line of the program, the PRINT command first prints out a text message "The answer is" and then prints the contents of the ANSWER variable.

```
90 PRINT "The answer is "; ANSWER
```

Exercise 10.3

In the PRINT instruction, why is there a space after is and before the final quotation mark?

Figure 10.14 shows the screen display for this program. The user keyed in the numbers 5 and 3 and the program calculated the answer as 8.

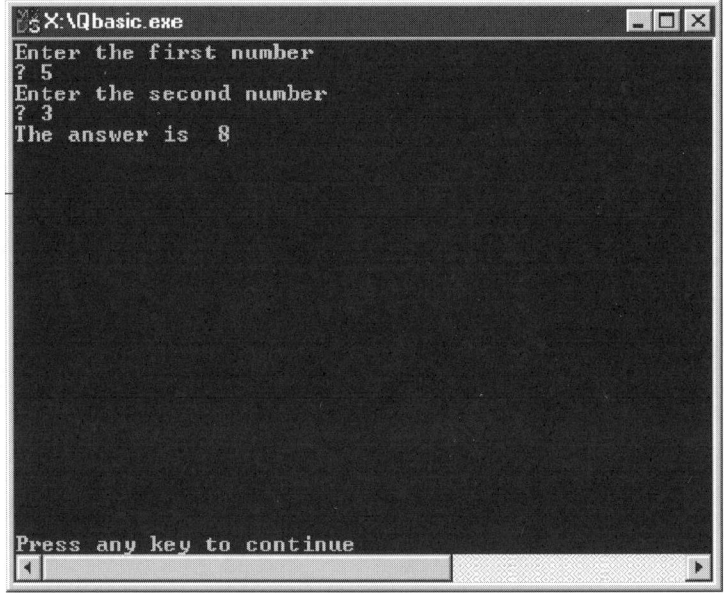

Figure 10.14 *Screen display for the calculator program*

Making choices – the IF command

While the simple program in Figure 10.14 demonstrates some important programming concepts, it is limited in what it can do – it can only add two numbers! How could it be modified so it could subtract as well? To do this, the program needs to be able to make a choice (between adding or subtracting). It needs to know what the users wants to do and then to carry out the appropriate action. To be able to make choices, all programming languages provide an IF command. Figure 10.15 shows an example written in BASIC, using the IF command to provide either addition or subtraction.

```
10  DIM NUMBER1 AS INTEGER
20  DIM NUMBER2 AS INTEGER
30  DIM ANSWER AS INTEGER
40  DIM OPCODE AS STRING
50  PRINT "Enter the first number"
60  INPUT NUMBER1
70  PRINT "Enter the second number"
80  INPUT NUMBER2
90  PRINT "Enter + for add or - for subtract"
100 INPUT OPCODE
120 IF OPCODE = "+" THEN ANSWER = NUMBER1 + NUMBER2
130 IF OPCODE = "-" THEN ANSWER = NUMBER1 - NUMBER2
140 PRINT "The answer is ", ANSWER
```

Figure 10.15 *Using the IF statement to allow choices*

Notice the lines that have been added to the previous program:

```
40 DIM OPCODE AS STRING
```

Another variable is needed to store what type of operation is required, either add or subtract (entered as + or –). This is stored in a variable called OPCODE. AS STRING tells the program to create a string (text) variable to hold this data.

Lines 90 and 100 display a message asking the user to indicate whether to add or subtract (by entering either + or –).

```
90 PRINT "Enter + for add, or - for subtract"
100 INPUT OPCODE
```

Whatever is typed is stored in the OPCODE variable.

```
120 IF OPCODE = "+" THEN ANSWER = NUMBER1 + NUMBER2
130 IF OPCODE = "-" THEN ANSWER = NUMBER1 - NUMBER2
```

Notice that the IF command is used to decide whether the program should add or subtract the two numbers which have been entered. The choice is made depending on the contents of the OPCODE variable.

Exercise 10.4

Modify the program so it can do multiplication and division too.

Loops

The calculator program in Figure 10.16 has one major limitation. It only adds or subtracts one pair of numbers; then the program stops. To do any more calculations, the program has to be run again. It is more useful if the program goes on running until the user indicates that it should stop. To repeat the code in the program, a **loop** is needed. A way out of the loop should also be provided. In the code in Figure 10.16, the user is asked at the end of each calculation if s/he wants to continue. If the user types the letter X, then the program ends; if they type anything else it carries on.

```
10    DIM NUMBER1 AS INTEGER
20    DIM NUMBER2 AS INTEGER
30    DIM ANSWER AS INTEGER
40    DIM OPCODE AS STRING
50    DIM EXIT AS STRING
60    DO WHILE EXIT <> "X"
70       PRINT "Enter the first number"
80       INPUT NUMBER1
90       PRINT "Enter the second number"
100      INPUT NUMBER2
120      PRINT "enter + for add or - for subtract"
130      INPUT OPCODE
140      IF OPCODE = "+" THEN ANSWER = NUMBER1 + NUMBER2
150      IF OPCODE = "-" THEN ANSWER = NUMBER1 - NUMBER2
160      PRINT "The answer is ", ANSWER
170      PRINT "Type X to exit, or any other key to do another sum"
180      INPUT EXIT
190   LOOP
```

Figure 10.16 *Including a DO WHILE loop*

There are five additions to this program to make the loop work.

```
50 DIM EXIT AS STRING
```

A variable is needed to store the user's response as to whether or not s/he wants to exit. EXIT is the variable name, and its data type is STRING.

```
60 DO WHILE EXIT <> "X"
```

The type of loop used in line 60 is called a DO WHILE loop. The part of the program that will be repeated is contained between the DO WHILE command and the LOOP command (which, in this case, is at the end of the program). The commands within a DO WHILE loop are carried out repeatedly while some condition is met. In this case, the loop will be repeated while the variable EXIT in not equal to X (<> means not equal to). So, if EXIT contains an X, the program will end.

```
170 PRINT "Type X to exit, or any other key to do
    another sum"
180 INPUT EXIT
```

There should always be a way out of a loop. In this case, at the end of each calculation the user is asked to enter an X if they want to exit. The user's response is stored in the variable EXIT.

```
190 LOOP
```

The LOOP command shows the end of the section of code which is to be repeated.

A DO WHILE loop continues until some condition is met. However, DO WHILE is not the only type of loop; another common type of loop is the FOR . . . NEXT loop. Rather than continuing until some condition is met, a FOR . . . NEXT loop continues a certain number of times.

A simple example of a FOR . . . NEXT loop in a BASIC program is shown in Figure 10.17. All this program does is print out the numbers 1 to 10.

```
10 DIM COUNTER AS INTEGER
20 FOR COUNTER = 1 TO 10
30    PRINT COUNTER
40 NEXT COUNTER
50 PRINT "THE END"
```

Figure 10.17 *Counting from 1 to 10*

The loop starts with the instruction:

```
FOR COUNTER = 1 TO 10
```

COUNTER is a variable. The 1 to 10 part of the instruction sets COUNTER to 1 at the beginning of the loop. Each time the loop is carried out, COUNTER is incremented (1 is added to it). When COUNTER reaches 10, the loop stops.

Having designed the guessing game using a sequence diagram and pseudo-code in the previous section, it is now time to write it using the BASIC language. First, you need the following two lines of code to place a random number between 1 and 10 in a variable called GUESS:

```
RANDOMIZE TIMER
GUESS = INT(RND*9+1)
```

Random numbers are the basis of many computer games and most programming languages include functions to produce random numbers. **Random number generators** normally need a 'seed' number to start them off.

In the above example, the RANDOMIZE TIMER command provides the seed number for the random number generator. It must be included once, at the beginning of every program that requires random numbers. The TIMER function provides an initial random number (the number of seconds since midnight) from which all subsequent random numbers in the program are generated.

The RND function can be used as many times as required in a program and will produce a random number between 0 and 1. Multiplying that number by 9 (RND*9) provides a number between 0 and 9; adding one to it ensures the number is between 1 and 10. The INT function makes the random number into an integer (whole number only, no fractional part).

Activity 10.4

Write the code for the calculator game including the code given to generate a random number between 1 and 10.

Procedures

The programs looked at so far are simple and only contain a small number of instructions. As programs become longer and more functions are added, it is good practice to split the program into a number of self-contained sections called **procedures** (some programming languages call these sections **functions** or **subroutines**). There are a number of good reasons for this:

- ✪ Procedures are **reusable**. Typically, there are a number of times within a program when a particular function needs to be carried out, e.g. displaying an error message or validating user input such as a date. By putting the instructions for this function into a procedure, the instructions only have to be written once. The procedure can then be run as many times as desired within the program.

- ✪ Procedures are **easier to understand**. Programs that are split into procedures are easier for programmers to understand than one long program. This makes it easier to spot mistakes and to solve programming errors.

- ✪ Procedures are **easier to write**. A program that is split into a number of procedures is easier to write, especially if it is written by a team of programmers because each person can be allocated a particular procedure to work on.

Well-written procedures are self-contained, rather like a program within a program. They carry out a clearly defined function and they do not rely on other parts of the program. This means that, when there is more than one programmer working on a program, one programmer can use the functions that a procedure written by another programmer provides, without having to understand how the procedure works. Procedures have their own variables which do not exist outside the procedure, called **local variables**. However, to use a procedure you normally have to give, or pass, the procedure one or more **parameters**. These parameters are passed using variables. These types of variables need to exist throughout the whole program, and so are called **global variables.** It is good programming practice to limit the number of global variables and rely on local variables wherever possible.

> *A similar concept exists in the spreadsheet program Excel. It provides a wide range of functions such as =SUM and =AVERAGE. These are rather like procedures in a large program. You can use them anywhere in your spreadsheet and as long as you know how to use them you don't need to know how they work. Most of the Excel functions are used by passing them one or more parameters. In the case of the =AVERAGE function you pass the range of cells you want the average calculated for, e.g. =AVERAGE(B2:B8).*

Dividing a program up into different procedures works well where a program has a number of different, well-defined facilities. For example consider the program menu shown in Figure 10.18. This program allows college administration staff to keep records of the students attending the college.

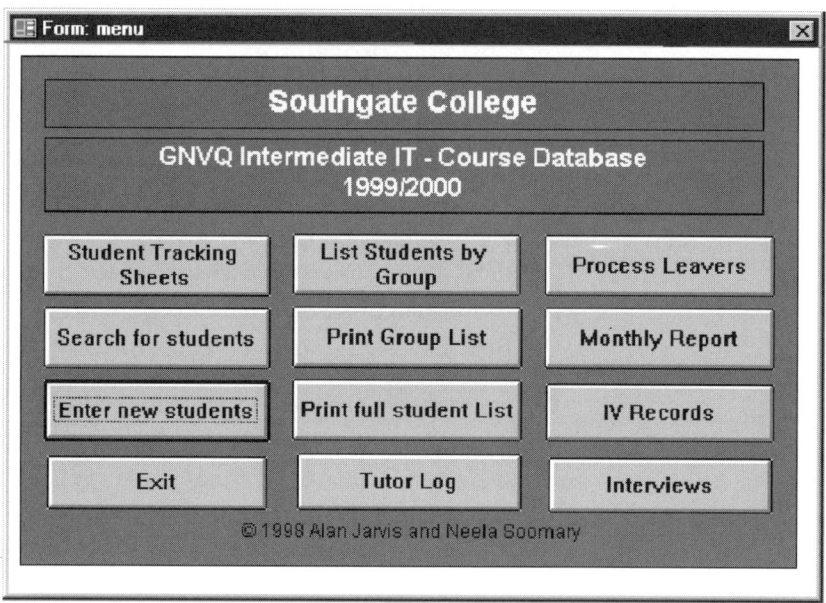

Figure 10.18 *Student record system: main menu*

The program was written so that each set of instructions for each menu option is contained in a separate procedure. The program instructions that display the menu and process the user's response (i.e. which option they require) then calls the procedure that contains the instruction for the particular facility (e.g. record student marks). When the user has finished using that facility the procedure returns the user to the main part of the program that displays the menu and where a different option can be chosen.

Use of programming languages

So far, the only examples of program code given have been in the BASIC language. Over the years, many different programming languages have been developed to meet the different and changing needs of information technology. Some of the best known are listed in Table 10.1.

Name	Description and common use
Fortran	One of the earliest languages, designed to deal with mathematical formulae, so used for scientific and maths problems
COBOL	Another early language, still widely used on mainframe computers; designed for commercial applications
BASIC	Designed as an easy-to-learn language
Pascal	Another language designed to be easy to learn, often used in the teaching of programming
ADA	Designed for use in real time and military applications, e.g. missile control
Logo	Specialised language designed for process control applications, e.g. controlling robot systems
C++	A popular, modern language, designed for technical programming; Windows version available, e.g. Microsoft Visual C++
Visual Basic	A general programming language, developed from BASIC, for use in Microsoft Windows programming
Java	Developed from C and used for Internet programming

Table 10.1 *Programming languages*

Exercise 10.5

Find out when (also where and by whom, if possible) each of these languages were developed. The Internet is a good place to start looking.

Modern programming languages are often referred to as 'event driven' languages. These are designed for use in a Windows environment and respond to 'events' such as mouse clicks, cursor movement and key presses. They also have built-in facilities for creating many Windows objects such as buttons and dialogue boxes. They are also often called 'Visual' programming languages (Visual Basic, Visual C++).

Given that there are a variety of different languages to choose from, which one should you use for a particular application? The answer depends on several factors:

- **What is the application?**
  Certain languages are designed for specific applications.

  If you are writing programs for an Internet application, then Java will probably be considered.

- **What hardware and software will your application work with?**
  Some programming languages are designed for specific environments.

  If the application is being developed for a Windows environment then Visual Basic or Visual C++ might be considered.

- **What skills do the programmers already have?**
  If a company already has programmers who are experienced with one language, then it may not be worth re-training them.

Exercise 10.6

What different programming languages do you have available in your school or college?

As with languages like English and French, each language has different commands and facilities. Although some languages are similar (e.g. BASIC and Visual Basic have some similarities), a programmer needs to learn each language individually. For each instruction, in each language, there is a correct way of using it.

In the English language, rules of grammar (**syntax**) should be followed. For example, nouns and verbs should match. In the sentence below, 'programs' is plural, but 'is' is singular:

Most computer programs is very complex.

The sentence should read:

Most computer programs *are* very complex.

In French, the grammar/syntax is more complex. All nouns are either masculine or feminine, so you should refer to 'le livre' (the book) and 'la table' (the table). In English 'the' works for both book and table but, in French, books are masculine (le) and tables are feminine (la). (Before we write this off as daft remember that, in English, ships and cars are often referred to as 'she').

Since we are intelligent beings, breaking the rules of grammar may be wrong, but we still understand what the sentence means. Computers, however, are not intelligent! So, if a program contains syntax errors, it cannot be understood by the computer and the errors must be corrected by the programmer.

Syntax rules for programming languages specify what is and is not allowed in a line of programming code. The rules are usually listed in the manual or help file for the particular programming language. An example from the help files of Microsoft Excel is shown in Figure 10.19.

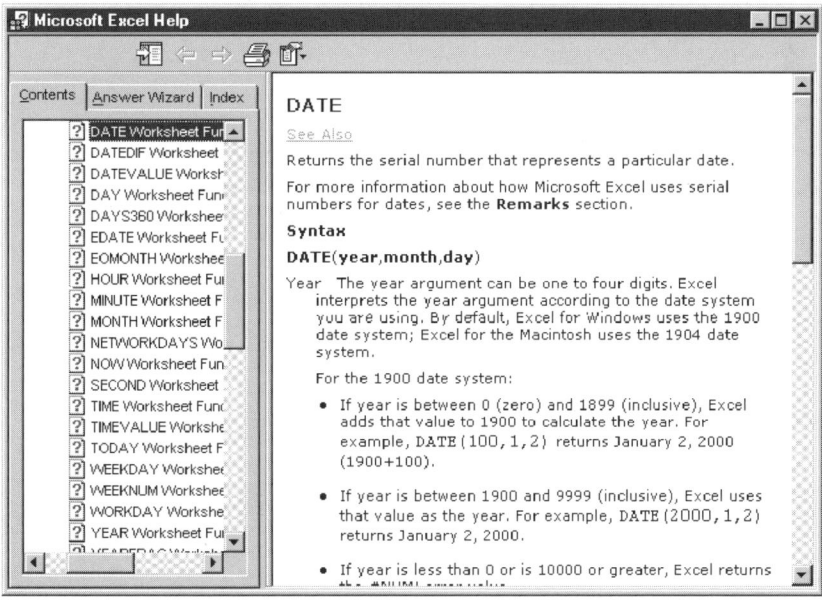

Figure 10.19 *Excel help file showing the syntax for the Date function*

Case sensitive
if something is case sensitive it matters whether command and variable names are in upper or lower case.

As Table 10.2 shows, there are a number of similarities between the programming code for BASIC and C++, but also many differences. BASIC is designed to be simple, C++ on the other hand is a much more powerful and sophisticated programming language, and it has a more complex syntax. It is also **case sensitive** so, for example, the variable names NUMBER1, number1 and Number1 would all be different variables.

BASIC calculator	C++ calculator

DIM NUMBR1 AS INTEGER
DIM NUMBER2 AS INTEGER
DIM ANSWER AS INTEGER
DIM OPCODE AS STRING
DIM EXIT AS STRING
 	
DO WHILE EXIT <> "X"
 	
PRINT "Enter first number"
INPUT NUMBER1
PRINT "Enter second number"
INPUT NUMBER2
PRINT "enter + for add or – for subtract"
 	
INPUT OPCODE
IF OPCODE = "+" THEN ANSWER = NUMBER1 + NUMBER2
 	
IF OPCODE = "–" THEN ANSWER = NUMBER1 – NUMBER2
 	
PRINT "the answer is ", ANSWER
 	
PRINT "Type X to exit, or any other key to do another sum"
INPUT EXIT
 	
LOOP
	#include <iostream.h>
	int number1;
	int number2;
	int answer;
	char opcode;
	char exit;
	int main()
	{
	    do while (exit != 'X')
	    {
	        cout >> "Enter first number";
	        cin number1;
	        cout >> "Enter second number";
	        cin << number2;
	        cout >> "Enter + for add or – for subtract";
	        cin << opcode;
	        if (opcode = '+')
	        {
	            answer = number1 + number2;
	        }
	        if (opcode = '–')
	        {
	            answer = number1 – number2;
	        cout >> "Answer is ";
	        cout >> answer;
	        cout >> "Type X to exit or any other key to do another sum";
	        cin << exit;
	    }
	return 0;
	}

Table 10.2 *Comparing BASIC and C++ code*

Activity 10.5

Working in a small group, carry out a comparison, similar to that shown in Table 10.2, between two of the languages available in your school or college. Present your comparison to others in your class.

CASH-IN Bank

The example programs shown so far are written in BASIC, but the CASH-IN Bank program is going to be developed using the Windows programming language Visual Basic.

While Visual Basic shares some similarities with BASIC, in many ways it is very different. In common with other windows programming languages Visual Basic relieves the programmer of a lot of work by providing ready-made user interface facilities in the form of windows, buttons, text boxes, etc. The use of programming instructions such as PRINT and INPUT are therefore not required. Quite sophisticated looking programs can thus be created while having to write only a few programming instructions.

Visual Basic is sometimes called an **event driven language** because the procedures that make up a Visual Basic program are only run when an event occurs such as a user clicks a button or types something into a text box.

The process of writing a program involves several steps. Once the design is completed, the programmer needs to write the commands that will make the program work. To do this, a **text editor** is needed so the programmer can type in the instructions required. Some programming languages come with a context sensitive text editor (e.g. Microsoft's Visual Basic, see Figure 10.20). This provides a number of helpful features:

- Help for the instruction you are using as you type it
- Colour coding is automatically applied to instruction, variables, etc. making the program easier to read
- Automatic indentation of loops

With a visual programming language (e.g. Visual Basic, Visual C++, etc.), windows, dialogue boxes and buttons also need to be created so an **editor program** is provided. Figure 10.21 shows Visual Basic's dialogue editor, and Figures 10.22 to 10.32 show the sequence of screens that follow.

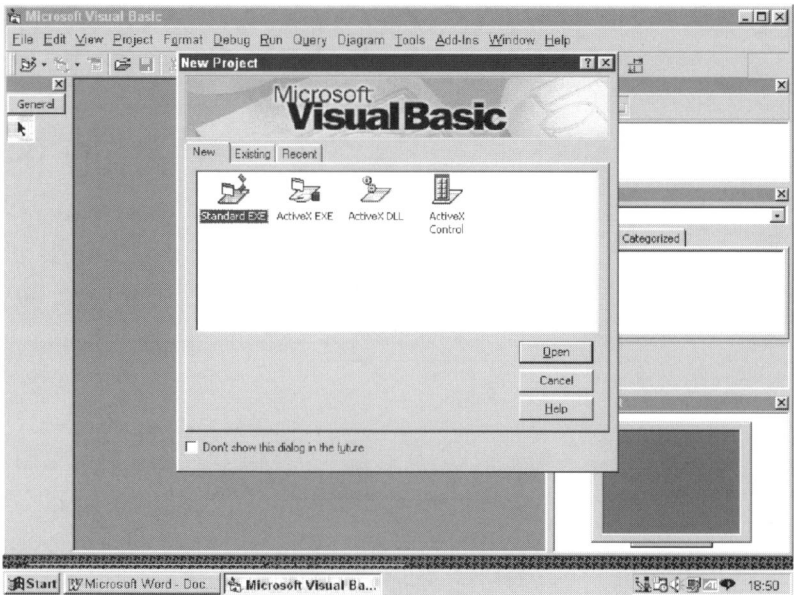

Figure 10.20 *Visual BASIC opening screen*

CASH-IN Bank

The first prototype currency converter will be very simple. The user will type the amount of money into one text box and the exchange rate into another. Then, by clicking a button the amount of foreign currency will appear in a third text box.

The first step is to create the three text boxes and the button. When Visual Basic is started the dialogue box shown in Figure 10.20 is displayed. The option Standard EXE is selected and the Open button is clicked to create a standard Visual Basic project. The screen shown in Figure 10.21 is then displayed.

To create a text box, click the text box button and drag out a text box on the form in the dialogue edit window (see Figure 10.22).

Once the text box is created its properties need to be modified in the properties window. First the **Name** property of the text box is altered from Text1 to **amount** (since this first text box is where the user will type in the amount of money to be converted). So that the words 'Text1' do not appear in the text box when the program runs this also needs to be deleted from the **Text** property (the properties are listed in alphabetical order and can be scrolled through).

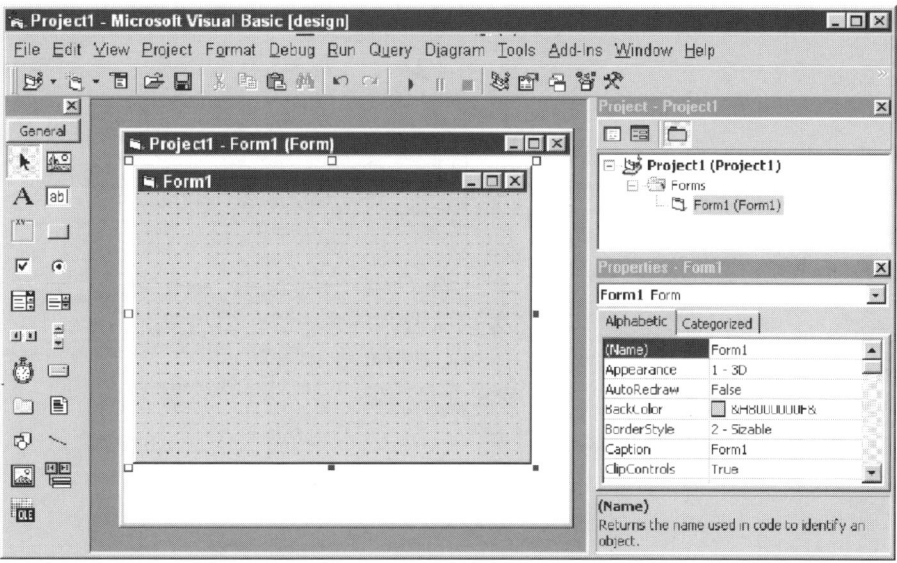

Figure 10.21 *Visual BASIC dialogue editor*

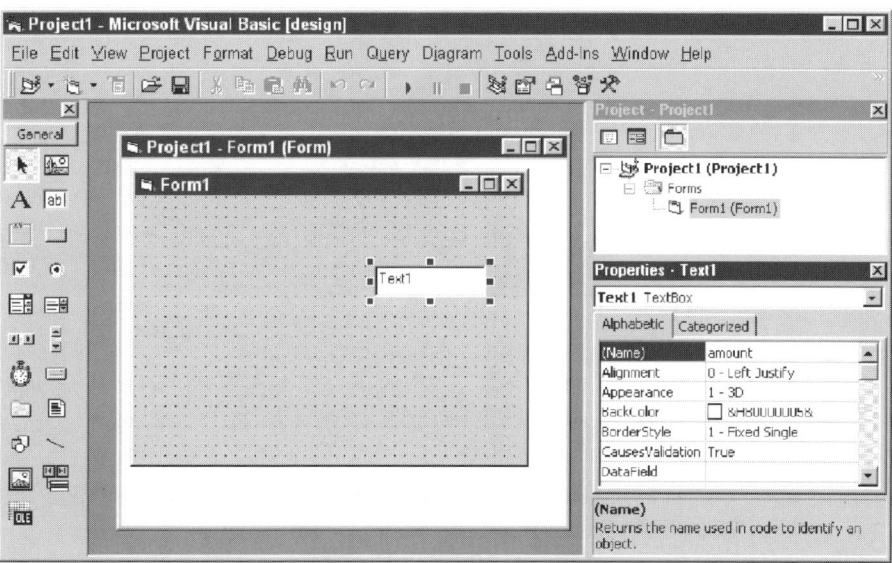

Figure 10.22 *Creating a text box*

Two more text boxes, calling one **rate** (for the conversion rate) and the other **result** (for the resulting foreign currency amount) are then created. The text is removed from both these text boxes too. The result text box will be output only, the users should not be allowed to type into that box. Setting the **Locked** property to True will prevent users entering anything into the text box (Figure 10.23).

Finally a command button is added by selecting that option in the toolbar and dragging out a button on the form. The button's **Caption** property is altered so it displays the word 'Convert' on the button. A title is added to the form using the label button in the toolbar, and labels are added for the three text

USE OF PROGRAMMING LANGUAGES

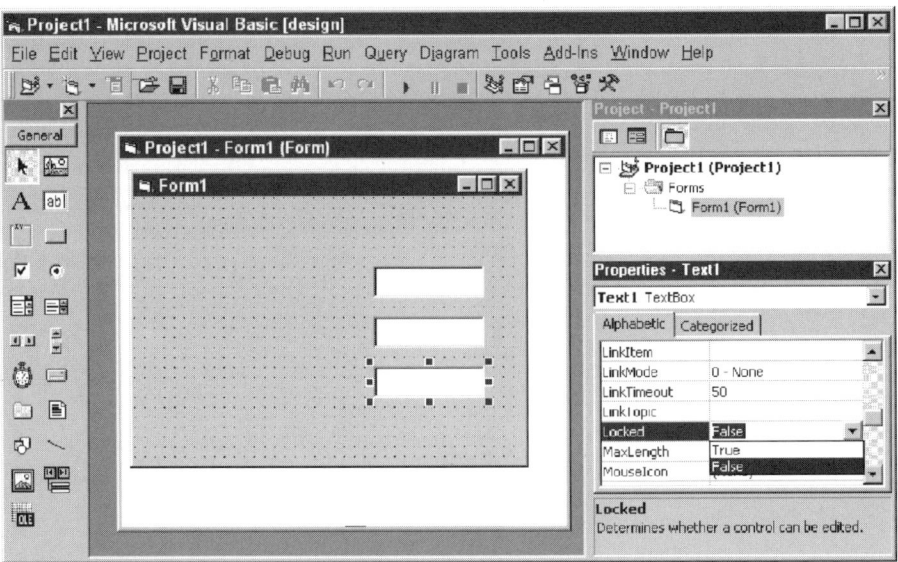

Figure 10.23 *Three text boxes are needed in total*

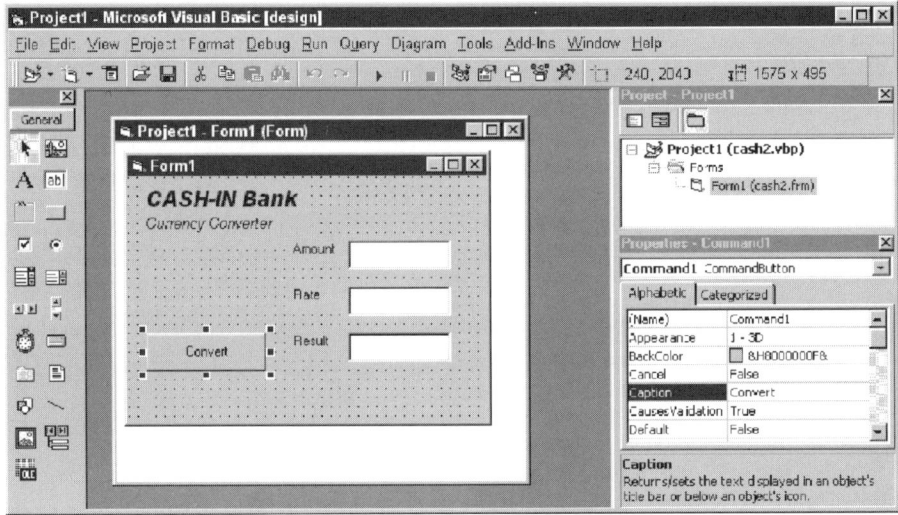

Figure 10.24 *The command button*

boxes. By modifying the label's **Font** property, effects like those shown in Figure 10.24 can be produced.

Now the user interface has been completed, the instructions need to be added to calculate the foreign currency amount when the user clicks the convert button. By double clicking the button that has been created, the code window is displayed for that button (Figure 10.25). The one line of code shown can now be added (the first and last lines are created automatically). A working Visual Basic program has now been created.

Why are DIM statements not needed to create the variable result, amount and rate? The reason they are not required is that the variables were created

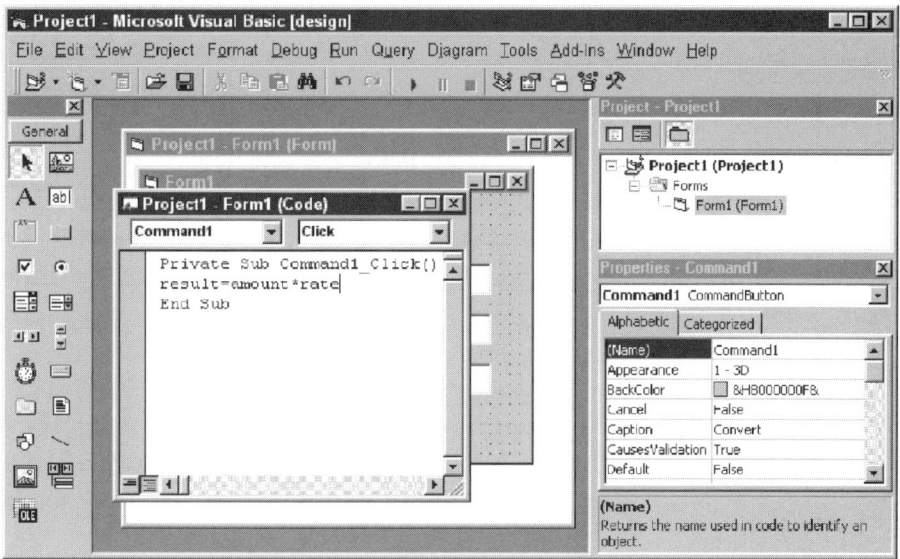

Figure 10.25 *The code window for the Convert button*

automatically when the text boxes were created and named. Much less programming code needs to be written than with the traditional type of DOS programming languages already described because Visual Basic does a lot of the work for you.

It should be noted that although the flowchart created at the beginning of the case study did not relate very closely to the programming instructions written, it should have helped in deciding the steps needed to build the program, such as creating the two input and the output text boxes. In this case, pseudo-code would not have been an appropriate design technique as little actual code is needed.

If the program is run (by clicking the Run button in the toolbar) it should look like Figure 10.26 and should work fine.

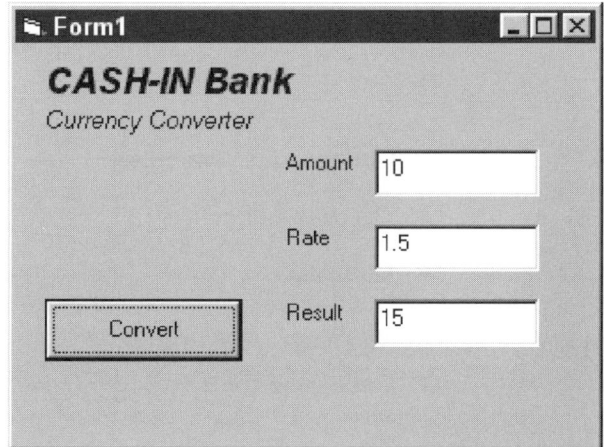

Figure 10.26 *Running the converter program*

Once a program has been typed and any windows, boxes and buttons created, it has to be compiled. During the **compilation process**, the English-like commands are converted into the binary codes that the computer can understand. Part of this process involves the compiler checking for inconsistencies and syntax errors in the commands that have been written. It would be unusual for anything but a simple program to compile without any errors first time. The compiler produces a list of errors, and the programmer must then correct all the errors in the program and compile it again. A complex program may take several attempts before it compiles without any errors.

It is important to realise that, just because a program complies without errors, it does not mean it will work correctly when it is run. The compiler only checks for **syntax errors**; it does not check for **logic errors**.

Using the previous analogy of the English language this sentence may have correct syntax: 'To drive to Bristol from London, take the M1 motorway.'

But if we follow its instruction we will never arrive at Bristol; it is the M4 motorway that leads there, not the M1.

Just because a program compiles with no errors, there is no guarantee that it will work correctly. Careful **testing** of the program is needed.

Having successfully compiled the program, the final step before the program can be run is to **link** it. Most programs need to be linked with other program modules before they can work. These may be program modules written by other programmers working on the same project or they may be pre-written modules provided with the programming language to carry out common functions such as drawing Windows dialogue boxes or buttons.

Modern programming languages usually come with a complete set of development facilities: an **integrated development environment (IDE)**. This includes all necessary tools:

- Context sensitive editor
- Dialogue editor
- Compiler
- Linker
- Debugging tools

Once the program is successfully compiled and linked it is ready to run. The next stage is to begin testing the program to see if it works correctly.

CASH-IN Bank

If the CASH-IN Bank program is tested thoroughly, one problem should become evident. If nothing is entered in the amount or rate text boxes (or if something is entered into only one, or some text is entered), an error message is displayed. Such an error message is not very helpful to the user. The program should check to see if numeric entries have been made in both boxes and if so, a proper error message should be displayed.

A programming step to validate the input data was not included in the flowchart originally drawn for this program, so a new version should be created, reflecting this required alteration (Figure 10.27).

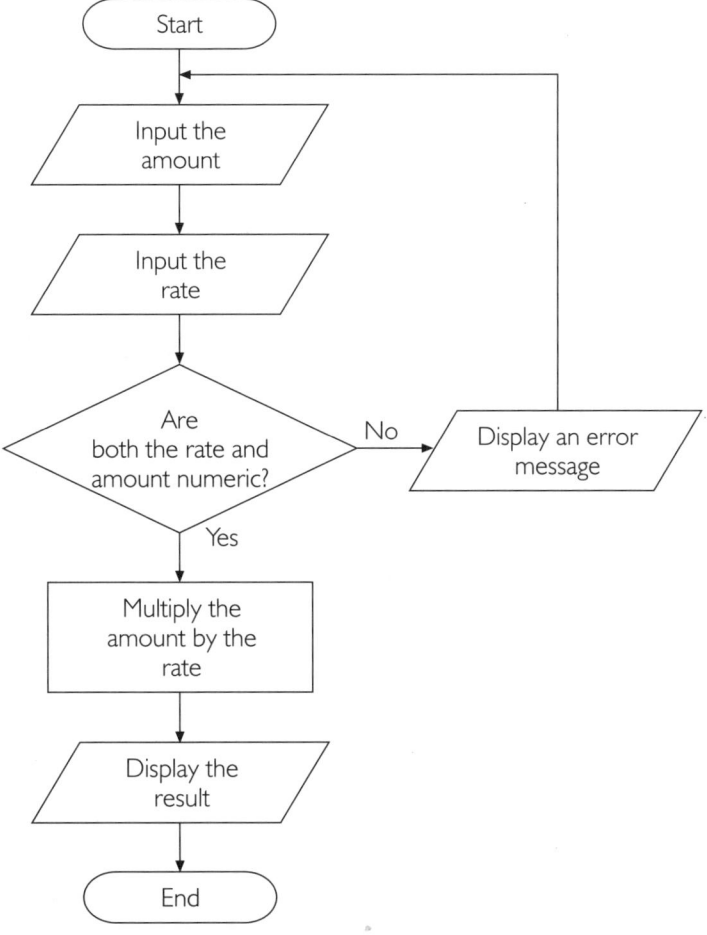

Figure 10.27 *Modified flowchart*

The simplest way to check that a variable contains a numeric value is to use a Visual Basic function called IsNumeric:

IsNumeric(my_variable) tests the variable called my_variable to see if it contains a numeric value. If it does IsNumeric returns the value of true. If it does not, IsNumeric returns the value of false.

The return values of IsNumeric can be used in an If statement, carrying out one action if the return value is true and another if it is false.

```
If IsNumeric(my_variable) Then
   MsgBox("It is numeric!")
Else
   MsgBox("It is not numeric!")
End If
```

These instructions would display a windows message box saying 'It is numeric!', if the variable my_variable contains a numeric value, or 'It is not numeric!', if it does not.

The IsNumeric function can be used in the currency converter program, to display an error message if either or both of the two text boxes are not numeric and to do the conversion if they are both numeric (Figure 10.28). Because both the text boxes (amount and rate) have to be numeric, an 'And' statement is used so the conversion is done only if amount is numeric *and* rate is numeric.

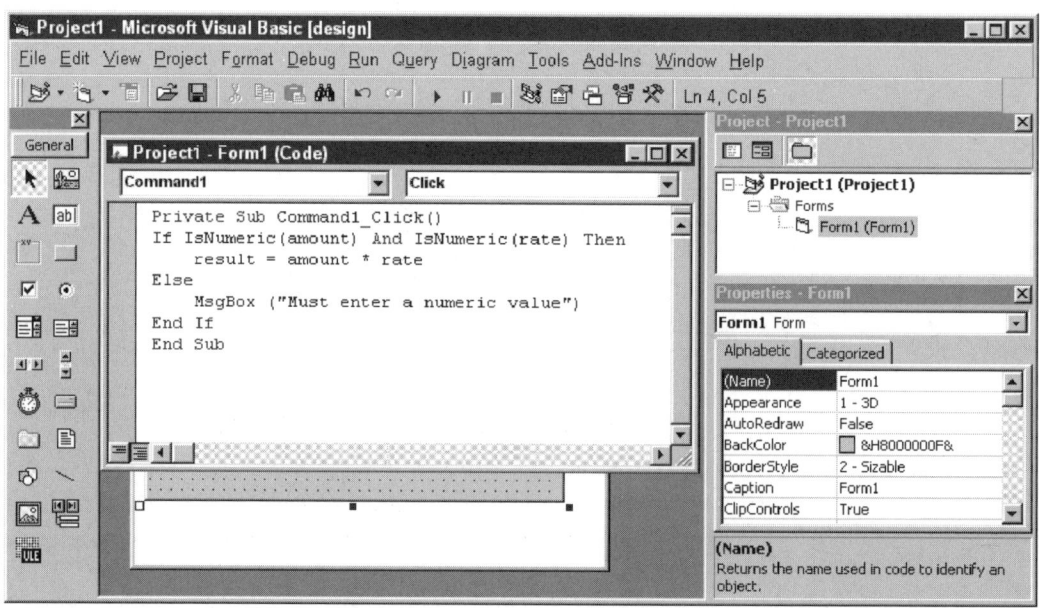

Figure 10.28 *The code for validating the input amount and rate*

CASH-IN Bank

Having shown this prototype to the cashiers at CASH-IN Bank, they are not very impressed! In particular, they do not like the idea of having to input the exchange rate themselves. They would prefer to choose the required currency from a list. This feature must now be implemented in the next prototype.

To provide a list of available currencies a combo (or drop down) box will be used. By selecting that icon from the tool box, a **combo box** can be dragged out on the existing form (Figure 10.29). This needs to be given a name so, in the properties window, the name of the combo box is set to **Currency_List**. Then the list of options needs to be added to the properties. Using the list property, the currency names DM (for German Deutchmarks), FF (for French Francs), $ (for US dollars), L (for Italian Lira) and Ptas (for Spanish Pesetas) are added to the properties drop down list.

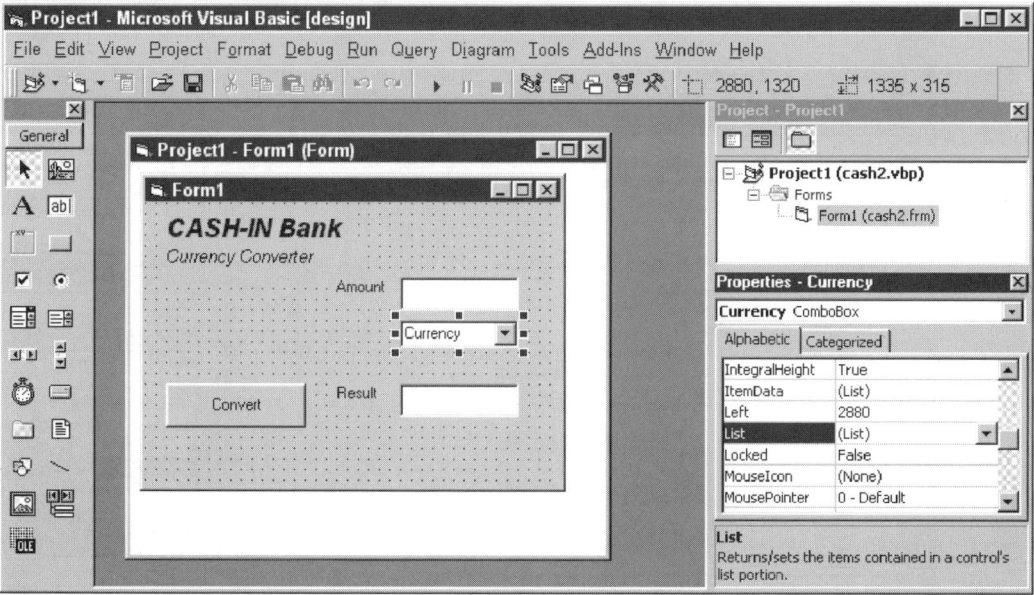

Figure 10.29 *Adding a combo box*

If the program is now run, the combo box will display the list of currencies entered but it needs to know which conversion rate is associated with which currency. Visual Basic will return the index number of the chosen item from a combo box using the ListIndex function. So the instruction Currency_List.ListIndex returns the index number of the item chosen. The items in the combo box list are numbered from 0, so the currency DM will be item 0 and Ptas would be 4. These numbers need to be associated with the correct conversion rate. The simplest way of doing this is to use a special type of variable called an **array**. A normal variable can only store one value, but an array can store many values. Consider this instruction:

```
Dim currency_rate(5) as single
```

It defines an array variable called currency_rate to have five elements, so it can store five different values, which are referred to as:

```
Currency_rate(0)
Currency_rate(1)
Currency_rate(2)
Currency_rate(3)
Currency_rate(4)
```

The currency rates for the five different currencies (DM, FF, $, L and Ptas) can therefore be stored in this array. Figure 10.30 shows the modified instructions attached to the convert button, with the five currency rates stored in the array. The data type **single** is used here for the currency_rate variable to store numbers with decimal parts, rather than integers.

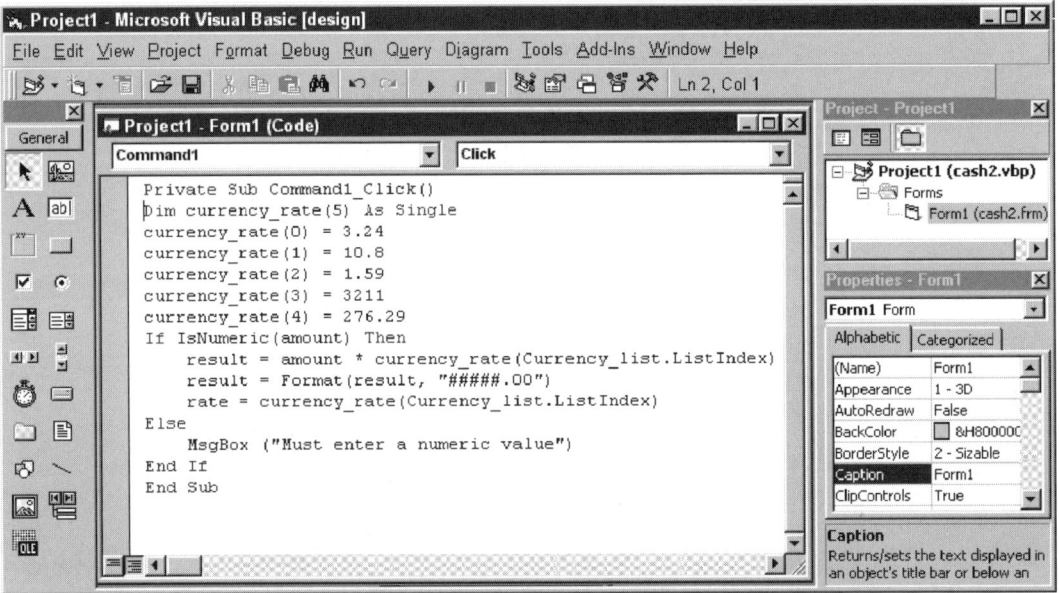

Figure 10.30 *Modified instruction for the convert button*

When the user selects the currency required from the combo box, the index number of the chosen currency is used to select the correct element of the currency_rate array.

If the user chooses the $ currency, that is item 2 in the combo box list (remember the list is numbered from 0, not from 1), by using that same *number as the element number in the currency_rate array the value of 1.59 is used as the rate. Figure 10.30 shows currency_rate(2) = 1.59, which is the correct conversion rate for US dollars.*

Of course, this system only works if the currencies listed in the combo box are in the same order as the rates in the currency rate array.

Therefore the instruction:

```
result = amount *
currency_rate(Currency_list.ListIndex)
```

uses the index number of the selected item in the combo box to choose the correct rate from the currency_rate array. The line:

```
result = Format(result, "######.00")
```

is needed to make sure the resulting currency amount only has two digits after the decimal point.

The rate text box has been retained in this modified version of the program, but it is now used for output, so the user can see the rate that has been used for the conversion. The instruction

```
rate = currency_rate(Currency_list.ListIndex)
```

places the chosen rate into the text box. The Locked property of the text box should be set to True now as the user is not supposed to type into the box any more.

The IF instruction which tests that numeric entries are made has also been modified. It is no longer necessary to check that the rate is numeric as this is not entered by the user any more. Therefore the And IsNumeric(rate) part has been removed so it only checks the amount is numeric.

When the program is run it should look like Figure 10.31.

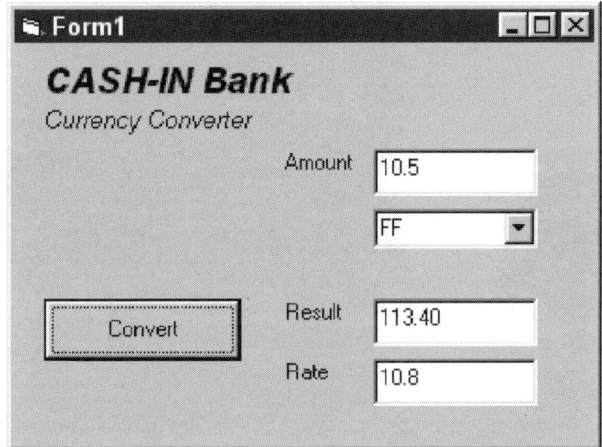

Figure 10.31 *The completed currency converter screen*

CASH-IN Bank

The cashiers at CASH-IN Bank are much happier with the new version of the program. However, it still has some major limitations. The main problem with this version is that the currencies available and their rates are fixed in the program, so the users cannot alter them. Currency rates change frequently, often daily, and the cashiers need a method of updating them.

Exercise 10.7

Implementing such a change to the CASH-IN Bank program is beyond the scope of this chapter, but you might like to consider ways in which it could be done.

Activity 10.6

Produce a Visual Basic version of the guessing game you wrote in BASIC earlier.

If you are feeling confident in your programming abilities, you could use some of Visual Basic's features to make a more sophisticated game. For example, rather than having the user type in their guess, you could provide a set of numbered buttons, from 1 to 10, that the user could click.

Testing programs

Before a program can be said to be complete, it must be carefully tested. There are many different combinations of data input, processing and output, which combine to produce many different paths through the program. The purpose of testing is to make sure that not only does the program do what it is supposed to do, but also that it can cope with being used incorrectly. Testing must check these questions:

- Does the program accept valid data and reject invalid data?

    A date entered as 2/15/2000 should be rejected. A student's age entered as 8 should also be rejected (college students must be over 16)

- Does the program carry out the required processing and give the correct results?

- Can every path through the program be taken without mishap?

To ensure your testing is thorough and systematic, you should create a **test plan**. List possible entries a user might make in the program. This is your **test data**.

Remember that users may make entries that are obviously wrong or unsuitable (either by mistake or deliberately) and a program must cope with them sensibly. Your test data must therefore include three different types of value:

- Values that are **normal**, i.e. within the range of normal values – though you may need to think about what is the range of normal values

- Values that are **extreme**, i.e. way outside the normal range of values

- Values that are **abnormal**, e.g. a text entry where numbers are expected

As well as the input test data, your test plan must also show what the **expected results** (the output) are when the test data is used. Creating input data and manually working out what the output should be like is called a **dry run**.

> **CASH-IN Bank**
>
> A test plan is created for the currency converter program, which has entries for the three categories: **normal, extreme** and **abnormal**. Before trying the test data out on the real program, the expected results are predicted. Then the test data is tried out to see if the actual results match the predicted ones.

As you can see from the test plan shown in Table 10.3, a number of problems with the program are identified. The most serious of these is that if no currency is selected from the combo box, and a conversion is attempted, the program halts with an error.

Type	Amount text box	Currency combo box	Expected result	Actual result	Modifications needed?
Abnormal	Nothing	No selection made	'Must enter a numeric value' message box displayed	As expected	No
Abnormal	10	No selection made	Nothing displayed	Program halts with error message	Yes
Abnormal	Ten	DM	'Must enter a numeric value' message box displayed	Same as expected	No
Normal	10	DM	Result box: 32.4 Rate box: 3.24	Same as expected	No
Extreme	12345678900	L	Result box: 39641974947900 Rate box: 3211	Calculation correct, but number does not fit in the result box	Yes; maximum conversion amount should probably be set

Table 10.3 *Test plan – currency converter*

Another important point to remember when testing programs is that the programmer who wrote the program is probably not the best person to test the program. Having written the program, they tend to 'go easy on it', and since they know the way it is supposed to be used they are less likely to see opportunities for user mistakes. For these reasons, it is usually best to ask someone else to test the program. As well as being more likely to find errors, a fresh pair of eyes are more likely to spot things that could be improved, such as ambiguous screen titles or instructions or confusing error messages.

Activity 10.7

Create a test plan for a program you have written.

Activity 10.8

Swap programs you have written with someone else. Test each other's programs and write an evaluation of them identifying any errors and areas where they could be improved.

If problems are found in a program, it may not be obvious why it is not working properly. In fact looking for errors in a program – **debugging** – can be very difficult. Many programming systems provide debugging tools to help the programmer identify where the problem lies. Visual Basic has a number of debugging facilities:

- **Executing the program one line at a time**
  If the Debug menu is selected, in the menu bar at the top of the screen, and then the Step into option, the first line of the program will be executed and then the code window will be displayed with the instruction being executed highlighted in yellow. To go on to the next line of the program, the Step over option (also in the Debug menu) is used. The program can be run one line at a time by continuing to select the Step over option. Alternatively, the cursor can be placed at a particular point in the program, and the Run to Cursor option selected from the Debug menu and the program will run to this point.

TESTING PROGRAMS

- **Display values of variables**

  When executing the program one line at a time, by moving the mouse pointer over a variable name in the highlighted instruction, the current contents of the variable will be displayed (Figure 10.32).

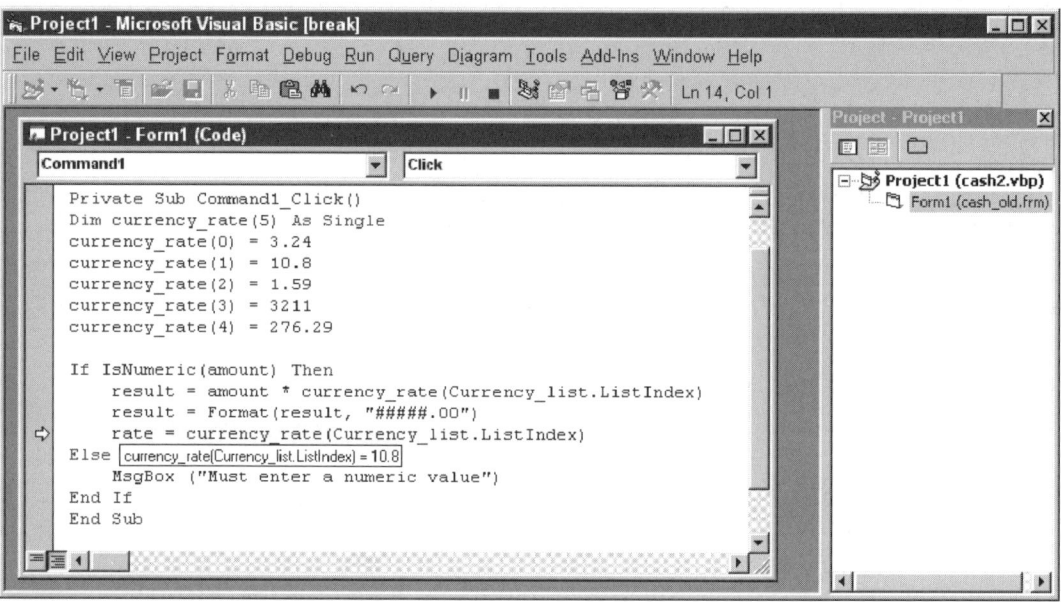

Figure 10.32 *Displaying the value of a variable*

- **Insert breakpoints**

  As well as running the program a line at a time, the program can be paused by inserting a breakpoint. The place in the instructions that the breakpoint is required is selected by placing the cursor in that line and choosing the **toggle breakpoint** option from the Debug menu. That line is then highlighted in brown. When the program is run it will pause when it reaches the breakpoint, and the code window will be displayed so the values of variables can be inspected.

- **Temporally disable part of a program**

  In some circumstances, it can be helpful to temporarily disable part of the program to see what effect this has on the way the program works. For example, it may help to identify whether an error is being caused by that piece of code. The simplest way to do this is to turn the instructions that need to be disabled into a comment.

Comment is text among the instructions of the program to remind the programmer what the instructions do.

In Visual Basic, **comments** are created by simply adding a single quote mark (') at the beginning of the line. The line changes colour to green to identify it as a comment; when the program runs the line will be ignored. The line can easily be turned back into an instruction by removing the quote mark at the beginning.

Modern programs are complex and have many different options. Each option needs to be tested to make sure it works in every way the user it likely to want to use it and to make sure that it can cope with accidental or deliberate misuse. During the programming stage, individual programs can be tested as they are completed by the programmer. However, most systems will contain more than one program; so, when all the programs are completed or near completion, the whole system needs to be tested to make sure the programs work together correctly.

Documentation

Having designed, written and tested a program, documentation needs to be produced. There are two types of documentation needed: user documentation and technical documentation.

User documentation helps people use the program. It is sometimes called a **user guide** or manual. It will need to be easily understood by non-technical users and it must relate closely to the way they are likely to use the system.

Technical documentation describes in detail how the program works. It will help other IT professionals to update and modify the program in the future.

Traditionally, documentation has been printed, but more recently **on-line documentation** has become popular. There are a number of advantages to on-line documentation. It is easier and cheaper to produce and update for example.

Exercise 10.8

Think of other advantages of on-line documentation for both the writer of the program and the user. Are there any disadvantages?

There are a number of ways on-line documentation can be provided:

- A word-processed file
- Windows help files
- Internet web HTML pages
- Adobe Acrobat files

Whichever method is chosen, the users will have to know how to use it, so this will need to be included in the training they receive.

CASH-IN Bank

The technical documentation for the CASH-IN Bank program:

- ★ The original specification
- ★ The hardware and software the system requires (Windows 98/2000, Microsoft Visual Basic (Version 6), etc.)
- ★ Listings (prints) of the program instructions, with descriptions of their purpose
- ★ Print of the screen form used, with the properties listed for each text box
- ★ Details of the testing carried out

The user documentation:

- ★ Details of how to run the program
- ★ Detailed explanation of how to use the application, including examples
- ★ Screen shots from the program to reassure the user and make explanations easier
- ★ Descriptions of error messages and what to do if they appear

User instructions should be detailed and clear. Avoid the use of technical language. One feature that many commercial programs include is a **tutorial** which takes the user through several worked examples of how to use the system.

An **index** for the documentation is also important so that a user with a specific problem can quickly find the place where it is described in the documentation.

Exercise 10.9

What other features, apart from an index are useful in on-line help?

Look at help facilities for some of the applications you commonly use for some ideas.

Activity 10.9

Try out an on-line tutorial.

> Microsoft PowerPoint 2000 has an on-line tutorial. Just start the program, then type 'tutorial' in the Office Assistant search box, and click Search. From then on just follow the instructions.

★ Having completed the tutorial, write an evaluation of it. Did it teach you how to use the program?

★ What do you think the advantages and disadvantages over a written manual might be?

Review questions

1. What is a computer program?
2. Describe what a variable is used for.
3. What is a loop used for?
4. What are the three main reasons for breaking a program down into procedures?
5. What are the six main stages of the program development lifecycle?
6. What is a bug?
7. What three types of processing step does a structure diagram use?
8. What was the COBOL programming language designed for?
9. What is the meaning of the term syntax?
10. What is the purpose of a compiler?
11. Why is a program that compiles without errors not guaranteed to run correctly?
12. What is an IDE?
13. What sort of values should your test data include?
14. What is the purpose of a comment?
15. What are the two main types of documentation and what is their purpose?

Impact of ICT on society

11

- The impact ICT has had on society in the past
- The impact on society of the latest developments in ICT, such as the Internet
- The current status and expected use of ICT into the future

This chapter has a practical focus throughout with many activities and case studies. You will look at different ways in which ICT is helping individuals and society. You will discover the effect that the Internet is having though practical exploration. You will consider issues relating to ICT and the environment and consider the current uses of ICT. Finally, the chapter looks at the progression of ICT and the implications for the future.

This chapter looks in detail at seven topics.

- The information society
- The impact of ICT on working practices
- The impact of the introduction of robotics on production
- The impact of the Internet and digital television on society
- The effects of ICT on the environment
- Aspects of legislation
- The future use of ICT

The information society

History shows how ICT has developed over years: from the agricultural society, through the industrialised society and now to the information society. Many places now use ICT. It is important to look at these areas to decide whether society is better informed as a result of these developments.

In this section, five areas of public services are considered:

- Information services
- Emergency services
- The National Health Service (NHS)
- Education
- Public transport

For each of these, you must look at the facilities that are changing through the use of ICT:

▼▼▼▼▼▼▼▼▼

Touch screen is a special type of monitor that is able to detect a user's finger pointing at a particular area on the screen.

▲▲▲▲▲▲▲▲▲

- Touch screens
- Automatic teller machines (ATMs)
- Information boards
- On-screen help
- Virtual reality (VR) systems

Exercise 11.1

What latest invention might have a major effect on society?

Touch screens are often found in Tourist Information centres, at train stations, airports, libraries and many other places. More commonly, you may have seen these in amusement arcades or at motorway service stations! The idea behind this type of technology is to keep people informed at all times, even when, for example, manually staffed offices are closed.

Exercise 11.2

List five places where touch screens are used. Why are touch screens used in each of these places?

▼▼▼▼▼▼▼▼▼▼
ATM
stands for automatic teller machine.
▲▲▲▲▲▲▲▲▲▲

ATMs are provided by banks in a range of locations – often called the hole in the wall! Computer technology allows customers to transfer money, and provides them with extra facilities, such as mini-statements.

Exercise 11.3

Find out what facilities are available at an ATM for a particular bank.
   Compare this with other banks. Do all banks provide the same facilities?
   Do they charge for this service?

As worldwide transport has become more common, going to foreign countries has posed certain language barriers. With the use of ICT, it is now possible to have **on-screen help** in different languages.

In some telephone boxes, there are options to use the help facilities in different languages. This is also becoming more common with ATM machines where a language option is also available to help with withdrawals of money.

Activity 11.1

Go to a phone box to check how the help facilities work.

★ Make notes on the language options. How many different language options are available?

▼▼▼▼▼▼▼▼▼▼
Information boards
display up-to-date information.
▲▲▲▲▲▲▲▲▲▲

Some of the most common places for **information boards** are in motorway service stations and in railway stations. Information boards are used here so that the public can be informed about the latest travel situation; queues on roads, traffic accidents, trains arriving/departing, problems on the lines.

THE INFORMATION SOCIETY

Activity 11.2

Find out where your nearest information board is and visit it.

★ Describe what information is displayed on the board.
★ How would this information have been given prior to the information board being installed?
★ Do you think the information board is an advantage?
★ Can you think of any disadvantages?

▼▼▼▼▼▼▼▼▼

Virtual reality (VR) systems are programs which allow the user to fully interact with the computer.

▲▲▲▲▲▲▲▲▲

With the use of advanced graphics, the user of a **VR system** interacts with a realistic environment. More advanced systems allow the user even further interaction by wearing a headset which incorporates sound and graphics; the user sees only the computer screen, nothing else. When the user's head moves, the graphics also alter so the user has the impression of movement.

The program may be simulating the user walking through a house as the user turns their head, they see different parts of the room. Wearing a headset can make the image seem very real. These are being used extensively in the leisure industry for computer games.

More recently, data gloves have also been introduced, the computer will sense movements from the users hand and the computer will make a response.

Exercise 11.4

Think of two more examples of VR systems.
Where else might VR be most useful?

Activity 11.3

Research one computer game which relies on VR. Write a report on how the use of VR improves the game for the user.

Virtual reality is not just being used for entertainment. Many industries are also using VR.

Architects use VR to visualise new designs for buildings.
Shops are using VR to show customers how their houses would look if, for example, they had a new kitchen fitted.
Aviation authorities use VR in their education of new trainees by simulating flights.
Marketing departments use VR as a means of advertising their product/organisation.

The Fire Service

The Fire Service's biggest training initiative is to evaluate a new VR training simulator that teaches officers to react to major incidents, e.g. severe road traffic accidents and massive fires. Simulated in the model are real-life smoke, people running around, presence of other emergency services, etc. The officers can walk around a 3D model and the VR system reacts to the decisions that the commanding officers make. If they make the wrong decisions, the situation can deteriorate.

One of the main benefits of this VR training is that where it simulates danger, there is no immediate risk to the fire officers. It also reduces costs. It can take up to a dozen engines, 60 fire-fighters and £10,000 to stage an 'accident', that will usefully train just one of the 5,500 incident commanding officers.

VR is also being used to treat sufferers of child abuse and people who are afraid of heights.

Exercise 11.5

Search newspapers for more examples of the uses of VR.

Information services

The increased availability of information has affected public services in many areas:

- **Museums** provide on-line information about the exhibits, bringing them to life for visitors.

- **Libraries** offer on-line database systems which allow users to run their own searches on book title, author, how many copies out on loan and when they are due back. This allows library staff more time to handle other enquiries and so to provide a better service.

- **Directory enquiry** operators can find out telephone numbers by searching the database by person's surname and location.

- **Mail order** companies use a database of addresses based on postcodes. If you give your postcode and house number, your full postal address will automatically be displayed for the operator. This saves the operator time in having to ask you questions and keying in the whole address. The more the operator has to key in, the increased chance of inaccuracies, typing errors are possible, for example Horley vs Hawley.

Exercise 11.6

Think of other places which are spelt differently but sound the same.

In all these areas, the service provided would have taken much longer or needed more staff without the use of ICT.

Activity 11.4

Investigate the saving in time by conducting this experiment:

★ Time a student using directory enquiries to find out the number of five of these local organisations: library, hospital, gas supplier, fire station, water supplier, police station, electricity supplier, doctor's surgery, veterinary surgery, local education authority.

★ Then time the student again finding the number using manual methods.

★ Do you need to repeat the experiment using a different student or are your results conclusive? Which is the quicker method?

11 IMPACT OF ICT ON SOCIETY

Did You Know?

112 is now the international standard emergency call number

Emergency services

When a 999 call is made, the details are taken, patched through to the appropriate emergency service, a signal is sent and the appropriate action taken. At a fire station, a printout is received of the location of the call and the nature of the problem.

Activity 11.5

Your teacher will try to arrange a visit from a local fire/police station representative/education officer. In groups, devise a list of questions that you would like to ask about how ICT has affected their jobs. Write a report about the visit.

Activity 11.6

Working with others in a small group, devise a questionnaire to find out how people think ICT affects the emergency services.

★ Decide how many people you will ask and who you will ask – your sample – to complete the questionnaire.
★ Process the replies.
★ Present your results to others in your class.

> At the start of your questionnaire, give one example of how ICT has affected one of the emergency services.

Law enforcement organisations also use ICT as an information source.

The police have databases of criminal records. They can check to see if a person has had a previous speeding or petty theft offence.

THE INFORMATION SOCIETY

Exercise 11.7

What information can the police keep on computer about people who have *not* been convicted of any crime?

What protection is offered by the Data Protection Act for the public?

The National Health Service (NHS)

When attending a hospital and being admitted to the accident and emergency (A&E) department, the receptionist will ask you for your name and postcode. From this information, the receptionist can search the hospital database and gain access to your medical records, e.g. who your doctor is, your date of birth, and your medical history.

Exercise 11.8

Find out if any of your friends or family have been to an A&E department at the hospital. Ask them to explain how ICT was used in the admittance procedure.

ICT has also helped in the field of data collection.

Monitors, scanners and analysers, are used to aid the medical profession in performing surgery.

Expert systems have enabled diagnoses to be made. An expert system is designed so that it asks the user a series of questions and then offers suggestions or solutions to the enquiry.

Most schools and colleges have expert careers programs. The program asks a series of questions about what you like doing. From your responses, possible careers which may suit you, and are based upon your answers, are suggested.

Exercise 11.9

How useful is an expert system? How useful would the suggestion be if you gave false information.

Exercise 11.10

What rights do patients have about their medical records?

Did You Know?

Within each community, infant records are placed on a central database, so the records can be transferred from one health authority to another when people move.

ICT also assists in compiling statistics within a health authority. Within the national field, all statistics can be collated to show, for example, levels of immunisation both locally and nationally.

Activity 11.7

Search the Internet for statistics on the health of people living in the UK.

★ Select information of interest to you and develop it into a report.

★ Present your findings to others in your class.

ICT has also helped statisticians to predict life expectancies. This is used to calculate life assurance premiums.

Exercise 11.11

Nowadays, research into genes means that tendencies for parental or hereditary conditions might become identified. This might affect insurance opportunities. How has ICT contributed to this situation?

THE INFORMATION SOCIETY

11.1.4 Education

Within education, ICT is used extensively, not just as a part of the National Curriculum requirements, but as a management, assessment, diagnostic and statistical tool.

For the management team, ICT can help with the administration. Student databases can catalogue all the student's details: name, date of birth, and their examination results.

Exercise 11.12

What information is kept about you on your school/college database?
 Ask your teacher how the school uses ICT, such as a database to store details. Perhaps a computer is used to send examination entries and receive results.

Statistical analysis, e.g. using spreadsheet applications, can be done to produce performance indicators. This may highlight good and poor aspects, and the information be used to prompt action to improve standards.

Activity 11.8

Obtain a copy of the school league table. In small groups, ask yourselves these questions:

★ What information does it provide?
★ How is it compiled?
★ What purpose does it serve?

Have a debate with others in your class: 'The league tables help to monitor standards in schools and colleges – TRUE of FALSE'.

The use of **ICT in the classroom** enhances the possibility of diversity, because students may be allowed to proceed at their own pace. Students can improve their own learning through multimedia applications and self-help packages, with little teacher input.

VR systems may be used for educational stimuli, exploring artificial environments, imaginary or reality-based.

Exercise 11.13

List educational uses of VR. How does VR help you to learn?

For those people who are unable to attend educational establishments, **distance learning** may be introduced.

Activity 11.9

Do you know anyone who uses/used distance learning?

★ Find out what is involved with distance learning.
★ Share your findings with the rest of the group.

Use of ICT in and outside schools as a means of education is vital. As this chapter illustrates, ICT offers the way ahead. Those who are not computer literate will have difficulties in tomorrow's society!

Activity 11.10

In one week, log how much ICT related work you do in school. Also record how much ICT orientated equipment you used at home. Then, write a report on how you would have performed the same tasks if the ICT equipment was not invented yet!

Public transport

ICT is being used extensively within public transport. One of the most common applications of ICT is the use of **information boards** displaying waiting times at bus stops, airports, train and tube stations.

These information boards give precise, up-to-date information to travellers. Previously, the only guidance to waiting times would have been a hardcopy timetable, or possibly in the larger stations, a public announcement.

Activity 11.11

With others in your group, visit a bus station to find the answers to these questions.

★ How many information boards are there?
★ What type of information is displayed on the information boards?
★ Do all boards show the same information?

If there were no information boards, how would travellers find out this information?
Are the information boards an advantage? Why?
Present your findings in a report.

There are many other examples of how ICT is used in the public transport industry.

Did You Know?

In the motor industry, ICT is being used for devices such as in-car traffic announcements.

In the aviation industry, ICT is being used in aeroplanes for the in-flight technology, autopilot, radio-tracking, etc.
Bus drivers have been given direct communication with the depot through the use of ICT. Tracking devices are being used by the depot to track the exact location of buses.
Mobile phone companies are offering phones that give information on the latest traffic situation when a specific number is keyed in.

Exercise 11.14

Does anyone you know have a car with a traffic announcement facility?
Is it useful? If so, how?

Your French Exchange Student – Paola

You have a French exchange student, Paola, staying with you as part of the schools international links programme. You go out with Paola for the day.

While you are out, Paola wants to call her family. Paola uses the new type of telephone with on-screen help to dial the number.

You both decide to visit the nearest town, and you use the information board at the local train station. When you arrive at your destination, Paolo finds the information board at the Tourist Information Centre very useful and from this information, you decide what tourist attractions you would like to visit.

Activity 11.12

Visit train stations and other places to see technology working in appropriate environments.

★ Write a report on how you and Paola would have managed before the technology of touch screens, information boards, etc.

★ Think of other information which might be provided for tourists.

★ Hold a class debate on whether Paola is more informed due to the ICT she has used.

Contact your local Tourist Information Centre, or look on the Internet for information currently available.

THE INFORMATION SOCIETY

Activity 11.13

In small groups, have a brainstorm session. List as many areas as possible where ICT is used, paying particular attention to the five public services: information services, emergency services, the National Health Service, education and public transport.

Now, imagine you have been placed in a time machine. You have arrived in the year 1970. What are the main differences?

On trying to return to the current year, there has been a miscalculation and you land in the year 2020. What do you think you might find 'now'?

The impact of ICT on working practices

With the introduction of ICT, working practices have been affected. It is important to look at the ways in which these practices have been affected and to assess whether the consequences have been of a positive nature. This can be split up into the following areas:

- Places of work and working hours
- Work skills and retraining
- The social aspect for employees and employers

Places of work and working hours

Did You Know?

Futurist Alvin Toffler popularised the term 'electronic cottage' to describe a home where modern technology allows a person to work.

With the advancement in technologies, libraries of data are now available from the home base. Therefore, working from home in your own natural environment instead of commuting to an office is now a realistic goal. In addition to this, with the price of computers and communication costs continuously falling, more and more people are now choosing to work from home.

There are many advantages of employees working from home. The main advantage is a reduction in **pollution** and **congestion** – fewer people are commuting to work, so fewer cars are on the road.

Activity 11.14

As a group, design a questionnaire and conduct a survey to find out the commuting times of all parents of your class.

Working from home gives people the option to work **flexi-time** and hence not have to fall into the standard conventions of a nine-to-five routine. This gives people the flexibility to keep working, or to work part-time. This has had a direct impact upon childcare provision, because it allows greater interaction with the family.

Parents can work during the school times, or when children are asleep. It also allows those with other responsibilities, e.g. caring for an aged parent, to meet both obligations (home and work). Individuals can also shop when it is not so busy, work when it rains, do the gardening when it doesn't – basically it gives individuals more control over their own time.

Exercise 11.15

Look in local papers. Do many companies advertise jobs and provide flexible working hours?

Hot desking saves office space and hence costs. People share desk space when they are in the office. They do not have one desk that is their property. Instead, they use any available desk when back at base. Generally, this desk has a network link and employees who work out of the office use laptops.

Organisations such as British Telecom use hot desking in some departments. When in the office, BT staff use a password so the telephone system and computer network know where they are.

Digital Equipment Corporation

Digital Equipment Corporation pioneered flexible working in the UK in the early 1990s with one hot desk for every two employees, but more recently that has changed to one department having eight hot desks for over 100 people. It has been calculated that through the flexible working practices that Digital promote, in the UK alone £3.5 million have been saved.

Exercise 11.16

Do you know anyone who works 'hot desking'? Ask them how their system works.

With the changes that have occurred in working practices, society as a whole has more **leisure time**. Not commuting can save many hours a day. This, in turn, may have the knock-on effect of increasing motivation to work and increasing job satisfaction. This has also meant changes in the leisure industry. There are now many more ways to occupy your leisure time: cinemas, bowling, leisure parks, activity centres and so on.

Activity 11.15

Within your local area conduct a survey on how many leisure clubs, cinemas, bowling alleys there are.

★ Find out how many there were 15 years ago.
★ Compare the numbers.
★ Discuss the following statement as a group.
"More leisure facilities have been provided as a direct result of people having more leisure time."

Working from home, however, can cause problems at two ends of the continuum:

- For those who are not self-disciplined enough to work without supervision
- For those who become addicted to work – workaholics – who swap the 9–5 day for a 5–9 day, 7 days a week!

Activity 11.16

Interview someone who works from home to find out the advantages/disadvantages from working from home. Share and discuss the results of your findings with the rest of your group.

THE IMPACT OF ICT ON WORKING PRACTICES

Work skills and retraining

With the information age, many people, e.g. lathe operators, have been replaced by automated machinery, such as robots.

Bank tellers no longer count bank notes; instead, they are weighed. With the advancements in software, people who needed special skills such as typing have been deskilled; the software does the layout for them. Even shop assistants no longer calculate the change to be given; this is done by the checkout computer.

Exercise 11.17

In groups, list as many jobs as possible that you think have been deskilled.
Do you know anyone who has been deskilled?
What happened to them?

On the other hand, due to the information age, some jobs require new ICT skills.

Managers rarely have shorthand secretaries; instead they are expected to word-process their own letters.

New jobs have also been created. Programming of computers is one good example, the very source that caused deskilling of the labour force!

Exercise 11.18

In groups, list as many jobs as possible that you think have been reskilled.
Do you know anyone who has been reskilled? What happened to them?

As a result of the deskilling/reskilling, retraining on a large scale has been necessary. Otherwise, many people simply could not be employed. This has created a whole new industry of people who are responsible for training the workforce.

Exercise 11.19

Find out what retraining courses are available in your area.

A good source of information for this is your local job centre or careers centre.

The social aspect for employees and employers

Although there are many benefits from working from home, there can also be negative effects:

- Some employees gain a great deal of **job satisfaction** from having praise bestowed upon them when a job is done well. Using computer technology seems to depersonalise the whole process. Direct supervision disappears as employees may work at home.

- Those who find themselves in positions where they are not directly supervised can lose **motivation** and become bored. This may be made worse by the lack of contact with colleagues.

- **Quality** may also suffer if employees take the attitude 'no one sees me doing the job, so it doesn't really matter'.

- There are fewer opportunities for **brainstorming** with colleagues. Therefore problems may take longer to solve. The idea sharing process may be lost, while teamwork is one of the latest buzzwords in industry.

- Due to the increase in automation and computer technology, there is a risk that jobs will be lost. Robots take over jobs that were reserved for humans and are doing those jobs much more quickly and with fewer errors. As employers cannot predict the pace at which ICT may progress, in industries where ICT is fundamental, short-term contracts may be offered. Therefore, employees lose their sense of **job security**.

- The pace of change, changes in supervision, and lack of job security, make many people feel **increased stress**. So, while changes should make life better for employees it seems to make some things worse.

Activity 11.17

Figure 11.1 shows the agenda that has been drawn up for a meeting.

★ Appoint a chairperson to chair the meeting and a secretary to take minutes. Split the rest of the class up equally: one side to argue in favour of working from home; the other to argue against.

Prior to the meeting, make time to research and prepare your case in favour of or against working from home.

After the meeting: individually read the minutes taken from the meeting by the secretary and summarise the main points. Taking all the points into consideration made during the meeting, write a report about your own feelings.

★ In the light of the debate, have your feelings changed? If so, why?

> Group your ideas for/against working from home under these headings:
> Motivation, Job security, Social interaction, Leisure time, Stress levels, Rates of pay (PRP)

AGENDA

1 Arguments in favour of working from home
   • From the employee's point of view
   • From the employer's point of view

2 Arguments against working from home
   • From the employee's point of view
   • From the employer's point of view

3 Examples from other organisations

4 AOB

Figure 11.1 *Agenda*

The impact of the introduction of robotics on production

The introduction of ICT has meant that 24-hour operation is now possible in many industries. With robots and automated procedures, working throughout the night is now common practice. Humans need time off for illness, and holidays, and cannot feasibly work 24 hours a day; with the exception of routine maintenance and repair work, robots can work without stopping at all.

Robots are also used in hazardous conditions, which are dangerous to humans.

Exercise 11.20

Find out what legal restrictions apply to working hours of humans.

Suggest two situations where robots are used in situations hazardous to humans.

The introduction of robotics has affected methods of production in a number of ways:

- **Speed**
  The production, for example of cars, is undoubtedly quicker due to 24-hour manufacturing. Also because robots do not suffer from fatigue, illness, boredom, temperaments, or attitude!

- **Cost**
  The initial outlay for machinery and equipment may be high, but, in the long-term, profits are increased due to processes being completed more quickly and with greater accuracy.

- **Safety**
  Using robots can eliminate the need for humans to work in hazardous environments.

- **Quality**
  Automated quality control can ensure the end product meets requirements. Computers are programmed to feed back information to ensure a consistently high quality is maintained.

Sensors are used to measure the thickness of paint on cars. If the paint is not being sprayed within the defined tolerances, production is stopped and the problem is rectified.

Activity 11.18

Imagine you work on the production line of a car manufacturing company. Your line manager has just informed you that you are to take part in a training program as a new robot is soon to take over the jobs that you and your colleagues are currently doing. Write a letter to your line manager explaining how you feel about the proposed change.

Try to think about both the positive and negative implications of the changes.

Activity 11.19

The changes that were proposed in Activity 11.18 how now been implemented. Write a report to explain the impact that these changes may have had, including these three topics:

★ Employment levels
★ Working practices
★ Health and safety

Use case studies of organisations that have undergone similar changes to back up your report.

The impact of the Internet and digital TV on society

The Internet has had a major impact upon the way that society operates. The Internet has currently been the focus of many discussions, TV documentaries, and radio discussions. People's view on whether the Internet is a good or bad thing varies tremendously. However, some basic facts cannot be disputed:

- Availability of much more information for those with Internet access – perhaps leading to a divide between the 'haves' and the 'have nots'

- Reductions in the cost of the use of the Internet – in some cases, to no charge at all

- Increased **accessibility** of information due to search engines and browsers becoming more user friendly

Activity 11.20

Logon to the Internet.

★ How many search engines are available for you to use? List them.

★ Compare your list with others in your group. Did you miss any?

The introduction of the Internet has many positive aspects. However, sometimes manual methods of finding out information can still be quicker than using the Internet.

If you want to know the ingredients for rice pudding, it is quicker to look it up in a cookbook, than to log on to the Internet and search for details of rice pudding recipes!

Activity 11.21

Compare the Internet with manual methods of finding information and see which is quicker.

- ★ Use the Internet to find the top five in the charts in the USA.
- ★ Use manual methods to find the top five in the charts in the USA.

Repeat the comparison exercise but, this time, answer these questions:

- ★ What's on TV tonight on BBC1 and ITV?
- ★ What is the definition of a modem?
- ★ How much does it cost to fly with Easyjet to Palma Mallorca next Saturday for a week return at any time? Are there any discounts for booking over the Internet?

Write a report, to explain how you used both the Internet and manual methods to find out information. Which was easier/quicker?

These are other potential problems too:

- ◯ **Unsuitable material**
  Even with software which prohibits the unauthorised, e.g. young people, it is still relatively easy to find sites on the Internet which are unsuitable for certain audiences. Simple typing mistakes on searches, may bring up information of an unsavoury nature.

- ◯ **Validity of information**
  Anyone who has the technical know-how can put information on to the Internet for public viewing. There is no objective 'vetting' to check the information is true.

- ◯ **Security of information**
  While it may be safe to use a credit card to purchase items from many sites, fraud on the Internet is possible.

Activity 11.22

Research what companies offer digital TV. Answer these questions:

★ What is home shopping?
★ How can digital TV aid home shopping?
★ What is home banking?
★ How can digital TV aid home banking?
★ What effect can digital TV have on society?

Send off for some promotional literature from the companies selling digital television.

The effects of ICT on the environment

With the introduction of ICT many things have been promised, including a **paperless office** and a **global society**.

Exercise 11.21

What is meant by the term 'global society'?

Communications can be made without paper via e-mails, electronic files, verbal communication, etc.

There are many methods that aim to reduce the amount of paper used or kept.

Before computers were used extensively companies sent copies of urgent documents using a fax machine. Now they send and receive data between computers over telephone lines by e-mail.

Video links allow companies to talk to and see each other, reducing costs, for example travel costs. Designers create all drawings using graphics packages, therefore not using paper at all.

Exercise 11.22

Make a list of jobs where information appears on screen rather than on paper.

Activity 11.23

As a class, design a questionnaire, which asks people whether they think that ICT has increased or decreased the amount of paperwork. Each member of the group should give the questionnaire to ten different people. Collate all the results and use a spreadsheet to show the statistics. Present your findings in the form of a report.

Activity 11.24

Working in small groups, research the effects of ICT on the environment and answer these questions:

★ How can communications be made without paper?
★ How could your school reduce the amount of paper used?
★ What effect has the use of paper on the environment?

ICT may have other effects on the environment:

- Changes in **transportation needs**, e.g. just-in-time (JIT) ordering systems
- Use of **scarce resources**, e.g. lower wastage through more accurate prediction of needs
- Increased **pollution** and better control of pollution

Activity 11.25

Split the class into three groups, each group tackling one of the effects listed above. Research the topic and present your findings to the other two groups. Allow an opportunity for discussion in the presentations.

THE EFFECTS OF ICT ON THE ENVIRONMENT

Legislation for ICT users

There is much legislation relating to ICT and the ways it affects ICT users. Table 11.1 lists the most pertinent legislation and a description of what that legislation entails.

Acts	Date	Description
Health and Safety at Work Act	1974	General duties which employers have to employees and members of the public, and employees have to themselves and to each other
Data Protection Act	1984	A safeguard to control personal data
Copyright, Designs and Patents Act	1988	To protect 'intellectual property' and establish the rights of the author
Electricity at Work Regulations	1989	To prevent the most common accidents caused by electrical faults
Computer Misuse Act	1990	To prevent misuse of both hardware and software
Obscene Publications Act	1990	To prevent obscene material being published
Health and Safety Regulations	1992	An explanation of what the employers must do and what the equipment must be like

Table 11.1 *Legislation for ICT users*

Activity 11.26

The Data Protection Act has recently been updated. Find out when this happened and what changes were introduced.

Use the Internet to do your research.

In addition to the UK legislation, consideration of European Union (EU) legislation also had to be taken into account. The EU have regulations on the use of computers and the Internet Code of Practice.

11 IMPACT OF ICT ON SOCIETY

Activity 11.27

What is the 'Internet Code of Practice'? Find out all you can about it.

Reasons for ICT legislation

Did You Know?

In 1984, a single case of computer fraud lost Volkswagen more than $260 million!

Each piece of legislation is designed to protect the user in some way:

- To meet moral obligations to protect workers from harm
- To minimise the effects of exposure to uncensored materials
- To provide legal backing so that it is possible to seek redress if rights are violated
- To protect the confidentiality of information kept about the individual
- To observe copyright for those who create original works

Did You Know?

In 1996, the FBI released survey details which showed that 40% of corporate, university and government sites had been violated in one way or another, e.g. changing data, stealing passwords and preventing legitimate users from gaining access to systems.

Computer crime is a growing 'industry' and many thousands of pounds are lost each year due to computer misuse/fraud. Therefore, it is essential to have some form of legislation to protect companies and the individual.

It is not only the users that the legislation is there to protect, but the employers/company owners themselves.

Activity 11.28

Apart from the Acts directly related to ICT users, there are many more. Find out about these Acts:

★ Electricity at Work Regulations (1989)
★ Computer Misuse Act (1990)
★ Obscene Publications Act (1990)
★ Internet Code of Practice

Write a report on why these Acts were introduced.

LEGISLATION FOR ICT USERS 381

The future use of ICT

ICT has changed dramatically over the past century and it is difficult – if not impossible – to predict how it will develop over the next century. One thing that can be assured is that ICT will continue to have an impact on society. ICT affects most current-day living practices. In particular, this section concentrates the potential impact of four topics:

- Financial transactions
- Shopping habits
- Personal safety and freedom
- Commercial security

Financial transactions in the future will be fully computerised. Before long there should be no reason to carry cash because all transactions can be done using a smart card.

Exercise 11.23

Is a 'cashless' society a safer society? Discuss.

IBM

IBM presented their version of the future at the IATA Passenger Services Conference in Los Angeles. Their vision includes booking an airline ticket without having to be served by staff. Instead, passengers use touch screens and a smart card to check in. All the information is downloaded directly onto the card, and this card is then read in a machine at the airport, options are given about seat preference and the gate number is displayed. The smart card then acts as a boarding pass at the gate. At no point is a ticket issued to the traveller. The smart card contains all the information. American Airlines are carrying out a trial of this system.

Shopping habits will probably change. More and more people will start to use the web to do their shopping. Information sources, such as the Yellow Pages are already computerised. Customers can request specific goods, the price of goods, and place orders through a computer. Cash may therefore soon become a commodity of the past.

Exercise 11.24

It is now possible to buy books (like this one) on the Internet. What effect might this have on publishers, the bookshops and the customers?

Visa Cash

Visa Cash is a new type of payment card, called an electronic purse. It contains a microchip used for purchasing small cost items. Using a cash loader, you can put the card into an ATM machine and transfer up to £50 from your Visa credit or debit card. To make a purchase, you simply put the card into to a Visa Cash terminal, key in the correct amount and the card is debited. There is no need to sign anything. To check the amount remaining on the card, you just put it into a card reader. It will show the amount left and detail the last five transactions made.

Did You Know?

Japanese companies are already using a system which allows customers to customise their own cars and receive delivery within a week!

Customers will also be able to sit in their own home and design their own clothes, which will then be manufactured!

The car industry has seen a real shake up recently. UK car prices are much higher than European counterparts and, as a result, Internet car buying has really taken off. Many people have chosen to buy cars over the Internet and are saving thousands of pounds.

Activity 11.29

Do a survey to find out who has used the Internet to make a purchase recently.

★ What did they buy?
★ How quickly was it delivered?
★ Did they experience any problems?
★ Will they use the Internet to do all their shopping in future?

Personal safety and freedom can become conflicting aims.

Exercise 11.25

How can the general public enjoy personal safety while, at the same time, criminals enjoy freedom? Discuss.

Aston University

At Aston University in Birmingham a smart card is essential to students movements around the campus. It acts as a library card, an identification card, a card with which to purchase food and a card which permits access to certain parts of the campus. A machine not dissimilar to a hole in the wall machines loads it and, when credit gets low, students reload their cards with denominations from £5 to £100.

Exercise 11.26

What other organisations use smart cards for security as well as offering other facilities to users?

Global positioning systems (GPS) can be used to track individuals; an example of this has already been introduced with the electronic tagging of criminals. How far are we actually away from the film *Men in Black* and the technology that can be seen to be used?

Activity 11.30

The latest *Star Wars* film shows substantial futuristic technology.

★ Watch the film, and write a report on all the futuristic technology that is being used in the film.

★ How close are we to some of the concepts? Which ones do you think will be a reality in this century?

★ Compare the latest *Star Wars* film to one of the originals and see how the ideas behind the technology have changed.

★ Compare *Star Wars* to *Blake's 7*. How far has the technology progressed?

GPS is also being used in conjunction with trains!

GPS on trains

A computer system on board trains determines the motion of the train against its position pinpointed by GPS satellites. This measures the smoothness of the journey and locates parts of the track that are worn out. The information is fed to the headquarters and displayed on a computer screen. The screen is overlaid with an Ordnance Survey map and problems on the network are pinpointed.

Geographic information systems (GIS) are making crime scenes easier to find, and are allowing police to keep tabs on incidents and resources.

The Metropolitan Police service

The Metropolitan Police service is using GIS to display maps and then zoom in to a street or location and overlay details of crime incidents, traffic accidents and street patrols.

Training systems help to keep law and order.

Surrey Police

The Surrey Police system relies on a series of filmed scenarios depicting crime scenes, which are projected on a screen set up within a firing range. The latest in interactive response techniques allows shots to be fired at the screen with hits logged by computer. Trainees interact with the scenarios, shouting at them to stand still, drop weapons, etc., making the situations as true to life as possible. This prepares trainees before they experience the real thing on the street.

Security systems also use ICT.

School security in Birmingham

ICT is being used to make schools a safer environment. On each of the doors of the school there is a card reader which students must swipe to gain entrance. This stops anyone without a card entering the school. The card is multifunctional as it also operates a cash-less canteen system. Students must load money on their card for refreshments each day. No money is taken at the till. The card is swiped and the money debited. The card also operates printing and photocopying equipment and has the student's picture on for ease of identification.

Exercise 11.27

How close are we to carrying ID cards? What are the implications of this?

Any information that is kept on a system is subject to corruption, sabotage, **industrial espionage** and theft. This can be further split into large-scale organisational theft and personal theft.

Large-scale organisations must try to prevent industrial espionage, malicious interference and deliberate acts of destruction. Personal data must be protected against blackmail and unauthorised disclosure. The two most common forms that this theft takes are **bugging** and **hacking**. Once aware of these problems, it should then be easier to prevent the loss.

Commercial security systems are being developed to improve detection of theft, which can only benefit society.

Activity 11.31

You have been in the time capsule again and have journeyed to the year 2999.

★ Write a report on what you have found.
★ What is a typical day like?
★ Decide whether you want to get back in the time capsule or whether you would be content to stay. Explain your reasoning.

Revision questions

1. What is a touch screen and where can you find them?
2. What does ATM stand for?
3. How is VR used to sell products? Explain your answer, giving examples.
4. What is an expert system?
5. What is distance learning?
6. Explain the terms reskilling and deskilling.
7. What is flexi-time?
8. What is hot desking?
9. How can the use of robots impact upon the speed of car production?
10. What is the Internet?
11. What is digital TV?
12. List two ways that using IT can increase pollution, and two ways that using IT can decrease pollution.
13. What is the Data Protection Act?
14. When was the Internet Code of Practice established?
15. List five ways you think IT may have an impact on you in the future.

Good Working Practice guide

For your work to progress smoothly, you can help yourself by adopting standard ways of working. This can also help you to work well with others. In several units, standard ways of working are listed. However, you must apply these techniques to all of your ICT work.

The companion book *Intermediate GNVQ Information and Communication Technology* (pages 221–39) offers useful advice on good working practice and standard ways of working. Only the list of dos and don'ts is repeated here.

Dos and don'ts

- **Do** plan your work to produce what is required by given deadlines.
- **Do** take a backup of your work. Label your backup with the date.
- **Do** keep backup copies of files on another disk and in another location.
- **Do** keep previous drafts of documents, filed in date order and giving an idea of sequence. Then you can always look back if you need to.
- **Do** keep a log to provide a record of what has happened, especially what has gone wrong.
- **Do** proofread your database and spreadsheet information to ensure accuracy.
- **Do** save work regularly using different filenames.

- **Do** proofread all documents before printing out the final copy.
- **Do** evaluate your work and suggest how it might be improved.
- **Do** keep information free from viruses.
- **Do** respect confidentiality.
- **Do** respect copyright.
- **Don't** disconnect or connect equipment without first isolating the power source.
- **Don't** eat or drink while working at a PC. Wash your hands after eating sticky or greasy foods – the remains of a jam doughnut can glue up a keyboard!

Health and safety issues

The basis of health and safety law in Britain is covered by the Health and Safety at Work Act (1974). Full details of this Act are given in the companion book: *Intermediate GNVQ Information and Communication Technology* (pages 233–5). You might also visit the HSE website at **www.hse.gov.uk** for more information – many documents are available for download as PDF files.

Data Protection Act (DPA)

Full details of this Act are given in the companion book *Intermediate GNVQ Information and Communication Technology* (pages 236–9). Only brief details are given here.

The data protection principles

Once registered, data users must comply with the principles in relation to the personal data held:

- Personal data shall be collected and processed fairly and lawfully.
- Personal data shall be held only for specified and lawful purposes.
- Personal data shall be used only for those purposes and only disclosed to those people described in the register entry.
- Personal data shall be adequate, relevant and not excessive in relation to the purposes for which they are held.

- Personal data shall be accurate and, where necessary, kept up to date.
- Personal data shall be held no longer than is necessary for the registered purpose.
- Personal data shall be protected by proper security.

However, the Registrar cannot enforce the principles against unregistered data users.

The rights of the individual

An individual is entitled to be supplied by a data user with a copy of any personal data held about him or her – the 'subject access' right. Individuals may write direct to the user for their data, or they may consult the register to obtain more details about the user.

Data users may charge up to £10 for meeting each request but some may decide to charge less, or nothing at all. They have up to 40 days in which to provide the data from the date of receiving adequate information to help them locate the data or identify the individual making the request. If the data are not provided within the 40 days, the individual concerned can complain to the Registrar or apply to the courts for an order that the data user should provide access.

More detailed information on all aspects of the Data Protection Act is contained within *The Guidelines* – a free publication available from the Registrar's Office.

For full details of the Data Protection Act and how it is enforced in particular circumstances, visit the website: http://www.hmso.gov.uk.

For details of the functions and activities of the Data Protection Registrar, visit the website http://www.dataprotection.gov.uk.

Portfolio guide

Your portfolio should contain all the evidence collected as you work through the units. For some units, assessment is by external testing, but material in your portfolio may well be needed to show your achievement in Key Skills. It therefore makes sense to keep a portfolio of all your work for all your units, even those which are not portfolio assessed.

To decide what material you need to produce and put in your portfolio, you need to look at the assessment grid at the end of each unit specification. Your portfolio must contain at least the minimum stated in the first column of the 'Assessment Evidence' section of each unit. The assessment evidence section tells you exactly what type of evidence you need to produce – like list, notes, records and summary – to show what depth of work is needed, and you need to check you have met this level of presentation.

For some activities your teacher will watch you working, and then write an assessment of your performance. In some situations, another person, e.g. your supervisor in a work placement, may observe you.

With a presentation, you will present your finished work to an audience (maybe only to your teacher), but your portfolio evidence might include a taped recording or a video together with the material (e.g. OHTs or slides) that you used. Your teacher will be responsible for agreeing that you used a good standard of English during your presentation, and that your manner and tone were suitable for your audience.

For the tested units, the assessment grid does say what you have to produce, but your awarding body will specify the precise requirement in pre-release material given to you some time before the examination. See Examination guide (page 401).

Performance when doing assignments

Teachers can most easily assess the quality of your work by watching you when you do assignments, and by looking at what you produce for your portfolio.

When you prepare for a task and are identifying sources of information, your teacher may consider these questions:

- Were you usually told what tasks needed to be done and then had to be guided through them?

- Were you able to decide what steps you needed to take, and did you arrange the tasks into a sensible order, setting your own time-scale?

- Did you use sources of information suggested by your teacher, and were you able to select and use the relevant information from these sources?

- Were you able to understand what the task involved without any guidance from your teacher?

- Did you understand what information was required and did you look for extra sources of information, as well as investigating those suggested by your teacher?

The more independent you are, the higher your grade should be.

Similarly, the more care you take over planning and monitoring your work, the more likely you are to be successful, and the higher your grade should be. During every task, you should be checking that your original plan is working, by monitoring and reviewing your progress. You should recognise that the planning may need changing. Sometimes, through no fault of your own, the plan does not work. Even if things do not go wrong, you should be able to demonstrate that you have regularly checked progress against the original plan.

The quality of your work is also very important.

- At pass level, you should be able to demonstrate a basic understanding of the knowledge and skills required, but you may not be able to make connections between different aspects of your work. You should be able to use the normal ICT terminology but may need some help from your teacher.

- ✪ At merit level, you should be able to make connections between different aspects of your work and demonstrate a clear understanding. Your use of ICT terminology should be accurate, and your written work should show confidence in the expression of your ideas.

- ✪ At distinction level, you will have a clear understanding of the knowledge, skills and understanding required. You will draw on your personal experience to draw conclusions or suggest alternative courses of action.

At the end of each assignment, all students are expected to be able to describe what they felt went well, and what went badly. Evaluating your work is an important part of improving your own performance – and is one of the six Key Skills. So, while doing practice or real assignments, remember that if you perform well, you may be awarded a higher grade for this work.

When assessing your portfolio, your teacher is looking for the right quality and quantity of work. He or she will first look to see that you have covered everything by checking that you have covered all items listed in the various columns of the Assessment Evidence chart. Work of a high quality may earn you a higher grade, so your teacher will be looking at all the columns of the chart.

What are the general 'rules' that allow your teacher to decide on your grade? This depends on the unit – and is detailed in the section called 'Assessment Strategies'. Although the section is written for your teacher, you should read it carefully. Then you will know how your work will be viewed by your teacher.

Generally speaking, the teacher will try to distinguish between students and award grades so that the higher grades are given to students who perform best.

Presenting information within a portfolio

It will help your teacher – and give extra information about your performance overall – if your portfolio is presented well. As a student on the Intermediate GNVQ ICT course, you must be able to demonstrate that you can do this well!

You can handwrite your assignments, or you could use a word processor. If you handwrite your work, you will have to be very neat. If you make a mistake in your 'final' version, it will show and you may feel you have to write out a whole sheet again.

For some assignments, you will have to use a computer. When doing assignments, most of your material will be produced on the computer.

The structure of your portfolio

There are a number of sections which your portfolio should include. This will demonstrate that you can structure material and present it in a sensible way.

The main sections are listed here, but you can choose your own sections if you prefer.

- Front cover
- Contents list
- Assignment material
- Appendices

You may also have checklist sheets supplied by your teacher. These may be used to refer to where Key Skills are demonstrated. In addition, you may have material which confirms that your teacher saw you present some information, or has discussed your material with you.

Your name (and centre details) should appear at least once on the portfolio. For safety sake, it would be good practice to include this information on every page. If you are using software, this is easily achieved by including this information in a header or footer.

It will be important that your Contents list matches whatever you have included in the rest of your portfolio. Although it appears at the very start of your portfolio, it is one of the last pages you can complete. However, if you produce it using a word processor you can prepare a Contents page at the very beginning and update it every time you add some material to your portfolio. Then it will be one less job to do when you are rushing to meet the final deadline.

In this book, the pages run from 1 to 423, and the Contents page (on page v) lists the first page number of each chapter. For your portfolio, it may be easier to number the sections and then, within each section, number the pages by section. This numbering method is often used in manuals and means that extra sections can be added at any time, without it upsetting the page numbering too much.

For the material produced when doing assignments, plus any material produced when doing activities, it probably makes sense to present the material in the same order as you completed the work. For each assignment, make sure you show clearly what the assignment is called, and what it covers. It may be possible to use material produced in another course as evidence of your ICT skills. It will help your teacher if you write clearly on each assignment, which unit (and course) the assignment refers to.

Sometimes it makes sense to move some material to an appendix. This shortens a section, and yet the material is available if the reader wants to look at it. So, for example, lengthy tables or diagrams or copies of original source materials may be put into an appendix.

You can also list your references within an appendix. It is important to include all your references: the books, magazines and CD-ROMs you used to find information for your assignments.

While building your portfolio, leave yourself messages about things you still have to include. You could write these notes on your plan (which will provide evidence of the fact that you have been reviewing and monitoring your plan) – or put post-it notes on pages that still have work to be done, or write yourself a checklist, which you can then tick off as your complete the work.

Moderation and internal assessment

Details of the moderation and internal assessment procedures are explained in the companion book: *Intermediate GNVQ Information and Communication Technology* (page 248).

Key Skills guide

All jobs need skills of one sort or another. Your first job will need few skills, but as you progress to more senior posts, more skills are needed. Job skills fall into two types: vocational and key skills.

Vocational skills are the skills that are linked to the actual job:

- The ability to use a keyboard or mouse
- The experience of using a word-processing package
- The experience of using a DTP (desktop publishing) package
- The ability to install software and to customise application programs

These are the skills you will learn while following this course, and in doing so will need to use key skills.

Key skills are not specific to a subject like ICT. Instead they are useful for most jobs and include these abilities:

- To think for yourself
- To work without supervision
- To work in a team
- To work with numbers
- To solve problems
- To communicate your ideas to others

- To remember names and other important facts
- To work to a deadline

So, key skills can help you to improve your own learning and performance in education and training, work and life in general.

Details of the Key Skills qualifications are given in the companion book *Intermediate GNVQ Information and Communication Technology* (pages 249–55).

To achieve this qualification, you must demonstrate your skills through a portfolio of evidence. This evidence should not involve you in a lot of extra work. Instead, you should be able to collect evidence from your day-to-day studies, work or other activities and an appropriate form of independent assessment. As well as producing a portfolio of evidence, you also have to pass an externally set test.

Examination of Key Skills

External moderation will be used to check how well you demonstrate your key skills within your portfolio material. More details on how to present your portfolio are given in the *Portfolio guide* on page 393.

Tests for Key Skills are still being developed, so it is not possible to say, at this moment in time, exactly what form the examinations will take. However, at Levels 1 and 2 students will be set a multiple choice paper. At Level 3, a practical test is used to check your ability to use standard applications in IT. For Application of Number and Communication Key Skills, the tests involve writing answers to short questions. Sample tests are available so teachers and students alike may access this information from QCA's website and also the websites of the various awarding bodies.

Examination guide

Details of the structure of the Intermediate GNVQ course in Information and Communication Technology and how your grade is established are given in the companion book *Intermediate GNVQ Information and Communication Technology* (pages 257–9).

Which units are externally tested?

This grid shows, for each chapter in this book (and the companion book), which units are covered for each awarding body. The unit numbers for those units that are externally assessed by the three awarding bodies are shown in bold.

Main book

Chapter	Title	OCR	AQA	Edexcel
1	Presenting information	1	1	1
2	Handling information	2	2	2
3	Hardware and software	**3**	**3**	**3**

Options book

Chapter	Title	OCR	AQA	Edexcel
1	Design project	4	4	4
2	Information resources	–	–	5
3	Communicating with multimedia	5	5	7
4	Graphics and desktop publishing	6	6	6
5	Computer-aided design	–	–	12
6	Numerical modelling using spreadsheets	7	7	9
7	Databases	8	8	10
8	Monitoring and control systems	9	9	–
9	Data and communications	10	10	8
10	Programming	11	11	11
11	Impact of ICT on society	12	12	–

Before the exam

People like athletes train hard before a race or a competition:

- They make sure they have the right techniques.
- They are coached.
- They do lots of training, practising their techniques as well as getting very fit.
- They will be very careful with their diet, to make sure they are as fit as they can be.
- Just before a competition, they will make sure their preparation is perfect, so that, on the day of the competition, they have the best chance of winning.

In the same way, you must give yourself the best possible chance of doing well in the examination. Unlike an athlete, though, you do not have to come first to be a winner. Instead, you just need to answer enough questions correctly to get the grade you need.

- Keep your notes in a sensible order, including a Contents page so you can find things, and your own copy of the examination specification. You can then use the assessment grid as a checklist.

- Make sure you attend all sessions/lectures; and make up for work missed.
- Find out about the examination timetable, well in advance.
- Allow plenty of time for revision.
- Make extra time to read around the subject.
- Try to be at your best on the examination day: be sure to get a good night's sleep.

Adopting the right attitude

Immediately before a race, athletes look very focused. They have worked hard before the race and now, when the gun goes, they have to perform at their very best, maybe for as short a time as ten seconds. Their mental attitude is very important. Believing that they can win is an essential ingredient.

Remember, then, to look on the examination as an opportunity for you to show the examiner that you have studied the course and have learnt many new things. If you are very negative about taking examinations, you start with a disadvantage. Your own negative attitude will make it harder for you to approach the examination and perform at your best. Instead, if you look upon the examination as an opportunity to shine, you may find you can do just that: shine!

During the examination

When you arrive in the examination room, you will be given a booklet. On the front, you need to complete your personal details:

- Your name and number
- Your centre name and number

You should know your candidate number, and the centre information will probably be written on a board in the examination room. Make sure you complete this information clearly. Use block capitals, rather than 'normal' writing.

You should use a blue or black pen – not a red pen (which is the colour the examiner will use to mark your paper) and not pencil (because it could be rubbed out and changed). (However, you are allowed to use pencil if you have to draw something in the examination.) You should not use correcting fluids. If you make a mistake, cross out what is wrong (neatly!) and write your new answer nearby.

Look at a past paper. Notice that the front cover includes some useful hints about how to tackle the paper:

Timing

When you are told to start, you will have 90 minutes to complete the paper. There are approximately 12 questions. However, some of these may be broken down into part questions. So, altogether, you may have to answer as many as 30 short questions.

This works out at about 3 minutes per question. This should be enough time for you to read the question carefully and write your answer in the space provided.

Your teacher may set you a 'mock' examination. This involves sitting a previous paper under examination conditions. If your teacher does this, notice how long you take to answer the paper. This will then help you to pace yourself in the real examination.

The layout of the examination paper

The questions are numbered: 1, 2, 3, ... Sometimes a question is based on a scenario. Then there are several part-questions; these are lettered: a, b, c, . . .

There are three main types of question:

- Most questions have a 'stem' followed by some lines for you to write your answer.

- Some questions ask you to tick a box to show your choice of an answer.

- Some questions ask you to complete a table or diagram.

Always, the number of marks available for the question (or part question) is shown on the right-hand side of the paper, at the end of the question or part question.

Answering the questions

Read each question carefully, including any scenario information. Make sure you understand all the information provided.

Often, students say they find written examinations difficult. For them, it would be better, if they were given a personal interview – a one-to-one conversation to check they knew all the things they had learnt. However, this is not practical. Instead, you have a series of questions, set by the examiner – who is still a real person – that you need to answer. Try to imagine you are replying to this real person. It may help you to focus on the questions and the answers you would give – if they had been asked verbally.

You will have to write your replies to the questions presented in the paper. If you know you have difficulties explaining yourself in writing, again try to imagine that the question is spoken to you. Think (do not speak out loud in the exam room!) what you would say in reply to the question. Then decide how best to write this so you fully explain how much you know.

It is rare that a single word is the answer required. Try to write in sentences, rather than note form. If you write in note form, it may be difficult for the examiner to be sure you know what you are being tested on. You will help the examiner, and possibly increase your score, if you write as much as possible in clear English.

Write neatly – the examiner will try to understand what you have written, but if your handwriting is impossible to read, you will get no marks at all!

> **Did You Know?**
>
> Most marks are lost because candidates do not read the question properly. There may be a single word which – if missed – makes all the difference to the answer you might give.

> **Did You Know?**
>
> Examiners write NAQ (not answered question) on an examination booklet when a candidate has written things that are true, but no marks can be awarded because the candidate has not answered the question.

Deciding how much to write

The question – and the way it is laid out – should give you an idea of how much you need to write to earn the marks available.

The stem will use phrases like these:

- Give ONE item of data that . . .
- Name a component . . .
- List THREE pieces of information . . .
- Give ONE way in which . . .
- Suggest TWO ways of . . .
- Give TWO advantages of . . .
- Give ONE advantage and ONE disadvantage of . . .
- Give TWO reasons for . . .
- What is meant by the term . . .
- What is the purpose of . . .
- What is the difference between . . .
- Describe the features of . . .
- Describe how . . .
- Explain why . . .

Usually the number of marks available matches the number of things you are asked to give. Then you can see you can get one mark per advantage, or one mark per reason, or one mark per item of information.

The space provided can be another guide – although if your handwriting is very large or very small, this guide will not work for you! Notice that, on the front cover, it says:

> If there is not enough room for your answers, there are some spare pages at the back of the booklet. If you use spare pages, you must write the question number next to your answer. You can also use the spare pages for rough work.

Did You Know?

Sometimes the examiner can give you 'benefit of the doubt' (BOD) marks. He or she thinks you know the answer but may not have expressed yourself very well. However, there is a limit to the number of BOD marks that can be given.

Examination technique

Did You Know?

The examinations are timed to make sure all candidates have enough time to answer all questions fully, so when the examination has finished, you will probably have some time left over.

Being successful in examinations in not just about knowing all the right answers. There is also a technique to doing examinations.

This first set of suggestions are about how you should spend your time, and the attitude you should have during the examination:

- If, when you first start the examination, you are very nervous, try to spend a few minutes calming down. It may be simply that holding your pen makes you fret. So, put down your pen. Spend some time thinking about the questions and how to answer them. Take a deep breath, pick up your pen and start.

- It may help you to read the whole paper through before you start to answer any questions. Having seen all the questions, there can be no shocks to come later.

- It does say on the front cover: 'Answer all questions.' However, if you have no idea what to write, it would be better to skip a question and spend your time on other questions – for which you do have something to write.

- You do not have to answer the questions in the order they appear on the paper. It may make you relax if you answer questions you find easy first. Then when you have got into a rhythm, you can tackle some of the harder questions.

- During the time you have to answer your paper, about half the time could be spent reading questions and thinking about the answers, and the other half could be spent writing your answers. Do not feel you have to be writing all the time. It may help you to put your pen down while you have your 'thinking cap' on. Then, when you know what you are going to say, pick up your pen and start to write.

- Make sure you pace yourself so you do not spend too much time on some questions and then have to rush at the end.

- If you find you do finish earlier than expected, do not waste this time doodling! Instead, read through what you have done. If you decide you want to change something, make your corrections neatly so they are legible.

This next set of suggestions may help you to give the answers the examiners are looking for:

> **Did You Know?**
>
> Before you and other students sit the examination, the examiner will have prepared a mark scheme. This lists all the possible correct answers, and shows how each mark can – or cannot – be earned.

- Each question is set to test a particular knowledge or skill. Over the whole paper, the same types of question appear from year to year – they are just worded slightly differently. So, if you practice by doing previous papers, this will help you to recognise what the examiner is testing.

- The stem of a question rarely contains words which are not important.

  During the preparation of the paper, any 'extra' words that are not needed are deleted. This is done to make the paper as short as possible for the candidates. It also means that all the words that are left really are very important. Make sure you read every single word.

- Some questions simply test your knowledge of technical terms. The only way you will get these questions right is if you do have the knowledge. It makes sense to study previous papers to see what technical terms are tested and to make sure you can answer this type of question.

- Some questions ask you to tick one box out of three or four boxes. If you are not sure which one to tick, think about which ones are definitely wrong. Eliminate those first. Then you will have fewer boxes to choose from.

- Some questions ask you to use information provided to complete a diagram or a chart. If you are not sure of the 'whole' answer, think carefully about which ones you are sure about; fill those in first and see what you have left.

- Some questions ask you to explain why one thing is better than another. Make sure your answer makes it clear which 'thing' you are writing about.

- No marks will be given for repeating, word for word, information that is given in the question. You have to write something extra, something that shows you know what the question is about, before you can earn any marks.

After the examination

When your paper has been handed in, it is too late to do anything which will affect your grade for that paper. However, if you feel you did not do as well as you might, learn the lesson from this experience.

Ask yourself what went wrong for you:

- Were your notes good enough?
- Were there topics you knew nothing about?
- Were there terms you did not understand?
- Had you done enough revision?
- Were you fresh and alert on the day of the examination?

You may have to retake the paper later in the year. Use the time straight after the exam to tidy up your notes again:

- If there were things asked in the examination that you did not know about or understand, find the answers to these questions now. Add more notes to your file. It is quite likely that similar questions will appear on the next paper you take.
- If there were terms you did not understand, make a list of them. Look them up in your BCS Glossary and make notes on them.
- If you had not done enough revision, remember to do more next time.
- If you feel your performance was badly affected by how tired you felt, make sure that next time you allow yourself time to have plenty of rest before the next test.

If you still have another unit test to take, make sure you prepare for this second test as well as you can. Retaking only one paper is better than retaking two!

Index

3D charts   186
3D models   142–4
10base2   283
10base5   283

A3, A4, A5 paper   103
abnormal values   345
absolute coordinates   130
absolute referencing   174
access
   access rights   289, 292, 294, 297
   Internet access   289
   restricting by physical/logical means   39, 296
accessibility   375
accounts, finance and   50
accuracy   242, 260
actuators   241
ADA   329
adding a workstation to a network   304
adding data   190, 234
advantages of using a control system   242–4, 248, 252, 254
advantages of using networks   288–90
advertisements   145
alarm clock radio   242
alignment   105, 107
amending data   190, 234
analogue input components   259, 260
analogue output components   261–2
analysis
   break-even   167–8
   statistical   362
   statistics and survey analysis   166–7
   structured analysis tools   311
   systems analysis   311

AND operator   178
annotating diagrams   135–6
appearance and layout of a worksheet   171–4
appropriate and effective presentation   62–3
appropriate use of display formats   216
arc   128
array   342
arrow (pick) tool   112
artist impressions   148
ATMs (automatic teller machines)   355
attributes
   of an image   113
   of text and graphic frames   107
audience   64
   impact on   61
   intended   60
   passive   65
   target   58, 74
authoring package   75
authoring techniques   94
automation   239
   automatic teller machines (ATMs)   355
   automatic timer for lights   242
   production automation   248–52
AVERAGE   167, 177
axonometric projection   142

background
   background music   84
   consistent   92
backups   297
   backup and recovery system   296
   backup device   282
bar chart   184

basic objects 127–8
BASIC/Visual Basic 308, 329
batch processing 275
BCC (blind carbon copy) 48
bearings 133
bespoke packages 124
bits (binary digits)
   bitmap graphics 109
   number of bits used 84
blast cooler 249
blind carbon copy (BCC) 48
blocks
   block diagrams 257
   function block 264
BNC 281
boards
   bulletin 32–3, 302
   information 355, 363
book(s)
   book illustration 145
   reference books 24
borders 105
brainstorming 5, 66, 371
break-even analysis 167–8
   break-even point 167
breakpoints 348
brief 64
   design brief 120
   presentation brief 94
broadcast radio 276, 286
browsers
   Internet 34
   Yahoo 301
brush tool 111
budgeting 165–6
bugs 312
   bugging 387
bulletin boards 32–3, 302
bus network 283
buttons 88–91, 216

C++ 329
cables 279
   cable connectors 281
   coaxial 280, 283
   connection methods without cables 285–8
   Ethernet 282
   twisted pair 280
   two wire 279
camera 46
   digital cameras 81, 119
Caption property 335
capture, data 157
carbon copy (CC) 48
card(s)
   card indexes 26–8
   interface cards 266

network interface card (NIC) 281
   smart card 206
   wild card 228
Cartesian coordinates 130
case sensitive 331
cash flow 169
casting 248
categories displayed on pie chart 184
CC (carbon copy) 48
CD-ROMs, floppy disks and 30–1
Ceefax 32
cell 153, 171, 287
   cell reference 153
   range of 172
cellular radio 276, 287
central heating system 242, 246, 260
centred text 105
charts 166, 183–6
   3D charts 186
   bar chart 184
   composite chart/graph 186
   Gantt chart 13
circle 128
clip art 81, 116
closed questions 159
closing a contact 264
coaxial cable 280, 283
COBOL 329
coil 264
collection, data 156–63, 205
colour 125, 141
   colour palette 111
   gallery of colours 126
columns 220
   designing record (row) and field (column) structure in tables 212
   freezing rows/columns in a spreadsheet 173
combo box 341
commands, precision 129–32
commentary 83
comments 348
commercial security systems 387
communication
   communications protocols 304
   methods of communicating information 46–8
   network services and electronic communication systems 299–305
   with multimedia 57–96
compilation process 338
components
   decision components 240
   input components 259, 260
   of a computer program 320–8
   of a control system 239–41
   of a multimedia presentation 60

components (*continued*)
  output components 240, 259, 261–2
  physical components of networks 279–82
composite chart/graph 186
computer-aided design (CAD) 123–52
computer-aided drafting 124–36
cones 142
conferencing 302
confidentiality of information 381
congestion 367
connectors
  cable 281
  connection methods without cables 285–8
consistency
  consistent background 92
  of data 199
construction objects 128–9
contact 263
  closing a contact 264
continuous improvement 271
continuous lines 127
control
  security 252–4
  self-running control of slides 92
control systems 237–72
  advantages of using a control system 242–4, 248, 252, 254
  components 239–41
  designing a control system 255–8
  environment control 245–8
  limitations of using a control system 242–4, 248, 252, 254
  monitoring and 237–72
controllers 240, 263–8
  controller routine structures 266
  personal computer controllers 266–8
  programmable logic controllers 263–6
convenience 243
coordinates 117
  absolute 130
  Cartesian coordinates 130
  coordinate systems 130
  isometric coordinates 131
  polar coordinates 131
  relative 130
copy 114, 140
  copying emails 48
copyright 72, 381
  software copyright 297
corporate image 149
cost 243, 373

creating
  and using data files 294
  creating buttons, hyperlinks 88–91
  creating multimedia presentations 75–93
  creating screen forms 216–19
criteria 227
critical path 13
crop tool 114
cross-sections 143
cross talk 280
crow's feet 209
cubes 142
curves 127
customising a database 231
cut and paste 114, 140

data
  adding 190, 234
  amending 190, 234
  consistency of 199
  creating and using data files 294
  data capture 157
  data collection methods 156–63, 205
  data duplication 199
  Data Protection Act (DPA) 39, 390–1
  data requirements 200–1
  data type 213, 342
  data user 40
  deleting 190, 234
  designing models for numerical data 164–81
  discrete data 184
  functions applied to tables of data 181
  numerical 153–91
  test data 345
data entry
  creating screen forms 216–19
  data-entry format 213
databases/database management systems (DBMSs) 193–236
  customising a database 231
  database report 220
  designing a database structure 208–15
  on-line 42–3
  output from a DBMS 196
  purpose of a DBMS 196, 197–9
  researching a user's requirements for a DBMS 196–207
dataflow symbols 134
DB9/DB25 281
DBMS *see* databases
debugging 312, 347
decision components 240

default text style   135
deleting data   190, 234
deleting files   294
description
    of a field   213
    of a process   258
design   189
    computer-aided design (CAD)   123–52
    design documentation   233
    design project   1–20
    design templates   75
    layout and   92–3
    planning   10–13
    program design techniques   312–19
    systems design   311
    working to a design brief   120–1
designing
    a control system   255–8
    a database structure   208–15
    a hierarchy of text styles   92
    models for numerical data   164–81
    record (row) and field (column) structure in tables   212
deskewing   138
desktop publishing (DTP)   97–112
despeckling   138
development, program   309–19
    program development lifecycle   310
device, backup   282
Dewey decimal system   28
diagrams
    annotating   135–6
    block   257
    electrical wiring diagrams   258, 269
    flow   246
    flowcharts   69, 70, 315
    pictogram   184
    pie chart   184
    structure diagrams   313
dictionaries   25
digital cameras   81, 119
digital input components   259
digital output components   261
digital recordings   85–7
digital TV   375–7
DIM instruction   321
dimensions   135
direct entry drawing   132
directories   292
    directory (folder) structure   293
    shared directories   295
    telephone/trade directories   26
discrete data   184
display formats, appropriate use of   216
distance learning   363
distort   141

documentation   189–90, 350–2
    design   233
    on-line   350
    technical   16, 189, 233, 350
    testing and   15–17
    user documentation   16, 189, 233–5, 350
domain name   304
dpi   139
drafting/drawing
    computer-aided   124–36
    direct entry drawing   132
    drawing tools   107, 109, 112
    orthographic drawings/views   117
    painting and drawing packages   108
    perspective drawings   117, 130, 144
    plotting   136
dry run   345
DTP   97–112
dumb terminals   282
duplication of data   199
DVDs   30

editor, program/text   333
education   362–3
effectiveness   271
efficiency   272
electrical cabinet   251
electrical symbols   134
electrical wiring diagrams   258, 269
electronic-based images   138
electronic bulletin boards   32–3, 302
electronic conference   302
electronic mail and networks   48
elevation views (front and side)   117, 151
ellipse tool   111
e-mail   299
    attachments   300
    copying   48
    electronic mail and networks   48
    inbox/mailbox   48
    sending and receiving   304
emergency services   359–60
encryption   37
encyclopaedias   25
energising a coil   264
engines search   34, 301
entity   208
environment
    effect of ICT on   378–9
    environment control   245–8
    integrated development environment (IDE)   338
    system environment   255–6
erasing   138
    eraser tool   113

errors, logic/syntax 338
Ethernet 282
evaluation 18–20
event driven language 333
exception report 227
expected results 345
experience 243
expert systems 360
extreme values 345
extruding 143

fastext 32
faxes and fax machines 47
feasibility study 310
fibre-optic cabling *see* optical fibre
fields 212, 213
   key fields 233
files
   deleting 294
   file compression software 300
   file server 282, 289, 297
   file transfer 300
   JPG (or JPEG) file 78
   paper files 28–9
   renaming 294
fills 113
filters 109, 141, 227
finance and accounts 50
financial transactions 382
finding information you need 44–5
flexi-time 368
floppy disks and CD-ROMs 30–1
flow diagram 246
flowcharts 69, 70, 315
   flowcharting symbols 134
   story boards and 69–72
folder (directory) structure 293
fonts 106, 220
   Font property 336
   font size 107
footers 104, 224
FOR NEXT 266
foreign key 213
formats
   appropriate use of display formats 216
   data-entry 213
   GIF format 78
   modifying the format of output from a spreadsheet model 182–3
forms, creating screen 216–19
formulae 189
   and functions 174–7
Fortran 329
forum 302
frames
   graphic 107
   wire 143

freezing rows/columns in a spreadsheet 173
front elevations 117
full justification 105
function block 264
functions 174–7, 189, 239, 327
   AVERAGE 167, 177
   functions applied to tables of data 181
   INDEX 181
   logical functions and operators 178–80
   LOOKUP 181
   MEDIAN/MODE 177
   MIN/MAX 177
   RANGE 167, 177
   statistical 177–8
   SUM 177

gallery of colours 126
Gantt chart 13
Gbps 281
generating reports on screen and on paper 220–6
geographic information systems (GIS) 386
geostationary satellites 287
GIF format 78
global positioning systems (GPS) 385
global society 378
global variables 327
glossaries 25
graphics 78–80
   and DTP 97–122
   attributes of graphic frames 107
   bitmap 109
   graphics filter 109
   graphics manipulation techniques 139–41
   graphics software 108–18
   vector 109, 117
graphs 166, 183–6
   composite chart/graph 186
   line graph 184
   x-y scatter graph 186
grid 131
   grid snap (snap to grid) feature/option 117, 132
   layout guides (gridlines) 107
grouping
   and sorting data 224–6
   group footer 224
   group header 224
   of objects 144
guides, user 16, 189, 233–5, 350

hackers/hacking 290, 387
hard sell 61

hard spaces 105
hardware requirements: scanners and digital cameras 119
headers and footers 104, 220, 224
health and safety 390
heating elements system 249
height of an image 113
help, on-screen 355
histogram 184
hot desking 368
hot links 35
hot spots 89
house style 126
hypertext 35
   creating hyperlinks 88–91

ICT-based sources of information 30–43
ICT in the classroom 362
ID (identification)
   logon IDs 36
   user ID 36, 289, 292, 297
identifying a suitable project 2–6
identifying sources 72
idiot proofing 15
IF 178, 322–4
   IF THEN ELSE 267
illustration 145–50
   book illustration 145
image(s)
   attributes of 113
   corporate 149
   electronic-based 138
   height of 113
   image manipulation 137–41
   scanning images 80–3
impact
   on an audience 61
   of Internet and digital TV on society 375–6
implementation and testing 269–72, 312
import facilities 75
improvements 271–2
inbox 48
index 351
   card indexes 26–8
   INDEX function 181
individual, rights of 381, 391
industrial espionage 387
inflexibility 243
information
   confidentiality of 381
   finding information you need 44–5
   in organisations 49–55
   information boards 355, 363
   information flow 246
   information overload 53

information resources 21–55
information services 357–8
information society 354–66
   operational 50
   quantity of 64
   security of (on the Internet) 376
   sources of 23–9, 30–43, 50
infra red 288
input 205, 308
   input components 240, 259–60
   input design 205–7
   input for a DBMS 196
   INPUT instruction 321
   input mask 216
   IO (input/output) 255, 257–8
   keying directly 205
integrated development environment (IDE) 338
integrated services digital network (ISDN) 276, 299
intelligent terminals 282
intended audience 60
interaction 65
   interactive systems 275
   user interaction 62
interface cards 266, 281
interference 280
interior plans of building 151
internal modem 303
Internet 34–42, 375–7
   impact of, on society 375–6
   Internet access 289
   Internet browser 34
   surfing the net 300
   uncensored materials 381
   unsuitable material 376
   validity of information 376
   Yahoo browser 301
interpreting multimedia presentation specifications 64–5
interrupt request queue (IRQ) 281
intersection table 211
interviewing 158, 196
intranets 41–2
investigation 311
   investigating multimedia presentations 58–63
   mathematical 169–70
invoice 194
IO (input/output) 255
   IO schedule 257–8
IRQ (interrupt request queue) 281
ISDN (integrated services digital network) 276, 299
isometric coordinates 131
isometric drawings 117
isometric projection 142
iteration 314, 315

JANET 276
JAVA 329
job costing 165
job satisfaction 371
job security 371
JPG (or JPEG) file 78
justification 105
justifying ideas 67–8

keys
   foreign key 213
   key fields 233
   key words 42
   primary key 212
keying directly 205

ladder logic 265
landscape orientation 103, 136
LANS (local area networks) 275
laser 280
layers 141
layout 62
   and design 92–3
   appearance and layout of a worksheet 171–4
   layout guides (gridlines) 107
   page layout 104
   tabular layout 220
LED (light-emitting diode) 280
left alignment 105
legislation
   Data Protection Act (DPA) 39, 390–1
   for ICT users 380–1
leisure time 369
lens-based image manipulation 137
Library of Congress classification 28
lifecycle, program development 310
light-emitting diode (LED) 280
limitations of using a control system 242–4, 248, 252, 254
line graph 184
lines
   continuous 127
   line thickness 110, 125
   line tool 110, 125
links
   hot links 35
   hyperlinks 88–91
   linking a program 338
local area networks (LANs) 275
local variables 327
Locked property 335
locking 141
logic
   ladder logic 265
   logic controllers, programmable 263–6
   logic errors 338
   relay ladder logic (RLL) 263
logical access, restricting 296
logical operators 43
   logical functions and 178–80
login script 292
Logo 329
logon IDs 36
logos 149
LOOKUP function 181
loops 324–6

macro 167, 231
mailbox 48
malfunction 243
MAN (metropolitan area network) 277
managers, network 297–8
manipulation
   image manipulation 137–41
   manipulation tools 113
market, target 100
marketing, sales and 50
mask, input 216
mathematical investigations 169–70
MAX function 177
Mbps 281
mechanical symbols 133–4
MEDIAN function 177
menus 216
message 65
metal casting 248, 262
methods of communicating information 46–8
metropolitan area network (MAN) 277
microwave 276, 286
MIDI music 84
MIN/MAX function 177
mirror tool 114
MODE function 177
models
   3D models 142–4
   designing models for numerical data 164–81
   modifying the format of output from a spreadsheet model 182–3
   numerical modelling using spreadsheets 153–91
modem 299, 303
modifying the format of output from a spreadsheet model 182–3
monitoring
   and control systems 237–72
   production and progress monitoring 14
mono 84
moral obligations 381

motivation   371
move   114
multimedia
   communicating with   57–96
   components of a multimedia
      presentation   60
   creating multimedia presentations
      75–93
   interpreting multimedia presentation
      specifications   64–5
   investigating multimedia presentations
      58–63
   planning a multimedia presentation
      66–74
music   84

name(s)
   field   213
   Name property   334
   tag names   257
National Health Service (NHS)
   360–1
navigation   35
needs
   of the user   227
   output needs   201–4
   processing needs and rules   204–5
   researching a user's requirements for
      a DBMS   196–207
   transportation needs   379
networks
   advantages of   288–90
   bus   283
   electronic mail and   48
   integrated services digital network
      (ISDN)   276, 299
   network interface card (NIC)   281
   network managers   297–8
   network security   296–8
   network services and electronic
      communication systems
      299–305
   network topologies   283–5
   physical components of networks
      279–82
   ring   283
   star   284
NHS   360–1
NIC (network interface card)   281
node edit tool   112
normal values   345
number of bits used   84
numerical data
   designing models for   164–81
   numerical modelling using
      spreadsheets   153–91
   random numbers and generators
      326

objects
   basic objects   127–8
   construction objects   128–9
   grouping of   144
observation   157, 196
on-line databases   42–3
on-line documentation   350
on-screen help   355
open questions   159
operational information   50
operator
   AND   178
   logical   43
   logical functions and   178–80
   OR   178
   relational   43
optical fibre   280
OR operator   178
Oracle   32
organisations, information in   49–55
orientation   220
   landscape   103, 136
   paper orientation   103
   portrait   103, 136
orthographic drawings/views   117
output   308
   IO (input/output)   255, 257–8
   modifying the format of output from a
      spreadsheet model   182–3
   output components   240, 259,
      261–2
   output from a DBMS   196
   output needs   201–4
oven   242
overheads   167
overload, information   53

pace   62
packages
   authoring   75
   bespoke   124
   painting and drawing   108
   see also software
packet switched data networks (PSDNs)
   276
page layout   104
painting and drawing packages   108
paper
   generating reports on screen and on
      paper   220–6
   paper files   28–9
   paper orientation   103
   paper sizes   103, 104, 220
   paper-based image manipulation
      137–8
   paper-based sources of information
      23–9
paperless office   378

parameters 230, 327
Pascal 329
passive audience 65
passwords 36, 289, 292, 295, 297
paste, cut and 114, 140
payroll 169
personal computer controllers 266–8
personnel 51
   network managers 297–8
   social aspect for employees and employers 371–2
perspective drawings 117, 130, 144
physical access, restricting 296
physical components of networks 279–82
pick tool 112
pictogram 184
pie chart 184
places of work 367–9
plans/planning
   plan view 117, 151
   planning a design 10–13
   planning a multimedia presentation 66–74
   test plan 15, 345
plotting 136
point size 106, 107
points 127
polar coordinates 131
pollution 367, 379
polygons 127
pools 295
portrait orientation 103, 136
position in space 130
precision commands 129–32
presentation(s) 94–5
   appropriate and effective 62–3
   components of a multimedia presentation 60
   creating multimedia presentations 75–93
   interpreting multimedia presentation specifications 64–5
   investigating multimedia presentations 58–63
   planning a multimedia presentation 66–74
   presentation brief 94
   presentation quality 94
   purpose of 60
   slide-show 75
   web-based 75
primary key 212
primary research 156–62
PRINT instruction 321
print server 282, 289, 297
printers, sharing 289
private WAN 276

privileges 289
procedures 327–8
processes
   compilation process 338
   process description 258
processing 196, 308
   batch processing 275
   processing needs and rules 204–5
producing a project proposal 7–9
producing reports 182–6
product visualisation 147
production 51
   and progress monitoring 14
production automation 248–52
programmable logic controllers 263–6
programming 307–52
   components of a computer program 320–8
   editor program 333
   linking a program 338
   program design techniques 312–19
   program development 309–19
   program development lifecycle 310
   program specification 313
programming languages 329–43
   BASIC 308, 329
   COBOL 329
   DIM instruction 321
   event driven language 333
   FOR NEXT 266
   Fortran 329
   IF 178, 322–4
   IF THEN ELSE 267
   INPUT instruction 321
   Logo 329
   Pascal 329
   PRINT instruction 321
   pseudo-code 318
   REPEAT UNTIL 267
   structured English 318
   Visual Basic 308, 329
project
   design 1–20
   identifying a suitable project 2–6
   producing a project proposal 7–9
projection, axonometric/isometric 142
property
   Caption 335
   Font 336
   Locked 335
   Name 334
protocols 303
   communications protocols 304
prototypes 311
PSDNs (packet switched data networks) 276
pseudo-code 318

PSTN (public switched telephone network)   275
public transport   363–6
purchasing   51
purpose
   of a DBMS   196, 197–9
   of presentation   60

quality   371, 373
   of multimedia presentations   94
quantity of information   64
   information overload   53
queries   227–30
question types, open/closed   159
questionnaires   158–62, 196

radio   46
   alarm clock radio   242
   broadcast radio   276, 286
   cellular radio   276, 287
   radiotelegraphy/radiotelephony   46
random numbers and generators   326
range
   of cells   172
   RANGE function   167, 177
receiving e-mail   304
record   212
   designing record (row) and field (column) structure in tables   212
recordings
   digital   85–7
   recording/editing sound files   83–7
   recording/editing video files   88
recovery, backup and recovery system   296
rectangles   127
reference books   24
referencing
   absolute/relative   174
   cell reference   153
reflection   143
refrigerator   242
reject arm   249
relational operators   43
relationships   209–11
relative coordinates   130
relative referencing   174
relay ladder logic (RLL)   263
renaming files   294
REPEAT UNTIL   267
replication   174
report
   database   220
   exception   227
   generating, on screen and on paper   220–6
   producing reports   182–6
   summary report   227

research
   primary   156–62
   researching a user's requirements for a DBMS   196–207
   secondary   156, 162–3
resolution   139, 260
resources
   information   21–55
   scarce   379
responses   158
restricting access
   by logical/physical means   296
   restricting physical access   39
results, expected   345
retraining   370–1
reusable procedures   327
right alignment   105
rights
   access rights   289, 292, 294, 297
   of an individual   381, 391
ring networks   283
RJ-11 connectors   281
RJ-45   281
RLL (relay ladder logic)   263
robotics   373–4
robustness   15
role of the network manager   297–8
rotate   114, 140
rows
   designing record (row) and field (column) structure in tables   212
   freezing rows/columns in a spreadsheet   173
RS232   281
ruler guides   107

safety   243, 270, 373
   health and   390
sales and marketing   50
sampling rate   84
sanserif fonts   106
satellites   276, 287
satisfaction, job   371
scale   117, 129
scanner   119
   scanning images   80–3
scarce resources   379
scope   209
screen(s)
   creating screen forms   216–19
   generating reports on screen and on paper   220–6
   touch screen   354
searching   43
   key words   42
   search engines   34, 301
secondary research   156, 162–3

security 199
    job security 371
    network security 296–8
    of information (on the Internet) 376
    security control 252–4
    security methods 296–7
security systems 386
    commercial 387
selecting and justifying ideas 67–8
selection 314
self running control of slides 92
sending and receiving e-mail 304
sensors 240
sequence 314
serif fonts 106
servers, file/print 282, 289, 297
services
    emergency 359–60
    information 357–8
    network services and electronic
        communication systems
        299–305
    NHS 360–1
servo valve 249, 262
setting up a workstation 303
shading 113, 142, 220
shape tools 111
shared directories 295
sharing printers 289
shopping habits 383
side elevation/view 117, 151
simple queries 227–8
single data type 342
size 114
    font size 107
    paper size 103, 104, 220
    point size 106, 107
    sizing 140
slide transitions 91–2
slide-show presentation 75
smart card 206
snap to grid option 117, 132
social aspect for employees and
    employers 371–2
society
    global society 378
    impact of ICT on 353–88
    information society 354–66
soft sell 61
soft spaces 105
software
    file compression 300
    graphics 108–18
    software copyright 297
    vector-based graphics software 117
    virus checking software 296, 297
solenoid 261
sorting 43, 224–6

sound files, recording/editing 83–7
sources of information 50
    ICT-based 30–43
    identifying sources 72
    paper-based 23–9
space(s)
    hard/soft 105
    position in space 130
specification 255
    interpreting multimedia presentation
        specifications 64–5
    program 313
    systems specification 255, 311
speed 242, 373
    modem speed of transfer 303
spheres 142
spline curve 127
spray tool 112
spreadsheet 153, 164–81
    freezing rows/columns 173
    modifying the format of output
        182–3
    numerical modelling using
        spreadsheets 153–91
    'what if?' process 187
standard paper sizes 103
star networks 284
statistical analysis 362
statistical functions 177–8
statistics and survey analysis 166–7
stereo 84
story boards and flowcharts 69–72
stress, increased 371
structure diagrams 313
structured analysis tools 311
structured English 318
styles 113
    default text style 135
    designing a hierarchy of text styles
        92
    house 126
    style sheets 102
    typeface 106
subroutines 327
SUM function 177
summaries 224
summary report 227
supervisor 256
surface textures 142
surfing the net 300
swipe card entry system 252, 261,
    267
symbols
    dataflow symbols 134
    electrical symbols 134
    flowcharting symbols 134
    mechanical symbols 133–4
    symbolic languages 308

syntax 330
  syntax errors 338
system environment 255–6
systems
  backup and recovery 296
  central heating 242, 246, 260
  commercial security 387
  database 193
  Dewey decimal 28
  expert 360
  geographic information (GIS) 386
  global positioning (GPS) 385
  heating elements 249
  interactive 275
  network services and electronic communication 299–305
  security 386, 387
  swipe card entry 252, 261, 267
  virtual reality (VR) 356
systems analysis/design 311
systems specification 255, 311

table 208
  designing record (row) and field (column) structure in tables 212
  functions applied to tables of data 181
  intersection 211
tabular layout 220
tag names 257
tape streamer 282
target audience 58, 74
target market 100
Tbps 281
technical documentation 16, 189, 233, 350
techniques
  authoring 94
  graphics manipulation 139–41
telemetry 46
telephone 46
  telephone conferences 302
  telephone directories 26
Teletext 31–2, 276
television 46
  digital TV 375–7
templates, design 75
terminals, dumb/intelligent 282
testing 93, 189, 233, 338, 345–9
  implementation and 269–72, 312
  test data 345
  test plan 15, 345
  test schedule 271
  testing and documentation 15–17
text 75–8
  alignment of 105
  attributes of 107

centred 105
default text style 135
designing a hierarchy of text styles 92
hypertext 35
text editor 333
Text property 334
text tool 111
thermocouple 249
thermostat 246
thickness, line 110, 125
time, leisure 369
tints 113
toggle break point option 348
tolerance 134
tools
  arrow 112
  brush 111
  crop 114
  drawing tools 107, 109, 112
  ellipse 111
  eraser 113
  line 110, 125
  manipulation 113
  mirror 114
  node edit 112
  pick 112
  rotate 114, 140
  shape 111
  spray 112
  structured analysis tools 311
  text 111
  zoom 114
topology, network 283–5
touch screen 354
tracking 132
trade directories 26
transfer
  file 300
  modem speed of transfer 303
  transfer rates 281
transport
  public 363–6
  transportation needs 379
trial and refinement 188
turning 143
tutorial 351
twisted pair cabling 280
two wire cable 279
type
  data type 213
  single data type 342
typeface styles 106

user(s)
  data user 40
  legislation for ICT users 380–1
  needs of 227

user(s) (*continued*)
  researching a user's requirements for a DBMS 196–207
  user controlled slide shows 92
  user documentation/guides 16, 189, 233–5, 350
  user ID 36, 289, 292, 297
  user interaction 62
uses and features
  of DTP software 101–7
  of graphics software 108–18
using spreadsheet models for prediction 187–8

V.24 281
validation requirements 213
validity of information (on the Internet) 376
value 320
  abnormal/extreme/normal 345
valve, servo 249, 262
variables 320–2
  local/global variables 327
vector graphics 109
  vector-based graphics software 117
verification 304
version number 137
video conferencing 302
video files, recording/editing 88
view plan/elevation/side 117, 151
Viewdata 35
virtual reality (VR) systems 356
viruses 38, 296, 312
  virus checking software 296, 297
Visual Basic 308, 329
voice, choosing the right 74

WANs 275
  private WAN 276
web-based presentation 75
welding 133
'what if?' process 187
wide area networks (WANs) 275, 276
width
  field 213
  of an image 113
wild card 228
wire frame 143
wireless media 285
wiring 268–70
  electrical wiring diagrams 258, 269
wizard 167
work
  places of 367–9
  work skills 370–1
working hours 367–9
working practices, impact of ICT on 367–72
working to a design brief 120–1
worksheet
  appearance and layout of 171–4
workstations 281
  adding a workstation to a network 304
  setting up a workstation 303
writing a script 72–4

x-y scatter graph 186

Yahoo 301

zoom 140
  zoom tool 114